Reminiscences

of

VICE ADMIRAL GEORGE C. DYER

U. S. Navy (Retired)

U. S. Naval Institute
Annapolis, Maryland
1973

Preface

This manuscript is the result of fifteen tape-recorded interviews with Vice Admiral George C. Dyer, U. S. Navy (Retired) at his home in Pendennis Mount, Annapolis, Maryland. They were all conducted by John T. Mason, Jr., for the Oral History Office in the U. S. Naval Institute and cover a period from April, 1969 to May, 1971.

Admiral Dyer has made some corrections to the original transcript. The entire manuscript has been retyped and an extensive index has been compiled.

This narrative should prove of considerable value to Naval historians. Admiral Dyer is the author of several naval biographies as well as other works in the field of Naval History. Because of this focus his observations have especial interest and pertinency.

VICE ADMIRAL GEORGE C. DYER, U. S. NAVY, RETIRED

VICE ADMIRAL GEORGE CARROLL DYER, former President Naval Academy Alumni Association, member of Board of Directors of the Retired Officers Association, and author of the standard text book on "Naval Logistics" was born in Minneapolis, Minnesota, on 27 April 1898, the son Harry Blair and Georgia Mortimer Dyer.

Appointed to the Naval Academy from Oregon, Vice Admiral Dyer entered the Naval Service on June 16, 1915 and graduated from the Naval Academy after a three year course on June 7th, 1918. World War I duty included instruction at the Submarine Base, New London, Connecticut, and duty in Submarine N-6 operating in the North Atlantic from that base.

In the next ten years, while in the junior grades, he served in Submarines N-5, N-7, R-1, R-5, and V-3, and commanded the D-3, L-10, and S-15. His first command of a submarine, the D-3, was when he was twenty-one years of age.

During the next decade, while in the middle grades, he attended postgraduate school at Annapolis, the Naval War College at Newport, Rhode Island, taught school at the Naval Academy, and served in the battleship ARIZONA, the heavy cruiser INDIANAPOLIS and on the Staff of COMMANDER DESTROYERS SCOUTING FORCE, U. S. FLEET. During this same period, he also commanded the submarine rescue ship, WIDGEON, the light minelayer GAMBLE and SUBMARINE DIVISION EIGHT.

In the immediate years before World War II, he served on the Staffs of COMMANDER BATTLE FORCE, PACIFIC FLEET, and then that of THE COMMANDER IN CHIEF, UNITED STATES FLEET, and as Executive Officer of the flagship of COMMANDER SCOUTING FORCE, the INDIANAPOLIS.

He was in the INDIANPOLIS at Johnston Island when the Pearl Harbor attack commenced. When Admiral Ernest J. King formed up his Staff in December 1941 and took over as COMMANDER IN CHIEF, U. S. FLEET and Chief of Naval Operations, Commander Dyer was ordered to that Staff.

In early 1943, as a captain, he was ordered as Chief of Staff to Rear Admiral Richard L. Conolly, COMMANDER AMPHIBIOUS BASES NORTH WEST AFRICA and served in the Mediterranean Area on that staff through the Tunisian, Sicilian and Italian campaigns. At Salerno, Italy, aboard the BISCAYNE in September 1943 he was machine gunned in the leg during a German air attack and was then invalided home.

When released from the hospital, in February 1944, he was ordered to command the light cruiser ASTORIA "THE MIGHTY NINETY," and fought that ship through the Philippine, Iwo Jima and Okinawa campaigns of the Pacific War.

V. Adm. G. C. Dyer, USN, Ret.   Page 2

In June 1945, Captain Dyer was ordered back to Washington and duty on Admiral King's Staff and served as Special Assistant to Admiral Richard S. Edwards, Deputy Commander in Chief.

When promoted to flag rank in November 1945, Rear Admiral Dyer became Chief of Logistic Plans in the Office of the Chief of Naval Operations, and later served as Chief of General Plans in the same office. Subsequent details prior to the Korean War included command of CRUISER DIVISION TEN and Deputy Commandant, National War College.

During the Korean War, Rear Admiral Dyer was COMMANDER UNITED NATIONS BLOCKADE AND ESCORT FORCE, a multi-national naval force of over a hundred ships with contingents from the Navies of Australia, Canada, Great Britain, Korea, Netherlands, New Zealand, Thailand and the United States.

Assignments subsequent to the Korean War were as COMMANDER TRAINING COMMAND, PACIFIC FLEET and COMMANDANT ELEVENTH NAVAL DISTRICT with headquarters in San Diego, California. While in this assignment, he suffered several strokes and was physically retired on 1 February 1955.

Besides "Naval Logistics," he wrote "On the Treadmill to Pearl Harbor," the story of the naval service of Admiral James Otto Richardson during the immediate pre-World War II period, and "The Amphibians Came to Conquer," an account of the life and naval service of Admiral Richmond Kelly Turner, Commander of the Amphibious Forces, Pacific Fleet during World War II.

United States decorations include the Distinguished Service Medal for exceptionally meritorious service during the Korean War, four Legions of Merit (three combat awards), a Bronze Star Medal with Combat "V," and a Purple Heart Medal for service during World War II. Campaign ribbons for naval service spanning World War I, World War II and the Korean War carry eleven "Battle Stars."

Foreign decorations include:- British Honorary Commander of the Military Division, Order of the British Empire; French Legion of Honor, Degree of Commander; Peruvian Cross of Naval Merit, Great Officer White; Thailand Most Exalted Order of the White Elephant, Degree of Knight Commader; Korean Order of Military Merit, Degree of Taiguk; and Italian Military Order of Merit.

Vice Admiral Dyer is a member of the Society of the Cincinnati, State of Virginia, and a member of the General Staff of the Military Order of the World Wars.

Married to Mary Adaline Shick of La Porte, Indiana, on April 2, 1921, they have three children and twelve grand children.

Home address is 4 Chase Road, Pendennis Mount, Annapolis, Maryland.

28 October 1966

Authorization

The U.S. Naval Institute is hereby authorized to make available to individuals, libraries, and other repositories of its choosing the transcripts of 15 oral history interviews concerning the life and career of the late Vice Admiral George C. Dyer, U.S. Navy (Retired). The interviews were recorded on 15 and 29 April, 26 May, 12 and 19 June, and 13 November 1969, 31 March, 15 April, 12 May, 15 October, 5 and 24 November, and 10 December 1970, 4 March and 11 May 1971 in collaboration with Dr. John T. Mason, Jr. for the U.S. Naval Institute.

Acting on behalf of the estate of the late Admiral Dyer, the undersigned does hereby release and assign to the U.S. Naval Institute all right, title, restriction, and interest in these interviews. The copyright of both the oral and transcribed versions shall be the sole property of the U.S. Naval Institute. The tape recordings of the interviews shall be the sole property of the U.S. Naval Institute.

Signed and sealed this 15th day of June 1988.

Adaline S. Dyer
Adaline S. Dyer
(Mrs. George C. Dyer)

DECLARATION OF TRUST

The undersigned does hereby appoint and designate as his (her) Trustee herein, the Secretary-Treasurer and Publisher of the United States Naval Institute to perform and discharge the following duties, powers, and privileges in connection with the possession and use of a certain taped interview between the undersigned and the Oral History Department of the United States Naval Institute.

1. Classification of Transcript.

    ( )a. If classified <u>OPEN</u>, the transcript(s) may be read or the recording(s) audited by the qualified personnel upon presentation of proper credentials, as determined by the Secretary-Treasurer of the U. S. Naval Institute.

    (X)b. If classified <u>PERMISSION REQUIRED TO CITE OR QUOTE</u>, the user will be required to obtain permission in writing from the interviewee prior to quoting or citing from either the transcript(s) or the recording(s).

    ( )c. If classified <u>PERMISSION REQUIRED</u>, permission must be obtained in writing from the interviewee before the transcribed interview(s) can be examined or the tape recording(s) audited.

    ( )d. If classified <u>CLOSED</u>, the transcribed interview(s) and the tape recording(s) will be sealed until a time specified by the interviewee. This may be until the death of the interviewee or for any specified number of years.

2. It is expressly understood that in giving this authorization, I am in no way precluded from placing such restrictions as I may desire upon use of the interview at any time during my lifetime, nor does this authorization in any way affect my rights to the copyright of my literary expressions that may be contained in the interview.

Witness my hand and seal this 3rd day of May 1973

George C Dyer

I hereby accept and consent to the foregoing Declaration of Trust and the powers therein conferred upon me as Trustee:

R E Bowler

Interview with Admiral George C. Dyer April 15, 1969
by John T. Mason, Jr. Annapolis, Maryland

Mr. Mason: Admiral, it's wonderful that you've consented to do this series on your fascinating career in the Navy. I've been wanting to do this for a very long time; at least four or five years, and at last the moment has arrived. I wonder if you'd begin, in a very informal way, to tell me something about your background. First, give me the date and place of your birth, and then something about your family, and from there, something about your early education.

Admiral Dyer: Well, I was born on the 27th of April, 1898, and that was just six days before my father left to go to the Spanish-American War. Actually, he left Minneapolis, Minnesota with the 13th Minnesota Regiment to go to San Francisco, where he was put on a transport and went out to Manila, where he participated in the siege of Manila, its capture and subsequent operations. I may say this, that my mother never let him forget his going away leaving her with two small boys to take care of.

Q: He deserted her at a crucial moment.

Dyer: With my brother, who was two years older than I; and it made a very marked impression on her. She never let him forget it.

When I was talking with my wife this morning about this interview, I said, "Well, how shall I start this interview off?" And she said, "Well, tell the story about how you happened to go to the Naval Academy." And that will illustrate a lot about my family. My brother and I were talking at the table--the dinner table--about what we were going to do when we grew up. This was when we were, I'd say, probably 10 and 12, or 9 and 11; and we had this long-winded discussion to which my father listened. When we finished, he raised his finger like this, and he said, "Well, I'll tell you what you're going to do. You (pointing at my brother, who was the older), are going to West Point; and you (pointing at me, the younger), are going to go to the Naval Academy." And that's what we did.

Q: Well, that certainly is a very revealing remark, isn't it?

Dyer: In regard to my family background--I'm sure the reason that my father decided our future in this way was that at that time, we were just as poor as church mice. He knew the value of education, and was very anxious that we get a college education. He had served in the Army in the National Guard, both before and during the Spanish-American War, and subsequent thereto. He was very fond of the Army. His younger brother who had been a private in Company I of the 13th Minnesota, which was the Regiment with which my father went to Manila by that time, was a first Lieutenant or a Captain in the Marine Corps. He knew that my uncle, who got his commission without a college degree, had been sent to college by the Marines, and by that time had a law degree out of Georgetown. He knew you could get a college degree if you had the necessary stuff behind you, and so, I think that was basically the reason why he made that decision.

Q: Yes, that certainly was in the time before scholarships were available, in the manner in which they are now.

Dyer: My family in particular the Dyer side; I know considerable about, because my grandmother Dyer was a great student of the family tree, and a great believer in family. The Dyer family in the earlier colonial days, and during the first half of the 19th century had really quite a substantial background.

Q: Where were they located, in New England?

Dyer: No, the branch that I belonged to of the Dyer family, basically is located in Franklin County, West Virginia. My great-grandfather, John J. Dyer moved from what was Virginia at that time to Iowa. When the state of Iowa was formed, he became the first Federal judge in Iowa.

Q: That was 1819, 1820.

Dyer: No, this was 1846. Iowa became a state, and my great grandfather Dyer was appointed by President Polk to be the first Federal judge. He served for nine years. He was ordered back to Washington in 1856 to some kind of a judicial conference, and en route, he contacted typhoid fever. He actually died over in Franklin, which was the family home, in 1856. The John J. Dyers' had a very large home in Dubuque, Iowa. I have a postcard here showing my great grandfather Dyer's home in Dubuque, Iowa. The postcard is dated 1907; later the home was taken over by the St. Joseph Academy, as their Administration Building, after having been the rectory of the Academy.

Q: It became the rectory of the Academy. Very interesting.

Dyer: My great grandfather, John J. Dyer graduated from the University of Virginia. This is his graduation book. You'll see there in the signatures of many of the famous contemporary Virginians. The Dyer family actually comes down from the group called the Roger Dyer family. There were three Dyer brothers who came over to America in the period well before the French-Indian War, but long after the Mayflower.

Q: From England?

Dyer: From England. One brother went to Providence, one went to Maine, and one went to Pennsylvania, and thence to Virginia. Actually my Dyer line moved from Pennsylvania into Virginia in 1747. My great-great grandfather's (Zebulon Dyer) house is still standing over there in Franklin, West Virginia: it's a very nice house. It was built in 1816, and is still being lived in.

Q: A member of the family, or has it passed out of the family?

Dyer: No, it is not being used by a member of the family, although there are members of the family who live in Franklin. None of them are in the house; it is being rented at the present time. I saw it about a year ago. When my great-grandfather (John J. Dyer) died, he left his widow, Lucy, a substantial sum of money. Before she died, she spent it all. She was raised in the southern style, she was a Virginia lady--so to speak--and she just went through all the money. Her three boys (Frank, Charles and William) did not go to college, and neither did any of my grandfather's three boys (Harry, Jesse and John). In other words, my father, and his two younger brothers. They had their problems financially. During my early youth, I can remember the financial problems that my family had.

My older brother was appointed to West Point, took his

examinations, and he was accepted. During the time he was waiting to go, he had an attack of acute appendicitus and died. When he died, my mother insisted that we leave where we were living; which was Hopkins, Minnesota, and go to some place else. So, father, who at that time was working for the Minneapolis Threshing Machine Company, in the collection department, got himself a job with another threshing machine company, which was called M. Rumley Company. Later it became the Advance Rumley Company, and now is the Allis-Chalmers Company. We went out to Portland, Oregon. I can remember the financial discussion about my father's new job very well. When father left the Minneapolis Threshing Machine Company he was getting $85 a month; and when he went to work for M. Rumley Company, he was getting $150 a month; which to my father and mother, in 1912, seemed like a lot of money.

Q: Well, it was. I mean, it bought a lot.

Dyer: It bought a lot more than it does now, but it wasn't a lot of money, in the real sense.

Q: Admiral, lap back and tell me how you reacted, how you felt when you were told, in no uncertain way, that you were going to the Academy.

Dyer: My reaction--which was entirely different from that

of the youth of today--I accepted it as a wise decision. I've never regretted it. I am just eternally grateful to my father for having made that decision. Because, when anybody asked me at that period of my youth what I was going to do when I grew up, I said I was going to go to the Naval Academy, just as though I was going to go. It took a bit of doing, both on my father's part, and on my part to get to the Naval Academy. He set a goal for me to achieve, and by George, I achieved it. The Navy has been very wonderful to me, and all I say is, I worked like a dog for the Navy.

Q: Well, tell me Admiral, is this characteristic of the kind of training you got generally?

Dyer: I was raised very strictly. Both my mother and father were strict disciplinarians. The Academy discipline was no burden at all for me. And I'll tell you one other insight-- when I went away to the Naval Academy, my mother said to me, "Now George, I don't want you to drink coffee, and I don't want you to smoke." And I've never done either. Despite the fact, that years later she said don't ever think anything about what I told you not to do; all I meant was not to do it until you reached maturity.

Q: Have reached the age of discretion.

Dyer: --Age of discretion. Yes, but I've never done either. I've been able to discipline myself, and that is a great asset, no matter what you're doing. I was raised in a family of discipline, and I don't say that I did not rebel against it at times; because I can remember scenes when I did. Ended up back of the woodshed with my father and a leather strap, but nevertheless, it schooled me well.

Q: You did learn from him, then to set goals and work for the goal; rather than lash around in an indefinite way.

Dyer: That's right; not know what I was going to do. When we went out to Portland, Oregon, my father was, of course, cut off from people he had grown up with--so to speak--because he was born in St. Paul, Minnesota, raised in Minneapolis, and then had moved to Hopkins, which is a suburb of Minneapolis. Now you can't tell Hopkins isn't part of Minneapolis because it's one of the inner-suburbs of Minneapolis. When we got out to Portland, Oregon, we knew no one at all. My father was very much concerned about getting an appointment to the Naval Academy for me. Senator Nelson of Minnesota had appointed my brother. My mother's father had been in politics a reasonable amount, and so together, they were able to get the appointment for my brother--from Senator Nelson. When I got out to Portland, the first thing that came along was that the local Congressman held a competetive examination for the Naval Academy during my senior year in high school. I took the examination. There were 13 boys who took that examination.

Q: For a single appointment?

Dyer: For a single appointment.

Q: Plus two alternates.

Dyer: I presume there were alternates but I do not remember it. Nothing was announced about the results of the examination, not only for days, but for weeks and months.

Q: Was it a Civil Service examination?

Dyer: Given by the civil service. Whether it was civil service, or not--we took it in the post office--and it was conducted by a civil service employee. I think the examination was an old examination sent out from the Naval Academy, but I don't know. In the interim before the results were announced; father made contact with a chap who had served in the same Regiment with him during the Spanish-American War, whose name was Ridgeway. Major Ridgeway knew the senator from Oregon, Senator Chamberlain, and in due time secured an appointment with him. They took me down to see Senator Chamberlain. It certainly was my first contact with any politician, much less with a senator . . .

Q: This was in his Portland office?

Dyer: It was in his Portland office. We had the appointment with the Senator, arrived, and were ushered in and Major Ridgeway sounded off. Senator Chamberlain, turned to me, and he said, "You know, the only thing that worries me about the appointment, I want someone who'll graduate from that S. O. B. institution. I've been a senator for six years, and I've never been able to get anybody to graduate from there. All my candidates get thrown out." He turned to me, he said, "Do you think you could graduate?" I gave the right answer, I said I surely could.

Q: That's really a commentary on the school system, as it was then in Oregon, isn't it?

Dyer: So, he said, "I'll give you the appointment." And he did. After I'd had the appointment, oh, maybe a couple of weeks or thereabouts the results of the Congressional contest were announced in the paper one night. And I had won the congressional appointment. The chap who passed second was Ross Dierdorff, who became my roommate at the Naval Academy. The chap who passed third that year was named Kinney, who entered in the class of '20 but bilged from that class into 1921 and then did not graduate.

Q: Did you have to come to a prep school then?

Dyer: No. To go back a little bit . . . My family lived in Minneapolis in the years immediately after father came back from the Spanish-American War. Then father got this job out in Hopkins, and we moved out to Hopkins. I was not six years old at that time, but when I became six I went to the grade school. In the meanwhile, my grandfather Mortimer, my mother's father bought a house for mother and father to live in in Hopkins. The house was what today would be roughly about two blocks from the school. It was actually one long block out in the country--they just hadn't sub-divided yet. I went to school there through grade school. At that time, Minnesota had a very fine school system. Starting with the fifth grade you had to take examination--state examinations in every subject. I still have my certificates down in the strong box in the cellar--my certificates from grades 5 through 8. I did the 8 grades in 6 years. It was a small school, a country school, and I have my graduation picture down below. There were five of us in the 8th grade graduating class, with our teacher, Miss Alexander. We called her "Miss Alexander, the great commander." I went to a four-room school house which handled the 8 grades, in other words, there were 2 grades in each room. The first two years of high school I also did in Hopkins. At the end of the second year, my brother died, and we went out to Portland, Oregon. When we lived in Hopkins, in the early days, my brother had a Saturday Evening Post route. He delivered the Saturday Evening Post, which at that time was a nickel--the boy paid 3 cents, he made 2 cents a copy--so brother was making between 50¢ and 60¢ a week. When he got older, he then picked up a Minneapolis paper route which paid him more. I took over the Saturday Evening Post route. As soon as we got out in Portland, I got myself a paper route. The first paper that I delivered was really a tabloid like the Daily News of New York. I had a small route, widely scattered over the whole section where we lived. The paper cost 30¢ a month, and the people that I was delivering to, unfortunately had a habit of moving out all the time. I was constantly losing my 30¢'s which I was to collect at the end of each month. So, it was not a very good route.

Q: That was very frustrating, wasn't it?

Dyer: Yes, but I worked at it and built it up about double the number, by going around and asking people to subscribe. Then, I applied for a route with the Portland JOURNAL, which was the afternoon paper. A very fine newspaper—it charged 90¢ a month, 3¢ a copy—I really made hay with the JOURNAL because I solicited a lot of people. I delivered 200 papers—which is a lot of papers. I'd make two runs with the wagon—I delivered them from a small red wagon. I was making a lot of money, and I was saving my money because at that time you had to deposit $485 at the Naval Academy to become a midshipman, to pay for your outfit. I felt sure that it would strain my father to provide the $485, and so I felt that I should provide a large share of it. Then, as I say, I established a reputation. I went to work for the Portland OREGONIAN, and delivered a morning newspaper—5¢ a copy, $1.50 a month. This was in 1914, and a 5¢ newspaper was something unusual. The people who took the paper were all reliable people and they all paid the paper boy. It was really a very fine thing. My mother objected to it because she got up every morning to get me started on my way. I used to leave the house at 5:30 or 5:40—I picked up the papers at 6 o'clock, and started delivering at 6 o'clock. She didn't like it very much.

Q: It didn't detract from you energies for school, though?

Dyer: No, no. As a matter of fact, I did not have any great problems in high school. I was never a "savoir" but

I was a diligent worker, and that made up for a lack of real brains, I'll say.

Q: Admiral, this whole episode of delivering magazines and then papers--this was a lesson for you, too, wasn't it--a study in human nature?

Dyer: Oh, yes. Anyhow, after I had gotten my appointment, the assistant-circulation manager of the Portland OREGONIAN was offered the job as the circulation manager of the Wichita BEACON. He persuaded my mother and father to let me go with him to Wichita, Kansas to work with him in the circulation of the Wichita BEACON. I was, then, about four months away from coming to the Academy. I mean, taking the examinations, and so forth. My mother and father let me go, and I went down to Wichita. I took the early examinations for the Naval Academy at the post office in Wichita in April 1915.

There hangs another story--They told you when you took the examinations that you wouldn't hear from them for another month or six weeks, but you would hear--I think it was--by the 25th of May. So the 25th of May came and went by, and I didn't get any word. I thought, of course, that I must not have passed. My father and mother of course--couldn't accept that. Anyhow, my father sent a telegram to his brother, who at that time was on duty in Washington. He was the aide to the Major General Commandant of the Marine Corps. The uncle (Captain Jesse F. Dyer, USMC) sent back word that I had passed. But I still didn't have any official notification. I waited another week, still didn't get any notification. So, father sent another telegram. This time I got a telegram down in Wichita, Kansas. I'll never forget it. This was about the 9th of June, it said, "You are authorized to report at the Naval Academy on June 7th. Wire if you intend to do so." Well, the 7th had already gone by, gone by before they ever sent the wire.

I got on my horses as soon as I could and entrained for Washington. My uncle was not in Washington when I arrived but he had arranged for a Major Carmody to meet me. He did, and took me down to the Army-Navy club, where I had lunch. He put me on the old electric trolley, and I got down here to Annapolis, where I was met by another Marine, an officer by the name of Underwood. At that time, (1915), the Marines had their bachelor officers quarters out in town. I spent the last night before I entered the Navy at the Marine bachelor officers quarters out here in town.

I came in to the Naval Academy the next morning, and got in line--they had a line of prospective Midshipmen all formed up before the Administration Building. This was on the 15th of June, 1915. I got up to the head of the line, and the clerk said, "Name?", and I said, "Dyer, George C." He looked at the list, and he said, "I guess you didn't pass, stand aside there." There was somebody behind me, so I stood aside. He processed all the rest of them. By that time, I had my telegram out, and I gave him the telegram. It said, "You are authorized to report on June 7th, wire if you intend to do so." He stood up and said, "Hey, Joe, here's the guy that didn't get the word." Well, that was my initial start in the Naval Academy.

Q: The one who didn't get the word. It took a lot of courage to come out here under those circumstances, and on your own.

Dyer: I was so glad I was finally here. Then, of course, they give you a physical examination. When I was a boy--my brother and I, and some others were lifting a telephone pole-- they were putting in telephones on our street--and somebody gave the word to "let go." I didn't get the word, and they dropped the telephone pole on my foot. It broke one of my toes. My mother didn't recognize it as a broken toe. Of course, I didn't know anything about it--it merely healed, a bit bent. When I got to the Naval Academy and had my physical examination, they said, "You've got a broken toe. I don't know if we can let you get by with this broken toe. When did

did this happen?" I said, "Well, this happened back in Hopkins about 1908, I guess." He said, "Ever bother you?," and I said, "No, it never has yet." Anyhow, I had a very bad moment, when the doctor said, "I don't know if we can let you get in with that broken toe, or not." But the Medical Board did pass me. And the toe has never bothered me yet.

To go back to the other side of the family--my mother's name was Mortimer, Georgia Mortimer. Her father, for a good many years, was the City Passenger Agent of the old Minneapolis and St. Louis Railroad, in Minneapolis. They lived at a very large place--640 5th Avenue, South in Minneapolis. I've been back there, and it is right down town now. There's a tremendous office building on the site. Grandfather Mortimer was a Civil War veteran and very much of a G. A. R. man. He was the State Commander of the G. A. R. for a number of years and always participated in G. A. R. meetings, and so forth. One of my early rememberances is of going down to the annual parade on the 4th of July, sitting up in an office window and seeing my grandfather lead the parade in Minneapolis. He was a very wonderful person, as far as I knew. He died in 1905, when I was seven years old. One of the horrendous things that I learned from that--before he died, and he died from what I believe at that time they called asthma--he couldn't get his breath. You might call it emphysema, or some other such thing. Mother took my brother and me in to see him, in the period just before he died. That is something you should never do with young children. Instead of having a very pleasant and wonderful rememberance of my grandfather, which I had always had before, I saw this person gasping for breath. I never had any desire to watch anybody die after that. My grandfather Mortimer was also English, and was always known in Minnesota as a Territoral Settler. He arrived in Minneapolis, from Montreal, before Minnesota became a state. I can remember going to the State Fair in Minneapolis to watch Dan Patch run his mile in 1:59 4/5, or whatever it was. He held the world's record. And being taken by my grandmother and my mother to a building and seeing a picture of my grandfather--larger than that one (2' 2" x 3') on the wall of this building where all the official Territorial Settlers had their pictures.

My grandfather Mortimers brother's name was George and that was actually from whom I got my name, George. Although, there are other George Dyer's in the Roger Dyer line. And my middle name is Carroll, which my grandmother Dyer was instrumental in my getting, because she was a Carroll--from the Charles Carroll of Carrolton's. So, she managed to get me my middle name, Carroll.

Q: What were the religious influences in your family?

Dyer: Very strong, very strong. I was just reading in this book today before you came--this is "Who Made Iowa," which has a great long song and dance about my great-grandfather, John J. Dyer. When my great-grandmother, Lucy Dyer, died, this article was printed in the Iowa historical record, it said--this was about her--but it says about her husband-- "Judge Dyer was a good deal of a man, and was regarded as one of the most prominent and influential citizens of Dubuque in those days. He, with General C. H. Booth was instrumental in organizing the Episcopal Church, and was regularly elected Senior Warden as long as he lived." My Grandfather Mortimer was also an Episcopalian, and also a Senior Warden at an Episcopal Church in Minneapolis. And I have been a member of the Vestry of three different Episcopal churches. I served in the Vestry when I was a Senior Lieutenant in Honolulu; in 1931-1934 and I served in the Vestry at St. John's, Bethesda on two occasions--when I was a Captain, and later when I was a Rear Admiral. I served on the Vestry of Christ Church, Coronado when I was a Rear Admiral and Commandant of the 11th Naval District out there. My feeling churchwise is very strong. I went to St. Margaret's Episcopal Church (Westminister) annual meeting here in Annapolis last Sunday. I'll not serve on the Vestry any longer, because I think it ought to be done by younger men. Nevertheless, I'm a strong Churchman, have been all my life; and have participated in many church programs in the Navy. If you want to ask about that, you talk with Chaplain Kelly, and he will tell you roughly that about 15 years ago, they had a program in the Navy trying to re-establish moral standards, and so forth in which I participated very actively. I have a very certificate from the Chief of Chaplains hanging in my study paying tribute to my efforts.

Q: Tell me, Admiral, something about the Academy days themselves.

Dyer: When I arrived at the Academy on 15 June 1915, it was in the midst of the Gouging Inquiry of 1915. They later had a Naval General Court Martial sitting here in that early summer, June. The Inquiry had resulted when a number of Midshipmen had broken into an academic department on the night before examinations, and lifted questions--if not actual examination papers. I think it was just questions, I think they made copies of the questions. They were all used to good advantage. In an effort to help, the questions were turned over to some of the wooden people in the class who were having academic troubles. Quite a number of the midshipmen who participated in the raids were dismissed; and a number were turned back a class because they had knowledge of it. There were a number of midshipmen in the Class of 1918, who were turned back into our class (1919), because they had knowledge of, or somehow or other had been contaminated by this gouging. My knowledge of this Inquiry is 100% heresay.

Q: Turned back, you mean, they repeated a year?

Dyer: Yes, they were turned back into the next class and repeated the work, yes. At that time, the Academy published a yearbook. I don't know if they still do, but I don't believe they do. I was just looking at the yearbooks for 1915, 1916, 1917, and 1918 for a different reason when the class of 1919 celebrated its 50th anniversary here last year. I wanted to get the names of the people who had been turned back into our class from the earlier classes. I went over and consulted the Naval Academy register. Those who were turned back for gouging or hazing are so listed, and those who were turned back for academic deficiences, or being on the border line, so to speak, they also were listed. I wasn't interested, particularly, in the numbers, although I would guess that there were about five that were dismissed for gouging and for hazing, and fifteen that were turned back. But, they weren't all turned back into our class. They were turned back--first class to second class, second class to third class, third class to fourth class which was my class.

During that summer, 1915, the ships that were taking the Midshipmen on the Midshipmen Practice Cruise remained out in the bay here while this Gouging Inquiry was going on so that all the Midshipmen would be available to testify. Because the Court didn't know how this inquiry would spread, and whom they would want as a witness. Those were the days before battleships carried airplanes or helicopters so the decision was made to keep all the upper class Midshipmen available. They permitted Upper Class Midshipmen to come in once or twice a week to the Naval Academy and to Annapolis to let them have liberty and recreation. The Upper Class Midshipmen carried on their midshipman cruise work right out in the bay on board ship. Some of these Upper Class Midshipmen used to land at the Academy docks and roam the Academy. Here were all the newly arrived plebes. The Upper Classmen really raised cain with us plebes, by hazing us. When my class came in to the Academy, we were assigned temporary roommates, alphabetically on the day we came in. My Plebe Summer roommate was a very fine Jewish midshipman, whose name was Edwin Friedman. I'm very sorry to say, but it's true, but due to the fact that I was living with him, our room received a tremendous amount of attention from the Upper Classmen. They really just gave him the very devil, and gave me some of it.

Q: There weren't many Jewish boys in the Navy then?

Dyer: There were very few, there were five in my class. Of the five, I thought there were three very wonderful people amongst those five. They all moved along the ladder of success, not in the Navy, but have done very well by themselves in the years subsequent to graduation. They all graduated. They all had anywhere from three to eight or nine years of commissioned service in the Navy. One was physically retired, because he got seasick. The other four resigned. One chap, is, probably, I think the wealthiest man in our class. He runs a tremendous home construction establishment, builds whole sub-divisions. He's one of the most generous persons that I've ever known. His name is Harry Goodwin. In 1915, Harry Goodwin scored the first touchdown against Army that the Navy had scored in a number of years. At that time they permitted plebes to play varsity football. Harry was the center, and he recovered an Army fumble and ran for a touchdown. The story is told of Harry--it's probably just a story--that the coach, whose name was Jonas Ingram, (Class of 1907) had offered any one that scored a touchdown against Army, either a bottle of champagne or $5. Harry took the $5, and made it grow.

My classmate, and very close friend--has been ever since--

Ed Friedman, really took an awful lot of abuse. Including drinking ink, and all that sort of thing.

I had not been in the Academy two hours, before I was in what was known as an elephant race. I was coming back from having picked up my complete outfit of uniform clothing with instructions to go right to my room and stencil everything with my name. I had the stencil. An upper classman, whose name was Harvey, out of the class of '17; met me and asked me what my name was where I was from, and so forth. Then he said, "Have you ever been in an elephant race?" Of course, I said, "No, I've never been in an elephant race." He said, "You're about to be in one." I went down right below the rotunda in Bancroft Hall, and there already gathered were roughly six or seven of my classmates. All were on their hands and knees, still in civilian clothes, with big piles of new uniforms and gear set off to the side, and all with one shoe off. With a newcomer, everything stopped, and I was put into line after taking off one shoe. The movement then started off by taking the shoe and hitting the man ahead of you on the rump. Then he passes the blow on to the one ahead of him. In the meantime, you have to keep crawling with one hand and two feet to the cheers of the onlookers. That started off the elephant race.

Of course, we arrived here in various physical conditions.

I don't think I was in bad physical condition, but I certainly wasn't in toughened condition.

During the hazing we received generally, the first thing we had to do was stoop-fallings, then knee bends, and then chinning yourself on your locker or the door of the room; and so forth until you were just exhausted. Then you had to do all kinds of other physical exercises. This hazing went on for several weeks. Long before the end of the summer, the news spread through the regiment to the plebes--somebody had taken this story to the Executive Officer, Lieutenant Commander Sinclair Gannon, later Admiral Gannon. Within a couple of days a formal investigation was underway. The head of the Board that investigated this, as far as I knew, was a Commander whose name was Price. He had a full beard and mustache, and so forth. I thought he was "older than Jehovah". But, I'm sure that he was not more than 45 or 48 years old. The Board swore you to tell the truth, the whole truth and nothing but the truth. You were then put on the stand and a much younger officer than Commander Price asked you many questions. I answered them all truthfully. I had been hazed tremendously, I didn't know anybody's name--I really didn't. They didn't ask me if I'd ever been in an elephant race. But I told them a lot of other things that happened in the room. I didn't know who Harvey was until after the end of plebe summer, when the Midshipmen came back and I was in the same company that he was. Then I learned who he was. Almost immediately following the investigation they had a hazing General Court Martial. The ships stayed on. But this time, after about four or five days, the ships shoved off on the delayed summer cruise. The poor culprits were left, and some of them were dismissed.

Q: It was really a serious problem in those days, wasn't it?

Dyer: Oh, tremendous. So, that was my introduction into the Naval Academy. One other story to tell--I don't presume that you know--there was a professor here named Charles Storr Alden, who some years later became Head of the Department of English. At the end of Plebe Summer, they gave all the plebes an examination in grammar. If I had a very weak subject, it was grammar. I came into the recitation room after taking the examination the next day, I was in Mr. Alden's section who at that time was just one of the professors--and we sat down. The Midshipman in charge of the section made his report. At that time the Midshipman in Charge of Section marched the Section in and reported all members of the section present or accounted for, then Professor Alden's first remark was, "Who is Midshipman Dyer?" Of course, I bounced up. And he said, "Where are you from, Mr. Dyer?" And I said, "I'm from Oregon." Because

I'd been appointed from Oregon. He said, "My what a long ways you'll have to go back." You can imagine what that did to my morale. This test counted as one mark of your first week in English. At that time you got daily marks and a weekly average mark. I don't know if the midshipmen still do or do not get weekly marks. In English we had five recitations a week--I don't know how bad my mark was in the test but when they posted the marks at the end of the first month, as they then did at the end of each month--you could tell what you got each week--my mark for that week was 2.5. (2.5 was the passing mark on a scale of 4.0). Fortunately, my mark was a little higher for the rest of the other weeks.

Q: Or you would have made that trip back.

Dyer: One other story to tell which is about mechanical drawing. I never was a good artist in mechanical drawing. They have a very useful and necessary course in mechanical drawing. After it gets on, you have various developments of it where you have to produce on the drawing board development of spheroids. This was, roughly, I would say about the middle of the second term. We had just gotten into this, and I thought that I understood it, but my instructor--whose name was Ralph Needham, (Class of 1907), he was a Senior Lieutenant at the time--put me on the weekly tree. If you were unsatisfactory in your work, you were posted over at Bancroft Hall at the end of the week. And I was on the tree with a 1.0, that's an awful low mark when 2.5 is passing and 4.0 is perfect. It takes a lot of higher marks to balance it. I went around and tried to talk to some of my savvy classmates in the mechanical drawing, and tried to comprehend the subject a bit more. By George, at the end of the second week, again I was on the tree with a 1.0. I was really in a panic. I again studied the book, and I got help from my classmates. In the middle of the third week, we took our regular monthly examination. At that time you had a monthly examination in every subject. The day after the monthly examination, we had regular class again. Lieutenant Needham was at my side every two or three minutes. I just thought this is really the coup d'etat. I'm about to be given the old "boot-o". On the following Monday, I went to class, and as soon as I arrived my instructor; Needham, turned the class over to one of the other instructors. He said, "You and I have a date with the Head of the Department." I was just petrified. We went down to the Head of the Department's office. He questioned me--the Gouging Inquiry was right in the back of his mind. I said, "No, sir." Did I feel that I understood this? And I said, "Yes, sir, I can't understand why I've been on the tree with 1.0; I think I understand it quite well." The Head of the Department said, "Well, I guess you do, you're the only one in the class who got a 4.0 in the examination." I was sent back to class. Ralph Needham told me years later--he was my division commander--the Head of the Department just gave him hell for giving me a 1.0, and I had been the only one who got a 4.0 in that examination. Which is a perfect mark, as you perhaps know. He had put me on the tree twice. For the third week, he had already entered the daily marks for the first couple of days before the examination. My weeks mark was reasonably good--I got something like a 3.2. The last week I got 4.0. Still, in daily averages I was unsat for the month, with that mark, and only my exam mark which counted 1/3 for the monthly mark made me sat for the month.

Q: How could he have made such an error?

Dyer: I don't know. When I had command of the S-15, he was my division commander. He used to tell everybody that story-- He would say, "He is the guy to whom I gave a couple of 1.0's." He gave me wonderful fitness reports for my command of the S-15. If I had written them myself they couldn't have been better.

One other story I want to tell about the Naval Academy. I was there during much of World War I. There were two officers there--Lieutenant Commander Max De Mott and Lieutenant Commander Granville B. Hoey. Hoey developed the Hoey navigation position plotter. This story--which went all around amongst the midshipmen goes as follows: Because of the war--every officer wanted to get to sea duty. The Academy was the last place in the world they wanted to be. At that time, Lieutenant Commander Hoey--he was my battalion commander--got himself slated for orders away from the Naval Academy. He came down from Washington and walked into Max De Mott's office, and he said, "Max, I've just come from the Bureau. They tell me up there, they have ordered everybody away from the Naval Academy except the sons-of-bitches, and the damn fools--which are you?"

Q: Which category?

Dyer: Yes, which category. I'd just like to mention just a little bit about my cruises when I was here at the Academy.

Q: Yes, they're always interesting. Summer cruises.

Dyer: The first cruise I took was in the old coal-burning battleship WISCONSIN. The second cruise I took was in the very new oil-burning battleship NEVADA. The thing that I remember most about that first cruise is we had to coal ship every time we got into port. Coaling was an "All Hands" evolution. Officers, men, everybody, including the Chaplain, was given a shovel. We shoveled these large bags full of coal, we whipped them up from the coal barge and over, and onto the deck and dumped the coal down into the canvas coal shoots leading to the storage compartments (coal bunkers) below decks. We had a lot of unlucky midshipmen down below who leveled off the coal as it came down. Coaling ship was a most arduous, interminable, dirty job. The coal dust got all over the ship--in to every nook and corner and into every pore of your sweating body. After coaling was the only time on those old ships that you could take a fresh water bath. All the rest of the time, you took salt water baths because fresh water was a scarce commodity. But after coaling, they gave you a fresh water bath. You needed it.

Q: You really had to clean out the pores, didn't you?

Dyer: Yes. The first Midshipman's Practice Cruise that we took, of course, was during World War I and we did not go to Europe, as had been the immediate past practice. We went to Guantanamo Bay, Cuba, and then on up to Portland, Maine, and to Boston, and finally down to Long Island. The old battleships in the Cruise Squadron had very limited refrigeration of food. On the trip up from Guantanamo to Portland, our ice machine failed; and all our fresh meat went bad. Of course, we were reduced to living on canned food, which they had an adequate supply--including beans. We had plenty of beans.

I only had two cruises, due to the fact that I was at the

Academy only three years. The second cruise I took was in the NEVADA. The NEVADA was one of our newest battleships. She was commanded by a very distinguished naval officer and gentleman--a Jewish gentleman, Captain Joseph Strauss. He later became Chief of the Bureau of Ordnance and then later a four-star Admiral, Commander-in-Chief of the Asiatic fleet when I was out in the China station. There are any number of things that I remember about that cruise, but the one thing that I remember mostest was . . . I was down on the fo'c'sle taking an afternoon constitutional. The ship was standing-in to Hampton Roads. All of a sudden, I heard, through a megaphone, some one saying, "Midshipman, first class on the fo'c'sle, lay up on the bridge on the double." I didn't know what I had done, but I layed up on the bridge on the double all the way at top speed. Just as I came up on the bridge deck, I did not duck low enough, and I hit my head on the hatch combing and I really thought I had knocked myself out. But I recovered from that, got up that last step on the ladder. When I reached the bridge, the Captain said to me, "Relieve the Officer of the Deck." The Officer of the Deck was a Naval Militia lieutenant--you see, they had Naval Militia in those days rather than Naval Reserve. The Officer of the Deck was a Senior Lieutenant. He was a school teacher from Minnesota. I looked up his name in preparation for this. His name was Lieutenant R. D. DeWolfe. I was the most embarrassed person in the world. In the first place, ordinarily when you are coming into port, you post your special coming-into-port details--that includes one of your better Officers of the Deck. Here I was a first class Midshipman with the chore of having the deck coming into Hampton Roads. I certainly had some trepidations about what I should or shouldn't do but I did what I felt I should; and I evidently survived. I didn't get relieved, I stayed on, 'til the end of the watch.

Q: In spite of the blow on the head, too.

Dyer: The ship was a very excellent ship and I was most lucky to have been assigned to it for my First Class Cruise. The executive officer was William D. Leahy of whom you have heard. Later, he became Chief of Naval Operations, and Chief of Staff to President Roosevelt during World War II. The navigator was Commander James O. Richardson, who later became Commander-in-Chief of the U. S. Fleet, and was relieved by Admiral Kimmel February 1, 1941. The chief engineer was O. L. Cox, who became Chief of the Bureau of Engineering. Lieutenant Commander W. L. Furlong was also aboard. He became Chief of the Bureau of Ordnance. Incidentally he is still alive at the age of 88. And Robert L. Ghormley was also aboard.

Q: Certainly all familiar names.

Dyer: They were all in the NEVADA, when I was on board as a First Class Midshipman. And another thing, that you will find it difficult to believe--there were only, including Warrant Officers, 21 officers on the NEVADA that summer.

Q: What was the complement of a battleship like that?

Dyer: The complement, normally was 40 officers. She had 21. They stripped all those ships to put the people on the ships that went to Europe. The ones they left, at least in that ship were really first class. We had a Commander Loomis as the Officer in Charge of the Midshipmen. He was the father of the officer, Kent Loomis, who is Judge Eller's assistant in the Naval History Division at the present time.

I'll never forget this--At morning quarters in those days they had prayers every morning. The first time that the NEVADA left Hampton Roads and went to sea after the midshipmen had reported aboard, we had a young Chaplain, an acting Chaplain. His name was E. K. Duff. The North Atlantic was a bit rough that morning off Hampton Roads. He got half way through his prayers, and then went over to the rail and parked his cookies. Came back and finished his prayers. This was much to the delight of the Midshipmen. He had a job to do and he did it despite his handicap.

Dyer 2 - 35

Interview with Admiral George C. Dyer April 29, 1969
By John T. Mason, Jr. Annapolis, Maryland

Mr. Mason: Admiral, I'm very happy indeed to be with you for this second interview. When I departed last time, we had agreed that you would begin with your World War I assignments. The first of which, I believe, involved training at the Submarine School.

Admiral Dyer: I think there's one thing I want to mention. When I reported up to the U. S. Submarine Base at New London, my orders leaving the Naval Academy had been addressed to Midshipman G. C. Dyer. One of the oddities of my orders, as far as I'm concerned, is that when I reported to the Commander of the submarine base; he endorsed my orders to Midshipman G. C. Dyer--despite the fact that I was wearing an Ensign's white service uniform. The reason that I was wearing white service, was that I had bought a full Marine Corps outfit, because I thought I was going into the Marine Corps. Only six days before graduation, I was told that I was to be an Ensign in the Navy, and I could not purchase and have made up any blue uniforms in the short interval of time remaining before graduation on 6 June, 1918. Of the ten ensigns from my class who went up to New London, Connecticut to go to the Submarine School, there were five of us who were in midshipman white service, with Ensign shoulder boards. That was the only way we could show that we were Ensigns, of which fact we were very proud. The others, of course, wore blue uniforms; because in New London, in early June, you still wear blues.

Q: Just a question: Were you disappointed that you didn't get the Marine Corps assignment, or delighted?

Dyer: Actually, I had a very strong desire to go into the Marine Corps. I think I may have said this previously, but if I haven't, I should--My Father's younger brother was in the Marine Corps. He was really my ideal of what a Marine officer ought to be. He had participated in a considerable number of Expeditionary Force landings and operations in the Central American countries. At the occupation of Vera Cruz, he had been in Mexico. During a period when naval officers were not entitled to wear a great many campaign ribbons, he had a lot of them. He had a Medal of Honor, and all the other necessary ribbons to indicate a very fine performance of duty. He was a handsome individual; he wore a goatee. I just thought nothing could be better than that my going into the Marine Corps. Once the decision was made contrary to my desires, I put the matter behind me and charged ahead.

Q: So, it was then, a matter of disappointment.

Dyer: Oh, I was extremely disappointed. There were quite a number in my class who put in to go into the Marine Corps. There were six of us who had our requests approved. When they called us in, and told us we would not go into the Marine Corps--the Commandant of Midshipmen (Captain Louis N. Nulton) said, "Gentlemen, what type of duty would you like to do?" Thomas C. Hart--later Admiral Hart, Commander-in-Chief of the Asiatic fleet at the time World War II started--had been down to the Naval Academy in recent months, and had given a talk on submarines operating in the Atlantic during World War I. At that time he was either a Captain or a Commander, I believe the latter.

Q: Oh, yes. Based on Southern Ireland.

Dyer: Our submarines were based both on the Azores and on Ireland. The K-boats were in the Azores, and the L-boats were in Ireland. Of that group of six midshipmen, who had put in for the Marine Corps, and been accepted for the Marine Corps--all six of us then and there requested submarine duty upon graduation. In addition, there were four others, who had previously requested submarine duty. All ten were all ordered to the U. S. Submarine School at the Submarine Base, New London. One of the remarkable things about this, as far as I am concerned, is that of those six, there were three of us who became Flag Officers. As you know, that is simply just a tremendous number, percentage-wise. Because, you have when you graduate an average less than one chance in twenty of becoming a Flag Officer.

Q: Who were the other two, Admiral?

Dyer: Sunshine Murray, who later was Commander, Submarine Force, Atlantic; and now is a retired four-star Admiral; and the other chap was Eliot H. Bryant, who retired as a Vice Admiral, the same as I. Bryant lived here in Annapolis, and died here in Annapolis 14 years ago. (1955)

We all went up there, and our first Commanding Officer was Commander John Rodgers--the famous naval aviator, who was also a submariner. He was the Commander, Submarine Base. The school was commanded by a chap whose name was Marsh. We had actually about $4\frac{1}{2}$ months in the school. During the time we were in the school as students--when our submarines based on New London were making patrols off the Atlantic coast, Cape Cod, and up towards Nova Scotia--they occasionally used the students to fill in for a vacancy in one of the junior officers billets. This started happening along about September, after we'd been at school about $2\frac{1}{2}$ or 3 months.

Q: On duty training you got?

Dyer: Yes, on duty training it was. The submarines were all

very small. I made two cruises in the N-boats. They both had two officer bunks, and 16 enlisted bunks. And they had four officers, and 32 men aboard. You worked on the hot bunk principle--you stood six hours on, and had six hours off, which, except when eating, you had to spend in your bunk.

When you were on watch submerged, which was most of the time during the daytime, you stood a half-hour watch at the periscope, and a half-hour watch at the diving controls. In other words, you had a man who manned the forward planes, and a man who manned the after planes. And your station was right in between these two diving plane operators. If you had the periscope watch--normally the submarine ran at 32 feet--you stuck up the periscope every three minutes and made a sweep around the horizon, which took 10 or 15 seconds, depending a bit on the weather. You took a look-see, and then "Down periscope" again, and then in three minutes again "Up periscope". It was really a very wearisome thing, because as the day grew to an end, the air in the submarine got just plain foul.

The "Lake" N type submarines didn't have any air purifying systems in those early type boats. While you started out the day fresh and with lots of energy, as the amount of oxygen in the boat was used up, it was more and more difficult to do what you had to do. Then during the night, it was necessary to lay to on the surface and charge the submarines' batteries in order that it could dive the next day and spend the long day submerged. When you came to the surface at dark, you charged your batteries on both engines roughly 'til 1 or 1:30, or 2 o'clock the next morning, depending on the state of the batteries. When the batteries were reasonably charged at the high rate you'd get under way on one engine and finish off your charge with the other engine. And that way you would shift your station in accordance with instructions received by radio or in accordance with a prearranged plan. Occasionally, if you were under orders to get to a certain position--particularly during periods when German submarines were known to be actually operating over on our side of the Atlantic, information came in that they had attacked or sunk some ship, and you were ordered somewhere near their position. Then you'd have to knock off charging your battery earlier and run on two engines in order to reach that particular position, before you dove the next morning.

Q: The danger to our submarines from the enemy on this side of the ocean, was largely from German submarines? Was it?

Dyer: Except when friendly transports or freighters took pot shots at you it was, entirely.

Q: Were there any German raiders?

Dyer: No German raiders of any kind that I knew of. Actually the number of sighting contacts by our submarines was very, very limited. No American submarine sank a German submarine during World War I. Several fired torpedoes at them, but no one made a hit.

Q: Our submarines operating off the coast were involved in convoy duty, were they?

Dyer: Oh, no, we weren't involved in convoy duty at all. We had only an anti-submarine mission, to locate the German submarines that were over here and sink them. But we didn't.

During the time that I was a student and one reason I got to take two cruises--there was a squadron torpedo officer, an officer whose name was H. D. Bode, of whom you may have heard . . .

Q: Howard Bode -- very well.

Dyer: He was the skipper of the CHICAGO at the time of the Battle of Savo Island.

Part of the instructions we received as students at the Submarine School was getting torpedoes ready to fire. The junior officer on the submarine was turned into a Torpedo Officer. That was one of the jobs that he normally had. I was taking this course along with all the rest of the class.

There were 20 officers in the class. My sub section of students were getting a torpedo ready to fire. When Lieutenant Bode-- at that time he was a senior Lieutenant--left at the end of the working day; he said, "I want you people to stay here until these torpedoes are ready." We were doing it all by ourselves without any enlisted help or supervision; in order to actually train us to do the chore. I thought it was just the way it should be done. We had received a lot of theoretical and practical instructions, we had been through getting torpedoes ready with enlisted men a lot of times; and it was time that we were doing it ourselves. As the hours of the night wore on, we ran various tests and one of the bloomin' torpedoes wouldn't pass the tests. Of course, we had to do certain things in order to get the torpedo ready for firing. One by one the students started drifting off, when they got very tired, went up to the officer quarters and turned in. Finally, long about 2:30 or 3 o'clock the next morning--in walks Lieutenant Bode. Ensign George Dyer was the only guy who was still there. He said, "You go up and get the rest of the students and get them all down here." I said, "Well, Mr. Bode, this torpedo is within about five minutes of being ready, and why don't you stay here and let me test it out, and then I'll go up to the quarters, and you can go up to the quarters and get those boys up." A lot of them were senior to me, you know. So, he stayed around.

I ran a final test of the torpedo and by great good luck the torpedo checked out. He was just as pleased as all get out. He became a very firm friend of George Dyer. Now, he was a very difficult man . . .

Q: Indeed I know that.

Dyer: He just raised cain with so many people as he moved through the Navy. He was always my friend, always spoke up for me, and told everybody what a fine officer I was. It all came from sticking with the job. He told that story a dozen times to everybody within sight. When I had finished checking out the torpedo, he said, "You deserve to go turn in, and I'll go up and get those so-and-sos out of their bunks." And he did, and made them come back down again. That was the kind of a guy he was. That incident has always stuck in my mind.

One of the most important things that happened while I was at the Submarine School was that all my class were promoted (temporarily) to Junior Lieutenants. We actually received our temporary promotions in October--looking at my orders I note that they are dated the 25th of October, 1918. In October 1918, I was only four months out of the Naval Academy, and it really was something. Normally Ensigns in those days, served three years before being promoted to Junior Lieutenants.

When I graduated from the school, I was ordered to the

USS N-6. At that time--nobody lived on board the submarines except when they were at sea. When alongside a dock or a tender, there was a watch that stayed awake overnight on the submarine. No officers or enlisted personnel lived on the submarines, they lived on the Submarine Base--except when you were at sea. The submarines Commanding Officers had offices, desks, and so forth in a large administration building.

Upon graduation from the Submarine School, I went down and reported to the skipper of the N-6. His name was Hap Hein. (H. R. Hein). He was the anchor man in the Class of 1910. When I reported, he said, "Take a seat," and so forth; pulled out a cigarette, offered me a cigarette; and I said, "No thank you, I don't smoke." At that time, I was not 21 years old. My father had told me that he would give me a gold watch and $100, if I didn't smoke 'til I was 21, and I was still working on that. Hap Hein said with great emphasis, pounding on the desk with both fists. "Don't ever start!"

Smoking was not permitted on board submarines in that era. And there was a good reason for that advice from my Captain. Because when we went out on these patrols, the enlisted personnel talked about their next smoke from the moment we left the dock until we got back in. They had a well supervised program--generally drawing cards from a deck which the Chief of the Boat handled and shuffled between each persons' drawing. Each sailorman drew a card. The Chief of the Boat kept a record of who had drawn what card. Where people tied, they had to cut again, and so forth and so on. The Chief of the Boat established a list of the 32 men and who'd be the first man off to the submarine when it docked again, so he could smoke. High positions on the list became a valuable right, I mean it could be bartered or sold; depending on how crazy, or nutty, or depraved the individual was. He would buy somebody else's right to be the first or second person off the boat. After the ship was back in from the six or eight days patrol--those were the patrols we were making--the sailormen would rush off the boat onto dock and have five minutes. Then they'd have to come back on again, and relieve somebody else, so he could rush off; until the submarine was all secured and everybody was off and up in the enlisted barracks except the watch. I watched this go on, and it did anything except encourage me to start smoking.

One other thing about Hap Hein--he told me this himself some years later--arose due to the fact that he was of foreign extraction (German). During the war period, some high authority put a secret service, it was not called F. B. I. at that time, agent on board his submarine as a member of the crew. This agent was to see if anything was subversive in nature. The agent came back and the only thing that he reported was that the crew was drinking the torpedo alcohol.

I was on the N-6 only for about a month, when I was ordered to the N-7. The explanation for that was--that in writing up my orders the Bureau of Navigation intended that I go to the N-7, instead of the N-6, but in copying the radio dispatch, the radio operator made an error and copied the "7" as "6". So I was shifted. My orders to the N-5--the submarine I went to next were dated the 10th of December, 1918. The skipper of the N-5 was someone who you perhaps knew, because he was the Secretary-Treasurer of the Naval Academy Athletic Association for many, many years--M. D. Gilmore, called "Gracey" Gilmore. He was of the Class of 1911. Gracey was just a wonderful skipper--he was one of the best Captain's that I ever had. I'll illustrate it with a couple of stories.

One . . . At the Submarine Base, New London, at the time I was there, there were five docks. The two lower docks were for battery charging and air charging. Only submarines that were actually having their batteries charged by a shore generator or their air pressure build-up by shore compressors were alongside those docks. When you finished your charge, you moved up to one of the other docks in order to make the charging dock available. Due to the fact that they had a lot of submarines, it was a constant merry-go-round with submarines shifting all the time. Also at the Submarine Base, New London-- it's on the Thames River--the current runs very swiftly so that it takes an appreciable amount of skill to bring your submarine alongside the dock. On Christmas morning, 1918, "Gracey" Gilmore told me--the N-5 had been alongside the dock all night charging batteries--to go down and get the N-5, and shift it up to one of the other docks. So I went down and backed out in the stream. I did not perform the evolution at all well; and took some time in backing and filling before I got the N-5 alongside the upstream dock where the N-5 was supposed to secure. I then went up to the officers quarters and reported to Captain Gilmore that the N-5 was alongside the number 2 dock. And he said, "Yes, I was watching you. You did a terrible job. I want you to go down to the N-5 again, back out, and make landings from now until I send word down for you to come in." This was Christmas morning, 1918. So, I went down, backed out, and made a landing; backed out, made another landing; backed out, made another landing--not all of them good or perfect or anything else, but they gradually got a little better. Along about half past 11, he sent one of the mess boys down, and said, "Bring her alongside and secure." Which I did. But he taught me an awful lot of ship handling in the Thames River and this has stood me in good stead all my Naval career.

Q: I imagine so.

Dyer: The N-boats were small boats, 155 feet long, 340 tons. They had hand steering that is there was a hand steering helm. One time, not too long after I came on board, I was bringing the boat alongside under Captain Gilmore's supervision. We came in, I put the rudder hard right, then the rudder hard left, and backed down on the outboard motor. Then I kicked her ahead again, put the rudder hard right, and so forth. I had done this, maybe twice; when Captain Gilmore said to me, "Dyer, you take the helm." So, I took the helm. He said, "Hard right rudder." So I put her hard right. "Hard left rudder." I put her hard left. "Hard right rudder." Boy, it came over slower that time, because those old rudders, you see, are put over by hand power. "Hard left, once more boy." And I just barely got it back. He said, "Now do you understand?" I understood.

That same Christmas day, 1918, was the first time I played bridge. "Gracey" Gilmore that afternoon, said, "Dyer, I know you don't play bridge. We only have three bridge players on board. We've got to have a fourth to play. You're going to learn how to play bridge this afternoon."

Q: He was a hard task master, wasn't he?

Dyer: He was a wonderful teacher, not a task master, in my opinion. He knew where the kernel of the problem lay and his efforts taught one to solve it. He taught me how to play bridge, starting right on Christmas day, 1918. He was a great bridge player, a very skillful one. I played with him years later; when I played far better bridge. I became very fond of him during our short cruise together in the N-5.

Not too long afterwards, (I see my orders read the 24th of January, 1919) I went to the N-7. The reason that I went to the N-7, the N-boats had been in commission only several years but they had been very hard-used during the war, and their batteries were starting to fall apart. The N-5 was ordered down to the Philadelphia Navy Yard to have the plates on her battery renewed. Since the N-5 would not require so many officers as an operating submarine, I was made available, and went to the N-7. My skipper in the N-7 was an officer who was called "Gobo" Haas, W. S. Haas, whose widow used to live here in Annapolis. He was out of the class of 1912 and a very fine gentleman. I had one experience with him that is worth recording . . .

In the period right after World War I was over, the Submarine Force continued the training programs and the operating programs, which they had had during the war, in so far as they were able to. At that time, in New London, they had an old merchant ship which was fitted with a great number of listening tubes--because listening for submarines was done at that time by tubes with ears on their ends. This training craft had at least a dozen of these six on a side. They were manned, of course, by enlisted personnel, who were being trained as listeners. A submarine from the Submarine Base was a noise-maker, steaming around the anchored training ship at various depths of water and putting its periscope up at prearranged intervals to establish a time bearing.

Q: What were they called, technically? These tubes.

Dyer: They were called listening tubes, and that were based in receiving and recording sound waves. If you'll look at the photographs of old submarines, you'll see up on the bow what they look like. I think when I finish, we'll go out to my study and look at a couple of these old photographs of the D-3, which was my first command.

Sensitive sound receivers were placed at each end of a hollow metal tube about five feet long and six to eight inches in diameter, placed horizontally two to three feet above the bow deck of the submarine. This tube was pivoted midway between two hard rubberoid balls or ears of various shapes that were at each end of the listening tube. The tube could be turned thru 360° from a station inside the hull of the submarine and centered on the bearing (direction) of the strongest sound waves.

Q: How effective were they?

Dyer: They worked.

Q: They worked.

Dyer: They certainly were far better than nothing. The submarines of that era had to make approaches on surface ships and fire exercise torpedoes based on only sound bearings as part of their regular yearly torpedo competition. Hits were more frequent than misses. If you got real close to something--like seven or eight hundred yards--then you could start to track the noise with great exactitude. The outside range was probably 2500 yards to 3000 yards, although it may have been greater in some of the newer submarines that were not at New London in 1918.

To tell this story about the N-7. . . The area outside the mouth of the Thames River in Long Island Sound was divided into submarine operating areas. This particular incident happened in Area 2S, which was area 2 south. There was 2 north and 2 south. I do not remember the name of the training ship--it was due to anchor in 2 north. The USS N-6, with Lieutenant W. C. Burgey (Class of 1914) commanding; was assigned to 2N. The N-6 was the noise-maker. She was directed to circle around the anchored training ship, with her periscope up, then pull it down at irregular intervals and then put it up again so that the training ship personnel could take a bearing and see how closely the men being trained as listeners and who were listening on these tubes were actually detecting the bearing and estimating the distance of the N-6. You understand the problem.

Q: Yes, I do.

Dyer: The N-7, which I was in, was out doing just ordinary personnel training in submerged submarine operators. In the period immediately after World War I, people were leaving the Service in large numbers; they were getting in very young people and they had to be trained. We were running through the operations of a training dive. We had made our dive in area 2 south, and we went through a series of exercises taking the ship up and down and leveling it off at various depths of water. Finally, the skipper, who used to sit on a tin bucket in the control room (there were only three officers in the ship at that time--these were the Skipper, a temporary naval officer named Skinner, and myself). He said, "Oh, come on Dyer, that's about the end of it, let's bring her up." And I said, "Well, Captain, there's one thing we haven't done; we haven't tested our "automatic blow" for quite some days, and I think we should test it." It was required by submarine regulations, that the automatic blow be tested once a week. So, he said, "Go on down and test it." Ordinarily the "automatic blow" on those submarines was set at 90 feet. I took the N-7 down to 90 feet, the automatic blowing of the ballast tanks commenced and up we came. As we came up and broke water at the surface, I was on the periscope and I swung around, and, my Lord, there was a periscope just on our port bow. No distance at all away it looked like to me. I hollered, "Blow everything," and "back emergency." The Captain jumped up, and ran over to the periscope. He said, to the controller man, "Hold down the circuit breakers." We backed with every bit of power we had. We had just been backing maybe 10 or 15 seconds when, zowie, we were hit and bowled over on our side. Then the N-6, which was underneath us, blew her ballast tanks and up she came; and down we slid stern end first to about 70 or 80 feet before we regained control. Our blowing or the ballast tanks then again took hold; we balanced fore and aft and rapidly came up on the surface. As soon as we got to the surface--and boy, was I glad to get to the surface--I opened the conning tower hatch, and climbed up onto the bridge. At that time, there were no gyro-repeaters on the N-boat bridges. They only had azimuth circles and a magnetic compass. I took azimuth bearings, and I had a quarter master there--he recorded the bearings--because it was important to find out where we were. Were we in 2 north, or was Burgy in the N-6 in 2 south? It turned out that they were about 700 yards in our area.

Just to show how close between life and death things can be, the N-6 and the N-7 were single hull submarines. There was only one water-tight door from the stern all the way to the bow. That was right in the center of the boat. The N-6 went through our forward main ballast tank and knocked off our keel, opened our hull up to within 5½ inches from the rivets that held the plates together at the bottom. The N-6 lost her bow. The bow, of course, was a false hull; and that dropped off. The actual submarine hull of the N-6 was not damaged, the hull of the N-7 was considerably damaged. Both of us found out as soon as possible that the other one wasn't sinking, and then we proceeded back in to port. They initially ordered a Board of Investigation, and then a Court of Inquiry. Then poor old Burgy got a general court martial.

Q: Having been out of his area?

Dyer: Out of his area. He resigned from the Navy in 1923. His General Court Martial was published at the Submarine Base, New London. I was present. That was the only time I ever saw, in the Navy, a public reprimand ceremony. They had everybody present, all the officers and all the men at the Submarine Base in dress uniform, lined them up with Lieutenant Burgy front and center in the assembly area. The Executive Officer then read off this public reprimand from the Secretary of the Navy. It was the only time I ever saw it. W. C. Burgy.

The skipper of the N-7 was just as tickled as could be with me. He wrote a very nice letter in regard to the collision and attached it to my fitness report. We broke water at just the right moment. If our blow valves on our automatic blow had not blown just the moment they did, and got us up there where I could see and start backing just at the moment I did, it would have been curtains for everyone in that ship.

Q: A real crash.

Dyer: When the N-7 was ordered down to the Navy Yard, Philadelphia to get her battery changed, I was ordered to the USS R-1. R-boats were a new class of submarines that were just going into commission.

Q: Were they larger in size?

Dyer: Oh, yes, they were considerably larger than the N-boats. The R-boats were 570 tons and 186 feet long. The Lake N-boats were 340 tons; they were 155 feet long and had Bush-Selzer engines with 600 horsepower. They were built at the Lake Torpedo Boat Company at Bridgeport, Connecticut. One of the things that I thought was quite unusual, I noticed in looking up the act of 30 June, 1914, authorizing the building of the N-boats, that it provided that the Secretary of the Navy was requested to consider the advisability of stationing four of the N type submarines on the Gulf Coast.

Q: Four on the Gulf?

Dyer: Yes, that was suggested in an Act of Congress. That was one of the most unusual things that I ever saw--in an Act of Congress.

Q: What would have provoked that?

Dyer: I presume that some Congressmen from the Gulf Coast felt that his constituents in the Gulf weren't getting adequate protection. This was done before the start of World War I, and before the German Submarine operations were going strong.

Q: Congress going in for Naval operations?

Dyer: Yes, I really thought that was something. Anyhow, I next went to the R-1.

One other thing that I should tell you that very much impressed me when I was in the N-boats. It happened on the practice war patrol that I made on the N-5 after the end of World War I. Temporarily on board the N-5 was an officer named Isaac Schlossbach. He was a K-boat sailor, and out of the Class of 1915. If you remember the name of the man who tried to go up to the North Pole in a submarine along in the early '30s--Wilkins. Ike Schlossbach was his submariner. Ike was a real something, as far as I was concerned. He was a large heavy-set chap. In rough weather he used to get out on the cross trees, which were just above the bridge on the N-boats and hang on by curling his legs and feet around the crow trees and reach down and touch the water as the submarine would roll from side to side.

Q: Something of a contortionist.

Dyer: He aroused my admiration at that time, because in rough weather I was delighted just to hang on standing on my two feet. Small submarines were awfully lively, and it was darn difficult to hang on.

I went up to Boston for duty in the R-1. My Skipper was G. W. D. Dashiell. In the first place, this was the first submarine that I had served on regularly that had four officers assigned. I was the fourth officer. Lieutenant Commander Dashiell used to keep telling me that I was the only other Naval Academy graduate aboard beside himself and that we must set the highest possible standard of performance of duty and that he and I had to run that submarine. The trouble was, that both the other officers were quite senior to me and much more experienced in submarines. I just thought it was quite an inappropriate way to try to run any ship--to have someone other than the skipper, the Executive Officer and the rules of seniority to run the ship.

One of the other things that also impressed me was the fact that we had a full Commander on board quite frequently as the R-1 was the Division flagship. The division commander was Commander Conant Taylor. He had been the Commanding Officer of the R-1 and then had gone over to Germany to bring back a German submarine. He was, I thought, a very effective individual. I had seen very few full Commanders, at that time in my career.

The CAMDEN was our theoretical tender, but we never lived in the tender. We lived on an old sailing ship, which was alongside the dock up there in the Boston Shipyard--at that time called the Boston Navy Yard. The thing about that ship which was most annoying was that both in the living quarters and in the wardroom, there was a very inadequate overhead. Actually, about five feet, so that one could not stand up straight when in there spaces. For instance, if you backed away from your chair at the wardroom mess table and stood up--you whamed your head. Everytime you got out of your bunk and stood up straight-- you whamed your head. I don't remember what the name of that craft was, but I do know that it really was a most uncomfortable ship to live on, but the R-boat ship companys' lived on board it.

After the R-1, I then went to the USS R-5, and Lieutenant Commander Eric L. Barr out of the Class of 1911 was the very capable skipper of the R-5. I made several practice war patrols while in the R-5. The second officer's name was William E. McClendon--an ex-sailor man and a very capable officer. He eventually became a full Commander in the Navy in the regular service. Then I came, and a classmate of mine, who formerly was senior to me, but became junior to me while we were at the Submarine Base, New London, through the action of a General Court Martial.

To tell this story. Four of my Class went down from New London to New York City to observe the celebration of the false armistice in November 1918. We went down by train, of course. I went down with my classmate, Eliot (Swede) Bryant. The crowds were hilarious and simply tremendous in New York City. It wasn't too late in the evening before I said to Swede, "Let's go back to the railroad station, [Pennsylvania at 34th]. It's going to take us a terrible long time to get back there because we were then north of Times Square. We wanted to catch the last train up to New London along the shore line that night. Swede was more than agreeable. We pushed our way slowly down Broadway to Times Square and then down the rest of the way to the Pennsylvania station, boarded the train and went back to New London. There were boats that met that N.Y. N.H. and H. train regularly, a motor sailor for the sailormen, and a motor launch for the officers. The train arrived in New London, roughly about 4 o'clock in the morning, and we went back up to the Submarine Base. Lo' and behold, when we had morning muster, two of my classmates, Charles L. Andrews, and H. Roy Whittaker, were not present. They didn't show up, and didn't show up, and soon were reported absent at morning muster. They finally arrived about the middle or late afternoon, I don't remember which. The Navy in that era was not a permissive organization. The Senior Officer present ordered the usual Board Investigation, followed by a general court martial. Both of these officers were sentenced to lose seniority in grade. Charlie Andrews who graduated 12 numbers senior to me, became junior to me. So, when we both ended up on the R-5 together, I was the senior. I was the third officer, and he was the fourth.

Q: That's the way some of us learn, you know.

Dyer: From what I hear, discipline is not as strict in the Navy anymore.

The next detail that I had, was on the S-2. I think that there's an interesting story about our early S boats that many of the modern submarines don't know . . .

Following World War I, we brought back four surrendered German submarines to this country. (U-111, UB 88, UB 148, UC 97) We sent over some of our very best people, for instance, Freeland A. Daubur out of the Class of 1909 was one of those who went over, and they brought back these submarines. They were, of course, examined inch by inch; and out of those submarines, we got what was known as the M. A. N. engine. This engine design was modified some, but the modified design we put into S-10 to 13, and a further modification into a good many of our later submarines. In any case, in 1919 the Navy Department turned to the three submarine construction yards that had been building submarines, which were all on the East Coast. They said to them, design a submarine of about 800-850 tons and build into it the highest surface speed, the highest submerged speed, the quickest diving time, the best depth control, the longest cruising radius and a lot of other desirable submarine qualities. Then we will run competetive tests between these three submarines. Depending on how well the submarines, from each building yard do, later contracts will go in proportion to each submarines merit. The S-1, which was the Fall River submarine, was 850 tons; the S-2 was the Bridgeport Lake Torpedo Boat Company submarine; and the S-3 was built by the Portsmouth Navy Yard. Those were the three principle submarine building yards. The submarines were much of the same size and displacement and in later years were all rated at 800 treaty tons under the 1921 Washington Limitation of Arms Treaty. The Fall River submarines, the USS S-1, was 219 feet long, and the S-2 was 207, and the S-3 was the longest one--231 feet.

Q: They were inspired somewhat by the German submarines?

Dyer: Actually, a good many of the capabilities of the German submarines were built into them. Particularly, the quick diving--the German submarines had much quicker diving than we did in 1918, and in the engines. The Lake Torpedo Boat Company had always used Bush-Selzer engines in their submarines for main propulsion.

When the S-2 was being built--Louis Hancock, Class of 1910 was her prospective skipper. He was lost in the SHENANDOAH disaster, September 1925. He came up to New London, talked to several other skippers and said he wanted to get someone as his Executive Officer or Chief Engineer who had done well in Bush-Selzer engines. And who had other things to recommend him. As a matter of fact, he happened to ask both "Gracey" Gilmore and Eric Barr, and they both recommended me. That's how I happened to go to the S-2. I had had quite a little luck with the Bush-Selzer engine. You had to have luck, because no amount of skill would make the darn things run well all the time.

Q: They were diesel, were they?

Dyer: They were diesels. I sent down to the S-2, which was building at the Lake Torpedo Boat Company, and spend about four months down there in Bridgeport, living at the University Club. My orders are dated the 23rd of July 1919, and my orders away are dated the 7th of November--so I was there August, September, October, and a short part of November. The Lake Torpedo Boat Company was a submarine building company, built around old man's

Lake's idea of submarines. He was one of the very early submariners. He never had enough financial resources to really operate a proper company, and I believe, that he was not particularly blessed with business ability. Such a combination of an inventor and a lack of businessman ability did not fit together for an easy financial life of the Lake Torpedo Boat Company.

Q: Very few Henry Fords, were there?

Dyer: The company had financial difficulties all the time.

My skipper, as I said was Louis Hancock. He was a very enterprising and capable officer. He and I lived up at the University Club in Bridgeport--both bachelors. The other two officers in the S-2 were an ex-enlisted man, an ex-gunner, named Albert J. Wheaton, and an electrical-gunner whose name was Biven M. Prewett. They were both excellent.

The S-2 had gone through all its test trials, and we had had some problems in connections with them, which I'll tell you about.

At that time, before a submarine could be accepted, the submarine had to go through a test run of 52 hours. You ran 48 hours at normal cruising speed, and at the end of that time, you ran 4 hours at full speed. The Bush-Selzer engine which was put in the S-2 had considerable more horsepower than the engines that were put in the S-1 and the S-2 because Lake was very anxious to develop a submarine that was faster than the ordinary 12½ to 13 knot submarine. The Bush-Selzer engine was a two cycle high speed engine. Actually the S-2 made 16½ knots, over the measured mile course, and that was a real feather in Simon Lakes cap.

When the Navy Departments' Board of Inspection and Survey came up from Washington and ran this first test, we ran the 48 hours with no great problem at all, and then started the final 4 hours of full power. We ran 3 hours and 50 minutes. We were within 10 minutes of the end of the test, when one cylinder of one engine dropped a spray valve. As you know, the fuel oil is sprayed into the cylinder by the spray valve. The constant pounding of this spray valve at very high speed had fractured it. It fell into the cylinder, and when it did, of course, it smashed everything that was inside the cylinder. That ended the first test. And the Board of Inspection and Survey went back to Washington.

We went all through this getting ready again for a crucial "final acceptance" engine test. The second time, when they came up, we got through the 48 hours, and then through the 4 hours. I certainly say, that the good Lord helped me through, because I sure prayed those last 4 hours. The engine was wonderful, at about 80 per cent of full power. It ran like a sewing machine. As soon as you got it up into full power, the engine labored. Only if you can listen to and realize how an engine can labor, you know how you can just sit there and pray that the thing will continue to hold together and deliver. Anyhow, we got through the engine test.

We came back in to port, and we had one more test to do, for acceptance of the S-2 by the Navy Department. And that was our deep dive. We went out the next day and made, at 200 feet, our test deep dive, and it was very successful. When we came back in, the Lake Torpedo Company top officials were down on the dock with the contract spread out on a proper table and equipped with a proper fountain pen. The top man from Lake said, "Captain, how's to sign for the boat?" I had followed him ashore. He had the pen in hand, the contract out, and had started to sign, and I said, "Captain, under the contract, the Lake Torpedo Company is required to deliver this boat with the battery fully charged, and the air banks fully charged. Since we've been out and have made the deep dive, the Lake Torpedo Boat Company banks need to recharge the air banks and to recharge the battery. I recommend that you not sign that contract until those things have been done." He laid down the pen and walked off leaving the Lake Company officials madder than a hornet. That was it. He said, "When you fulfill the contract, I'll sign it."

We went back up to the University Club. We had fully

expected the next day that we would shove off for the Navy Yard, New York where we would fit out for active service. All personal preparations had been made by us. The University Club was giving Captain Hancock and myself a party that night. Captain Hancock was quite a party-er, I'll tell you. At the end of this dinner, which they had given us, we then retired to the card room to play poker. The poker card room was good sized about the size of our living room here at 4 Chase Road, with a big table covered with a green cloth. I was sitting right at this far end, away from the entrance and there were big heavy curtains across the entrance. Along about 11:00, I suddenly realized that someone was looking at me. I looked up, and there, with his head sticking through the curtain, was Chief Gunner Biven M. Prewett. He beckoned to me with his fingers. I went over and through the curtains to the hallway. Bevin whispered to me, "Both main motors are burned out." I said nothing to Captain Hancock, but I went rapidly with the Electrical Gunner to the S-2. The S-2 had had a fire in the motor room. What had happened in any motor, as you know, there are riser bars between the copper bars that make up the motor. The riser bars had worked loose, had started scraping the brushes, had gotten burning hot and fired, and started the fire. The copper had all melted and started throwing itself around. And the S-2 had had a good size motor room fire. The copper was all over the bulk head. The wreckage was widespread. I was down in the S-2 a couple of hours. About 1:30 or 2 o'clock in the morning, I went back to the Club to make a report to the skipper. He was still there, and they were still playing poker. I called him out, and I said, "Captain, both main motors are burned out." He said, "How long will it take to fix it?" I said, "About four months." They were manufactured by the Diehl Motor Company, and I wouldn't want to blaspheme the Diehl Motor Company--but they had had trouble with their motors. He said, "You really mean that?" I said, "Four months." He said, "I'm not going to stay around here for four months. You want to stay around here for four months?" I said, "Lord, no." He said, "What do you want to do?" I said, "Well, I'd like to have a submarine command." He said, "When I sober up, I'll go down to the Navy Department in Washington and see what I can do."

I went up to my room and turned in--I was tired and dirty. I'd been climbing all over the motors and everything. I took a bath, and turned in.

The next morning, I got up, went down to the boat. No skipper. I went in to see the Inspector of Machinery, who was the senior naval officer at the Lake Torpedo Boat Company--his name was Raymond G. Thomas, called "Roaring Bull" Thomas. He, of course, had heard about the S-2 casualty. He kept asking me, "Where's Hancock, where's Hancock?" He was a senior Lieutenant Commander, and I was a very young junior Lieutenant. He scared me. I kept saying, "Well, I haven't seen the skipper this morning." "Roaring Bull" would then say, "When he comes in, I want to see him immediately." The day went on, and the skipper never showed up. Along about the end of the working day, I got hold of Al Wheaton. I said, "How's to go up to the police station, and see if you can locate our skipper." So he went off, and about a half an hour later, called back and said, "No, they don't know anything about him." I worried through the night, and made up my mind that the next morning I was going to have to report his absence.

The day after the casualty to the motors, I had drafted the necessary dispatches and notified the Bureau of Engineering in the Navy Department which controlled all the private building yards at that time, and notified the Commandant of the Third Naval District, the Board of Inspection and Survey and everybody else concerned.

Q: About the motors?

Dyer: About the motors being burned out. I notified the Commander, Submarine Force--except it was Commander, Control Force at that time--and the Immediate Superior in Command--everybody. But, I was talking about the skipper--

The next morning I went in to Lieutenant Commander Thomas' office, and I said, "I'm sorry to report, but Captain Hancock isn't present." "Where was he, yesterday?" "I don't know, he wasn't present yesterday." He said, "Have you made a report?" I said, "I have it here in my hand." He took it, laid it on his desk, and said, "What have you done to locate him?" I said, "Well, I had a contact with the police in Bridgeport, and haven't located him." He said, "Well you better locate him, and get him back on board, or I'll send this thing in. If he isn't here by the end of working hours today, it's going in."

I went back to the office, about 11 o'clock the telephone rang, and it was the Chief of Police at New Haven. He said, "Do you know an officer whose name is Lieutenant Hancock?" I said, "Yes, he's my Captain." He said, "Have you got $500?" I said, "No, I don't know that I've got $500, but I can raise it, I'm sure of that." He said, "If you want to get him out of jail, it's $500."

I got on the next train, and went up to New Haven. I went up to the Police Station. They told me that Captain Hancock had taken his car up there. They had closed out a bar on him, he'd gotten mad at this turn of events, backed his car up, and driven his car right into the front of the bar.

Q: Boy, he really was on a toot, wasn't he?

Dyer: By the time I got there he was sobering up. I had collected all the money available from Biven Prewett, Wheaton and myself, and several people up at the University Club-- I had $500 cash. We put the $500 down, and I got him out of jail.

On the train back--his car, of course, was a wreck and had been hauled off to the junk yard--we rode the train back to Bridgeport, he said, "I'm going to take the night train to Washington. I've decided I'm going to go into lighter than air. You still want to get a command?" I said, "I sure do." He said, "I'll see what I can do for you." So, he went down to Washington, got his orders to lighter than air training, came back to Bridgeport with his orders in his hand, was detached and soon gone.

Q: This wasn't held against him, his A. W. O. L. for two days?

Dyer: Thomas never sent in the report.

When Captain Hancock came back to Bridgeport, I met him and he said, "You're going to go command the D-3." Well, that's how I went to command the D-3.

Q: May I ask you a question about the S-2, and these defective motors. You said the Lake people were standing there at the dock, wanting to have the contract signed and the submarine turned over to the Navy. Were they, perhaps, aware of any problem?

Dyer: Oh, I don't think so at all.

Q: Why were they rushing things then?

Dyer: The contract with the Navy Department provided a bonus for every day they beat any other of the two submarines going into commission. The Lake Torpedo Boat Company was very anxious to collect that bonus. The earlier the boat was accepted, the bigger the bonus.

Q: I see. Well, that explains that very well.

Dyer: That explains that. Despite the delay, the S-2 was not the last one to go into commission. She was delayed five months. I guessed four months, it actually took five months before she was ready to go. The S-1 was commissioned June the 5th, 1920; the S-2 was commissioned May the 25th, 1920. In other words, she beat the S-1 even with the five months delay. While the S-3 went into commission on January the 30th, 1919.

I went to the D-3, which, at that time, was in commission in reserve. One point that I think should be made is, that at that time in the Navy--in other words in late 1919, early 1920-- we had a tremendous number of submarines in commission, in commission in reserve, or building, in the over one hundred submarines with Commanding Officers listed in the Naval Directory.

Q: Why was this? Because of stepped up production during the War?

Dyer: You see the German submarines had been tremendously successful during World War I--had almost won the war, as a matter of fact. Anyone who really knows how close the British were to being starved into yielding knows how close the German submarines came to winning World War I.

Q: Admiral Sims deals with this in his book. Very adequately, I think.

Dyer: On January 1, 1919; which was only six weeks after the war ended; we had nearly 100 submarines in commission. We had six A-boats, three B-boats, five C-boats, three D-boats, two E-boats, four G-boats, two H-boats, one M-boat, and seven N-boats. We had eight K-boats, part of them were in the Azores. We had eleven L-boats, part of them were in Norfolk and four on the West Coast. We had 16 O-boats, we had 20 R-boats, and we had three AAA-boats--the double hulled A-boats. In addition we had the S-1, S-2, and S-3 building. A tremendous number of submarines. The Navy Department, I'm sure, was very hard pressed to provide people--competent in any way--to command and operate them.

Q: Do you have any special knowledge of the difficulties with enlistments at that time?

Dyer: On, my next story is about that.

Q: Oh, I see, fine.

Dyer: When I reported on board the USS D-3 in early November 1919, there were five enlisted men attached to that submarine. Two of them were Chief Petty Officers and one was a First Class Petty Officer, one was a fireman, and one was an apprentice seaman. That was all that was left, everybody else had been paid off, and had not shipped over. These three petty officers, either hadn't been paid off due to the fact that their enlistments had been so spaced that they were still in the Service, or they had re-enlisted.

Another thing was--there was only one officer attached to the D-3. You were it, you were everything. You had all the chores to do. When you took a cruise the Chief Gunner, the so-called Chief of the Boat--was the one with whom I stood watch and watch on any extended cruise. I was just trying to think this morning of the Chief of the Boat's name--his name was Grimes. He was the Chief of the Boat. He was a wonderful Chief Petty Officer, and taught me a great deal.

Q: That must have been a thrill--to get your own ship.

Dyer: I was proud as a peacock, and also diligent, let us

say.

Q: Well, that's what got you there in the first place.

Dyer: Two of my classmates had gone through the Submarine School with me, one was Eliot (Swede) Bryant, and the other was Johnny Reynolds. They became the skippers of the E-1, and the E-2 respectively. These submarines were transferred out of the Submarine Base in New London to the Submarine Base, Hampton Roads. I thought it would be very nice if I got a detail-- we were all bachelors--down there at Hampton Roads. Particularly after they wrote me and told me what a fine place the Submarine Base there was, and so forth and so on. They lived at the old Piney Beach Hotel, which was a hotel that had been built at the time of the Jamestown exposition, the 1907 exposition.

Q: In commemoration of the landing of the first settlers.

Dyer: Yes, they had an exposition down there in 1907, and the Senior Officers of the Navy are still living in the exposition building built at that time.

Interview with Admiral George C. Dyer　　　　May 26, 1969
by John T. Mason, Jr.　　　　　　　　　　　Annapolis, Maryland

Mr. Mason: Admiral, last time you broke off just as you were about to launch forth into one of the exciting events in your career--which was your first command, your command of the submarine D-3.

Admiral Dyer: It was a very exciting period for me. I was darn young, I was 21½ years old. I was just simply amazed that I had such a command, and I was really anxious to do a good job in it. The D-3, which had originally been the SALMON, had been renamed the D-3 when they felt they had run out of good fish names and started to give submarines letters and numbers. The D-3 was, of course, an extremely small submarine, 288 tons, 155 feet long. She had a number of unusual features about her. She had four torpedo tubes and forward of the torpedo tubes she had a hard, hard nose cone with two slots that could be rotated. The nose cone had to be rotated in order to put a torpedo tube slot opposite the torpedo tube. We had two slots, and carried four 18" torpedoes.

Q: It was synchronized, was it? I mean, the motion.

Dyer: The D-3 had a very hard nose, contrary to later submarines, such as the N-boats that had a very delicate bow

~~shields~~ because they had long false hull shields that went forward of the torpedo tubes. (These shields had to retract in board prior to firing torpedoes). With the soft nose or bow you were likely to dent the false hull shield as you made your landings alongside a dock or a tender. Then when you fired a torpedo, it could be deflected from a true course by the hull shield.

The D-3 also had only one set of water tight doors in its full length, which was 135 feet. That was between the control room and the engine room. The D-3 had received, the year prior to when I had command of her, diesel engines, of very low horsepower (240 HP). Actually we could only make eight knots on the surface. We could make more speed submerged with our motors and battery than we could on the surface. They were NLSECO (New London Ship & Engine Co.) engines and they ran like a sewing machine, and we never had any great problem with them.

Our Division Commander who was out of the Class of 1907 was Commander Harold M. Bemis. He also was the Division Commander of the E-boats and I believe, the N-boats. The D-3 was his flagship.

Not very long after I came on board, the Division Commander said that he wanted the three submarines in the division, D-1, D-2, and D-3 to go on a recruiting tour. Actually, he gave us permission to choose where we wanted to go as long as it was within the First and Second Naval Districts. (New England). At about that time there was a Second Naval District-- there no longer is one. I picked out small towns along the Maine coast and one town in Rhode Island, to go to. While my contemporaries in the D-1 and the D-2, picked out the larger towns to recruit in.

Q: Where was the headquarters for number two?

Dyer: We were based at New London, Connecticut; on the Thames River, at the Submarine Base at New London.

Q: I meant Naval District Two.

Dyer: Oh, Naval District Two consisted of the Naval activities in Connecticut and Rhode Island.

Q: But Newport was the base?

Dyer: Newport, Rhode Island was the Commandant's Headquarters. The Second Naval District was abolished shortly after World War I ended. Now they have a Commander, Naval Base, Newport who operates under the Command of the Commandant, First Naval District in Boston.

In any case, we went into these small towns, and secured alongside their docks, where ordinarily there were some fishing craft also secured. The mere presence of a submarine, small though it was, excited interest in the town. And the fact that we were there, became known in the town. An hour or so after we would arrive, a fairly steady stream of people came down to the docks to look at the submarine and many would ask to come aboard. We had some A board signs--which they still use in the recruiting service. We had the three enlisted men who had some background of service who acted at the recruiters. At least, they made the initial approach. Surprisingly enough, in roughly ten days, of recruiting--we recruited twelve men.

We brought them right on board, and put them into uniform. We had brought various uniforms along with us, of course, never quite the right size, but uniforms, and the Chief Gunners Mate, Grimes, was very handy with the needle. He altered the uniforms, where necessary, or where he thought it was necessary. Perhaps where he thought it was urgent. In any case, we recruited the people right on board.

Q: And so an enlistment was an immediate thing?

Dyer: Immediate enlistment. It was subject to a confirmatory medical examination when we got back to the Submarine Base, New London. I was authorized to have the men examined by a local doctor of the port and to pay the local doctor for the examination. This we did. The physical requirements were put on a form, which the doctors could read and follow. When we got a man who wanted to enlist, we took him to the doctor. By and large, the men that we enlisted all stayed in the Service, except one man. He was thrown out after we got back to the Submarine Base at New London. We were not permitted to enlist a married man; and he turned out to be married, although he had denied it when we took him.

Q: How could you accomodate 17 men on such a small vessel?

Dyer: Well, we had on that submarine berths for 16 men, and 4 officers. And there was only one officer regularly assigned, and 5 men; so we could put 12 more on with no problem whatsoever. Using all the berths.

When we got back to New London, my Division Commander, who was Commander Roscoe C. Grady, really upset me. I got back with these 12 men, and I was, of course, visualizing having a full crew. Because 16 was a full crew. Instead of that, he said, "I'm going to divide them up amongst all the boats in the Division.

Q: The others hadn't been that successful.

Dyer: One had recruited none, and one had recruited one. I came back with really a catch.

Q: Good pickings among the Maine citizens.

Dyer: As far as recruiting is concerned, there were only two groups of people to work on. First, the boys who had turned 17 since the end of World War I, and who could be recruited and were sound material. And, secondly, we got a number of men who had not been drafted during World War I, although perhaps they had been eligible for the draft. They had had a tinge of conscience is what I would call it, that they hadn't participated in the war. So, they wanted to get into a military service.

Q: When it was a bit safer.

Dyer: Perhaps it wasn't that reason. But I was amazed that we did get some people that were 21, 22 years old that as far as my knowledge went, had been eligible, and so forth and so on--but hadn't been in World War I.

Q: What were the times at that point? Was employment good, in industry?

Dyer: As you know, in 1919 we were starting to move into less than full employment. Although the actual so-called depression didn't begin until '21 when we had a very considerable drop down in employment and business.

We got these young men, and of course, not having the advantages of going through recruit training where they teach them to keep clean and to take care of their uniforms, and all that sort of thing--which is just an essential for a young American--we had great trouble with these people. Tried to teach them those things, and at the same time tried to teach them technically how to live under very difficult circumstances--which was living on board the submarine.

One thing that I want to mention also is--that at that time a qualified submarine man got a dollar a dive to the maximum of $15 a month. When I came on board, there had been a period when the D-3 under her previous Commanding Officer, was only making five or six dives a month. The three most valuable people I had on board were very much disgruntled. So, I made up my mind the day I arrived that that month I was going to make 15 dives. And every other month I was going to be on board I was going to make 15 dives. And I did. That endeared me to my leading men like nothing else I could have done.

Also, I made the D-3 available to men on the other submarines of the Division so they could make a dive on my submarine with temporary duty orders and get the dollar, and I could carry out training for myself in making approaches on ships proceeding along Long Island Sound. There approaches, with simulated torpedo firings developed my eyes for estimating angles on the bow, distances, and use of the "Is Was", a hand device used in firing torpedoes.

You think of a dollar as nothing, but a sailor man in 1919, a dollar was something. And it was something to George C. Dyer, too. I didn't get it, no officers got it, only enlisted men got it.

It was not until June 1920 that a Chief Petty Officer with acting appointment received $99 a month, and a Chief Petty Officer with permanent appointment received $126.00. In 1919, our Chief Petty Officers received less than that and the other ratings tailed off to $21.00 a month for an apprentice seaman.

I'd take the D-3 out, and take about as many men as I could. I would take only qualified submarine men. I'd put all the new recruits who were just excess weight off, and I'd take all the qualified men from the D-2, and D-1; and even I took men from the N-boats--who for one reason or another had not gotten their maximum number of dives, and took them out and made the dive for them. And they got the dollar.

I did other things--I fired practice torpedoes while the other D boats didn't or not as often. The D-3 had a fixed periscope, which meant that you had to be on an absolute level in order to really make a decent approach on a target. Because if you got the least bit angled down by the stern, which the D-3 was very apt to do, you couldn't see anything except the sky. Because the periscope was fixed. It was the last class of submarines that had the fixed periscopes. All the rest had eye pieces that could be elevated or depressed. If the submarine got a little angled up, you just turn the glass a little down. If you got a little angled down, you turned the glass up.

I learned to operate something called the "Is-Was". The "Is-Was" was a gadget spelled just like it sounds. When you were making an approach, you took this "Is-Was"--which had a compass nose on it, an inner dial with another compass nose on it, and a speed dial all made out of celluloid, and a range scale. You set the range which you estimated the target was at, you set the angle which you estimated that you were on the bow of the target, you put in the estimated speed of the target, and then you whirled this thing around; and out came the course that you were supposed to steer in order to make a collision course approach.

Of course, you didn't want to engender a collision, so you regulated your speed. The "Is-Was" had nothing to tell your required speed. Everytime you took a look, you made a refinement on the "Is-Was". And you regulated your speed so as to bring you in a firing position. This was most valuable training for me because previously I had had only theoretical training and observed previous Commanding Officers make approaches.

In the other submarines that I had served in, I had never gotten up to be senior enough to operate the "Is-Was". The skipper and the Exec were the ones who make the approach normally in the old days. I had never reached the stage of being an Exec on an operating submarine. I was always down about the third or fourth echelon because I was very junior. I had studied the "Is-was" and so forth. I got to use it, and it turned out to be a tremendous value, and I'll tell you why a little later.

After I'd been in the D-3 four or five months, a classmate of mine named John Reynolds, whose widow just spent the last week-end with us, who had gone through the Submarine School the same time that I had--got command of an E-boat. The E-boats were based at Norfolk. He and I were both bachelors. John wrote up to me, he'd just gotten the command. He said: "I've just gotten command and you've had that command for four or five months. How about asking to come down here to Norfolk and get command of one of these big L-boats?" So, nothing daunted, I put in a request requesting transfer to a command based at the Submarine Base, Hampton Roads. Actually, in no time at all, I was ordered in command of the L-10 down there. She, of course, was a much larger submarine. (450 tons, 167 feet long). She had been overseas in World War I and I was just tickled to death. Anyhow, I went down to Hampton Roads and took command of the L-10, in early April of 1920. I stayed in command of the L-10 until--well, not too long--August, 1920.

About in July, my Division Commander--who was James C. Van de Carr received a letter from the Submarine Detail Officer, Bureau of Navigation which in effect said--"Lieutenant Junior Grade George C. Dyer is two years out of the Naval Academy, and he's never been in big ships. Therefore we are going to order him into big ships." I thought that was good. I was happy as a lark, because my belief was that I should get into big ships. While the Submarine Detail Officer was talking over the phone to Lieutenant Commander Van de Carr, he sent for me and said, "What big ship to you want to go to?" That was the PENNSYLVANIA. And so he said "He wants to go to the Fleet Flag." So, my orders were issued to go to the PENNSYLVANIA. While he was on the phone, I said, "I have been out two years, and I have never been on any leave. I would like some leave before I go to the PENNSYLVANIA." He told this to the Detail Officer, and the Detail Officer said, "How much leave does he want?" A month was the maximum you could get, so I said, "I want a month." Actually the Bureau authorized Van de Carr to issue me orders for a months leave. And told him when Dyer comes back, he goes to the PENNSYLVANIA.

I shoved off from Hampton Roads and went out to Chicago, where my mother and father were living. After I had been there just a day or so, I got a warning telegram from the Bureau of Navigation, now Bureau of Naval Personnel, which said, "Upon your return to the L-10, you are going to be ordered to a submarine in a division bound for the Asiatic Station." Actually I was down in La Porte, Indiana where my present wife lived when this telegram came through. My mother called me on the phone, the telegram had come during the day time, and she told me she had a telegram, and what should she do, and I said, "Open it, and read it." So, she read it to me.

I went back up to Chicago. Of course, my father and I talked about it. Father had been out on the Asiatic Station. He said, "The first thing you should do before you go out to the Asiatic station is to get married." He said that's no place for a bachelor to be. That was very sound advice, I tell you. So, I said, "There's only one girl I want to marry, and that's Adaline Shick. And she's already sent back my ring," and she had. He said, "Well you better take it and go back and see her." So, I did just that.

I got a second telegram from the Department cancelling my leave and directing me to come via the Bureau of Navigation (Naval Personnel) before I reported back to the L-10 to get relieved. So, I went into Washington--I had never been into the Navy Department or the Bureau of Navigation before. I found my way into the Detail Office. Finally, to the Submarine

Detail Officer, who, of course, I didn't know from Adam's old ox. The Detail Officer said to me, "We have a vacancy for an Executive Officer of an S-boat. We cannot let you go to big ships. You've got to go back into submarines. We need officers who had a previous command and who can serve as Executive Officer of the great big new S-boats." They were big, compared with all the other submarines. He said, "You can go to either the S-7, or the S-15." I said, "Who is the skipper of the S-7?" And he said, "Zemke". I said, "I will go to the S-15." He said, "Fine, I'll put you down for the S-15. You got back to Norfolk. I will get your orders out, and by the time you get relieved of command of the L-10, you can then go to the S-15."

I left, and went down below, and had walked down Constitution Avenue three or four blocks before I realized I didn't know who the skipper of the S-15 was.

Q: But you didn't want to be with the other one?

Dyer: I knew darn well I didn't want to be with Eric F. Zemke. He had been in the R-boats when I was in the R-boats.

I walked back up, and knocked at the door. At that time the Bureau of Navigation had all swinging doors. These little half swinging doors.

Q: Like a saloon door?

Dyer: Like a saloon door. I knocked and went in. This Commander was there, and I said, "Sir, would you mind telling me who is going to be the Commanding Officer of the S-15?" The Detail Officer got up and said, "Ha, ha, ha, ha." He walked through the next swinging door to his boss, told this story, and then went on and I stood there for about five minutes--feeling like a nitwit. Finally he came back and said, "Doc Lee is the prospective skipper of the S-15." D. R. Lee was called Doc Lee. Well, of course, it was a wonderful choice.

Q: Had you known him?

Dyer: I didn't know Doc Lee, but I knew I didn't want to be with Zemke. So, then I went to the S-15.

There's one more story I want to tell you about the L-10, before I leave the L-10. The Division Commander had been operating in the war zone and he wanted all of the L-boats to carry out practice war patrols. He wrote up a regular war operation order for the submarines in his division. We would leave the Submarine Base and go out thru the Capes into a designated "Operating" Area. We had orders to make approaches on all merchant ships coming into Hampton Roads passing through our area--which was roughly an area sixty miles square and 150 to 250 miles eastward from Hampton Roads. Two or three of the other L-boats had gone out and had not stayed the full length of their patrol which was either six or eight days. They had not made their approaches close enough so that they could read the names of the merchant ships which they had made their approach on, by passing close astern, and reading the names. Which is what the practice instructions called upon them to do. He gave me a big pep talk before I went out the first time, and I said to myself, "Nobody else has done this. By george, George Dyer's going out there and give it a full due."

Another thing I want to tell you, I was a Junior Lieutenant at that time; and my Executive Officer was a Senior Lieutenant whose name was T. T. Patterson--out of the class of 1916. He was three years senior to me at the Naval Academy. The reason that he was my Exec, was that I was a "qualified for submarine command" officer, and he was not a "qualified for submarine officer." You had to be "qualified" in order to command a submarine. I qualified when I was in the R-boats. I had qualified with Eric Barr--who was the skipper of the R-5. He had qualified me, and put it on my fitness report that I was "qualified to command." That was essential to have a command. You had to take a qualifying test, and had certain written things that you turned in, and you had to be approved by your division commander. Any reasonably effective naval officer could become qualified if he did the work. But he had to have time to do it. Patterson graduated from the Submarine School, and had been ordered direct to the L-10. He actually relieved me when I was detached as the skipper of the L-10. He became qualified during the period that I was in the L-10. Of course, I was very anxious to have him qualify because I was as embarrassed as all get out to have an officer so senior to me as my Exec.

When I came to the Naval Academy to teach school in 1934, Patterson was the Secretary to the Admiral. He was a Commander, I was a Lieutenant Commander at that time. He recalled the days when I had been his skipper.

I went out on this cruise--this supposedly eight day cruise. We arrived on station, I sighted a merchant ship, and made my first approach, reached firing position, simulating firing torpedoes by firing water slugs, then passed close under her stern, read her name, wrote it down, logged it, and felt that I had accomplished the first chore in my war patrol mission.

Q: When this was done, was the merchant ship warned of this?

Dyer: Oh, no, she wasn't aware in any way.

Q: She wasn't aware of it.

Dyer: Not aware in any way, no.

Q: She certainly would be now. With radar.

Dyer: I really wouldn't be able to give an answer on that.

To the best of my knowledge, when I left submarines--submarines were still making approaches unbeknowst on merchant ships in order to gain appropriate skill. But they may very well be sending them a message now. But radar has no capability to detect a submerged submarine insofaras I know radar.

I had just finished this approach, let the merchant ship get well clear and then surfaced and started up the battery charge with the engines, and up came the pharmacists mate. He said, "Captain I've got a man on board I think has acute appendicitis." Then I went down below and talked with the man who was in his bunk. He was moaning and groaning, and feeling very poorly. To one who is completely ignorant of medicine as it is practiced, he seemed to me like a legitimate appendicitus man. Boy, I could have just murdered him. But I decided the thing for me to do was to crank up the submarine, take it back into port, drop him, and go back out on my patrol. After I had gotten reasonably well started on our way back to Hampton Roads, I sent a dispatch to my division commander telling him that I was returning to port, the reason why, and told him my estimated time or arrival. I asked him to have an ambulance meet the L-10. One of the things that the medical book said was that if a patient had acute appendicitis the worst thing that you could do was to give him a cathartic. I read that, and the corpsman read that, and we decided that that was something that we just couldn't do.

The L-10 took the patient back to port and the ambulance was down on the dock, we lifted him up the forward hatch lashed to a stretcher and put him in the ambulance. The division commander was down at the dock, of course. I gave him the dope, I'd made this one approach, and so forth and so on. He said, "Go on back out." I said, "I'm going just as fast as I can go."

The L-10 was maybe fifty miles out from the Base which was about five hours, when I received a dispatch from the Division Commander that said, "Mans bowels moved, feeling fine."

Q: The man should have been able to help you with the symtoms. Probably didn't.

Dyer: I really don't know, I was so mad at him. Anyhow, in due time, I was detached from the L-10 at Norfolk.

I went up to the S-15, which was building in Bridgeport, Connecticut at the Lake Torpedo Boat Company. She was some months away from being ready to be commissioned. During that period when the S-15 had not yet been accepted by the Navy, (she was accepted by the Navy on the 15th of December, 1920), I had received my orders to take my examinations for permanent Junior Lieutenant before a regular Naval Examing Board sitting at the

Navy Yard, Brooklyn.

I was a temporary Junior Lieutenant because of my promotion during World War I. Prior to the War, Ensigns served normally three years, and then they were eligible for examination, promoted to Junior Lieutenant. You generally had your examinations, needed to prove yourself qualified professionally ahead of time. In order that, if you failed the first time, you could take your re-examinations and still make your number and get your increased pay on time. I was ordered down to the Navy Yard, Brooklyn, New York, where there was a permanent examining board. There were two different ways for an officer to take his examinations; one was a temporary examination where you took the written examination on board ship under a Supervisory Board, that had no power to mark the papers or do anything else. It did ensure that the officer wrote the examination without receiving any outside help. The Supervisory Board merely supervised you during the time that you were taking the examination. This was by far the most common method.

The other way was a permanent examining board. In those days the Bureau of Navigation had three or four of them strategically located at Navy Yard or Receiving Ships around the country to which you reported. If you failed your examination before a permanent examining board, you lost six months seniority. This was automatic. You really were on the spot, when you appeared before a permanent Examining Board to take the examination. The senior member of the Board I reported to was a Commodore, Commodore Charles M. Fahr. It was the first time I had ever seen a Commodore. He was a retired Commodore, who had been ordered to active duty. The officer who directly handled me was a Captain, Andre Proctor, anchor man in the Class of 1893.

I took the examination. The Commodore had two assistants. There were four or five of us, including officers taking the examination for Senior Lieutenant and Lieutenant Commander. Commodore Fahr or Captain Proctor would come around, read over one's shoulder, and as we lifted our pens but before we had a question or had finished writing on a subject, he'd pick up our paper and take it away and say, "That's enough for that." A little enervating, let's us say, because you get worried as he looks over your shoulder, seeing something's wrong.

Q: You can't have a second thought.

Dyer: That's right. I worked at the exam. One thing that Captain Proctor was very meticulous about was our navigation examinations. Due to the fact that I had served on board seven submarines, and been the official navigator on four of them, I had done a lot of navigating. I really had no problem with the navigation examination. The problem that I had was one where I was in the southern hemisphere, which to me makes everything backwards from navigating in the northern hemisphere. I was required to cross a moonsight and a sun-sight to get my position. Of course, sun-sights are common as all get out; but moon sights just really aren't. Because the moon, very frequently, isn't available at the time that the sun is. So you very rarely cross a sunsight and a moonsight. Anyhow that's what I had--along with a fix from three star sights and some piloting. But navigation was a real crux of the promotion examination. If you got that part, Captain Proctor gave you a fair breeze in the other examinations.

Naval Officers, as you know, took examinations in roughly a dozen subjects. When I finished off my navigation examination real well in the latter examinations, Captain kept saying, "Oh, that's enough, that's enough. Don't write anymore on that question, that's enough."

When I had finished all the examinations, the Commodore called me in, and he said, "Congratulations, Mr. Dyer, you passed last Tuesday." Tuesday was the day I took my navigation examination.

Q: Oh, I see.

Dyer: One officer who took the examination the same time I did, failed and lost six months seniority. So, I thought I was very, very lucky.

On this examination hangs a long story, and I'll tell it to you now because it ties in to my going down to the Brooklyn Navy Yard for my promotion examinations. Although later I will want to go back to the S-15 a bit. After the S-15 had been on the China Station for some months--there were only three officers in the ship. The skipper--who was Doc Lee, myself, who was the Exec navigator, and chief engineer, and an Ensign whose name was George Hern. The latter was an ex-enlisted man and a very capable one. The skipper--who was a bachelor--decided that George and I would stand the duty every other day, which was a bit of a burden. I was a newly married man.

One day when I had the duty in October, 1922, in came a very long-winded dispatch from the Navy Department--just pages of coded groups. So, I sat down and started de-coding it. I didn't get very far in the decoding before I realized it was a message of some personal importance to the skipper. I got hold of a messenger--the skipper was in Manila--the S-15 was in Cavite. At that time, you went from Cavite to Manila either by steam launch or by motor boat, and the boats ran at infrequent intervals. I sent this enlisted man ashore in Manila to look up Captain Lee, and tell him to come back on board right away.

So, this long-winded dispatch from the Chief of Naval Operations to the Commander-in-Chief of the Asiatic station-- who was Admiral Thomas Washington--started out that the such and such tugboat company had put in a claim for the salvage value of the USS S-15. Claiming that the S-15 had been firmly aground on Hell's Rock, coming in through the East River and Hell's Gate heading enroute down from Bridgeport to the Brooklyn yard. (The S-15 was to be "fitted out" at the Brooklyn Navy Yard). And that the tugboat had pulled the S-15 back afloat from its grounded position. Therefore, the tugboat had salvaged the S-15. And that the Bureau had carefully examined the Ships Log of that date, and had found no mention of this incident. If the incident was true, and since the matter was coming to court trial, the Navy Department required the presence of the Commanding Officer, the Officer of the Deck, and the Navigator in court in New York City. And that the Commander-in-Chief of the Asiatic Station should arrange the necessary reliefs and provide transportation. The dispatch was very long but this is a very short summary of what the dispatch said.

The first thing that I did was to send for the Chief of the Boat. The Chief of the Boat was Bullis--an old chief gunners mate who was just wonderful. I said, "Bullis read this dispatch." And he read it, and he said, "Well, Mr. Dyer, it's true. You weren't on board, and you didn't know anything about it. Nobody has ever said anything about it, but it's just as true as it can be. The steering gear jammed when we were coming through Hell's Gate, and the S-15 swung left and ran on this blooming rock and we couldn't get her off."

Q: Very strong current there.

Dyer: Bullis continued, "We did everything we could. This tug came along, and the skipper said, 'Hey, throw me a line.' So this tug threw us two lines, and got squared away, and pulled us off." So, there's the story as it was.

About a couple of hours later, the skipper walked on board--having been told by this sailor man to come back immediately. He came back, and of course, there was a copy of the dispatch to the Division Commander, and to the Flotilla Commander. About the time that the skipper arrived back, there was a dispatch from the Commander-in-Chief of the Asiatic station, Admiral Thomas Washington, four star Admiral, for the skipper, the navigator, the Officer of the Deck, the Division Commander, and the Flotilla Commander to report on board together and immediately.

When that dispatch arrived, the Flotilla Commander, I do not actually remember whether it was Tommy Hart or Zeno Briggs, but I believe Zeno Briggs. I know the division commander was Ralph C. Needham. Anyhow, off we went to the Fleet Flag ship, which was over in Manila Bay. My skipper said about the S-15. "Sure it's true, I didn't think it worth reporting."

The Commander-in-Chief made the immediate decision in his cabin after there had been a review of the facts. I had been dismissed from the conference since I wasn't on board the S-15 when the grounding occurred. I never knew anything about the grounding. No one had ever said a word to me about it. I was the navigator. The Captain said he was the Officer of the Deck. A Lieutenant (junior grade) named Kinnear actually had signed the log for that watch but the skipper said he had the conn and that actually gave him the responsibility at the time of the grounding. The Commander-in-Chief said to Lieutenant D. R. Lee, "You are going to be relieved as of tomorrow morning. I'm going to start you back to the States on the S. S. . . . " He turned to the Division Commander and said, "Whom do you recommend as his relief?" The Division Commander said, "My recommendation is Lieutenant, junior grade Dyer." So, I relieved Doc Lee the next morning.

I was Junior Lieutenant and in the Squadron there were a number of Senior Lieutenants, who were Execs and who hadn't had command of boats but who would have been happy to command the S-15. I really was on the spot.

Q: They didn't love you for that.

Dyer: They didn't love me for that at all. The reason the Division Commander had recommended me, I'm sure, was that the

S-15--I was the Chief Engineer, in addition to being Exec--had won the engineering trophy for the whole Navy. There were over a hundred submarines in the Navy, and we'd won the trophy for the whole Navy. Also, when he went to sea with us, which he did very frequently--because we were the Flag Ship of the division--when we made approaches, Doc Lee just couldn't make an approach. He couldn't run that 'Is-Was', and I could. So, he made the first approach and we got a miss with our torpedo and a zero score in our torpedo competition. After that approach he turned to me and said, "I'm never going to make another approach. You're going to make every approach." I made every approach thereafter and I got a hit every time during that competition year. The Division Commander saw this happen. He was on board and witnessed it. I think that helped him make the decision. Anyhow, he made it, and I became the skipper of the S-15.

I want to tell you a couple of other stories, yarns. When the S-15 was getting ready to conduct its trials in 1920, the "Trial Captain" hired by the Lake Torpedo Boat Company, was a chap named Joseph Eliot Austin. He was out of the class of 1908. He had been in the Navy and been in submarines and had resigned in the period after World War I was over. He had been hired as the "Trial Captain." We used to take the S-15 out and conduct the various trials that were required by the contract. This chap Austin was not a good handler of submarines either on the surface or submerged. He was so slow in making up his mind, so poor in handling the submarine. He gave my Captain the fits. Finally Doc Lee came in to port after a day of frustration and said to me, "I'm never going out on the S-15 until I'm the Commanding Officer. You go out and bear with him." So, I went out. We went out time after time, after time, after time. Every day we went out and tested something. Finally, we went out to make our 200 foot dive, one of the final tests before the Official Board of Inspection and Survey tests. When we got out, not too far off of Bridgeport, I was amazed. Austin said he was going to make a stationary dive because he did not want to risk--there was only a comparatively limited 200 foot depth area in this particular spot not too far off Bridgeport--making a running dive and getting out of this 200 foot depth area. He said he wasn't sure enough of his navigation. By George, he got out and he fiddle-faddled around, and fiddle-faddled around, and fiddle-faddled around--trying to get the S-15 started down towards her 200 foot depth. All of a sudden--the submarines were all like that, they developed air pockets if you'd wait too long, or fill your tanks too rapidly--the S-15 just stood on her tail and down she went stern first until the tail hit the bottom. She tipped up on a tremendous angle, and one of the civilian crew cried out, "The acid's coming out." Because at that time, if you tipped the cells of the battery at too great

an angle, the acid would run out. It was his guess of the angle--
fortunately his guess was wrong. But, everything loose in that
submarines, and there was lots of loose gear, went down towards
the tail. The crew all beat it forward to get forward of where
the acid might come down, from the forward battery compartment.
There was nobody left in the control compartment except Lieutenant (jg) Kinnear and myself. Kinnear was the next senior officer in the S-15. He and I both ended up on the after bulkhead
of the control compartment. Of course, oil and loose gear all
over everything including us. Finally, I said, "Let me stand
on your shoulders." He stood there, pushed my legs, and I was
able to get up so that I stood on his shoulders. When I stood
on his shoulders I was just able to reach the controlls on the
motors--and this is another thing that's a real oddity. In
order to go ahead, you pull the controlls back. I had been
trying to get that changed ever since I'd been in that submarine--the S-15. Trying to get the controls changed so that when
you wanted to go forward, you threw the controlls forward.

If I'd had had to push them forward, I couldn't have done
this. I was just able to get to them and pull them back, and
kick the motors ahead. As soon as the motors took hold, they
tended to plane the S-15 back up on the surface. Our nose had
already come out. And we came up and had the diving planes
moving, I got to the air controls and blew all the main ballast

tanks with air, and got all of the water out. The civilian crew filtered back into the control room and things were brought under control.

When we came back, I told the skipper in detail about this incident. He sat down and wrote an official letter. As a result of it, Naval Operations or someone in Washington insisted that the Lake Torpedo Boat Company fire Austin. And they did.

The next time I saw Austin--I went to a football game in Honolulu on New Years Day in the early 1930's. They used to have a big football game each January first. Mrs. Dyer and I went in and sat down in two seats and two people came in and sat down next to us and it was Austin and his wife. If that wasn't a coincidence. Later, I took the Honolulu Naval Reserve Unit, which Lieutenant Commander Austin headed, and while on that cruise, my commission as a Lieutenant Commander came in, and Austin administered the Oath of Allegiance to me.

That's my story about the S-15 and her trials with the Lake Torpedo Boat Company.

We went into commission and went up to Portsmouth yard for our post-commissioning repairs and alterations. When you put a new submarine into commission there are always some things that the builder doesn't do which the government undertakes to do on its own. When we got into Portsmouth yard, my skipper, Doc Lee said, "I'm going to go on leave." He was in the Class of '13. He said, "I've never been on leave of any length since I graduated. I went through the war without leave. I'm going to put in and get 30 days leave." So he did. He put in a request which had to go to the Bureau of Navigation. The Bureau approved all 30 days leave requests. When the leave papers came back, he said, "Oh, I'm not going to go on leave right away." He let his approved request for leave lay in the "incoming" basket for days. I thought that was funny. I said to him, "What are you trying to do, persuade some girl to get married or something?" He didn't ever let me know.

Eventually the submarines were due to go into dry dock, and he shoved off on his leave. He came from Kentucky, and he went back to Kentucky on leave.

They put the four submarines, S-14, 15, 16, and 17 into dry dock at the same time. When they started to pump down, the S-15 started to take an angle and fall on its side. They pumped back up, and the dry dock Officer checked and centered the S-15 real closely. They pumped down again--over she tipped on her side again. This time they sent divers down. The divers said that the duct keel was all torn loose from the hull and bent outward at an angle of about 30° for about 40 feet back from the bow. I don't know whether you know what a duct keel is or not. In order to move water from one trimming tank on a submarine to another, the water is pumped down from the bow trimming tank through the duct keel and up into the after trim tank. There are valves on the bottom of each ballast and trim tank and by opening or closing the correct valves, you can move the water through the duct keel from one tank to another. You can also move fuel oil through a duct keel and the S-15 was fitted to carry fuel oil in its main ballast tank.

As a matter of fact, in the S-boats, when we took these long trips like going from the Panama to San Pedro, Pearl Harbor to Guam, or from Manila to Shanghai--we had to take fuel in our ballast tanks. And we handled it through the duct keel.

To continue with the docking, some divers with acetylene torches were sent down. They had to cut off the forward part of the duct keel that had been wrenched awry. Eventually the Navy Yard, Portsmouth, had to build the S-15 a new duct keel.

The Commandant of the Portsmouth Navy Yard, (Captain Louis R. de Steigner) always held a conference every Friday of the Commanding Officers of all ships that were in his yard for repairs. You had an opportunity to voice any complaint you might wish to make against any part of the yard, or anything the yard was doing; or suggest anything that might help them do a better job.

The Commandant asked me, "When did the S-15 run aground?" I stood up there, perfectly honestly, and said, "It's never run aground." He said, "How long have you been on her?" I said, "I helped build her, put her through her trials, and been on her ever since." I didn't mention, perfectly unintentionally, that I had been off the submarine when she was proceeding from Bridgeport down to New York--that was when she ran aground. The Commandant accepted that with considerable disbelief, but he couldn't prove otherwise. So they just fixed up the duct keel.

When the skipper came back, I told him about this and he never said a word about having run aground. He never at that time batted an eye--about the S-15 having run aground. But, she had.

Q: Was this ultimately discovered that she had?

Dyer: I just told you about that. That was why I relieved D. R. Lee, through her having run aground in Hell Gate.

I had a very good cruise out there on the China station. When I came back from my cruise in the Asiatic Station, the ARGONNE, on which I was a working passenger, had gotten as far as Corinto, Nicaragua and I had not received any orders to my next duty station. I was getting concerned about this. My Flotilla Commander, Captain Zeno Briggs, (incidentally, he's still alive--he's about the third or fourth oldest living graduate of the Naval Academy) . . .

Q: He's not as old as Jackson.

Dyer: No, he's 10 years younger than Admiral Jackson. About

92, I think he is, he may be 93.

Q: Jackson was just 103.

Dyer: Well, Captain Zeno's about 93. Anyhow, when we got into Corinto, Nicaragua; my previous Flotilla Commander, Captain Zeno Briggs, who had also been relieved, (by Captain J. R. Defrees), was on board the ARGONNE with me. My orders for my next duty hadn't come in, so he sent a dispatch from the ARGONNE to the Department. In fact, he wrote a very flowery dispatch about me.

My dispatch orders came back. I was ordered to the Naval Recruiting Station, Detroit, Michigan, as Recruiting Officer and as Officer-Inspector of the Naval Reserves in the state of Michigan. Well, if they had hauled off and kicked me in the kahonees, I couldn't have been more upset. Because, it was my opinion that by and large officers that are ordered to recruiting duty are not what I would call, the so-called 'cream of the crop', and I felt that the way the Bureau was looking at my record, they had definitely downgraded me.

Q: No, I think not. This is kind of a side track, isn't it?

Dyer: Yes, I felt I had been sidetracked. My Flotilla Commander sent back another dispatch. The Bureau of Navigation sent him a dispatch which he didn't quite understand. But they said, we are doing you a favor when we are doing this. When Captain Briggs returned to Washington, he became the sub-head of the #2 recruiting division in the Bureau. So, somebody had figured that he was doing Captain Zeno a great favor by ordering an officer of whom Captain Zeno thought very highly as one of his subordinates.

Q: What were they doing to the officer?

Dyer: I went out to Detroit, and I spent two years out there. The Navy had competitive recruiting at that time. There were roughly 35 Naval recruiting stations in the United States. Detroit was next to the bottom in the competition. I went to work, traveled all over Michigan, spoke from the end of a Recruiting truck to getherings of three, five, or ten, spoke at any meeting that needed a speaker and did everything else to stir up interest and enthusiasm for the Navy. At the end of a year, Detroit was third in the competition and the next year we were first in the recruiting competition.

Q: And you were actually competing with Henry Ford, and other people in the automobile industry.

Dyer: Yes. Some of the things I'd like to mention in regard to that--I soon decided, as far as I was concerned, a far more interesting aspect of my duty was my additional duty as Inspector-

Instructor of the Naval Reserves. I also decided that there was comparatively little professional advancement to be gained in the recruiting field as far as an individual Recruiting Officer was concerned. I just didn't see how I really could get anything out of it. That was borne out later when I saw my fitness reports--which were made out by a Rear Admiral named Courtney, Charles E. Courtney. Did you ever hear of him?

Q: Oh, yes, I've heard of him.

Dyer: Handsome Charlie Courtney. Well Handsome Charlie was my boss--he was the top man. He really didn't care a coopala about the recruiting officers working for him.

The Naval Reserve was in a very sad situation. On the 31st of December, 1921, the Organized Naval Reserve fell apart because Congress had not appropriated any money to pay the officers and men for any drills in the rest of the fiscal year or for its next fiscal year. There was an 18 months hiatus from the 1st of January '22 until the start of the next fiscal year, the 1st of July of '23, before there was any unit whose members were in a paid status in the Naval Reserve. With the result that there were very few on the rolls. Of course, the Congress became aware of this horrendous mistake and they rectified it in due time. But here was this shambles. On the other hand, on the 1st of July, 1923--which was roughly eight months before I had arrived, they had started to pick up the pieces and put them back together in the Inspector-Instructor's job.

The first thing that the Navy Department decided, and this is for reasons about which I do not know anything, they decided that everybody who was to come back into a paid status in the Naval Reserve--in other words, being paid for drills, you understand--which is an earmark or the National Guard and the Naval Reserve--

Q: Certainly one of the principle incentives too.

Dyer: Yes. Each officer had to take an examination to prove that he was qualified for the rank that he currently held because, as the Bureau said, officers had been promoted beyond their capabilities during World War I. If they thought they had been promoted beyond their capabilities during World War I, they should look at the Navy after World War II.

All these poor chaps who were anxious to go back to drilling and who liked the Navy, and all that sort of thing--here they were faced with an across the board professional examination. So, I set up schools there in Detroit, and also in Flint, Michigan; and out in Benton Harbor where we had another naval reserve unit. All the Naval Reserve units in Michigan had gathered for their regular weekly drill on Monday nights. Well, I couldn't be every place on Monday night, so the Naval Reserve had to change the drill nights if I was going to conduct school in Navigation, Ordnance, Gunnery, Military Law, etc. They continued to drill in Detroit on Monday night, where there were the most Naval Reservists. And drill at these other places on Tuesday, Wednesday, and Thursday. Another Reserve unit was set up in Lansing eventually.

And so, there were three or four nights a week that I was on the road going from here to there and some place else holding drills and conducting school. These people appreciated that beyond mention, they thought it was simply wonderful. I mean, I never received such thanks from people. I conducted schools in a dozen different subjects. One place they didn't know anything about navigation, another place they didn't know anything about engineering, another place they didn't know anything about military law, the others didn't know about international law, didn't know anything about ordnance, etc. A tremendous school--generally I would have school in two or three subjects each night in which I would give a half-hour talk, and then answer questions for five or six minutes, then a break for five or six minutes; and then we'd do another subject. I did this for two years. We formed some very fine new units in Michigan with excellent people in them. As a matter of fact, two of the Reserve Officers out of the Detroit units became Presidents, or whatever it is they have in the Naval Reserve Officers Association--Milt Wortley, and George Akers. They both became Captains during World War II, and had wonderful tours of active duty, and later became Presidents of the Naval Reserve Officers Association.

There were a lot of others who did well both in Civilian Careers and in the Navy. There's a chap, now a member of the Naval Academy Alumni Association Board of Trustees who comes from Detroit who was a Reserve Ensign while I was out there, Rear Admiral Leon J. Jacobi, U. S. Naval Reserve. Of course, he's retired now.

The only immediate recompense that I gained from that job was that it helped me professionally, because when you have to teach a subject you have to study it and you become more knowledgeable in it.

Q: I'm sure it was awfully rigorous having to teach like that. Different subjects in the same evening.

Dyer: One other story that I want to tell--When I went out to Detroit, there was a Chief Petty Officer who handled the financial accounts for the recruiting station. The Recruiting Officer handles a lot of money because he pays prospective enlistees for meals, provides for overnight lodging and then for their transportation to go from Detroit down to the Great Lakes Naval

Training Station. When I relieved the officer (Lieutenant Commander, Jere H. Brooks, out of the Class of 1907), who was the previous Recruiting Officer, he said, "Well, I don't pay any attention to this financial business. Ward, the Chief Yeoman takes care of it. I pay no attention to it." I said, "Yes, but you're the responsible person." He said, "Oh, that's a lot of hokum. Ward's good and honest."

I took over the money myself, and I took over the safe and changed the combination. About four months after I came on board, I received a letter from the Commandant of the 9th Naval District. He said, "You're being nominated to be a member of the general court martial for Lieutenant William H. Ferguson." He was a classmate of mine, who was Recruiting Officer down at Kansas City. He let the Chief Petty Officer who had the money when he took over as Recruiting Officer keep control of it, but the Chief ran away with the money. So, Ferguson was court martialed and lost seniority. Of course, he had a comparatively difficult naval career, because of a mistake in judgment at this early date. I've often thought of that.

Ward, later became, I believe, a Lieutenant, Supply Corps, after initially becoming a pay clerk. I followed him that long. Ward was a very responsible individual, and I'm sure would have been all right if I'd let him have the money.

But I didn't.

I wrote back to the Commandant of the Ninth Naval District and said that I didn't think I should sit on the court because Ferguson was a classmate and I didn't feel it was fair to ask one classmate to sit on a court martial of another. I did not actually sit as a member of the court. But Ferguson was court martialed and found guilty.

Q: All of this, Admiral, shows what you can do with a job that didn't look like very much when you went to it.

Dyer: In early 1926 I received a letter from Lieutenant Commander Charlie Lockwood--of whom you know--And he said, "I'm going to have command of the USS V-3." She, of course, was a great big submarine, 2,000 tons, 300 feet long, and due for Commissioning at the Navy Yard, Portsmouth. He said, "How about going with me on the V-3?" He did not mention what job I would have. He had been the skipper of the G-1 when I first graduated from the Submarine School, and then skipper of the S-14, when I had been in the S-15. I just had the highest opinion in the world of Charlie Lockwood. He was a bachelor, he was a very hard working man, he was extremely intelligent, and he just struck my eye. When he asked me to go with him, I wrote back and said I would be delighted. Then he wrote me another letter and said, "I'm sure that you felt that you were going to be the Exec. You have been the skipper of three submarines so far. You aren't even going to be the Exec, nor are you going to be the Chief Engineer. John Twomey in '17 is going to be the Chief Engineer, Bert Rodgers in '16 is going to be the Exec. You'll be the Electrical Officer." I said, "To travel with you, I'll do anything." So, I became the Electrical Officer on the USS V-3.

About a year after the V-3 was commissioned, (May 22, 1926), John Twomey moved up to the carrier LEXINGTON (CU2) which was a building, and I relieved him as Chief Engineer. I was the Chief Engineer until I was detached in June 1928. Jimmy Compton '16 relieved Bert Rodgers as Executive Officer. You probably know of Rodgers--he became a Flag Officer and Commander Amphibious Forces, Pacific, after a very fine war record. He was an excellent Executive Officer. Captain Jimmy Compton lives just outside of Annapolis.

I had a wonderful cruise in the V-3, and one that did me a great deal of good in many ways. In the first place, I had never served under Charlie Lockwood before. I had been in the same organization with him, and he knew me by reputation, but I had never been in the same ship with him. He kept all of his officers on their toes and moving ahead.

When he came back from England. . . He was in England as U. S. Naval Attache when World War II started for the United

States. In April 1942, he was promoted to rear Admiral and assigned as Commander Submarines, Southwest Pacific. So, when he came back to the U. S. he reported into Admiral King's Headquarters for briefing on his new duty. I was on Admiral King's staff at the time as Operational Intelligence Officer (E-35) and Intelligence Officer Officer (F-11). Charlie came around to my office and said, "How about going with me out to Australia and be my Chief of Staff?" Of course, I said, "I'll be delighted, but you will have to spring me. I will not spring myself." So he came back about a day later and he said, "I'm sorry, but you're not springable. If a little later you can come, no matter who's there, I'll want to have you." But of course, I never went as his Chief of Staff.

After my cruise with him in the V-3, we became firm and fast friends. He was, I'm sure, helpful in my becoming a Flag Officer. And I'm eternally grateful. I'll tell you some stories about Charlie . . .

Q: Fine. Do you have all of his seven books?

Dyer: No I don't. But I reviewed two of them for the SHIPMATE, and one for the Naval Institute. Actually, I did not like his HONDA book; because, in my opinion, he did not stress adequately the derelictions of duty of those who were involved as I said in my review.

I want to tell you one other story about the S-15, because it ties in with Charlie Lockwood. When I was in the S-15, the junior officer was an Ensign whose name was Glascock--I will not mention what his nickname was. When the submarines were operating in Manila Bay, we used to get underway from Cavite and stand out to the diving area. We had to run about three miles to get where we could dive, because the water wasn't deep enough. Also, we had to get past the steamer lanes, running from Corregidor Island into Manila Harbor.

We would stand out of Cairte on a North Westerly course for our daily training exercises. Our working hours in the Philippines were a bit different. Instead of working an 8 a.m. to 4 p.m. day, we worked a 7 a.m. to 3 p.m. day, because of the tremendous heat and the submarines got so bloomin' hot later in the day. Normally we were standing out, 5, 10, or 15 minutes after 7 in the morning. One, two or three merchant ships were normally standing in, and they were making an 8 o'clock arrival in Manila. So, we would have them on our port hand. Therefore, under the International Rules of the Road, we would have the right of way.

I believed very strongly ever since I had been a Commanding Officer when I was young--I was still young, but I was comparatively seasoned that a Commander Officer must train his subordinate officers. Every day my other officers were alternated in taking out the S-15, preparing the ship for diving, and diving it. I merely stood by as an observer. I did not stand up on the bridge, I stood down on the gun's sponson just forward of the bridge, so that I wouldn't be kabitzing everything that they did.

When Glascock would have his day to take the submarine out--of course, the Navigator, who was Kinnear would stand up beside him on the bridge as he should. These great big 12,000 to 20,000 ton merchant ships would come from the port hand. The submarine, S-15, was 800 tons. Old Glascock would hold his right of way, hold his right of way, and hold his right of way until Kinnear would just have catfits. Finally Kinnear would call down and say, "Captain you've got to do something." Well, when the Navigator said I had to do something, I did something. What I normally did was either swing hard left rudder, or I stopped, shifted to motors and backed. And I let the bloomin' merchant ship go charging on in to Manila. Well, this type of performance persisted, and persisted. I had long talks with Glascock, trying to reason him out of his procedures. I explained the realistic procedure to him. He was an ex-Chief Quartermaster; he had spent his life as an enlisted man on the bridge. He had been told all this 47 different times, but we couldn't get him to do any different than to hold his right of way. Finally I wrote a letter to my Division Commander and said, "Ensign Glascock is tempermentally unsuited for submarine

...ty. He can never, as far as I can see, be declared qualified ...or command. And he should be sent to other duty." The Division Commander approved it, the Flotilla Commander approved it, ...nd Glascock was transfered to a Yangtze River gunboat, the ...SS Sacramento.

So Glascock did a cruise on a gunboat in Southern China. ...hen he was due to come back to the United States, having completed his cruise on the China Station, Glascock sits down and ...rites an official letter and asks that he be ordered to the ...ubmarine School. And says that he was sure that the reason ...hat he hadn't been qualified for command in submarines was ...hat he had never gone through the Submarine School. So, a ...ery foolish Bureau of Navigation ordered him into the Submarine School. Charlie Lockwood was a member of the Board of Investigation or Court of Inquiry that investigated the sinking of the S-51. Glascock was the Officer of the Deck of the S-51 when she was rammed and sunk. He was holding his right or way, which he had, on the City of RALEIGH.

Q: He never learned that brinkmanship doesn't pay.

Dyer: That's the end of my story. That's right.

Dyer 4 - 120

Interview with Admiral George C. Dyer   June 12, 1969
by John T. Mason, Jr.   Annapolis, Maryland

Mr. Mason: Admiral, last time when we broke off in Interview #3, you had been dealing with your submarine career in the Philippines largely. I think now you're ready to talk about your assignment on the battleship ARIZONA.

Admiral Dyer: Actually I have told you before about how I once had orders to the PENNSYLVANIA. Those orders were cancelled, instead I was ordered to the Exec of the S-15.

Mason: Yes, you told me how eager you were to serve on the PENNSYLVANIA.

Dyer: That's right. So I kept putting in requests at regular intervals for duty on board a battleship. By this time, which was 1928, I had been in the V-3 from 1926 to '28. I had been out of the Naval Academy 10 years, and I felt that I really should move on from submarines.

Q: You were becoming too much of a specialist, weren't you?

Dyer: During that period, 1926-1928, a letter came out from the Department directing all officers of certain seniority to take an aviation physical examination. If they were physically qualified, the Department urged them to put in for aviation training duty. Captain Lockwood, who was my skipper; and one of the officers on board named Johnny Dix, who was a senior Lieutenant and I all went over and took this aviation physical. Captain Lockwood passed the physical. I did not pass the physical unqualifiedly. They told me they could get a waiver on the disabilities which I had--which was being too skinny and a slight deficiency in depth perception.

I did not request aviation training. I went home and told my wife about this letter, and that I had taken the physical examination. She urged me not to put in for aviation. I might say at that time, of course, submariners were not drawing any extra pay; and the aviators were. That 50% extra pay looked awfully big to me.

The Department ordered Charlie Lockwood to take initial training at the Naval Air Station, San Diego. He went over there on a regular schedule, and they put him through a course of sprouts. The day came when he was to solo. A number of the officers from the V-3 went over to watch him solo. Charlie came down in what is known as a 'hot landing', and bounced about a hundred feet in the air. He went charging off again, came back down again. The second time he only bounced about 30 or 40 feet in the air. They decided he had better stay in submarines.

Q: That didn't encourage you to seek that kind of a career. Were you tempted to do it however, in terms of your own advancement? Thinking of the future role of aircraft in the Navy.

Dyer: I wish I could say the answer to that was "yes." Actually, what enticed me at the moment was the thought of that 50% extra pay. I had three children, and I was getting roughly about $350 a month. It just seemed like an awful lot of money that I was missing.

I was very anxious to broaden my knowledge of the Navy. As a matter of fact, that was one of the reasons why I wanted to go into battleships. Eventually my orders came through. I was ordered, and went to the ARIZONA.

When I came on board, they told me that I was going to have the electrical division. One thing that I remember very distinctly is that the electrical division had 58 men in it. Fifty-eight men seemed to me like a lot of men. Since that number of men was about twice what an S boat had on board.

Q: Small complements.

Dyer: Small complements, and so forth. I had a very interesting cruise on the ARIZONA.

Q: Who was skipper?

Dyer: The first skipper was Captain Victor A. Kimberly, out of the Class of 1899. He was a bachelor, very capable and he also was a stamp collector as I am so that helped break the ice. The second one was Ward K. Wortman, and I say this-- probably the most incompetent officer of the rank of Captain I ever served. He was just absolutely worthless, in my very humble opinion.

I was standing watch, of course, down in the engine room. We were at sea engaged in maneuvers very shortly after I came aboard. Over the voice tube from the bridge--at that time they had voice tubes--the Captain was on the other end and he wanted to speak to Lieutenant Dyer. I said, "Yes, sir." He said, "I'm told you can work the mooring board." I said, "Yes, sir." He said, "Run all the way up here." I was in dungarees, I came up on the bridge, completely out of breath, of course.

They had some very simple maneuvers, and I put it on the board, and worked the solution. He turned to the Exec, Commander F. La Frenz (Class of 1907) and he said, "I want Dyer's battle station to be up here on the bridge so he can work this mooring board."

Do you know what a mooring board is?

Q: No.

Dyer: A mooring board gives you a solution to go from where you are to where you want to go. It is something like an 'Is-Was', which I told you about. The experience that I had with the 'Is-Was' made me able to work a mooring board with no great difficulty.

A ship would be, say ordinarily, 500 yards astern of the ship ahead of it in column, as far as a battleship was concerned. An order would come out for all ships to get on an echelon of 30 degrees. All you needed was the solution of a very simple mooring board problem, depending on the speed of the guide, what speed you had available, and the position you were to get to--to figure out what course and speed you should take. If you didn't do that; you could end up very embarassingly too far ahead, too far behind, too slow to get there, or some other embarrassing thing. Discomfit the Admiral who was conducting the maneuvers.

Q: I would take it that the Australian carrier MELBOURNE was lacking in the mooring board.

Dyer: As I remember it, she was working at night, which in the days before radar made it a bit more difficult.

That's how I happened to stand a lot of duty on the bridge of the ARIZONA. What they did in those days--they had two kinds of exercises. One was to train Execs and Captains the other was to train Officers of the deck. They would put out a signal that the Officer of the deck would take the "conn." Therefore he would control the ship in its maneuvers. He also had the assistance of the regular team that was on the bridge. Or they'd say the Captain would have the "conn" and he would control the actual movement of the ship.

Q: Admiral, I take it from what you said that the ability to operate the mooring board was a specialized one that not many officers had.

Dyer: In 1927-28, they were working it in to professional examinations for promotion. In other words, they were commencing to require officers to work mooring board problems on their professional examinations. At that time, officers took long-winded professional examinations. For instance, going from Junior Lieutenant to Lieutenant, and from Lieutenant to Lieutenant Commander, normally it took a steady week of writing. By that, I mean Monday through Saturday, on different subjects. You were examined in ten subjects altogether. Navigation (theoretical and practical), seamanship, gunnery, aviation, electrical engineering, steam engineering, military law, international law and strategy and tactics. So, you had to do a tremendous amount of studying.

I think one of the greatest mistakes the Navy ever made

roughly ten years ago, they knocked off professional examinations. These had required officers to study. Whether you're 20, or 30, or 40 or 50, it does you good to stick your head in a book and try to get something out of it.

Shifting my battle station to the bridge sort of varied my experience in the ARIZONA. I had anticipated being in the engineroom, where I badly needed training in engineering—steam engineering since my previous engineering training had always been in diesel engineering.

One thing that happened in the ARIZONA—when I came aboard and became a member of the Wardroom Mess—at that time the Wardroom Mess in the ARIZONA was collecting $25 a month mess bill from each officer. I had come out of submarines, and our normal mess bill was about $12.50 a month. You want to realize that, at least I, and I believe about 95% of the rest of the officers—were living very close hauled financially. Because we didn't have very much. So that paying $25.00 was quite a financial change for me.

Q: Does it indicate the food was better?

Dyer: The answer was it was costing more. I have a long-winded story. I'll tell you about that. I was the junior member that sat at the head wardroom table. The Exec sits at the head of the #1 table in the Wardroom Mess. I sat at the foot--I was the junior member at that table. I groused about the cost, and about the food, and the service of it. At that time it's changed now--at the end of each month they held an election as to who'd be the next Mess Treasurer of the Wardroom Mess. The Mess Treasurer not only collected the money, and expended it, but he arranged the menu and he supervised the boys--the stewards and mess attendants.

Q: Just a kind of an extra chore.

Dyer: Yes, an extra chore. I had a lot of opinions in regard to the Wardroom Mess and expressed them too freely. At the end of the first month, I was elected the Mess Treasurer. The first thing that I did was consult with my wife, and together we made up a week's menu. Then I held a consultation with the Chief Steward; a great big black man about 6 foot 3 or 4, who weighed about 260 pounds. His last name was James.

I told him hereafter I will do all the buying. I'll do all the buying not only ashore, but the buying that we do from the Paymaster. The Wardroom Mess, of course, buys from the Paymaster the things that the Paymaster carries in his stock for the General Mess which the Wardroom Mess can use. So, I started that. As a matter of fact, I'd been a very busy boy on board submarines. There'd always been a great deal for me to do. I found that in this assignment as Electrical Officer in the ARIZONA. I had working for me a tremendous number of people, some of whom were very highly qualified. I did not have enough work to keep me busy, so I was very happy that I had this job as Mess Treasurer. I turned to on it, and tried to do a good job.

The new menus which my wife made out were a great success. The daily expense book that I kept to show how much I was spending indicated that actually we were running at a cost of about $19 to $20 a month; instead of $25. Which with the number of people we had in the mess, (35), meant that the mess was running roughly 150 to 200 dollars less per month on overall expenditures.

Q: Did you actually go into the market place?

Dyer: Went into the market and bought what I had to buy.

Q: Did you have the help of your wife in doing this?

Dyer: The answer to that is, I had a lot of advice from her. But she did not go along.

The Chief Steward was completely upset, terribly upset. So, at the end of the first month when the books were all balanced out, actually the mess had cost something like $19.70. Instead of collecting $25 for the next month--we always collected on pay day--which was the first Monday in those days--I collected

$20. Figuring that I would be able to run it that cheap, or cheaper, the next month.

I was acquiring experience, I didn't have too much experience in this thing, I was acquiring some.

Q: And there were no squawks from the men?

Dyer: Oh, I got re-elected unaimously, no competitors, no complaints. Everybody was very pleased.

About the end of two weeks of the second month, the Chief Steward came in to see me. He said, "Mr. Dyer, I'd like to have a heart-to-heart talk with you." He said, "How much do you aim to run this mess for?" I said, "I aim to run it, probably for about $18.50 a month. We'll collect $20 and we'll gradually build up a little reserve here. (Because the mess had been just skimping along). I don't like this not having a little reserve, so if we want to have a party we'll have money to give the party. I aim to build up a little reserve." He came back with a reply immediately. He said, "If I take these here menus which you and you's wife makes out, and give you everythin' thats on those menus--if I guarantee that this mess will be run for a little less than $18 and a half per month-- how about letting me run this? I'se the Chief Steward. Everybody's making fun of me. You's doing my work." I said, "I think you have a point, I have been doing your work. But I've been doing it because I wanted to show you that it could be done better and cheaper. That sounds like a good bargain, $18.50. I agree."

Every month I served in the ship from then on, I was re-elected. I was in the ship a year, and I served as mess treasurer of the Wardroom Mess every month except the first. We ran the mess for $18.50, or a little less--a few dimes each time.

We arrived in Norfolk, where the ship was going to modernize. The ARIZONA was going to have the additional water tight protect put on her, and get new liners in the turrets, new boilers, and all that sort of thing. About a year and a half job.

The dentist on board (Lieutenant Commander J. D. Halleck), incidentally Dr. Gordon who lives here in town was the junior medical officer on the ARIZONA at that time--received a letter from the Department saying he was going to stay in the ARIZONA while the ship was being modernized. Most of the Line officers were being ordered away. They were keeping just a skeleton crew of officers. The dentist had rented an unfurnished apartment and gone into Norfolk to buy furniture. Of course, he had to have credit arrangements. So he had gone up to the credit department of this furniture store. The credit man told him, "You're the second officer that's been in here today from the ARIZONA. However, the other officer was a great big colored fellow. He bought a lot more furniture than you did. In fact he bought about $1800 worth of furniture, and he paid $1400 cash on the purchase."

I thought that I had cut James short, but I hadn't cut him short enough, I can tell you that. Otherwise he never would have been able to pay that much cash on a furniture purchase. This happened in the era when Chief Petty Officers drew $99 or $126, depending on whether they were temporary or permanent Chief Petty Officers and $157.50 after 16 years service. James wouldn't have been able to save that kind of money.

Q: You really had cut down on his income.

Dyer: I had cut down on his income pretty hard.

Q: So that was in lieu of tips?

Dyer: It was something like that. I've never forgotten this experience and how difficult it is for a Line officer to really determine what a large mess will cost.

I had a very pleasant year in the ARIZONA. When we got around to the East Coast and into the Norfolk yard--we had participated in the Fleet Problem that year, I was detached and ordered up to the Naval Academy to the Post Graduate School.

There were 120 students in the Line Post Graudate which I was in. The head of the school was Captain Albert T. Church who was an E. D. O. and out of Admiral Numitz' Class, 1905. The Exec, Cary W. MacGruder, was a very famous naval officer. His older brother was a Flag officer. You've probably heard of T. Pickett MacGruder--that's his older brother, Cary became a Commodore during the war.

Not very long after we had arrived in Annapolis at the PG School, and before we had start our years work, Commander MacGruder gave the Class a talk. Incidentially one of the courses that you took in the General Line School was in mooring boards. It was taught by Dickie Knight, Admiral Knight's sons. Admiral Knight wrote the book on SEAMANSHIP studied by generations of midshipmen. His son, Lieutenant Commander R. H. Knight, Jr. taught the mooring board along with several other officers.

Q: Were there electives in this course?

Dyer: No, you took a set course. It was purely a professional course, and an excellent one.

Commander MacGruder told us that the officers who stood in the top ten in the General Line Class would go directly to the Naval War College when they left. I don't know how many, but there were roughly a dozen "star" men in that group of 120 who had "starred" at the Naval Academy. And there were some very bright officers who had transferred into the regular Navy after World War I. Of course, I had not "starred". I stood right in the middle of my class. However, I wanted very much to go to the Naval War College. I studied, I don't think I ever studied harder for a longer period of time. I graduated number ten. I really was extremely proud. I just was bursting out all over Because I ended up number ten.

I'll tell you a little story about that. At our 51st Class of 1919 get-together, one of the classmates who showed up for it, was a chap whose name is Abie Stein. After the class had finished up at the General Line School we were to have the graduation exercises the next day--the Stein's had a cocktail party. Abie had been held over for a re-examination. Abie's trouble was that he nursed the bottle, instead of studying. And so did his wife.

Q: It's a bad combination.

Dyer: When Adaline and I arrived at this party, Abie and his wife were at the door. Greeting me, she said, "I heard you graduated number ten." I said, "Yes, I did, and I'm delighted." She said, "My Abie is brighter drunk, than you are sober." And that was true, most probably. She has passed to her reward, and he has a very fine number two Mrs. Stein. He teaches school down in Virginia. He was not selected to Commander, but has done extremely well since he retired. He has been on the wagon now for twenty years or more, and doesn't touch a drop. I never see Abie that I don't think of this story and it is just as true as it can be.

Another person in the General Line Group in 1929-1930 that's here in Annapolis is Admiral Sherway Clark. He's of the class of '22. There was a very good group in the General Line School the year that I was there. Arleigh Burke was here in the Ordnance PG course that year.

I then went up to the Naval War College, and spent a year up there. That was, I think, one of the most fruitful years I ever had in my whole naval career.

Q: Was that also a set course?

Dyer: The answer to that is--by and large it was a set course. You had to turn in what we call term papers. Which now have been given a much more classy educational name, copied after universities, and so forth. You could pick any subject you wanted for your term paper.

Q: What is it, a dissertation now?

Dyer: A dissertation. It had to deal with reasonable national problems that had some relation to military matters, or naval matters. It couldn't be on the antics of a fly--you couldn't write that sort of a paper. It was a very much worthwhile exercise.

They had a very fine group of people on the staff. Admiral Hewitt was one person that you know--he was on the staff while I was up there.

Was Spruance, by any chance?

Dyer: He was up there on the staff, but not while I was there, he came afterwards.

Glassford, Draemel, Tommy Withers, and Alan Kirk were all on the staff. The first President of Naval War College they had while I was up there was Rear Admiral Harris Laning, who was an ex-Chief of the Bureau of Naval Personnel. Later, he had a three star job at sea, Commander Cruisers, Scouting Force. A very fine person. He had on his staff before I left up there an officer who had been skipper of the REINA MERCEDES, when I was at the Naval Academy as a midshipman. His name was H. H. Christy. He was called "Horrible Hannibal" Christy. He was senior to the President of the Naval War College on the list of Rear Admirals.

Just a footnote, Admiral. You know about these things. Why some of these horrible nicknames the naval officers get?

Dyer: I don't know.

I heard one the other day--Muddy Waters.

Dyer: Whiskey Riggs, right up in Washington.

In looking over the list of people that were up there, I have quite a dissertation in my Kelly Turner book on--What The Bureau's System of Ordering People to the Naval War College Was--in the period when I was there, the middle 30s. And I won't repeat that here. By and large, as it appeared to me at the time, there was a very fine group of Captains. They had a very miscellaneous lot of Commanders a few people that would make you shudder to look at them, as far as their professional ability was concerned. A fair group of Lieutenant Commanders, including Dick Conolly in 1914, and they had a pretty good group of senior lieutenants. I notice of my Junior War College Class that were up there, four besides myself became Flag officers. (Conolly, Von Heinburg, Tuggle Korns). Which considering it was 15 years ahead of their promotion to Flag rank was pretty good job of looking into the future. We had some dillys of really worthless Commanders.

I'll tell you one of the first things that happened to me when I went there. We were at a cocktail party when a chap came in whom I didn't know from Adam's off ox. He introduced himself as the head fireman of the Newport, Rhode Island Fire Department. It wasn't too long before he was standing up on a chair and saying, "The firemen are going to have their annual ball ten days from now." He wanted to extend an invitation to all the War College officers to attend that ball. He gave us all the details of where it was to be held, and so forth. I actually swallowed it hook, line, and sinker. It wasn't until the next morning that I found out that this was Ditty Box Mayo--Admiral Mayo's son--a Commander in the Navy and a member of the Senior Class who had extended this invitation.

Q: This was just as a big joke.

Dyer: Yes. You can tell from his nickname, Ditty Box Mayo, that his classmates and contemporaries had sized him up very properly. He was sitting on his ditty box all the time, and not doing much worthwhile.

I had a very interesting thing happen to me up there. At that time, they played one big Fleet problem each year. A Red-Blue ⌊Great Britain, United States⌋ problem, or a Blue-Orange (Japan) problem which they played each year. At that time, the members of the junior class were assigned as operational aides to members of the senior War College class. One Rear Admiral who was taking the senior course told me this story himself. His name is Arthur Jappy Hepburn. He later became Commander-in-Chief of the United States Fleet.

He told me that the previous year when he was at sea, he had received a dispatch from the Chief of the Bureau of Navigation which said, "I have had an inquiry from the Senior

Member of the Selection Board that is considering Line Captains for Flag Officer asking if Captain Hepburn was selected would he request the Senior Naval War College course for his next assignment?" The Chief of Bureau wanted an answer. Hepburn said, "I knew what the answer to that was. I'd be delighted." So he was there at the Naval War College.

Q: Sort of a package deal.

Dyer: That's right, a package deal.

I worked as his Operations Officer during the course of this problem. Not too long after this problem was over, Tommy Withers--who was an old submariner and who was on the staff--sent for me. He said, "As you know, when Admiral Hepburn leaves here, he's going to be Commander Submarine Force. He is considering taking you along on his staff. Would you like to go?" I knew the answer to that one, too. "I'd be delighted."

This happened along about April when you play the big Fleet problem or early May. And about the time that you start to get notice of what's going to happen to you for your next duty assignment. Since your course ran out in early June, people started getting their orders, and I didn't get any orders. I didn't get anything. I didn't even say anything to my wife about it. Time went on, and still I didn't hear anything about it. Finally, as far as I could see I was about the only member of the junior class who didn't have any orders. Just about that time, my classmate up there--name of Von Heimburg, "Count" Von Heimburg--announced that he was going to marry Commander Glassford's daughter. As a matter of fact, I was one of the ushers at the wedding. The next thing I knew, the Count tells me he's going on Hepburn's staff.

I hot footed it up to my friend Tommy Withers, and I said, "What's happened to my going on Admiral Hepburn's staff?" He said, "Well, after all, Glassford kept talking to us about his son-in-law. So Count Von Heimburg is going to go instead of you."

Here it was pretty near time for us to graduate, and I didn't have an assignment. Next thing I knew I had a telephone call from Bureau of Naval Personnel. It was the Submarine Detail Officer. He said, "We're in need of some people who will take the deep sea diving school course, and then go out and command submarine rescue ships. Those submarine rescue ships are at the present time all commanded by ex-enlisted personnel. We've gotten a number of complaints from Division Commanders and Flotilla Commanders. We're going to clean house, and put in all Academy graduates in these ships. Would you be willing to go down to the deep sea diving school?" I said, "I'd be delighted."

So I was detached and went down to Washington where the deep sea diving school was. I took a course in deep sea diving. Then I went out to Pearl Harbor.

I relieved--actually an old shipmate of mine who had been in the V-3 with me--Lieutenant Johnny Dix, who was an ex-Chief Quartermaster, as the skipper. The WIDEGON was a converted mine-sweeper. About 500 tons of diving gear, decompression chambers, two bow and two stern anchors, large air compressors, everything else. At that time, which was 1931, 32, 33, the Navy was really on its uppers because it didn't have any money. Of course, we were living on a pay cut, and a pay freeze. The first year we were cut 8 1/3%, the second year we were cut 12½%, and so we were living on very thin money rations personally. And very thin rations for operating ships. So the WIDGEON not only did the normal duties that might be expected of a diving ship, but she did a lot of other chores. They were trying to make one ship do the work of two.

I did a lot of tugboat handling of ships over at the Ten-Ten dry dock. Ordinarily, they would have used a yard tug. They did have one yard tug, but they needed two tugs, and I was the second tug. Any time that the SEA GULL couldn't operate-- the SEA GULL was the submarine tender, I took over her chores.

I had two years there in commander of the WIDGEON. Two very wonderful years. Some very fine people served with me.

One of them was a very renowned deep sea diver, a Chief Gunner whose name was Clarence L. Tibbals. Believe it or not--There's a Clarence L. Tibbals award given each year to a Midshipman when he graduates. I just was amazed. I was at the Naval Academy when they made the presentation of awards this year. I think the award is just wonderful. Tibbals was a very fine person. He not only was extremely competent professionally, but he was a very wonderful Naval Officer. Tibbals is one of the few naval officers that Congress has voted a financial renumeration to for extraordinary services rendered. These services were in connection with the salvage of the USS S-4. He was the Chief Gunner when I went to the WIDGEON. He was soon relieved by another Chief Gunner by the name of Walter J. Love.

I had a very wonderful Machinist in the WIDGEON. Actually, he was the second Machinist to serve in the WIDGEON with me. The first one's names was Jesse S. Hooper--a great big overweight gentleman. Then I got a freshly made machinist whose name was Michael Hurley. Of course, a Machinist was not qualified by previous training to stand any watches on deck when the ship was underway. But I taught young Hurley to stand a deck watch, and to navigate, and do a lot of other things. He has told me, in fact he has written me that during World War II after he was promoted to commissioned rank, he was called on to do a large number of deck officer chores and he'd say,

"Thank God for George Dyer." Because I'd taught him. As a Machinist, he then became a Line Officer, retired as a Commander in the Navy. I think probably a darn good one. He was a very good Machinist. He learned easily, and willingly. He had a lot of innate ability. All he needed was the opportunity.

I had a perfectly worthless Bosun out there, that finally got court martialed and kicked out of the Navy. His name was Edward R. Palmer. He was relieved by a Chief Boatswain named John L. Hunter, who became a Lieutenant Commander during World War II and retired as such. He also was very capable and excellent.

So I was fortunate to have such good people on a small ship like that. We had only 41 men, 4 officers. The WIDGEON did quite a little diving work and some salvage work.

One of the things that I did that I will never forget—I stayed up the longest that I've ever stayed up in my life. I stayed up for five days and five nights. And that's 120 hours.

Q: Were you conscious at the end?

Dyer: I was just barely conscious. I got the ship back into the harbor.

The S-4 had sunk by accident, and then she had been

raised after days and months of effort. When she had been raised, somebody had the very excellent idea that she ought to be sent around to wherever they had diving ships stationed. She should be sunk again, and then salvage ships should raise her, using their equipment, testing out their equipment, and giving the submarine rescue ship an actual submarine to work on.

Sometime in 1932, 1933, I don't remember exactly when it was, the S-4 showed up at Pearl Harbor. The Flotilla Commander scheduled this submarine salvage exercise. The basic instructions required that the S-4 be put down in 80 feet of water. At that time, 200 feet was largely the end of the rope--as far as diving was concerned.

For instance, when I graduated from the deep sea diving school, I was qualified to dive 200 feet, which was as great a depth as they qualified people. A few people had gone deeper-- don't misunderstand me. The Deep Sea Diving School did not qualify people at depths over 200 feet nor did graduates do diving beyond that depth because of the tremendous length of time it took to get people safely back up from the bottom--$5\frac{1}{2}$ hours. So that it was just impractical to operate at deeper depths.

We put the S-4 down on the bottom off the Ewa Plantation Mill. After she had been put down, I laid a four anchor mooring around her. And I put the WIDGEON in the center of the moor. Then the WIDGEON started putting divers down, to run these heavy chains. The ends of the chains were secured to her great big 12" hawsers in order for the large pontoons to provide the necessary life to get the S-4 started up from the bottom.

The first thing you have to do is tunnel underneath the submarine (the S-4) in order to run the chains underneath. Due to the fact that we were tunnelling coral, it was a major time consuming operation. It took just days longer than it took to tunnel under normal circumstances such as under hard sand, or in mud.

We had been over the S-4 about four hours, when I could see the divers' bubbles were working out towards seaward. The S-4 was working to seaward. We were about a mile off shore from the head at Ewa Plantation Mill. There was a big tower down there at Ewa to mark where we had put the S-4 down. So the WIDGEON had to pick up the old moorings and lay a new mooring, a four hour job, because the S-4 was working into deeper and deeper water. Every time a diver went down--the first time it was at 80 feet, the next time he went down to 86 feet. The next time he went down to 92, and so forth. And it takes longer, and longer, and longer to get your divers safely back up. We just had to decompress each diver more slowly.

Eventually at the end of roughly 60 hours, $2\frac{1}{2}$ days, we had the chains through. We ran our hawsers. As soon as we took a strain on the hawsers, the hawsers parted. They had acquired dry rot out there in Hawaii where they had been stowed in tanks, for some period prior to the time I got out there. We had some spare hawsers. We ran the spare hawsers. And then what happened-- the first one of the chains was wearing on the coral, working on the coral due to the sea, wore through this great big five inch chain. The submarine was working out to sea--finally was in about 130 odd feet of water. I had already shifted my moorings three times. We couldn't make the connection between the chain that was through under the S-4 and the line that was coming down with the sister hooks on it, because the sea and swell were picking up.

All my divers were exhausted. Needless to say, I was exhausted. So finally I turned to this chap, Baron--William P. Baron. At that time, he was a Gunner's Mate, first class. He is now a retired Lieutenant Commander in the Navy. I said, "Baron will you make one more try?" He said, "Captain, I sure will." He'd been down twice before, but hadn't been able to make this vital connection. He was a diver 'par excellence', just super. He went down and made that connection, and we got that blooming S-4 up. The time was roughly 4 days, and 16 hours after we had put her down. Then I had to tow the S-4 back into Pearl Harbor.

I never went home. I had one of the men call up my wife and tell her I'd be home in another 24 hours.

Q: That was a lesson that made an indeliable impression, didn't it?

Dyer: Yes. You should have known this chap Baron. He became a Warrant Gunner in 1933 and was a Chief Gunner when World War II started. He became a Lieutenant Commander. The law requires that officers with his background be retired after 30 years, and so he was retired. He went back to his little home town in New Hampshire, where he first became what we would call an alderman. Then he became the Mayor. Then he became a member of the State of New Hampshire Assembly, and then was re-elected. Just doing extremely well, when he had a stroke--somewhat like I did. He then resigned from the Legislature. He's down in Florida each winter. He comes to New Hampshire and I see him every summer. He comes over to see me. I owe him the greatest debt of gratitude. I never will be able to repay him.

While this and a number of other things were happening, who should turn up as the Flotilla Commander out in Pearl Harbor--my Flotilla Commander, Submarine squadron 4--but Captain Ward K. Wortman, my former skipper in the ARIZONA.

Q: Your friend.

Dyer: It was at the time of the Massey trouble. Have you ever heard of the Massey trouble?

Q: Oh, yes, Thalia Massey.

Dyer: You know that very worthless Captain Wortman--darn if he didn't, in my opinion, take the wrong attitude in everything, in regard to what the Navy should do in the Thalia Massey case. I was so upset by him, I just couldn't stomach it. This was not an individualistic feeling on my part. Finally the Department decided to relieve Captain Wortman, and they sent out Captain Hugo Osterhaus. I don't know whether you know Hugo Osterhaus. He was one of the famous Captains of the Navy, out of the Class of 1900. His father was a Flag officer before him, Commander-in-Chief of the Atlantic Fleet.

Hugo was a very stern personality. Old Hugo certainly gave the Submarine Base at Pearl Harbor a cleaning.

One of the things that happened after Captain Osterhaus arrived out there was in connection with the annual Fleet Problem. They always sent out the problem well ahead of time, and invited all Commander Officers to put in an Estimate of the Situation and a solution to the problem. I forwarded my solution to my Flotilla Commander, Captain Osterhaus. All of the solutions were forwarded up the chain of command to the Commander in Chief.

Captain Hugo sent for me and he said, "You know I haven't had time to prepare a solution. I've looked at your solution. I like it very much. Would you consider my taking over your solution, having it re-typed, and a few changes made here and there, and submitting it? Whether Lieutenant George Dyer submits one or not won't make any difference. But if Captain Osterhaus doesn't submit one, the Fleet Staff will say: 'Why in the hell didn't Osterhaus submit a solution?'" And this was perfectly true. I said, "Why I'd be delighted. I've had my mental exercise in the actual working out of the problem." And that was true.

He forwarded the solution. Of course, when you put in a solution, you postulate what both sides will do. As a matter of fact, it turned out the Force that the WIDGEON and Captain Osterhaus' submarines were on did largely what my solution suggested. The other Force didn't do what I said they'd do at all. But, it turned out extremely well. Captain Osterhaus was very happy about it.

He's still alive. He's one of the oldest living Naval Officers. He's out of the class of 1900 and lives at the Army-Navy Club. About once a year I go over and see him and talk to him.

Q: Over in Washington?

Dyer: Yes. This tells part of the story of my command of the submarine rescue ship WIDGEON. At the end of two years, I was ready to trade and travel. In 1933, selection list came out in late May or early June. If you weren't selected that year and had been passed over the year before, you were due for retirement as of the 30th of June. So the officers in this category needed a relief real quick. When the list actually came out--the list came out by dispatch--there's an officer by the name of J. M. Miller, out of the class of 1912, who was the skipper of the GAMBLE, which was a light minelayer. She was operating out of Pearl Harbor. When I discovered that Miller was not on this list, was not being picked up, I went up and saw my friend Captain Hugo. I said, "Captain Osterhaus, I'd like to have command of the GAMBLE. And they have to have a relief right away quick for Lieutenant Commander Miller because he has to retire on the 30th. Will you help me to get command of the GAMBLE?" He said, "I sure will." He ran for his car and off he went to 1010 Dock, where the OGLALA was secured.

He went there to see Rear Admiral Watts, who was Commander, Mine Force. He came back, and in about another 20 minutes, the WIDGEON got a message from the OGLALA, Flag ship of the Mine Force . . . "Lieutenant Dyer, report on board to see the Admiral."

I hot footed it over there to the OGLALA, and went in

to see Rear Admiral William C. Watts. The first question he asked, "Why would you like to have command of the GAMBLE?" I said, "I like to have command and I have been trained in command. I've had four smaller commands, the D-3, the L-10, the S-15 and the WIDGEON. I'm a Senior Lieutenant, but I'm a darn good one. I think it'd be nice if you broke the ice, and asked that Senior Lieutenant be ordered to command the GAMBLE, rather than waiting and getting any Lieutenant Commander the Bureau might order." He said, "Well, you have a point. You go over and talk to Commander McClaren." Commander John Walter McClaren was the Division Commander--J. W. McClaren out of the class of '11. He was a bit taken aback when I asked for command of the GAMBLE, but he was very much impressed by the fact that I'd had four commands. He said, "My Flag ship needs something done to it. Maybe you're the guy to do it."

Before the day was out, Commander, Mine Force sent a dispatch into the Bureau of Navigation recommending I be ordered. Be George, I was ordered. I reported on board, and I'll tell you two stories on that.

In due time, I relieved Lieutenant Commander Miller. I had an unpleasant incident before I relieved, but I'll tell you about that second. Because this one is very amusing.

After the relief ceremony and Lieutenant Commander Miller had left the ship, I gathered the officers of the ship, of whom there were five beside myself in the wardroom. I told them in some detail of the more important things that I wanted done. And there were a lot of things that I wanted to get done. One young officer, Ole Hanson, Ensign H. O. Hanson--said, "Captain, I'm sure we can do everything you want to have us do, if you just don't require us to play bridge in the morning."

Q: You mean, this had been the custom?

Dyer: This had been the custom in this ship, yes. I'll tell you another story about Ole Hanson which is very amusing. In those days, the short range battle practice was fired at targets at a slowly changing range. You moved down a range on a course parallel to the targets course, slowly closing the target, you passed abreast of the target at between 1200 and 1400 yards-- firing your guns as rapidly as you could sight and fire resulting a very high rate of fire. The objective was to get the maximum number of hits in the minimum time. In that era, if you did not get a satisfactory score, the ship received a Board of Investigation. So that the pressure was really on. And the USS GAMBLE had had a Board of Investigation in 1932-33. Ole Hanson, who was a fresh caught Ensign out of the class of '30-- and this was in 1933--was the Gunnery Officer in the GAMBLE. During the previous year, a destroyer, the CHILDS, (DD241), had developed a system of gunfire getting the maximum number of hits in the minimum time. They had done very well in short range practice the year before. The system was simple. The gun pointers kept their firing circuit keys closed all the time, relying on the pointer and the trainer to keep the gun on target all the time. As soon as the breech was closed, off went the gun. It was called the CHILDS system. And the ship ran up a tremendous score, under this system.

The Judge Advocate was examining Ole Hanson in regard to the system of gunnery training used in the USS GAMBLE. And he asked, "Mr. Hanson, did you use the CHILD'S system?" Ole replied, "I used a man's system."

Too tell the unhappy incident before I relieved will take a little longer. When I reported on board, at that time, in that era, the Commanding Officer was directly responsible--personally financially responsible--for the expenditures made in feeding the crew. This was the crew's mess. In other words, the mess ran on a dollars and cents basis, the dollars and cents being given to each ship by the Bureau of Supplies and Accounts in the Navy Department in Washington. The amount of money depended on the number of men in the crew, the larger ships receiving less money per man than smaller ships.

Q: But you'd had plenty of training in that.

Dyer: Yes. If the mess ran short of funds, the Commanding

Officer was personally responsible for the shortage. Every year there'd be letters going out, requiring them to kick in so much money here and there to make up the shortage.

So, when I reported on the GAMBLE, I did one of the first things that you did in those dark days when taking command was to take an inventory of the supplies that were in the crew's mess. How many . . .

Q: Sacks of beans?

Dyer: Yes, sacks of beans, and cans of pears, and bottles of ketchup, and everything else that was in the mess. And it was all stored in the crew's mess storeroom except refrigerated supplies and fresh vegetables. They had a separate storeroom set aside with lock and key. They had a storekeeper in charge of it. Normally, he was a Chief Commissary Steward.

I went down to the storeroom to take this inventory, with a great big inventory sheet in hand. Every item is listed, and you check off how many are there, if they have any. The storekeeper--the first couple of things he pulled out, I examined them, and they were all there. He started just showing me the fronts of large cartons, or large boxes with the various cans in them. I let him do that for 8 or 10 boxes. Then I said, "Just pull it out and set it down on the deck, and I'll count it." So, he did. Actually, only about half of it was there.

He said, "Some mistake, must have missed that." The next one he pulled out, just to show the front of it. I told him to set it down on deck and I would count the cans. There was another shortage. It ended up by my counting every can and every bit of meat in the whole inventory. The inventory was some $500 short. Of course, Miller, the officer I relieved became financially responsible for that shortage. I started out with a brand new inventory. The Chief Commissary Steward received a general court martial. They didn't do anything more to Miller because he was being retired anyway, except to require him to foot the shortage.

Q: The storekeeper had been making off with it?

Dyer: Yes, selling it ashore. Those were the things you learned by doing your job the way it was supposed to be done. Not taking short cuts.

As a matter of fact, a very good friend of mine, and an officer of whom I think the very highest--named Ralph H. Roberts, classmate, came out to Pearl Harbor and took command of another one of the ships in the division, the USS RAMSEY. He did not take his initial inventory. In other words, he took the inventory sheet as it was handed to him and signed his name to it. About two or three months later a new Chief Commissary Steward came in to relieve the other one, and he did take an inventory and found a shortage. Ralph got stuck with the shortage. It was less than Miller got stuck with, but it was about two hundred dollars.

Q: And that came out of the man's pocket.

Dyer: That's right.

Q: Why that immediate and personal responsibility for something like that?

Dyer: To insure the government's interest. The responsibility for all equipment on board used to be very personal. The Commanding Officer signed for all movable articles and subordinate officers signed to him. The Commanding Officer had a personal responsibility. I think it's a great mistake that he no longer has this responsibility. Since he has an impersonal responsibility, nobody is really responsible. So the result is the so called "slippage." It is tremendous these days, and very costly to the Navy and thus to the United States Government.

In 1933, you couldn't expend a hawser, you couldn't expend a heaving line without an official survey. All articles were the personal responsibility of some officer in the chain of line command.

During the year that I was in the GAMBLE and after some experience in mine laying, and after much thought on the problem,

I rewrote THE TACTICAL INSTRUCTIONS FOR MINE LAYING. The Division Commander--Commander McClaren--never forgot that. Not only because he got a degree of credit, for his contributions to which I made reference but due to the fact that the experimental mine laying exercises and drills were done during his tour of duty and he had great pride in his professional qualifications. He was most helpful over the years after I left the GAMBLE.

In 1934, I came here to the Naval Academy, and taught school for two years. Just about the end of two years in 1936--one day a Commander came down into the Seamanship office. I was teaching Seamanship and Navigation. Charlie Lockwood was head of my section, in the Seamanship Department. He had asked for me. At that time, that was the way you got duty in the Naval Academy. Somebody asked for you to come.

Q: Was that a desired duty?

Dyer: Highly desired duty.

Q: Why? Because it afforded the opportunity to be with your family?

Dyer: No. I think that that was part of it. But by and large, it offered an opportunity to learn and to study. To advance yourself in your professional background knowledge by wide reading, by submitting yourself to searching questions by midshipmen, by having contact with the educational leaders in the institutions in the Washington area.

Q: While you taught.

Dyer: Yes. It also offerred a chance to do a little thinking. It was highly advantageous. At the time that I was at the Naval Academy, there were six of the class of 1919 on duty. Herrmann, Callaghan, Briscoe, Dyer, Hungerford and Stein-- my good friend, Abie Stein. Four of the six became Flag officers on the active list.

Amongst the senior officers at the Naval Academy in 1934-36 who became Flag officers, there was Ralston S. Holmes, Forde A. Todd, Russell Willson, who was my Head of Department, H. Kent Hewitt; Ike (Robert C.) Giffen; Monroe Kelly, Jules James, Bryson Bruce. It was an extremely desirable detail, and it was kept so by a selective process. Contact with first rate officers is most valuable, if you have an open mind and a desire to learn.

At the end of two years, 1936, I was slated to be the Midshipmen Executive Officer on the WYOMING to take a European cruise. I had taken a European cruise the year before in the WYOMING, but not as Midshipman Exec. I was the number two that year. I had prepared all my cruise orders and plans for all the Midshipman training.

One day a Commander walked into the Seamanship office and said, "Who is Lieutenant Commander Dyer?" I was pointed out and he came over and sat down beside me, and started to ask me questions. Largely professional questions. I answered them the best I could. They covered a broad range. I couldn't see what he was trying to get at. I thought I better just keep my thoughts to myself and keep answering the questions. He asked me 20, 25, I don't know, maybe 30 questions. He finally got up, and said, "Thanks a lot." Out he went.

Q: I think I would have asked for an explanation.

Dyer: After he'd gone, I said, "Who in the world was that?" Someone said, "That was "Chips" Carpender." He introduced himself to me but his name didn't mean anything to me. Arthur S. Carpender.

A couple nights later, my wife and I were up in Washington to a dinner with the McClaren's--my old Division Commander. Mrs. McClaren said to my wife, "Isn't it nice that you're going on Admiral Richardson's staff?" Of course, my wife didn't know anything about it, and she rushes over to me, "What's this?" I said, "I don't know anything about it."

Carpender was going to be Admiral Richardson's Chief of Staff. Richardson, prospective Commander Destroyers, Scouting Force, had told him to look around and locate some other staff officers. He had seen Commander McClaren, and said, "Who do you recommend for staff officers for Richardson's staff?" He said, "I recommend George Dyer. Go down to the Naval Academy and talk with him." So, he had come down.

I really had a knotty problem. When this possible assignment came through, the Head of the Department of Seamanship objected very seriously. He said I was all prepared to go on the cruise with all the orders and plans. He didn't think that I should accept a new detail, and that I should go on the cruise. He said, "You go over and see Admiral Sellers." Sellers was the Superintendent. I went over and sang my song and dance. Admiral Sellers wasn't impressed. He said, "Oh, you're all set, and I'm all set, and I'm not about to get upset." So, I didn't know what to do. Finally I said, "Admiral if I could find an officer who was as acceptable to you, as I am, one who would pick up this chore and do a first class job, would you permit me to go?" He said, "Well, I'll think about it. You start finding someone."

I got Swede Momsen. (C. A. Momsen). Swede, as you know, was extremely capable, very willing, a thoroughly competent naval officer. Swede was delighted. He was about the right seniority, his class was just junior to mine. Swede decided he would welcome the opportunity. So in a few days I went back to see the Superintendent, and Admiral Sellers said, "O.K."

So, I got sprung, and went out to San Diego, and reported in on Admiral Richardson's staff.

Interview with Admiral George C. Dyer　　　Annapolis, Maryland

by John T. Mason, Jr.　　　　　　　　　　　June 19, 1969

Mr. Mason: Admiral are we all set?

Admiral Dyer: Yes sir. I finally got sprung from the Naval Academy. I drove to San Diego. The officer whom my boss-- Rear Admiral James O. Richardson, was going to relieve as Commander, Destroyers Scouting Force was Rear Admiral Sinclair Gannon. I got out there three or four days before my orders called for me to report because I was anxious to get aboard, and to get fully indoctrinated. I did, and Admiral Gannon was very helpful and wonderful to me. I, therefore, felt that I was reasonably well prepared to take over the job as Flag Secretary. In many reliefs of Flag commands by new Flag staffs, the individual reliefs are done without too much detailed turnover. Occasionally, there are quite obvious gaps that later appear due to this limited turnover.

This story I have told in the Naval Institute, it is no new story, but I will tell it again for this record.

After we had relieved, Admiral Richardson gathered the staff in his quarters--his cabin. He outlined several objectives within the destroyers that he would hope to accomplish during his tour of duty. We all listened to it, made notes in regard to it, and decided what we as members of his staff would have to do in order to try to accomplish these objectives.

Early in the next forenoon--I'd say about nine o'clock in the morning--the Admiral sent up a hand written order which he was going to issue as the new Commander Destroyers. It was the first order--the one which every relieving Admiral was required by Navy Regulations to issue when he assumed command, naming the officers of his staff and setting forth some basic data. It's purely routine. The Admiral wished a staff conference in regards to it at 11 o'clock. In addition, there was a second hand written order. So, I read the second one. It was an order which said that one of the problems which the destroyers suffered from was lack of real attention by the officers and men to the chores at hand, and it just appeared to the new commander that there was too much of--not only regular leave and liberty, but of granting of special privileges in relation there to. He thought that a closer rein on this sort of activity would result in a greater productive effort in the destroyer organization. That's the sum and substance of what it said.

At 11 o'clock we all filed in. The actual first meeting that the staff had had, other than when Admiral Richardson had sounded off on what he hoped to accomplish. The routine first order was approved by all members of the staff. The Admiral then turned to his second order.

He started right with the Chief of Staff, who was a Commander named "Chips" Carpender, whom you may know, later became Vice Admiral "Chips" Carpender, Commander, Naval Forces Southwest Pacific, and a very fine gentleman. He said, "Chips, what do you think of the order?" Chips thought it had some merit, some good points, "Even he wouldn't have written it just the way the Admiral had written it. But the point was there. A problem to do something about." Admiral Richardson then went down the staff starting with the next senior after the Chief of Staff. And by and large they all thought it was fine. If they expressed any doubts, it was of extremely limited kind. He finally got down to me--I was next to the junior. He said, "Dyer, what do you think of it?" And I said, "It stinks." He said, "You really mean that?" I said, "Yes, sir." He said, "Why does it stink?" And I said, "Admiral, if you had been here for three months and made up your mind that that was what was happening within the force which you commanded, and wanted to take that remedial action which you have proposed, this proposal order would be quite all right. But, you're absolutely a new broom. You don't have any justification for the statements made. You're casting aspersions without any evidence, on a group of very fine people, as far as I know, who are going to have to work for you very hard. Certainly this staff can provide no evidence because none of us are officers who have served in the Destroyer Force recently. I just think that it's a terrible order." So the proposed order was bandied around a bit. Then Admiral Richardson went to the junior officer, who was Walter E. Linaweaver, the Flag Lieutenant. Linney sort of rode a very careful middle course without taking any strong position one way or the other. So, at the end of the conference, the Admiral said, "Thank you very much for your advice and opinions. I'll give the order some more thought." I had no more than gotten up to the Flag Secretary's office when there was a "buzz buzz" from the Admiral. I went down to his Cabin, I died a thousand deaths on the way down there. Here was my first job on the staff, my first conference with my new boss . . .

Q: And you had spoken your piece.

Dyer: I thought I am really about to get a tremendous dressing down which I well deserve. I walked in, and the Admiral was sitting over at his desk. I walked across to his desk and he said, "Look," and he pointed down to the waste paper basket. There were the pieces of paper all torn up of the order which he had written. He said, "I wrote that order knowing that it stank. I wanted to find out from whom in my staff I could get an honest opinion. One of the necessary things for a Flag Officer is to get honest opinions from his staff.

If he can't get honest opinions from his staff he really can't operate. He doesn't have enough eyes, he can't hear everything. He can't be every place, he can't see everything, he can't talk to everybody. He's got to have his staff--people have got to see things, hear things, and tell him. They've got to tell him honestly, just the way it is. I now know that I have one person on my staff that will tell me just how it is. I won't always agree with you. Now don't expect because you won this first victory that I will always agree with you. I will know at least that I'm getting an honest opinion from you. That's a very valuable thing for a Flag officer." That was a wonderful lesson to me. I couldn't have had a better lesson. I was a Lieutenant Commander at the time.

When I became the Division Commander--which I'll tell you about later, Commander Submarine Division 8--I got all my Commanding Officers together. One of whom lives right out here in Annapolis, Willard A. Saunders. He has mentioned this to me two or three times--the fact that I said, "You're my Commanding Officers. I don't have any staff (except for an engineer). You're the people who must tell me right straight no matter how things are. What gives, and what doesn't give. So that I can make an intelligent decision. I can't make an intelligent decision unless I have the facts. You're the people who have to give me the facts."

It made a tremendous impression on Willard Saunders. He has mentioned it half a dozen times. Admiral Richardsons' dictum made a tremendous impression on me. I never assembled a staff that not only did I say it once and early, but I would say it at later times, that they had to tell me things as they saw them. And not expect me to buy everything they said. Because my judgment on the same evidence might be different than theirs. But they had to provide the evidence. I would make the decisions.

Q: That is still a rather unusual thing, isn't it, in the Navy?

Dyer: The article that I wrote for the Naval Institute was titled, <u>Learn To Say "No" To The Admiral</u>. It had a good circulation. They received a lot of requests for additional copies. Some young fellows still mention it to me. It does make a point.

That got me off on the staff on the right foot. I had a very wonderful year in the staff.

Another thing to go back, and I mentioned this before-- the ability to handle the mooring board. What an asset that was! I was the Secretary, and not the Operations Officer. But I could handle the mooring board.

When Admiral Richardson would get out in Fleet exercises

with his 21 destroyers all tagging along behind him--it was very difficult to visualize from the lead ship how things appeared from the rear ship several miles behind. We were in the RICHMOND, which was a light cruiser Flagship, and would be steaming along at 18 or 20 knots. To visualize what had to be done, course and speed had to be taken to get that rear tail destroyer of yours on the outer flank to get it clear of other ships in the Fleet or Force formation when you carried out a maneuver that was difficult. When the Fleet was assembled in a sort of Battle of Jutland formation, there are many other ships and forces as well as the "enemy" to consider. If you have learned to handle the mooring board with skill, you can draw your tail right out on the mooring board, and with the help of a range finder right above the Flag bridge--a little short range finder--you take a distance and bearing of your tail ships, whichever was you wish to turn--you've got to drag that tail around-- then you can really use the mooring board, and you can maneuver that fast moving formation and put it safely where it can carry out its mission.

Two or three times when we had the maneuvers, as they had in those days, Fleet maneuvers--the battle line, the cruisers, and the destroyers, and everything else--the Boss admiral would tell us to move from here to there. I would give my Admiral the course and speed to go from here to there quickly and without embarrassment to the Battle Line or the Cruisers. The first few times I did this--of course, he had his little doubts that it was going to work out well. When it did work out well, time after time, he got so he had the greatest faith in this mooring board solution which I would produce.

I'm sure that's the reason why, in fact, I know that's the reason why, three years later when he went to be Commander Battle Force--the first thing that he did was to ask me if I'd go along with him. He said, "You relieved me of so much worry during the last cruise. I know I'll just sleep well if I've got you there doing that old 'is-was' thing of yours." Which just shows how a little talent can really be used to be very helpful.

We did any number of interesting things. One especially interesting operation that we did when we were in the RICHMOND for the Fleet Problem. A classmate of mine whose name was Mentz--and who was called "Egg" Mentz, because he had a head which was shaped just exactly like an egg--was the Navigator. The problem called for the RICHMOND to swoop down on French Frigate Shoals, which is about 500 miles northwest of Oahu in the Hawaiian Islands. It was suspected that the enemy force might be stationing a seaplane tender at French Frigate Shoals and conducting air searches from there with its assigned patrol planes. We were, of course, told to wipe out the tender and its planes.

French Frigate Shoals is a large shoal area. There are no islands there, it's purely a shoal area. By and large, it's pretty well avoided by shipping, because it is a dangerous unmarked shoal area.

In order to do this raid on French Frigate Shoals so that we wouldn't be sighted by the enemy search planes, we had to approach it at night from a point 300 miles away. Running as we were at speeds between 25 and 38 knots, moving down from the North and heading directly towards the shoal area, where there were not any lights or bell buoys or anything else--your navigating had to be darn accurate. Your star sights had to be better than good in order to determine your exact position.

First I took any number of sun sights in the late afternoon before we started our approach. Then as long as I could get a horizon, I took star sights. I had a position. Of course, the skipper of the RICHMOND was just as much interested. It was his ship, and it was the ship that was going to run aground, if any ship ran aground. He was darn interested in what her position was at all times. My navigation and that of the ship's navigators were not just a little bit different, they were quite a ways different.

The actual time that the Admiral had set for the RICHMOND to get to French Frigate Shoals was 45 minutes after first light.

I don't know of any 45 minute period in my life except perhaps when I was wrestling with the S-4--that I had a greater trepidation. Here we were dashing through the night bell bent for a shoal area with not a sign of anything in sight. With my navigation showing us less far south than the navigator's navigation. In other words, he had us much closer to the shoal than I did. The Admiral wanted us to maintain high speed up until the last minute so that our attack would be a surprise attack, and that we could actually shell the sea planes before they got off the water, as well as destroy the seaplane tender.

The operation worked perfectly and the RICHMOND came in just as hoped for. We caught, not all of the planes, but we caught most of the planes on the water. Of course, we caught the seaplane tender. It was a very successful part of a Fleet Problem, which redounded to the Admiral's credit. Which redounded to my credit, because of the navigation. Poor old "Egg" Mentz he just got the dickens from his Captain, S. F. Heim.

I had been navigating ever since I graduated, and the good Lord had blessed me with good eyes, which are an essential part of good navigating.

Q: How extensive are those shoals in that area?

Dyer: They cover a space of roughly 20 miles. They're spread on a northwest southeast basis. They're about two to four miles wide. We were coming down from the north.

In 1937, we were out on one of the monthly problems that they used to play--tactical problems. Vice Admiral Horne was in the SARATOGA, as Commander, Aircraft Battle Force. We were off the California coast at a fair distance, and the weather was blowy with a deep swell. The destroyers had been given a search mission. It was during a period when Admiral Richardson, who was Commander Destroyers, was back in Washington sitting on the Selection Board. Captain D. W. Bagley, who was the senior Squadron Commander in the destroyers, was the acting Commander for the Destroyers Scouting Force. We had been pushing into the sea, and the destroyers were coming up on radio and telling us of their rough water problems. We had had some problems in the Flagship which was the DEWEY carrying away three sponsons, and bashing out bridge windows. So we were gradually slowing down the destroyers "Speed of advance". Slowing down, and slowing down some more. We had started out searching at say 21 knots, and by the time this incident happened we were making about 14 knots and just holding the destroyers together with our eye teeth, as they ploughed into the heavy seas.

Along came the great big SARATOGA, 10 times bigger than any destroyers--in fact 20 times. She came on through the scouting line, and as she got about abreast of the DEWEY, she sent over this snazzy message which said, "What is holding back your scouting line?" Captain Bagley wrestled with that one for some time before he could think of an answer. He finally ended up by saying, "I've had damage reports from this ship and that ship, and, in the Flagship, we have carried away three sponsons and so forth. We're doing the best we can." And we were.

We had a very interesting Fleet Problem that year. It had to do with Hawaii, but I can't remember what the exact nature of the Fleet Problem was. It was during that year, that the carriers did make air raids on Pearl Harbor as part of advancing the problem interests of their Commander.

Things went along pretty well with the Destroyer Command during the twelve months, I served in that duty. As a matter of fact, when my Admiral was ordered from that job, he was ordered as the Assistant Chief of Naval Operations, which was very unusual as he was a junior Rear Admiral. His first sea command as a Rear Admiral was as Commander Destroyers, Scouting Force.

My Admiral (Richardson) had attended a Fleet conference in San Pedro Harbor on Long Beach Harbor and was returning to the head, riding in a barge with Admiral Tarrant, when my next detail after I left the Destroyer Staff was determined.

Admiral Tarrant is right here in Annapolis. He is 92

years old.

Q: Does he live here now?

Dyer: Yes, he's 92 years old. He was a Vice Admiral at the time. He said to Admiral Richardson, "If I could get someone who would just clean up my Flagship, I could be wholly happy." Admiral Richardson said, "My staff is going to be broken up when I leave. It's my guess that I have a young officer on my staff who might just do that job for you." Admiral Tarrant asked what the name was and so forth. Admiral Richardson told him, "George Dyer."

In due time, I had orders to the INDIANAPOLIS, which was a very fine ship. A beautiful ship. I always thought the INDIANAPOLIS was probably the most beautiful ship I ever served in. She had wonderful lines. She had been Flagship for a good long time. I was ordered to be the First Lieutenant and Damage Control Officer of the INDIANAPOLIS. I was delighted because I knew practically nothing about damage control, except the little that I had learned in the ARIZONA. So, I was delighted to have that detail. Of course, the First Lieutenant is the housekeeper of the ship.

When I went on board, there were things that I was not to happy about. I could easily understand why Admiral Tarrant wasn't too happy about some things in the ship.

The Executive Officer of the INDIANNAPOLIS was Commander Oscar Badger, of whom you probably know. He was a very capable, very fine person, with a very strong personality, and was a great driver. The Commanding Officer was Captain Thomas Kinkaid-- He was Commander, 7th Fleet during World War II, out of the class of 1908 and the first officer in that class to be a four star Admiral, and a very wonderful person.

Actually I was amazed--Oscar Badger hated paper work. With the result, I would suggest that things should be done, and he wouldn't get out the memorandum, the Executive Officer's memorandum which would get this thing started. Nothing would happen for a day or so, and I'd say, "Commander, how about this so and so." He'd say, "You get out the memorandum."

Eventually I got out--well, I had a file of them, about 40 memorandums. About half of them, in my opinion, should have been issued by the Executive Officer. So, as First Lieutenant I got them out, and he was happy, and so I was happy about it.

It was the period of June, 1937 to June, 1938, and the Navy was starting to expand, and starting to do many new and exciting things. It was a very interesting period to be aboard ship. There were lots of more realistic gunnery and damage control exercises, monthly tactical exercises, quarterly tactical exercises, and annual Fleet Problems. We were really doing many things to make the Navy and the Fleet ready for war.

The INDIANAPOLIS had a berth at Long Beach Harbor, a very limited berth. The INDIANAPOLIS and the CHICAGO were in this inner-berth.

Q: They were sister ships.

Dyer: They were both heavy cruisers, but they were not sister ships. It was a very interesting and good training detail for me. When the ship was coming in to anchor or to moor, the First Lieutenant on a heavy cruiser was always down on the forecastle. The INDIANAPOLIS was moored in an inner berth in Long Beach Harbor in any kind of wind or weather. It called for a high degree of seamanship skill by the Exec, who normally handled the ship, or by the Skipper, to bring us exactly into that berth, and for the INDIANAPOLIS to actually make her mooring smartly. It also called for a high degree of skill by the men down on deck in handling the lines, to run the mooring lines to the mooring buoy and by the men on the buoy to secure the anchor chain to the mooring buoy.

I learned a great deal during that period in the INDIANAPOLIS. Several things happened then. The Division Commander of Cruiser Division Five to which the INDIANAPOLIS was assigned was Rear Admiral John Downes, who was about the fourth or fifth generation of John Downes' in the Navy.

Q: Like the Alexander Sharps'.

Dyer: Yes. Admiral Downes was a very fine person. He was the officer who actually conducted the cleanliness and the damage control inspections of the INDIANAPOLIS. By that I mean, he conducted the regular quarterly inspections and the annual inspection. After the first quarterly inspection, in writing the inspection report--Admiral Tarrant had evidently spoken to Admiral Downes about the INDIANAPOLIS--Because Admiral Downes in writing up his report on his inspection said, "It now appears that, at long last, the long awaited shipkeeper of the INDIANAPOLIS has arrived." When that report got over to the ship, Commander Badger immediately saw it, and he sent for me. He just raised cain with me. He said, "I don't see what in the devil you've done here that made the INDIANAPOLIS any different, than when Alan McCann was the First Lieutenant."

In any case, the INDIANAPOLIS did very well in their ship cleanliness inspections, and in their Damage Control Inspections. I learned a little bit about damage control, and about big ships.

One thing that did come out. Captain Kinkaid had a real sense of the eternal fitness of things. Oscar Badger used to give the Heads of the Departments the dickens a great part of the time. They were a bunch of pretty good officers. There were four of us, and one other one became a Flag officer, that was C. C. ("Chick") Hartman, the Navigator. J. J. Vatterron, the Gunney Officer died when he was a Commander, and H. W. Turney, the Chief Engineer ran his ship aground in the Bay of Fundy.

The Heads of Departments used to have some pretty hot and heavy go-rounds with Oscar Badger. The Captain (Kinkaid) used to get us all in his cabin, and sort out the meat of the matter, and make the hard decisions in a way that left us satisfied, and I think left Commander Badger satisfied. That called for real skill, and Captain Kinkaid had it.

I was always grateful for Captain Kinkaids' decisions because I was the senior one of the Heads of Departments, and generally the leader in the fray with Oscar trying to get him off of our backs. It called for a bit of doing. I was eternally grateful to Captain Kinkaid for his chore in doing it. And he did it.

I know that he gave me some very wonderful fitness reports, and they were very helpful.

After I'd been in the INDIANAPOLIS about a year, I received a letter from the Submarine Detail Officer, Commander E. E. "Swede" Hazlett. I thought I had shaken submarines from my back.

Q: Thought you'd had enough of that?

Dyer: No, but I felt that it was not the largest aspect of

the Navy, and that I would like to be in that larger aspect. The Detail Officer said that he examined all of the records of the Lieutenant Commanders, who had had submarine service, and who had had not less than two submarine commands; in order to make up a list of prospective Division Commanders for submarines. He had come up with a list of four that he considered the best, and that he had gotten the approval of Captain Chester Nimitz, at that time Bureau of Navigation Detail Officer, to order those four back into submarines. And that I was one of those four.

So, I was ordered to command Submarine Division Eight. Submarine Division Eight was based in Pearl Harbor. My wife and I went out to Pearl Harbor. Actually we were there only about six months until late 1938. At the end of six months, the Department made the decision that my division was going to go out of commission. Actually, I had command of two divisions. I had command of Experimental Division Two, and Submarine Division Eight. They were going to put Submarine Division Eight out of commission. The four submarines in it were to be taken back to the Philadelphia Navy Yard, and there put out of commission. Submarine Division II stayed in Pearl Harbor.

So, in December, we cranked up, and cruised back to the West Coast, and around through the Panama Canal, up through

Miami, and then on up to Philadelphia.

Q: During that six months, do you recall anything of significance vis-a-vis Nimitz?

Dyer: No, he wasn't there in Pearl Harbor. He was in command of a Cruiser Division, Cruiser Division Two, I believe. The Squadron Commander was Captain Frank W. Scanland, an old submariner of many years standing, and a very fine person. There were two Division Commanders, other than myself. I relieved Nino Gregory, who's right here in town--Rear Admiral J. W. Gregory. One of the others was Cassin Young, who was lost in the SAN FRANCISCO. He was Exec of the SAN FRANCISCO, when she was so badly hit. And Commander James Fife had command of Submarine Division Twelve with his flag in the Nautilus until Scott Umstead relieved him. I had been shipmates with Scott in the Philippines. He commanded the S-17 at that time.

In 1938, the submarines were carrying out an active program of making submarine approaches, and firing torpedoes, and shooting their deck gun. Approach conditions had greatly improved for the submarines. When I was there from '31 to '33, they had to shoot at the WIDGEON or the SEA GULL. The maximum speed that the WIDGEON and the SEA GULL could cruise at was about ten knots with a fair breeze behind them. There was very little variation in speed. By the time I was a Division Commander in Pearl Harbor, we had a destroyer as our target.

Therefore, a far higher and greater variation of speeds was available. In other words, if you know the target can only make ten knots as a maximum, and is probably making somewhere between eight and ten--you could split it at nine, and almost shoot your torpedo to hit no matter what. But if the target can make from eight to twenty-eight knots, and you've got to estimate the speed from her bow wave, you have a much more difficult problem. Another thing is that you don't have anywhere near as long to make up your mind about doing things against a fast moving target. If you're attacking a fast target, he'll run over you, or run by, and he'll be gone if you don't take the right course and speed almost immediately after you sight and dive. While with a slower target, you've got a lot more time to think, and to maneuver into position, and to make a good approach. So, it was far better training. The submarines were getting better training, because there were better targets ships for them to practice with.

I came back to the East Coast with the Submarine Division Eight and started to put the Division out of commission in January 1939. I was ordered down from Philadelphia to the Bureau of Navigation in the Planning Staff. On that Planning Staff at that time was Captain T. S. (Ring) Wilkinson, who later became Vice Admiral Wilkinson; Commander H. H. (Heine) Good, later he became Rear Admiral Good; and Commander D. E.

(Dan) Barbey who was the War Plans Officer, and who commanded the Amphibious Forces in the Southwest Pacific during W. W. II. The Planning Staff handled all the advanced planning, and then in addition Dan Barbey--who was part of the Planning Staff--handled the war plans. He had an assistant, Frank Stickney, who was a Lieutenant Commander at that time. It was a very interesting detail.

It was the only time in all my life that I appeared over at the Naval Affairs Committee in the House of Representatives, to be questioned in regard in certain personnel matters that were then being proposed by the Bureau of Navigation, later called the Bureau of Naval Personnel.

Q: Who was your chief inquisitor, Carl Vinson?

Dyer: That's right. He was the Chairman of the committee, and a very knowledgeable individual. He knew so much more about the Navy than I did, particularly insofar as related to personnel matters. There was just no comparison. He did, I think, a wonderful job for the Services. Because he knew their good points, and their weak points. He constantly prodded them in their weak areas, and he supported them in their strong areas.

I am delighted that they have named Vinson Hall for Mr. Vinson. I think he's just one of the many great people that come along that the American people in general are blessed with and who represent them in Congress.

I had not been on the job too long--a couple of months when one day the Chief of Bureau, Rear Admiral James O. Richardson called me into his office and said, "My Flag Lieutenant," (whose name was John Blue), "is going on a month's leave, and I'd like to have you come in and take over as Flag Lieutenant while he's gone." And, so I did.

At that time, the Assistant Chief of Bureau was Captain Frank Jack Fletcher, later Admiral. Captain Fletcher, for years, whenever he was introducing me to anyone he always said, "I want you to meet an officer who was always making me do something." Captain Fletcher was an officer who I thought had wonderful judgment, but he had a tendency not to do things. He was really very amusing. I used to give him the old gun-ho. And he would always respond. I, of course, got to know him very well, and to like him very much.

It was during that month, March 1939, that Admiral Richardson went over to the White House with Admiral Leahy. While they were there, the President told him that he was going to go to sea and be Commander, Battle Force with four stars. When he came back from the office, I was there to greet him--that being a Flag Lieutenant's job. He was all smiles, and could not have been in a happier frame of mind. He told me the news immediately as well as to Captain Fletcher.

A little later that afternoon, he called me into his office, and said, "I'm going to do something that I know that Adaline will hate me for. I'm going to ask you to go to sea with me, when I go to sea, in June." Of course, I'd just come from sea. We had rented a house out in Chevy Chase. We had never owned furniture in all our Navy life. We had bought a full houseful of furniture, and were in the process of paying for it. It just really got us close hauled financially. This was six weeks or two months before I actually went to sea. Anyhow, I said, I'd be delighted." And I was.

I went home that night, and I said to my Mary Adaline, "How'd you like to move to Long Beach?" Oh, boy, she didn't think she'd like to move to Long Beach. But she was really just wonderful, really the light of my life. She took it in splendid style, and said, "If it's good for you, it's good for me, and I'll be just delighted."

In late May, I was detached, and went on out to Long Beach. One other thing I would like to mention here is that Admiral Richardson--this was two to five days later after he had asked me to go to sea with him, I don't recall exactly--called me into his office, and he said, "My Chief of Staff is going to be Captain Sherwoode A. Taffinder, (later Vice Admiral Taffinder), my Operations Officer is going to be Bernhard H. Bieri. I knew Captain Taffinder, because he was a well known Captain at the time. I did not know Captain Bieri. He said, "I want you to pick out the rest of the staff--the Line officers of the staff. The Bureau will pick out the Doctor, and the Paymaster, and the Naval Constructor." In that era, we still had naval constructors.

That meant that I should suggest a candidate for the Gunnery Officer, the Communication Officer, and the assistant Operations Officer. I picked out Commander Ernest E. Herrmann, a classmate of mine, who later became a Rear Admiral for the gunnery detail. He was Head of the Postgraduate School when he died. For the Communications Officers, I picked out Lieutenant Commander Maurice E. Curts (Germany) who later became Commander-in-Chief, Pacific Fleet. He lives over in Washington. For the assistant Operations Officer, I picked out Commander Marcy M. Dupre, who became Captain Bieri's assistant. I also picked out Lieutenant Tom Eddy as the Admirals Flag Lieutenant. Tom had been the Commanding Officer of the S-27, when I had command of Submarine Division Eight.

We took over in June 1939. Admiral Richardson relieved Admiral Kalbfus, who then became President of the Naval War College. We had six months in the staff of Commander, Battle Force.

It was during that 1939 year, that in the Fleet, we first started to form task groups with carriers at the center. It was Admiral Richardson's and Captain Bieri's initative that got that started, as far as I know the story.

Q: Was Admiral King out there somewhere too at that time?

Dyer: Admiral King was in the Department on the General Board at that time. He did not become Commander-in-Chief of the Atlantic Fleet until early 1941, (1 February 1941). And we are talking about the last six months of 1939. Admiral King had been at sea in 1937 as Commander Aircraft Base Force and later was Commander Aircraft, Battle Force until relieved by Vice Admiral C. A. Blakely in the summer of 1939.

On 6 January 1940, Admiral Richardson took command of the United States Fleet. At that time, the United States Fleet included the units that were in the Atlantic, and they had so included them for some years. It was not until '41, when Admiral Kimmel took over from Admiral Richardson that the Atlantic Fleet was changed into an independent Fleet, and Admiral Kimmel took command of only the Pacific Fleet, while Admiral Richardson had had command of the United States Fleet.

Q: It was a very difficult command, wasn't it, a dual command in two oceans?

Dyer: It was difficult. The Patrol Force, U. S. Fleet had been established in October, 1940. The Patrol Force, U. S.

Fleet became the U. S. Atlantic Fleet, about the last day of January, 1941 or on 1 February 1941. When Admiral Kimmel took over, I was ordered to the heavy cruiser INDIANAPOLIS.

Before I move on to that, I want to tell you one more thing. During the period that Admiral Richardson was the Commander-in-Chief of the United States Fleet, he objected very strongly to the Fleet being based in Pearl Harbor.

One of the reasons that I feel, I do not know, but I feel, influenced him in this regard was that as long as the Fleet was in Pearl Harbor, he insisted that the patrol planes search for the Japanese every day. We had PatWing Two based on Pearl Harbor. There were 60 patrol planes in this Patrol Wing, and search every day they did, out to 300 miles. Now we did not have enough planes available to completely search around $360°$ of the circle.

Normally when you're searching out 300 miles, you have to figure out that to sight a ship as small as a surfaced submarine on that 300 mile arc, you have to have a plane about every 30-40 miles on that arc. You take the amount of distance in the perimeter of your 300 miles circle, and you estimate the visibility and find out how many planes you ought to have to prevent a single ship from slipping in between two aircraft searching. A thorough search required far more aircraft than were available on a seven day a week basis, since the aircraft required regular upkeep and overhaul. CINCUS and PATWING TWO didn't have half enough. PATWING TWO never could search even 180°, but it searched, day after day after day out to 300 miles.

They particular arc of the search was set as follows: If you had the CINCUS staff duty, roughly sometimes between an hour and an hour and a half before the planes were due to take off; the Staff Duty Officer made the determination of what sector they were to search. He was influenced by what had been searched yesterday, what the weather was, and a lot of other things including his own predelictions. No pattern was followed, and the Japanese couldn't know what the pattern was, because nobody knew. By and large, the Staff Duty Officer kept it to himself until just before the dispatch went over to the Pat Wing 2, telling them what sector to search.

About every three months, probably more often, the Pat Wing 2 people would come up through Commander Scouting Force with a tremendous beef on this tiresome search. In the first place, they were wearing out their planes fast. They were having tremendous trouble complying with the Commander-in-Chief's order which was that a minimum number of planes would be made available. (six) The number above that minimum changed from time to time, depending upon the total number of planes actually available to Pat Wing 2. If they crashed two planes, then the daily quota might come down. If they got some replacements from the United States then it went up. It was not a fixed number, only a fixed minimum. Roughly in the area from 6 to 10 planes would go out and search each day. They got off at 5:30 in the morning, or thereabouts, and searched. They'd frequently got back late in the afternoon having been detoured by squalls or by investigation of ships sighted. It was a long hard pull. They objected, and they had 47 different reasons. Every time that they wrote such a letter, if it started with the Squadron Commander, it went through the Pat Wing Commander with a strong favorable endorsement. ComScoPac would give it a strong favorable endorsement, and then it would get over to the Commander-in Chief. Then we would have a battle royal on the staff as to what we should do.

At different times, we had different Naval Aviators on the staff--Art Davis is the best known one. He later became the Secretary to the Joint Chiefs of Staff--Arthur C. Davis. The other ones name was O. B. Hardison. He was the first one. They, of course, supported the aviators point of view, and argued to kill this daily search. There were two people, Captain Bieri and myself who were strong to keep the search going on. The Admiral who made the final decision was by george, of the same opinion, that the planes were going to keep flying.

Q: What was his basic reason for this policy?

Dyer: The necessity of it. Protective, if you had the Fleet there, you had to have a daily search to protect it from Japanese air attack. You had to know something about the seas around Hawaii. If you couldn't know it 100%, by george, it was better to know 50%, than it was to know nothing.

Q: There was a great deal of realism back of his thinking?

Dyer: Yes, all you had to do was think of what could happen if you didn't have any search. As I say, we used to battle for it, but Admiral Richardson kept it going.

Of course, Admiral Kimmel cancelled it three weeks after he got there.

Q: Why wasn't it possible to get replacements for these planes? Were they all going to Europe?

Dyer: The answer to that was. Not in the Navy. We were giving them away to other powers. The war had already started in Europe. We were making lend-lease shipments. The number of planes being manufactured was relatively small. You can't fly something until you can get it. Then actually you've got to break it in. They just didn't exist.

The Admiral wrote any number of letters, everybody did, recommending more aircraft. But they just didn't exist. Initially they didn't exist money-wise. And even in '40, money was not thrown out the window like it's thrown out today. One who has not lived through an era where things don't exist that you need, doesn't really have an appreciation of this factor.

Another thing, the flyers were saying the air reconnaissance was ruining their training program. In other words, they wanted to train an aviator to do more than one thing, and that was a very realistic approach to making a well qualified naval aviator.

We had to, at least I was one of the ones who thought we had to do this air search job. And we did it.

Q: You must have been heavily influenced by the political situation as it was developing.

Dyer: I didn't give a two hoopalas about the political situation. I was just young enough not to care. I'm sure the Admiral was very much influenced.

I've written a book which is called ON THE TREADMILL TO PEARL HARBOR, which tells this story, in considerable detail, with all the references.

I was simply amazed to find out that the files of Pat Wing 2, which was the main patrol reconnaissance squadron in Pearl Harbor, no longer existed. They had been burned, destroyed. So that someone who wants to make the same study now, it's no longer possible.

Q: How could a thing like that happen?

Dyer: Very simple. The boss man in the Department of Defense, he didn't care a hoopala about historical records. He has an order out which says that our depositories can have only so many million cubic feet of space. For instance, all pay or disbursement checks must be saved for so many months because there's a law to that effect. As you expand your services, as you expand your government--the whole federal government has expanded tremendously--the number of checks increase just tremendously. I've been up there to the Mechanicsburg Depository any number of times, and seen this stuff in trucks roll in. If trucks of stuff roll in to the Depository and they can't increase stowage space; then they had to burn or throw away other things that were already in the Depository. People who have no historical interest at all, it's just a piece of paper, get rid of it.

When I started on my book on Kelly Turner, I had to get from as Assistant Secretary of Defense a "hold" order to keep the Amphibious Force, South Pacific files from being burned. Now that order is still in effect fortunately. Once my book is published, it no longer has validity. Then all those files will be burned.

Q: And yet they save old checks.

Dyer: They only save them for two years. I'm referring to

files of shipboard papers they've been saving for 30 years or more. I mean '42 to '72, '39 to '69.

Q: From the historian's point of view, it seems that records that pertain to a major conflict would take precedence over records of a peace time era.

Dyer: The present practice, from a historians point of view is just criminal. I'm not arguing for the burn policy, I've argued against it until I'm black in the face. Just barely was able to get a "hold" order on Admiral Turner's things. It makes historical research much more difficult with the passage of time.

Q: Indeed it does.

Dyer: When I came up for orders--Admiral Richardson was leaving the staff. I was ordered back to the Bureau of Navigation which by that time had become the Bureau of Naval Personnel.

Q: You want to, perhaps at this point, give me a portrait of Admiral Richardson? Whom you admired greatly.

Dyer: Oh, I just think he's out of this world. We saw him this last week--Tuesday. He's 91 the 18th of this September (1969).

He was a long rangy Texan, a very good looking man. He

was a man of tremendous energy. He had an extremely keen mind, great determination, great character. He called things the way they were. On the other hand, he had a very human touch, was full of funny stories. He loved golf, played anytime that he could. He had really a sort of fundamental dislike for newspaper people. He had had a very broad experience in the Navy primarily in the field of engineering and gunnery. He was in the NEVADA as Navigator when I was a Midshipman, and then as Executive officer after I had finished the summer cruise. I did not know him personally then, he didn't know me. I did know the Skipper, who was Joseph Strauss; and the Exec who later was Admiral Leahy; and the Midshipman Commander, who was Commander Sam Colby Loomis. Those people, plus some of the younger officers, I did know.

This is something that is worth telling. When Admiral Richardson was a Lieutenant Commander, he came up for selection to Commander and was not selected. He didn't know why, and certainly I don't know why--because he later became Commander-in-Chief of the United States Fleet. Anyhow, he missed the boat on his first selection to Commander. Very fortunately he was with some good people at the time. In other words, Captain Strauss, who became a four star Admiral; and Admiral Leahy, who became a five star Admiral. The next year he was selected, and from there he went right on up.

There was an officer out of the Class of 1890, who had

a similar thing happen; Captain Frank H. Scofield. He also later became Commander-in-Chief of the United States Fleet, having failed of selection to Captain.

Whenever I had a friend who misses the selection boat, I always tell him this story. It may console him a bit, and prevent him from giving up hope.

Admiral Richardson was a postgraduate in engineering. He was one of the early engineers in the Postgraduate School. He was out of the Naval Academy class of 1902. He did duty both in the Bureau of Engineering and in the Bureau of Ordnance. He became Chief of the Bureau of Navigation. He had a tremendous galaxy of friends. If there were people who didn't like him, entirely different from Admiral Turner, I've yet to find a person who spoke ill of Admiral Richardson. That's quite a broad statement, but in my opinion essentially so.

Q: Admiral, do you think he truly regretted being frank in his opinions as expressed to the President?

Dyer: I think that he midjudged Franklin D. Roosevelt in how much criticism of himself he would take. He had been in the Department when the President was the Assistant Secretary of the Navy. Had been on parties with him, and all that sort of thing. I think that he midjudged FDR. I don't think it would have changed an iota what Admiral Richardson did, because he was a person who believed in being frank with one's seniors.

Q: As you indicated in that incident. I would think that there is a possibility that the President changed in attitude, too, from the time he was Assistant Secretary until he became the overall Chief of everything.

Dyer: That's right. I think that Mr. Roosevelt was perhaps impatient of people who differed with him, much more as he got more secure in the position. Then he became less patient.

Q: This is probably a very sound observation of him as President.

Dyer: I had the duty as the Staff Duty Officer, when the dispatch came in ordering Admiral Richardson to be relieved by Admiral Kimmel. First I'll go back, and tell a little background.

Admiral Richardson had come back from Washington where he had had his conference with the President, and had said that he had been told that he would remain as a Commander-in-Chief for one more year. Purely as an aside, Admiral Stark has confirmed that promise to me--that Admiral Richardson was told that he would have command of the Fleet for one more year.

Admiral Stark's story is that when Admiral Richardson left Washington that he (Stark) had no idea that the President had been upset by what Richardson had said, because he had not participated in the conference, and therefore did not know, of the interchange between the two people. The thing that Admiral Stark was completely surprised with was, some 24 to 36 hours after Admiral Richardson had left Washington--that the President called him--Admiral Stark, and said, "I want J. O. relieved." That's Admiral Stark's story.

The dispatch came in, Admiral Richardson having told all the members of his staff that he'd been told they would be around for another year, that they might make their plans accordingly--here came his orders that he was leaving, on the 31st of January 1941. I got on my horse and buggy and went out to the golf links. It was on a Sunday. Admiral Richardson was playing golf as usual. I delivered this dispatch to him, and his remark was, "My God, they can't do that to me." Needless to say, they did.

There's one other little story that I should tell in relation to his relief too, that's of interest to Navy people. Peck Snyder, who was two classes senior to Admiral Richardson-- Richardson was '02, and Peck Snyder was '00--had been Commander Battle Force. In other words, he was number one subordinate. Then they ordered in Admiral Kimmel, who was out of the class of '04. They did not issue any change of orders to Admiral Snyder. He told Admiral Richardson, and I'm sure he told others that he was perfectly willing to serve under Admiral Richardson; but that he was unwilling to serve under Admiral Kimmel. So, he was relieved, and Admiral Pye became Commander Battle Force. That has a real story behind it. I think had Admiral Snyder stayed in the job, and when Admiral Kimmel was summarily relieved in December 1941 had stepped up into Admiral Kimmel shoes on a temporary basis--that the decision by Admiral Pye not to make the first bombing raid against the Marshalls in early '42, would not have been made. They were just two different kinds of people. Admiral Pye was a great theoretical tactician, and Admiral Snyder was a great--in my opinion--fighting sailor. He had determination.

That is not an original thought with me. I've heard other people voice the same opinion, but I am very definitely of that opinion.

I don't know whether you know the background of this story about the raid on the Marshalls but if you don't, I'll tell it to you right now.

Our war plans--our WPL 5--called for a raid on the Marshall Islands, as one of our early acts in the war against the Japanese. Having been set on our rear ends by the Japanese attack on Pearl Harbor, there was a great deal of feeling in the Fleet amongst the officers of the Fleet that the least that we could do would be to go down and take a smack at them.

About a week after the Japanese attack, we shoved off a goodly part of the combatant Fleet, headed for the Marshalls. We had a carrier, the LEXINGTON, we had the cruisers of Cruiser Division Five. I was present in the INDIANAPOLIS as the Executive Officer and we had the destroyers with Captain Dick Conolly, who later became Admiral Conolly, Squadron Commander of the destroyers. This is a long-winded story but, I think quite interesting.

After a ten day run, we were due to make the raid on the Marshalls at next daylight. About four o'clock of that previous afternoon; Admiral Wilson Brown, who was Commander, Scouting Force ordered everybody all buttoned up. We went to battle readiness--condition one--worked up to 28 knots, and started in. We had been running in about four hours, maybe five hours, it was getting dark--Commander Turner Joy, who was Wilson Brown's Operation Officer came down from the Flag bridge onto the ship's bridge where I was, and showed me a dispatch. The dispatch was from CinCPacFlt to the Task Force Commander, Vice Admiral Wilson Brown, saying the operation is cancelled, swing north towards Wake Island. Await any further instructions. I looked at that, and if somebody had hauled off and kicked me right in the cajones, I wouldn't. . . here we were all enthused that at last we were going to do something. The American people were saying--where's the Fleet, where's our

Fleet? There we were--going to do something. And here it was being cancelled.

Turner said, "The Admiral hasn't seen this, what do you think we ought to do with it?" I said, "I think you ought to tear up that dispatch and drop it over the side. The American people have been asking where the Fleet is, and it's up to us to show them where the Fleet is. We can't fight this war without taking chances. Sure this is chancy. By george, it's the thing to do. Possibilities are tremendous, and the Japs can't be defending everywhere. I don't see why we shouldn't go on in." Turner Joy disappeared, and a little while later he came back.

He said, "I'm going to take it in to the Admiral." He had shown it to his Chief of Staff. The Chief of Staff was an old woman, if I ever knew one, a bachelor. You'd think he'd been a fire eater, but instead of that, he wasn't. I said, "Let me show the dispatch to my boss. He was Captain E. W. Hanson, who was a fine fighting man. Captain Hanson said, "Tear the damn thing up." Commander Turner Joy went in and talked with his Admiral. The result of this conversation was that they sent the CINCPAC dispatch out to Captain Frederick Sherman, who was the skipper of the LEXINGTON, and to Captain Richard F. Conolly, who was the Squadron Commander of the destroyers. Admiral Wilson Browns dispatch read, "The following received, what is your recommendation?" Both of them came back with essentially the same recommendation, although it was not in exactly the same words. Frederick Sherman was short and to the point. He said, "Nuts, let us go on in." Captain Conolly said, "It would be a terrible thing if we cancelled this operation, and I strongly recommend that we continue the operation."

But we didn't. A little while later we changed course to the North, slowed down, opened up the ships, and so forth.

Admiral Pye who had relieved Kimmel temporarily, before Nimitz arrived, had just visualized the Japanese Fleet all over the Pacific Ocean. He had had a scare fight, and insisted that this not be done. I talked with any number of people that served on the Commander-in-Chief's staff at the time--I was told there was only one other senior officer who recommended that the operation be cancelled. All the rest were against its cancellation. It nevertheless, was cancelled. The cancellation was, of course, a tremendous disappointment to the fighting men of the Pacific Fleet.

Q: Wilson Brown wasn't willing, once it was brought to his attention, to forget about it?

Dyer: He just wasn't that kind of a guy.

Q: That must have been a jolt to morale.

Dyer: Oh, terrible, the starch just went out of everybody.

When I got my orders to duty in the Bureau of Naval Personnel from the CINCUS Staff, I asked the Chief of Staff, who by that time I think was Admiral Taffinder--he got promoted a few months after the staff was formed--if I could sent a dispatch into the Department, and request other assignment than the Bureau of Naval Personnel. I didn't want to go ashore. He said, "Sure, why not?"

I sent a dispatch, and said, "In reference to the Bureaus dispatch, I request sea assignment, any ship, any ocean." That dispatch came in, and by that time Captain Carpender was the BUPERS Detail Officer. He received that dispatch, and took it in to Admiral Nimitz who was Chief of the Bureau of Naval Personnel, and he said, "You know, I'm so sick of these people who only want one certain detail, one certain ship, one certain place to be. Here's an officer who says any ship, any ocean, and no delimitation of what kind of a detail. I think we ought to give him the best detail that's available." Admiral Nimitz said, "I think so too. Give it to him." So, I was ordered to the Exec of the INDIANAPOLIS, and it was the best detail that was available, or could be available at any time.

Every officer who had been Executive Officer of the INDIANAPOLIS, with one exception, and he went crazy, had become a Flag officer. There's nothing like moving into a job where the shoes of the people before you, have produced success. So, I was ordered Exec of the INDIANAPOLIS.

Q: What is that intangible something you express, moving into the shoes of men who make it? There's something intangible about that.

Dyer: Very much so. At least in the Navy that I grew up in, certain details were dead-end details. Certain details were details that produced people that moved ahead. Whether the detail was such, the challenge was such, or the performance was such--whatever it was, there were those details. There were those details in the Department. You could sit down and look at the Navy Department schematic drawing of assignments, and look into certain of those details. A very high percentage of the people that had had it, had moved along. Another detail, a very high percentage of the people--that was a dead-end. So, getting a good detail was highly desirable.

The Exec of the INDIANAPOLIS couldn't have been a better detail, and I was very grateful that I received it. I received it really by laying my head on the block, because they could have given me the TUSCARORA in southeast South America. I wouldn't have had a single comback.

Vice Admiral George C. Dyer by John T. Mason, Jr.

At his home in Pendennis Mount November 13, 1969

Annapolis, Maryland

Mr. Mason: Good to see you looking so well, Admiral after a long summer intervening.

When we broke off last time, you told me that you wanted to make some remarks about the disaster at Pearl Harbor.

Admiral Dyer: That's correct. I got back to Washington and became Admiral King's secretary about 10 January, 1942. To explain this a bit--in pre-World War II days in the Navy, the Flag Secretary was the Legal Officer, the Intelligence Officer, the Public Relations Officer, and in addition he was the Secretary.

About 24 or 48 hours after I had reported in, Admiral King called me in and said, "This Pearl Harbor disaster has a terrible smell. Something went completely wrong with our intelligence activities. I want you, in addition to your other work, to make a study, interrogate people--all within the Department here and come up with a report to me. I would like to have a report in about four or five days, or certainly no longer than a week."

Q: In addition to your other work?

Dyer: Yes. I was getting down to the office at seven, and leaving at nine or ten at nights; and this was really a chore. I tried to learn as much as I could, and interrogate a lot of people. Eventually I reduced at all to writing and came up with a piece of paper.

I'm saying this to indicate that my nose was pushed into the Pearl Harbor disaster fairly early in the game.

Q: While it was all fresh.

Dyer: That's right. Many years later after I was retired, I was asked to undertake by the Director of Naval History, Admiral John Heffernan at the time, (1956), was to do a book on Admiral James O. Richardson who was the Commander-in-Chief of the United States Fleet up until the first of February, 1941. I did the book called, ON THE TREADMILL TO PEARL HARBOR. It has not been published, because Admiral Richardson so requested. However, it will be.

By 1956, the Pearl Harbor investigation had been held. I sat down and read the 41 volumes of the Pearl Harbor report. I'm sure there probably is not more than 20 people in the United States that have done that. It's a major operation, but the 41 volumes have no index, so that in order to obtain not only the basic story, but the background and the interplay of personalities, it was necessary to read it all if one wanted to cover the 1940-1941 period thoroughly.

Q: This was at the instigation of the President, wasn't it?

Dyer: The investigation was held after the war was over when people could talk because of pressure in the Congress, I believe. It was held starting in November 1945 and ran for roughly four of five months.

Then in 1960, I started the book on Admiral Turner. He was the War Plans Officer in Naval Operations and one of Admiral Stark's principle advisors. He had a very real part to play in this and a responsibility, and some regrets in regard to what he had and what he hadn't done.

Again, I went back to the Pearl Harbor investigation and read parts of it this time that I thought were pertinent. So, I do have some knowledge in regard to what has been said by a lot of people.

When I left Admiral Richardson's staff, which was on the first of February 1941, I went to the INDIANAPOLIS as Executive Officer. As the summer dragged on and things got more and more tense between the United States and Japan, I finally got the heads (about August 1941) of the Departments of the INDIANAPOLIS together and said, "It is my opinion that we are not maintaining the proper state of readiness in this ship for what may very well happen to it, and that is a sudden surprise attack on Pearl

Harbor." They all reared back and said, "We're doing just exactly what the Commander-in-Chief's orders are." And that was true. The point that I made was that every Naval Officer and certainly everybody who was in a top spot, either the skipper or the exec of the ship, has a responsibility to do of and beyond what the orders tell him to do. He has the responsibility to do the right thing.

Q: To use his own gray matter?

Dyer: That's right. I said, "We are maintaining a condition four watch." Which meant a watch and four with one fourth of the crew on board, when we were in port. It meant having half the anti-aircraft battery manned, having half the ammunition passers and internal communications manned. It meant having about a quarter of the anti-aircraft fire control manned. I just thought that wasn't enough. I got practically no support from the Heads of the Departments, but I went in to see my skipper. His name was E. W. Hanson, out of the class of 1911.

Much to my pleasure he said, "I've just been hoping that you'd come in and say something like this to me. I think it's most inadequate what we're doing." I said, "Let's do what we think's right." He said, "I'm all for it. So, I had no problem at all with him. In fact, he was at least 110% in support of what I thought we should do.

So, we shifted the watches to what we called a "modified condition two." In other words--everybody was on watch two days out of four instead of one day out of four, and in port we could man 100% of our anti-aircraft battery, all of its fire control, have our ammunition supply system largely manned. Either the skipper or I were aboard ship all the time.

Understand that the INDIANAPOLIS, which had a wartime complement of about 1300; at this time had about 700 people on board; just a little bit better than half. When you only had a quarter of them on board, you had just a shadow of what you really should have. We shifted to the modified condition two watch, which meant that where we were in port, only half the officers and crew had shore leave or liberty instead of 3/4s.

This hadn't been going on 48 hours, when I got word from Mrs. Dyer. She said, "All the wives have been calling me, asking me, 'What's the INDIANAPOLIS trying to do, fight the war all by itself? Fight some war that doesn't exist?' Their husbands aren't coming home and they're upset." I said, "I'm sorry, but that's the way it is in the good ship INDIANAPOLIS."

Things got tauter and tauter on board ship and more people disgruntled and more disgruntled. When I handed the skipper the dispatch saying, "Air raid, Pearl Harbor. This is not a drill," we were at Johnston Island. He said to me, "You and I are lucky this dispatch came. In another week, the crew would have thrown us overboard." That's the way it was.

In my opinion, one of Admiral Kimmel's great derelictions was the failure to maintain the proper state of readiness in his ships.

If you'll read the Pearl Harbor Report with any degree of carefulness, you'll find that it was minutes and minutes and minutes after the initial attack came and the Japs had dropped their bombs before there was a gun that could shoot. The reason was that the proper condition of readiness was not being maintained.

They didn't have the proper fire control gear manned. Sure they had a bunch of ammunition sitting up alongside the gun and a few people that were standing there; but they didn't have fully manned guns crews or fully manned ammunition crews. And things just didn't happen.

Q: What about the air reconnaissance?

Dyer: That's the second thing I'm going to talk about.

That's point number one--Admiral Kimmel failed to maintain a proper state of readiness in the United States Pacific Fleet.

When Admiral Richardson was relieved, Admiral Kimmel only relieved him, in fact, of command of the Pacific Fleet. Admiral King became Commander-in-Chief of the Atlantic Fleet.

The U. S. Fleet ceased to exist from that moment, except as a paper organization. Admiral Richardson had been actually in command of the U. S. Fleet, and he had everything under his wings in the Atlantic and Pacific. Kimmel had only the Pacific Fleet, although paper wise, he was CinC U. S. Fleet.

The second point is that although Admiral Richardson had maintained air reconnaissance around Pearl Harbor for distance of 300 miles from May through 5 December 1940, and Admiral Kimmel had not instituted such an air reconnaissance despite the deterioration of our relations with Japan in the latter half of 1941.

Patrol Wing 2--with about 60 VPB planes was the principla naval air patrol and reconnaissance force that existed in Pearl Harbor. Admiral Richardson in May 1940 had started requiring this 300 mile air reconnaissance, every day, seven days a week. The fly boys just bitterly opposed it, for what they thought were perfectly logical reasons.

The air arm of the Navy was expanding extremely rapidly. They were getting all kinds of new graduates from the schools which also were expanding at break neck speed. They had to be trained to be in the tradition of the reconnaissance force and the tradition of the naval aviator at that time. They were trained to be a well-rounded naval aviator, so that they could do lots of things instead of being able to do one thing quite well. That concept had not been purchased, not only by the aviators, but by a lot of other people in the Navy. They wanted every naval officer to be a well-rounded naval officer and to be able to do practically anything. That takes time, effort, and a tremendous amount of training.

Commander, Patrol Wing Two, about every six weeks or two months, would come up through the chain of command with a long-winded three or four page letter telling how he was not doing his job of training his aviators properly because all his efforts were going into this blooming air reconnaissance and that he was wearing out his planes. They were making long flights. They took off normally at day break to seven o'clock in the morning and got back in the afternoon. It was a tremendous grind, but it was necessary.

Another thing mentioned was the inadequacy of the search, because they had a comparitively low number of planes. They could not cover 360° of search, they couldn't even cover 180°. What happened was that they would cover only a limited sector. That sector was determined by the Staff Duty Officer on the CincUS staff. So that no one knew in the patrol wing until the dispatch--or actually a wigwag signal message--went from the Flag ship over to Ford Island telling them what sector to cover. It varied from day to day because each Duty Officer would look at what had been done yesterday and decided on his own estimate of the situation. Nobody knew what they were going to do. It was constantly changing.

Pat Wing Two would send in these letters asking that the daily air reconnaissance be cancelled. The Pat wing letter would come up through Wilson Brown, Commander Scouting Force, and he was sympathetic with it. He would recommend the darn thing be cancelled. We'd have a staff conference. The naval aviators that we had on the staff-Hardison was the first one, Art Davis was the second one--would tell about the horrendous effects that this tremendous air effort was having on the personal training of young aviators. And what deleterious effects it was having on the planes of the patrol wing. Each time it came right down to a dog fight on the staff. Admiral Bernhard Bieri--who's right up here in Washington now--was the Operations Officer, would fight it tooth and toe nail. Admiral Taffinder, who was the Chief of Staff, his position was sort of on the fence--sometimes he'd lean one way and sometimes he'd lean the other. Other people on the staff took various positions. The Admiral had to make the decision. Each time he said, "No, we're going to continue it." Continue it we did, until 5 December 1940 when the Chief of Naval Operations, Admiral H. R. Stark, wrote that it wasn't necessary "at this time."

In my opinion, had we continued the air reconnaissance up until 31 January 1941, had Admiral Kimmel continued it, there never would have been an air attack disaster at Pearl Harbor.

Our aviators in Pat Wing Two could tell where they had been, but they never knew until early morning where they were going to search that particular day. So, there was no way for that information to get out to the Japanese or be given to the Japanese ahead of time. I say again, in my opinion, had the air reconnaissance been continued; there would never have been a Japanese air attack on Pearl Harbor.

What I started to say before this diversion what that about ten or twelve years ago I found out that somebody had burned all the records of Patrol Wing Two. They don't even exist anymore. I located some of their letters in CincUS file in the National Archives.

That's another thing that's happened. If you want to go over to the National Archives and research this matter, they put a girl in there to sit with you while you go through the titles and look. She looks at her watch about every five minutes, which is certainly not helpful, as far as a researcher is concerned.

Q: What does her presence guarantee?

Dyer: That you won't steal what you see because they have lost an awful lot. Perhaps they're justified but I just think they ought to check their researchers more carefully.

Another thing is that our Naval files have been gone through time after time and reduced--just like the files in Naval Operations. Every once in a while you find these girls who don't know anything about anything working on this reduction. They're going through those files, and they're supposed to reduce them from utilizing 7,300 cubic feet to say 3,400 cubic feet. So, they take things out and throw them away.

Q: They're just arbitrary about it?

Dyer: They've got a job to do and so they carry it out. They look and if it doesn't report something that they, out of a very limited knowledge think is important, out it goes.

Q: Aren't such archives in the hands of an historian?

Dyer: The answer to that is no, repeat no, repeat no, capital NO. The chap who is the head of things over there is at least Civil Service qualified I presume, as an archivist, but that's about it.

Q: So, your point is . . .

Dyer: . . . that Admiral Kimmel just completely missed the boat when he failed to stand up under pressures--there were great pressures not to continue this air reconnaissance and by not issuing the order to start it up when the situation with Japan tightened up in the summer of 1940.

Q: What role does Admiral Stark play in this? Did he not have knowledge of this lessening of the vigilance?

Dyer: I do not actually know the answer to that. His was the deciding influence to discontinue on 5 December 1940. He has said their was no air reconnaissance on 7 December 1941 and it surely was within the perogative of Admiral Kimmel to start it up whenever he felt the compelling need of it. He has said that he did not know. I presume that since a copy of all the Commander in Chief's orders--there was an order in regard to this--that his office got a copy of the discontinuance on December 5, 1940. Some subordinate did. Whether he personally was aware of the order. I don't know.

The third point that I find fault with Admiral Kimmel is that he did everything that he could to discourage officers and men from bringing their families out to Pearl Harbor. He did not bring Mrs. Kimmel out.

When the question of a greater degree of readiness of the ships and so forth was raised, he turned it aside. This is all heresay as far as I'm concerned. I never participated in any discussion of this in any way with Admiral Kimmel. He did this saying, if he brought all the ships up to a modified condition two watch, people would say, he could do it because his family wasn't out here.

Mrs. Dyer was out in Honolulu. Thousands of officers and men had their wives out there. His wife's absence provided Admiral Kimmel with an excuse, in my opinion, for not doing his job properly. Had his wife been there--explain it to her and get her to work along with it, just like I tried to explain it to my wife to get her to talk to the people and say why these things had to be done. It is my very humble opinion, that women play a tremendous part in such things. If you can just get them to work with you, you've accomplished a great deal. You can sell something through your wife many times that you can't sell yourself.

Q: Indeed you can.

Dyer: It was a fundamental error. He should have brought his wife out there and put her to work on the other wives. Having her back in the states was just no good at all.

I, in no way by naming these three points, wish to infer that he was the only person that had responsibilites. What I say is, that his defenders have by and large instead of taking a realistic point of view and saying, "Yes, there are things that he didn't do," have tried to paint him lily white. And he's far from lily white.

I've been asked several times, "How do I apportion the responsibility?" I have replied, "I think 40% of it belonged to Admiral Kimmel, 40% belonged to Admiral Stark, and 20% to the President." That's just the way I feel.

Q: The ultimate responsibility has to rest with him because of his decision vis-a-vis Richardson.

Dyer: That's right. That's a fact.

I really don't know where to go from there.

Q: I think you go to Admiral King's staff.

Dyer: About three weeks after I reported into Admiral King's staff; Admiral Russell Wilson, who was the Chief of Staff, called me in. He said, "The Admiral is going to have Commander George Russell, who was his Secretary when he was CinC Atlantic, ordered into relieve you."

I felt pretty low and didn't know what I had or had not done. And then he added, "He's going to retain you in the staff. Admiral Edwards has already asked for you to come work for him." Edwards was the Assistant Chief of Staff for Operations. He said, "You'll probably go to work for Admiral Edwards."

I don't know to this day, what I did, or didn't do. Except that I had expressed strong opinions in regard to things to Admiral King, which I learned afterwards he liked, so I felt sure it was not that. I just don't know what it was.

It took about three weeks before George Russell, who was

at sea in the Atlantic, showed up in Washington. So, I held the job about six weeks.

Q: What did that entail, actually, as Secretary?

Dyer: A Secretary handles the office. He's really the administrative officer. As I said, in addition in the old staffs; he was the Intelligence Officer, the Judge Advocate--in other words, he handled the law problems, and he was the Public Relations Officer.

Q: As Admiral King conceived the office, what was it?

Dyer: I handled all of those in the time that I was his Secretary.

As a matter of fact, about a week after they had told me that I was going to be Admiral Dickie Edwards' Assistant; he came into the office and said, "I can't wait any longer. I've got to have an assistant today."

This was about ten minutes after seven in the morning. He said, "Who do you recommend?" I said, "The only place that I know that you can get an officer today is at the Naval Academy." He said, "Get one."

I got out the roster down here at the Academy and looked over it and found my classmate, John Greybill Crawford, who was down here. I went in and told Admiral Edwards and he said,

"Get him here. Do you recommend him?" I said, "Yes." He said, "Get him here."

I called up BuPers and said, "I've got orders from the Commander in Chief to have Commander Crawford ordered up here today. I'd like to get him here today. I will get him on the phone and get him alerted." They said, "All right."

So, I called him. He was down in Annapolis. He hadn't even left home. It wasn't eight o'clock yet. I said, "Dick, you're ordered up to Admiral King's staff and he wants you here today. I'm sure that you won't have a relief, but you better come on up here. Get here right after lunch."

So, he arrived. Walked in the office about half past one and took over, and went into report to Admiral Edwards. So, that job as Assistant Operations Officer evaporated.

When Commander Russell showed up, we went into see the Admiral. He said, "I'm not going to have time to be the Intelligence Officer." Admiral King said, "All right. Dyer, you be the Intelligence Officer." I said, "I would like to be in the plans division." Admiral King said, "All right. You can be one of the assistant plans officers and the Intelligence Officer." That's what I wanted him to say.

I did about three months in that dual capacity. One day Admiral King buzzed for me. I went in and he said, "You go down and take over the operational intelligence office in addition to your present duties."

Q: Always in addition?

Dyer: That section was headed by a Rear Admiral. His name was Rear Admiral Frank T. Leighton. I walked down to his office.

In addition, Admiral King had said, "You relieve Admiral Leighton and I want Admiral Leighton out of the Navy Department before four-thirty this afternoon." That's Admiral King's way he operated.

Q: With orders to go somewhere else?

Dyer: He was being thrown out on his heels.

So, I went down there. Here was poor old Rear Admiral Leighton out of the Class of 1909. I was a Commander out of the Class of 1919. I said, "Sir, I have orders from Admiral King to relieve you today. You're to be out of the Department by four o'clock." Of course, there was very little he could say.

Q: Had he been deficient in the job?

Dyer: I express no opinion at all. I'm merely reporting the incident as I saw it.

I worked on the relieving job along with him until about

four o'clock. Then I said, "Sir, I'm ready to relieve you." So, he got under way and went up and saw Vice Admiral Russell Wilson and I guess Admiral King. He ended up as Commandant Eighth Naval District.

When I got a look around, there were two Captains in the office. I was a Commander. The two Captains were assistants to Admiral Leighton.

So, I hot-footed up to Rear Admiral Dickie Edwards. I said, "I've got two Captains in that office." He said, "Get rid of them before tomorrow morning."

Q: How disruptive to the morale of an institution.

Dyer: I called up the Detail Officer and said, "I have orders from Admiral King that they're to be detached today." I went in and told them both the unexpected news that they were to be detached. I said, "You better get in touch with the Detail Officer and find out where you're going to be sent." So, out they went and I never saw them after that day.

So, I picked up that job along with the others. Then, later I was given orders as the Navy Department Security Officer. When I left, which was in February 1943, four Captains relieved me. One of them took over security, one took over operational intelligence, one of them took over the assistant plans desk, and the fourth took over the basic duty of Intelligence Officer.

Q: It could not have been very pleasant functioning with that kind of Sword of Damocles over your head all the time.

Dyer: I'll tell you one story about Rear Admiral Frederick Sherman, who later went on to have a very wonderful combat career. Rear Admiral Frederick Sherman came into Washington after the Lexington, which he commanded, had been sunk. He relieved Rear Admiral Edwards as Assistant Chief of Staff for Operations, when Admiral Edwards fleeted up and became the Deputy Chief of Staff. He was a naval aviator, class of 1910; an extremely capable man. I served with him out in the Pacific in 1944-45; I thought he was just wonderful out there.

The system that was in existence in Admiral King's Headquarters was that I, as Operational Intelligence Officer, every morning at roughly quarter of eight, went in and briefed the Assistant Chief of Staff for Operations and the Deputy Chief of Staff, Admiral Edwards, in regard to what had happened in the submarine sinking picture since six or seven o'clock the night before.

I walked in one morning to make my report and Admiral Sherman wasn't there. So, I said to Captain F. S. Lowe, who had become the operational assistant to the Assistant

Chief of Staff for Operations, "Where's Admiral Sherman?" He just looked at me and said, "Well, he isn't here, is he?" I said, "No." I went out and waited about five minutes and came back.

I wanted Admiral Sherman to get this report because Admiral King normally at 8:15 had all the officers concerned with submarine sinkings and other operational matters in and I made a full blown operational intelligence report then. But I wanted these officers who were senior to me and who were particularly interested in the submarine sinking area to be briefed in advance. So, if Admiral King asked them a question, they would be alert to the situation and be able to answer.

Q: They'd have chance to think about it.

Dyer: Yes. I came back in about five minutes and Admiral Sherman still wasn't there. So, I said to Frog Lowe, "Are you going to take the advance briefing?" He said, "Yes." He got up and went into Admiral Edwards' office and I sounded off. When I finished, Frog Lowe went on out. And I said, "Where's Admiral Sherman?" Admiral Edwards just said, "I don't think he'll be back."

Admiral Sherman had been there when I left the office at half past seven or quarter of eight the night before.

Later that evening he had had some discussion with Admiral King. Admiral King had thrown him out. He actually went out to the Pacific and did a wonderful combat job.

When I came back from the Pacific, two and a half years later, I was ordered back to the Headquarters. I went in to see Admiral Edwards who had become the Deputy Commander in Chief. I said, "Why in the world hasn't Admiral Sherman become a three star Admiral?" Three stars were springing up all around. I said, "He's doing a marvelous job out there. He just couldn't be doing a better job. I can't see why he hasn't been given three stars." Admiral Edwards said to me, "You go in and tell the old man." So, I did.

I went in and I said the same thing to Admiral King. I said, "Here's an officer who's been in combat longer than most people by far. He's been out in combat ever since he left here in July or August of '42. He's been out there in combat, and hasn't been promoted. Why not?" He was promoted in a week from that time.

Q: Just had to be called to his attention again.

Dyer: He had to be pressed by someone in whom he had some reliance. As I said, I always got along fine with Admiral King. I had a number of conferences with him during the post war period. He never told me why he booted me out of the Secretarys' job, and I don't know to this day.

Q: Was that an extremely effective way in which to handle men?

Dyer: I'll tell you, it sets a standard. You've got to cut the mustard right. He set the highest kind of a standard and people that didn't meet his standard--he threw them out.

Q: In contrast--Admiral Nimitz set the highest standard, too, didn't he? But he didn't act that way.

Dyer: When I went up to see Admiral Nimitz in 1963 or 1964, I was talking to him about Admiral Ghormley, when Ghormley was Commander South Pacific Force. Admiral Nimitz told me this, "One of the toughest things that I ever did in my service career was to fire Admiral Ghormley. I had known him for nearly forty years, ever since we were Midshipmen at the same time. I have always had the highest opinion of him. He had done the most wonderful job all through his naval career. I was one of those that recommended that he be sent down to the South Pacific Command. Yet, I became convinced that he had to be taken out. So, I picked Admiral Halsey to go down and relieve him. When Admiral Ghormley came back, he came in my office at Pearl Harbor. He stood there before me and tears rolled down his cheeks. He said, 'Chester, why was I relieved?' I then had the most difficult time trying to explain frankly, yet kindly, why I had relieved him."

Q: This in itself, this story is a contrast with King's way of acting.

Dyer: I don't know a single top flight military leader that hasn't had to make those decisions.

Q: Naturally.

Dyer: They're never easy to make. There's no easy way to get rid of a subordinate, that I know of. Generally, you're fairly close to your subordinates. They are entitled to an explanation if they ask for one. You have to be fairly sure of your grounds before you do it. You have to answer to your own conscience. You have to be true to yourself. That's what makes it difficult. Are you setting an impossible standard? Are you asking too much of an individual? Or are you doing something that is for the good of the Service? It's a difficult problem.

Q: One more question in this vein. I was told by a Flag Secretary that many of the conferences between Admirals King and Nimitz in San Francisco or on the West Coast during the war were devoted in large measure to discussions about where they could put this person or that person, the senior officer who was inadequate in his present assignment. This apparently shows the softening and the compassionate nature of Nimitz involved in this.

Dyer: Yes. No question about it, he was a lot more compassionate than Admiral King. He took sometimes a long time to do something that needed to be done right away.

To go on from there . . .

Q: Can you tell me a little about some of your duties on the COMINCH staff? Don't skip over them too rapidly. Tell me about your chart room activity, which I know a little about.

Dyer: One of the things that I did as the Operationals Intelligence Officer was in the F-35. I had the numbers F-11 and F-35. F-11 was in the plans division and F-35 was in the operations division.

One of the findings which I came up with as a result of the very hurried and brief and inadequate examination of the Pearl Harbor disaster which I had made in January, February 1942 was that the intelligence people had been shoved off into a corner. By and large, nobody had paid adequate attention to them in the pre-Pearl Harbor period. In fact, there are only two people that I know--I'm sure there are others--had respectable billets in the Office of Naval Intelligence, as distinguished from duty as Naval Attaches, who ever really got anywhere in the Navy. One of them was Admiral Spruance--who is the exception that proves any rule you want to make. He had a Four in Naval Intelligence about 1927-1929. The other was Admiral Jonas Ingram who was in Naval Intelligence when I was at the Naval Academy--about 1934-36. Both became four star Admirals. But, by and large, the Office of Naval Intelligence was used as a depository for people who either were coming up for selection and nobody thought they were going to be selected, or people who had failed of selection and the Bureau of Navigation wanted some place to put them for a year or two before they retired. At that time, normally, you were passed over just twice. Once passed over, then you had a year more to do; and if you were not picked up the next time, you were retired.

Very few really first class people were in the Office of Naval Intelligence until 1939 or 1940, when someone impressed on the Bureau of Navigation the importance of intelligence to the Navy. This generalization certainly doesn't include the Director of Naval Intelligence. Generally, he, unfortunately, was a person who knew very little about intelligence. He became a Flag Officer through other endeavor; and then was named Director of Naval Intelligence.

Q: And didn't stay too long.

Dyer: Didn't stay too long and didn't know much about what was going on underneath him.

One recommendation that I came out with was that (ONI) intelligence should be part of the operations section of Naval Operations. Actually, when they reorganized naval operations in 1945 that was the way it started out. It is no longer. It is back as a separate division. We are too far away from the war. For a number of years after naval operations was reorganized, intelligence was part of naval operations.

In making me both F-11 and F-35, the idea was to have somebody who was in the intelligence picture who was also in the plans and operations section. So, that's the way I functioned. My chore was to insure that the operations people were kept abreast of everything we knew or thought we knew in intelligence.

At that time, we were still reading some of the Japanese codes. The idea was to insure that while the information was not so widely dispersed that it would get into the fringes and eventually get back to the Japanese that we were doing this breaking of their codes, but that the intelligence would be adequately dispersed so that people that were in operations would be abreast of this intelligence data. It was a very fuzzy area. That's what I worked at.

The operational war room was actually more or less of a side activity. It was one place where information which was available either as a result of high level operational reports or as a result of intelligence reports was assembled; except that no MAGIC was taken into the operational war room. MAGIC being the decoded Japanese dispatches.

Q: Did you have any cognizance or responsibility for the operational war room in the White House?

Dyer: Not the slightest.

Q: Did you furnish information to them?

Dyer: The only way that I furnished information was through the Joint Intelligence Committee--of which I was a member-- It got out a daily poop sheet which was circulated over to the White House. Actually, the Joint Intelligence Committee was largely window dressing; because it did not have the MAGIC available.

I can tell you a little story which is amusing in regard to the Joint Intelligence Committee. The head of the Army intelligence division, the G-2, was Major General George V.

Strong. He was a permanent Major General when the war started for the United States. He was a very wonderful person. We used to have Joint meetings. Together with one assistant, I would go over to the regular meetings. We would decide things. These were mainly administrative matters. Occasionally, they were in the actual intelligence field. But all had a great bearing on the intelligence field.

Roughly about June the 15th, 1943; Admiral King buzzed for me one day and I went in. He said, "I have a complaint against you." I said, "I'm sorry. Who's the complaint from?" And he said, "From General Strong." I said, "I'm doubly sorry. I have great admiration for General Strong and I thought we were getting along tremendously well." He said, "General Strong objects very strongly to having what he thinks we should do Jointly, vetoed by a Commander in the United States Navy." After all, he was a permanent Major General with some seniority.

That was typical, when I was Secretary to Admiral King. I was a Commander and the secretarys to the Air Force and the Army were both Brigadier Generals. They were laps ahead of us.

Admiral King said, "I said to General Strong, 'would you be any happier if Dyer was a Captain?' General Strong said, 'Yes, I'd be a little happier.'" So Admiral King said, "You're about to become a Captain. Hold up your right hand and I'll swear you in." And, I became a Captain. I was the second person in my class to become a Captain; Logan Ramsey who as the Duty Officer in Patrol Wings at Pearl Harbor on 7 December, 1941, and who had sent the message, "Air Raid Pearl Harbor. This is not a drill," and who had done a marvelous job in defending Midway, was promoted to Captain on 11 June 1942 and I made it on 17 June 1942.

Actually, I thought our differences were very minimum. And I thought that we worked extremely well together. Maybe I worked better after I became a Captain, I don't know. But I was very grateful to him after that.

Q: Would you go down a Tangential path once again and tell me, in your opinion, why did ONI fall into that less favorable catagory you mentioned before?

Dyer: In the first place, when I reported the first time on the Destroyer, Scouting Force staff, became the Flag Secretary, and took over the intelligence duties, my Admiral said to me, after outlining what he expected me to do as a Secretary, "Now as to your intelligence duty--the only intelligence that I am interested in, is who is going to get what job when. If you can tell me that, I'll be very much interested in it." That was by and large true of how many naval officers rated intelligence.

I think that was probably true of 95% of the naval officers of that peacetime era. And this was a peacetime era. The only so-called intelligence that they wanted to know was who was going to get what job when. There is very little in peacetime that arouses one in regard to intelligence.

Now, when the world is in sort of a strange state, intelligence is a matter of interest to a great many people.

Q: But in a former peacetime, everything was more or less above board.

Dyer: That's right. So, you could work very hard and yet you could produce practically nothing that you could say vitally important to the Navy.

If you were in gunnery, you could produce a good score. Everybody was interested in a good score in gunnery.

If you were in communications, you handled dispatches rapidly and that sort of thing. Everybody was interested in getting a dispatch right soon after it was sent.

You had something that immediately produced a favorable reaction, if it was done well. In intelligence, that was not true. By and large, it just didn't arouse people's interest. People went down to Peru, or down to the Argentine, or over to France, or down to Italy, or even to the Soviet Union. That was actually the best detail there was--the intelligence officer to the Soviet Union. They had some very good first class people. The Naval Attaches worked hard at their jobs--but many times produced very little of value to the Navy.

Q: There was a certain amount of espionage involved in that assignment.

Dyer: That's right.

There are two things which the Navy learned, and I hope learned well during World War II. One is that logistics is tremendously important, and the other is that intelligence is tremendously important. Those two things were not at all accepted in the pre-World War II Navy.

I got the greatest pleasure out of planning operations. I enjoyed planning. There were roughly ten or twelve people in plans. I think I was next to the junior one when I moved in. When I became a Captain all of a sudden, I became somewhat more senior. I was right down at the bottom of the list, because they had some very first class people in plans. I enjoyed that very much and we did a number of plans. The one that I perhaps had the actual largest amount of planning effort in was in our invasion of North Africa and the west coast of Morocco.

Q: What sort of tools did you have at your beck and call? What sort of information did you deal with and under who's command were you formulating these?

Dyer: Admiral Turner was the Assistant Chief of Staff for Plans. The plans division was divided into two main sections, one was Pacific and the other was Atlantic. Whenever a specific planning job was to be done, the junior ones could be shifted. I did planning in the Pacific and I did planning in the Atlantic. And so did a lot of other people. There were certain hard-core people who stayed in those sections, and the others were fluid and could be used for the job that was to be done.

I'll tell you a little story about planning for the Solomon Islands operation at Guadalcanal, which took place the 7th and 8th of August, 1942. When that operation was in the early planning stage, I was trying to scout out information in regard to Guadalcanal and the other Solomon Islands, and trying to do it at the same time in such a way as would not pinpoint that as a place of particular interest. I searched everything, and there was only a modest amount of information available.

Our recent naval intelligence in regard to the Solomons was zero point zero due to the fact that about a year and a half before we went in there Admiral Stark had gotten out an order saying, "In no way was the Pacific fleet to show any interests in the Solomons."

Q: What was the thinking back of that?

Dyer: I think that the basic reason behind that was that they felt that the Japanese might interpret it as a gesture as to how we might be planning to conduct a war.

Q: It was literal then?

Dyer: Literal, I quote it in my book on Kelly Turner; quote the order.

There was an intelligence organization of sorts in Washington called the Office of Strategic Services; the OSS. It was headed by a Colonel William J. Donovan who had command of the 69th regiment during World War I. He came from New York. Colonel Donovan.

I gave the OSS a number of places that I was interested in getting information about the Ellis Islands, the Gilberts Islands, the Solomons Islands, New Guinea, and so forth, everything that covered that part of the ocean. So, it was a real shotgun blast, pinpointing nowhere.

Colonel Donovan's outfit was supposed to turn out all this information. One day Colonel Donovan called me and said,

"There's a real hotshot on the Solomons. He's out in Chicago. I got a phone call, and he will call you at ten o'clock. He'll give you all the dope." I said, "All right."

Q: Was he guessing something?

Dyer: No, this chap came on the wire. I listened to him for about two minutes, and then I wrote a note to my secretary. I had a chap taking shorthand as this came in over the telephone.

Q: It wasn't monitored?

Dyer: No. I said, "Get me the Encyclopedia Britannica," which we had there in the office. He broke it out. I wrote on a piece of paper--Solomons Islands. This chap was still talking on the phone. I had connected up his conversation with what I had read before, and I was able to locate what he was reading from the Encyclopedia Britannica. I broke in and said, "You're reading from the Encyclopedia Britannica on page 787. You're now on line five from the bottom."

Q: He must have dropped his jaw.

Dyer: I'm no longer interested in carrying on this conversation. Thank you very much, good bye." I hung up. So, then I called Colonel Donovan. I said, "We're not very bright over here, but at least we read the standard references. We don't need to have any long distant telephone calls from Chicago--somebody to read the Encyclopedia Britannica over here." As a matter of fact, I made a lot of numbers with him by just that. He was always very careful thereafter when he produced anything for me. It was really something that was worthwhile. The OSS produced more trash than any organization I ever came up against.

Q: That was OSS?

Dyer: OSS.

Q: What cooperation and what value did you get from the Army's G-2?

Dyer: Army G-2 was excellent, in that they had a great deal more fundamental information than naval intelligence had. They had done their homework over the years, and produced standard treatises of practically anywhere in the world. Not every place, but an awful lot of places. Their standard work was far superior to ONI, with the exception of a few places. ONI had had some ambitious and capable chaps who had turned out a proper study here and there.

Q: Did you have contact, at that point, with young Captain Dean Rusk of G-2?

Dyer: Never knowledgable, no, not to my knowledge.

Q: He was a part of their staff.

Dyer: Yes, I know that. But, I never knew him.

That was a very interesting part--we did the planning on the Solomons operation. You want to understand that the Solomons Islands operation was planned for the initial landings to be in the Santa Cruz Islands. Guadacanal was never mentioned. Tulagi was mentioned, but not Guadacanal. Guadacanal only got into the picture roughly a month before the actual landing.

Q: Was this an attempt to surround Rabaul?

Dyer: The reason we went into Guadalcanal is that the Japanese moved from Tulagi into Guadalcanal. The theory was that if the Japanese thought it was worthwhile, we probably should think it was worthwhile. And it was. It provided land area to put proper land air bases. In fact, we put three of them there before it was all over, down on Guadalcanal. Far better than Santa Cruz, which after any number of looksees, was decided as an impossible place for land air bases.

That is something that is often not known--that the initial invasion objectives down there were Santa Cruz and Tulagi; not Guadalcanal at all. Of course, the big landing was on Guadalcanal. The secondary landing was on Tulagi. The Santa Cruz operation which was called Huddle, never got into the picture; except as a great bone of contention in that the Joint Chiefs every once in a while would send a dispatch down to Admiral Ghormley and ask, "When are you going to land on Santa Cruz? And carry out the rest of our orders?" Because the JCS orders didn't get changed right away.

Q: You said, also, one of your additional duties was that of security officer for the department.

Dyer: Let me tell you about that, that really was something.

When we started the planning for the landing in North Africa, it, of course, was a highly secret operation. As far as the Navy Department was concerned, it continued to be a highly secret operation. Very few people down in working level knew anything about it. They knew we were getting ready for an operation and certain things had to be done, but where it was going to be, they just didn't know.

Then reports started coming in. Young fellows would come in and say, "My Army counterpart or Lieutenant John Jones, or something like that, tells me we're going to land in North Africa." This alarmed Admiral King just tremendously. Because I told him. I said, "The Army is just spreading this news all over Washington."

He and General Marshall and General Arnold got together. The Joint Chiefs came up with a directive which directed the Army and the Navy to establish a Security Officer for their Department. One of the side tasks, the initial task, was to find out how many officers in each Department knew something about the North African landing. We laid our cards on the table. I was terribly embarrassed when I took this report in to Admiral King that some 61 officers had some knowledge of this landing. He just raised cain with me.

About 24 hours later, he sent for me again and said, "Do you know what the Army number is?" I said, "I don't have any knowledge Admiral. I'll bet it's close to 600." He said, "600? It's 1342. You can forget what I said yesterday."

Q: Why had he laced you out? It wasn't your . . .

Dyer: The Intelligence Officer on a staff also handles security, but I was not designated as a Security Officer of the Navy Department, only the COMNICH organization. Intelligence Officers had always handled security during the peace time years.

Or course, we in the Navy went around patting ourselves on the back. We had so few. The Army then really tightened things up. They tightened things up with a full thumbscrew.

Nobody would admit to knowing anything, for most of the rest of the time that I was in the Department. The Army was very cozy with any piece of information they had. It had a very salutary effect.

The way they handled future operations, both the Army and the Navy, (I know it was done in the Navy and I was told it was done in the Army) we established books on operations. We got into the code name business very strongly.

Q: North Africa had a name too.

Dyer: Oh, yes. They all had code names.

When you got any information, you had to sign the book. You could pass the information on only to people who's signatures were already on the book. If you brought in four planning officers, the four planning officers were given the dope and signed the book. Then they could talk with each other, they could talk with anybody else whose signature was above them in the book, in regard to this operation. You couldn't talk to anybody below that list or not in that list, unless you went up to the top man and got his permission to inform somebody else. It was a real task. Particularly as the number of operations multiplied.

One thing that most people don't appreciate is that in the early days very few people gave a great deal of thought to logistics. When you talk about logistics, you're talking about a multiheaded endeavor. It really cuts across the line of everybody, and everything.

When you have to start shipping things in June to be in Australia in September, you have to tell a lot of people. You have to establish a time schedule and a deadline.

Q: You've got to at least tell them a fragment of the story.

Dyer: Yes. It really got to be a tremendous chore, and very difficult with the passing of time.

Q: Just a remark, if I may add one. I don't recall operations after North Africa, the regulations being quite as stringent as for that one particular one. It virtually put me out of business and my three or four colleagues for a day or two, as civilians we were charged with the Secretary's chart room. We had to get there before day break to go through dispatches. This order came through and we were not allowed to see even confidential dispatches--our jobs. Depended--- So, the solution whether it was a feasible one or not, was to have an officer take the dispatches and read the data off the dispatches to us. Then we operated on that basis.

Dyer: Captain Ray Thurber, a classmate of mine, took over the Security job when I left there. Ray has told me a number of times, he's dead now, of this tremendous problem he had.

There are a number of other things that I could mention about the planning operations.

Q: Do, please.

Dyer: The great problem in planning the early operations, the two that I principally remember I've already named, the Guadalcanal and the North African operations, was that we did not have the resources available to plan with any broad sweep. We had to plan with the greatest of detail because there was so little that you could actually make available to participate in those operations. It involved a far more detailed planning than was true later in the war, when we had fairly generous resources and the planning at the higher levels could be on the broad sweep basis. Neither of those operations could be planned that way. They had to be planned down to the last detail to be sure that you had a ship that could carry a man to go to a place. You couldn't say--we're going to ship out the 43rd division to go here. We had to plan at the highest level, had to plan down to the last hundred men, and to the last piece of equipment. So, it was a much more detailed planning job, than it was later in the war.

When I got back in July of '45, the planning then in

COMINCH was planning for the invasion of Japan, was an extremely broad brush planning at that level. There were tens of thousands of ships, tens of thousands of airplanes, and so forth and so on.

Q: And the whole process had been perfected.

Dyer: That's right. The greatest lack of planning appreciation, in my opinion, particularly for Guadalcanal, was in the follow up.

We planned the initial invasion with great exactness, but there was no real planning at the COMINCH level about what would happen one week, three weeks, or six weeks after the troops had landed. After the Marines had gone ashore at Guadalcanal, no one at the highest level had figured out where the next thirty days rations or the next thirty days supply of ammunition, or anything was going to come from or how to get it there way across the Pacific; and so forth. That was not planned for at COMINCH. Therefore, it put the actual people on the spot--in other words, the people that were in Guadalcanal--at a great disadvantage.

The people that were down in the South Pacific were just grabbing at straws to put that campaign together after the initial effort. The initial effort went very well.

Q: In connection with plans, sir, how much of it was done

at the series of Quebec conferences and so forth; at that level?

Dyer: None of the detail planning. The question at those levels was--were the resources in general available, and was it sound from a strategical point of view.

The initial agreement, which was fully accepted by the Navy, was that the war in Europe had priority. Germany was the main enemy. The Navy Department and the planners from the Navy Department put forth a tremendous effort to get the necessary, let us say, weasel words into the agreements; to permit something to be done in the Pacific. It was only the fact that they had a few weasel words in, that gave Admiral King something to work on in the Joint Chiefs to really get the Pacific campaign started.

Q: Focusing on the Pacific campaign itself for a moment, how much authority and how much initiative was exerted by Admiral Nimitz in some of these operations?

Dyer: Admiral Nimitz exerted a great deal of authority in regards to how exactly the operations would be carried out. He also influenced, to a considerable extent, the 'when' it could be carried out and when the resources would be available so that it could be carried out. He influenced the 'where' in detail, but not the 'where' in general.

Q: Being specific now with Kwajalein--did he make the decision on that?

Dyer: Very much so. In other words. The decision was to go into the Marshalls. That was made at the Joint Chiefs level. The decision as to 'how' we would do the Marshalls, whether we would head for Wotje and Mille, which were two of the favorite objectives on the eastern end of the Marshalls; or whether we would go right to the heart of the Marshalls, Kwajalein--that decision was made by Admiral Nimitz personally. And I might say, largely against the advice of most of his subordinates. He made a wonderful decision when he made that one.

Q: Do you know on what it was predicated? Wasn't it contrary to the advice of his . . .

Dyer: It was predicated on his belief that if we successfully seized Kwajalein, that we would save ourselves having to do two operations--one on the fringes and one in the center. And that actually, if we were going to do the fringes, it was a real question as to whether we had adequate resources to do both of the fringe atolls at the same time. While there was no real question that we had enough resources to do one.

My voice is running out, so I think I'll stop.

Vice Admiral George C. Dyer, USN, Ret.   Annapolis, Maryland
by John T. Mason, Jr.   March 31, 1970

Mr. Mason: Wonderful to see you this morning, Admiral. Last time you gave me a very interesting account of the manifold duties you had on the staff of Admiral King in the Department in Washington. Today I expect you want to turn your attention to the next major assignment which was to the Mediterranean.

Admiral Dyer: I have a number of things that I remember quite well in regard to not only going over to the Mediterranean, but what we did over there.

The first thing that I think is an interesting anecdote, probably not too many people are knowledgable in regard to it. This was in regard to the planning for the initial landing in North Africa, which operation I did not participate in except in a planning capacity. The planning conferences were held alternately in the War Plans Division of the Navy and over in the War Plans Division of the General Staff of the Army. There were a limited number of people at these conferences, generally 12 or 14.

Q: Who presided over the planning?

Dyer: Initially for conferences in the Navy Department, Admiral Edwards was at the head of the table. Later Admiral Turner as the senior Navy planner was at the head of the table. The only two Army planners that I can remember at the head of the table were Brigadier General John E. Hull and Brigadier General Thomas T. Hardy. Quite frequently Admiral Hewitt came up from Norfolk. General Patton was at the meetings also. It was a very knowledgable and worthwhile group. They were dealing with the many thousands of problems that arose in connection with doing that initial invasion.

The planning had been going on for about six weeks or two months, at least the planning that I was participating in, and one day Admiral Russell Wilson, who was the Chief of Staff, called me in. He said, "Admiral King is disturbed because of the remark that he overheard at a cocktail party in regard to the North African invasion." TORCH, it was called. He said, "I'm sure he wants to talk to you about that."

When I got into Admiral King's office he said to me, "Dyer, how many people in the Navy Department know the whereabouts of this invasion that is going to take place?"

When you're doing an invasion, there are literally hundreds of people that have to know that something is going to happen, but they don't have to know where or when it's going to happen.

I said, "If I had to guess right quick, I'd say 25." He said, "That's too many." I said, "It may be too many, but you've got an awful lot of people that are directly concerned with things that they could do well only if they know where this operation is going to occur. He said, "I've talked to General Marshall about this and we have decided that the Joint Chiefs of Staff are going to set up what's called a Joint Security Committee. You are going to be the senior Navy member of that Joint Security Committee. Your first chore is to find out in the Navy Department, who knows about this thing. In other words, we've got to impress on the people who do know the need for secrecy. We've got to find out how many people really know about it."

Q: How far in advance of the actual invasion was this?

Dyer: This was, if I had to guess, about six weeks to two months before. In other words, planning had been going on for about four months and this was about half way through it.

He said, "Draw up a statement for people to sign which will impress on them, when they sign it, the necessity of keeping a tight lip on this problem."

So I went back and wrestled with the problem and talked with a number of other officers. I talked with Admiral Edwards, I remember. I don't remember talking with Admiral Turner, I very possibly did.

We drafted a statement and I got a book and ran copies of the statement printed at the top of each page. I took it around to the people that I knew, knew about the particulars of the invasion, where and when it was going to occur. I got them all to sign this statement. Each person that signed it had to say in the statement, "To my knowledge the following people also have similar knowledge." So that way we expanded the list.

I was just simply amazed because when I had run this matter down. It took two or three days going from person to person, to the neglect of practically everything else, that I turned up with 61 signatures in the Navy Department. Admiral King was getting madder by the moment. But when the Army turned up 1100 and some odd, we looked pretty good. After he found that out, I didn't get any more brickbats thrown at me nor did the other people. Actually, the knowledge had been held very very tightly within the Navy Department.

That was a very interesting sidelight. As you know, or perhaps don't know, Drew Pearson, a week before the invasion in his predictions of things to come, predicted that we would invade North Africa. I would gladly have shot him.

Q: Did this mean that Admiral King henceforth was even stricter about news leaking out for other operations?

Dyer: No, I don't think that he was any stricter. But I think that having to sign for this information and being faced with all the pains and penalities of revealing it, without getting permission from the person who had given you permission before you passed it on to anybody else, while it cluttered things up a bit, nevertheless it did hold down the dissemination of planning information very tightly.

A little side issue on that, which is perhaps of interest. As you know, Whitehill had come down to write the history of the Cominch staff. He couldn't sign the book because he hadn't been told, which is an indication of how inadequately he was able to do his job. The idea was excellent; I still think it was excellent. We brought him down to write a history of the staff. To write a history, you've got to know what's happening.

Q: Indeed you do, otherwise it isn't worth much.

Dyer: That's right. The idea was also to write the various pros and cons that were influencing--why decisions were taken this way and why they were taken that way. Unfortunately, Admiral King wouldn't let Whitehill function. That's a little side issue.

One thing that I remember about the planning was that the Navy of course was very much interested in places the Army wanted to be landed in North Africa, the beach gradiants, tide conditions, and everything else. We would go into this in great detail at some of these planning conferences.

General Patton would always end up by saying, "Well, it's all very interesting but the Navy will never land you where you want to land or when you want to land." His statement, for that landing, turned out to be 100 percent correct, with just minor exceptions.

Q: What about the question of landing craft and so forth, the adequacy of it?

Dyer: The North Africa invasion was made with none of the landing craft that we had later, insofar as our Navy was concerned. We had the small landing boats, but we did not have the landing craft.

There is one other thing of interest that I was directly involved in. That was an intelligence aspect. In the period before the invasion of North Africa, there was a man, his name I do not recall, who was in the weather prognosis business. He was a far out boy who always claimed that anywhere from a week to a month before the day that by getting certain data together, he could predict the weather.

The great problem along the northwest coast of Africa is the height of the swells. Very frequently you have swells so high that you couldn't possibly make a landing in small craft. We didn't have any LSTs, LCTs, or LCILs to land there. We were landing the small LCVPs from the transports. We had to have reasonable weather in order to land those craft.

Q: If we had had LSTs, it would have been an easier matter?

Dyer: Far easier, yes.

From the weather predictions that we were getting and from the reconnaissance we were running with our own submarines and so on, the weather reports from various places were extremely important. Naturally, it was a matter of great moment to Admiral Hewitt, who was in command of the naval force that was going to land in Morocco.

About two or three days before they were to land, and as one of my daily chores was to read various operational information dispatches that were sent out by the Army and the Army Air Force. Lo and behold, here was a weather dispatch which had been sent out by the Army Air Force. This far out weatherman was operating under the aegis of the Army Air Force. This very alarming dispatch, saying the swells were going to be so many feet high, which was $2\frac{1}{2}$ to 3 times as high as we were predicting they were going to be. Just to read the dispatch would scare you to death.

I got the dispatch and I actually ran down to where our aerologist, Lieutenant Commander Howard T. Orville, was and said, "What's the background of this?" He was as surprised as I was. He'd never seen the dispatch, he'd never had a chance to talk about it before it was sent, he didn't know anything about it, and he was in complete disagreement with it.

It had gone off to General Patton. He was riding in the same ship with Admiral Hewitt. So the only thing that we could do was to originate a dispatch saying that this did not represent COMINCH point of view and we confirmed what we'd said about the height of the swells in the last prediction.

Admiral Hewitt wrote about this in one of the articles that he's written about the landing in Northwest Africa for the Naval Institute. He said, in this article, that the dispatch didn't particularly perturb him. I've always had a little difficulty accepting that because it was an alarming dispatch, and if I'd gotten it, I certainly would have been perturbed.

Of course, the amphibious went on in on schedule and the dispatch was 100 percent wrong.

Q: How near was the actual situation to what . . .

Dyer: It was extremely close, the predictions which had been made by Lieutenant Commander Orville were extremely close and quite satisfactory.

It just shows what can happen. Had Admiral Hewitt been a more excitable man that he was, and not as much a seaman as he was, he could have very well delayed the invasion.

Q: Admiral, this is quite a tangent but perhaps you can throw some light on it. Recently I've been talking with Admiral Deyo, also with General Krulak. Both of them were in the China area toward the end of the thirties, and were aware of Japanese developments with landing craft. Actually, both of them sent intelligence to this effect in photographs back to the Navy Department. Why was it that we were not more ready with our own landing craft?

Dyer: I think primarily it was a question of funds. If you would like to read a little bit of the background of that, you can read Chapter Six of my book, "THE AMPHIBIONS CAME TO CONQUER." The chap that lives right across the street here, Captain Daggett, tells a very interesting story about our building efforts. He was the Officer in Charge of landing craft in the Bureau of Construction and Repair during 1939-41. In writing his story into this book, I have gone into the history of the stringent financial limitations under which the Navy Department was operating in connections with building landing craft and the background of the efforts of the Navy to get landing craft and the very limited funds that the landing craft development section had in the 1939, 1940, early 1941 period.

Q: And appropriations committees couldn't be convinced of the need?

Dyer: You had the same trouble with them perhaps then, perhaps you had even more trouble that you have now. Where it's very difficult to appropriate money for something that you can't actually see, you can't visualize it, you don't know anything about it. By and large our Congress, our Navy for that matter, knew very little about amphibious warfare in 1941.

I have a whole chapter on this development of amphibious warfare and some of the early Naval officers and early Marine officers who actually worked on this problem.

There's an officer here in town, Rear Admiral Walter

Ansel who was an early toiler in the amphibious warfare development. Do you know Walter Ansel?

Q: No, but I'm going to.

Dyer: He's a classmate of mine. He was one of the earliest amphibious students at the Marine Corps Amphibious Schools. He helped to write one of the first books on amphibious operations. He's since done a book on HITLER INVADES ENGLAND, which got excellent reviews.

It will be worth talking with him. He can tell you many more things than I can tell you about the problems in the Nineteen Thirties.

I'll say basically, and this is an overall picture, in the two or three years before World War II the Navy had a small number of officers who were very much interested in amphibious warfare who made great efforts to develop craft which would facilitate the handling of the amphibious problem. They were very closely held down by financial limitations. There just wasn't money.

We actually got our designs for our first amphibious craft, large amphibious craft, from the British.

That's too broad a problem to get into.

Q: And you weren't immediately concerned.

Dyer: I wasn't immediately concerned with it.

To go back to the invasion of North Africa--After that was over, and the decision was made to go into Sicily, they formed up an amphibious command which was to have a series of seven amphibious bases across North Africa. The officer who was named to command this amphibious command was Rear Admiral Richard Conolly.

I was on Admiral King's staff and I had been there a year. The day that I was there a year, I sat down and wrote a memorandum to Admiral King. It was a memorandum of the type that he demanded. It had to all be on one side of one sheet of ordinary note paper. It said, 1. "The officers who are serving on the Commander in Chief's staff should bring to that staff combat experience, in order that orders that go out from the Commander in Chief's staff will be based on what we have learned from the war up to date."

The second paragraph was that, "The Commander in Chief should have on his staff only capable and ambitious officers. If they have five cents worth of ambition as an officer, they don't want to be on shore duty in Washington."

The third paragraph, which was the meat of the memo said that, "I recommend that no regular officer, below Flag rank, be required to serve on the Commander in Chief's staff more than twelve months, so that there would be a constant turnover, with officers with fresh combat experience coming into the staff, and capable and ambitious officers getting a chance to serve at sea."

I sent it up through the chain of the staff. Everybody thought it was wonderful. Ernie buzzed for me, and I went in.

Q: It was, in fact, a resignation, wasn't it?

Dyer: He was holding this piece of paper up as I walked across this long, long room. I finally got up to his desk. I was a Captain by that time, I said, Captain Dyer, sir." He said, "You would be the son of a bitch that wants to break up my staff." But, he approved it.

Q: He did approve it?

Dyer: You had no trouble with Ernie, if you had the facts down and you had a logical recommendation. That was the wonderful thing about the man. He didn't like it but, by George, he put, "Approved, E. J. King." He approved it and handed it back to me.

I went back and got on the phone and called my classmate, Johnny Roper, over at the Bureau of Personnel and said, "This piece of paper's been approved. As of this date, it applies to only one person." And it did. That was George

C. Dyer.

I had arrived on the staff fifth; I was the fifth officer to report in. I had completed my twelve months. The other four were gone with the wind.

Johnny said, "Where do you want to go?" I said, "I want to go somewhere in the Pacific and I'd like to have a command." About half an hour later he called back and said, "You're slated to go down to Australia in command of a submarine squadron." I'd been a submarine division commander.

I said, "Not I, sit there on the beach and tell the other boys to go out close until you can see the white of their eyes and then shoot, not I. I want to go somewhere where I'll see some of this action." So he said, "We can give you an amphibious command." I said, "That will be fine. You pick out the biggest amphibious ship that you can give me and I'll take it."

I went up and saw Admiral Edwards. He was an old submariner. I told him what I had done. I felt a certain tinge of remorse, let us say. He said, "You just relax. In the first place, you haven't got Ernie's word that you can leave yet, have you?" I said, "No, he's signed the note. I'm eligible." He said, "You just relax. I'll look around." So I relaxed, a little uncomfortably.

Four of five days later, in walked Captain Conolly. He

was still a Captain. He said, "I'm about to be promoted to flag rank and go over to the Mediterranean."

By that time, the background for the invasion of Sicily was starting to form up in the plans division.

He said, "We're going to do the invasion of Sicily. Wouldn't you like to go along as my Chief of Staff?" I said, "Nothing would please me more." So, I went along as his Chief of Staff.

Q: You had no trouble being sprung from COMINCH?

Dyer: Oh, yes. Dickie Edwards had smoothed the way on that.

They told me I had to get in a relief. I had to get somebody that was qualified in this and somebody that qualified in that.

Q: You had to get a second George Dyer.

Dyer: Ended up by four people, four people took part of my job.

The primary one was officer by the name of Smith-Hutton. He was a Japanese language student, a very astute individual. He was a prisoner of war and he was coming back on the first prisoner of war exchange ship. So, he was bound to be available. He didn't have to be sprung out of any place in order to get a relief, so he was ideal. I suggested him to Admiral

Charles M. Cooke who had relieved Admiral Turner by that time. He was acceptable to him. The Chief of Staff accepted him, and Commander Smith-Hutton came in and took over.

Then they said I had to get somebody to handle the security features of the job. I got Captain H. Ray Thurber in my class, who came in from Admiral Halsey's staff. (He died just within the last year and a half.)

Captain T. T. Patterson came in and relieved me of the handling of the various Japanese language decodes and that sort of thing.

That's a rather interesting background story; it's just a story. When I was in the USS L-10, I was a junior Lieutenant, T. T. Patterson was a senior Lieutenant. He was my executive officer. It was one of the most embarassing circumstances that I ever operated in. He was a new graduate from the submarine school, not qualified for command. As soon as he became qualified for command, he was slated to relieve me. During the two or three months before he was qualified, I was in an embarrassing circumstance of having an officer who was not only senior to me, but was a rank senior to me, as my executive officer.

Q: Pretty hard to ignore that, isn't it?

Dyer: Terribly, it's a very difficult situation.

I went over to North Africa. I flew over with Admiral Hewitt and Admiral Conolly.

Q: Had you known Conolly?

Dyer: I had never known him at all on a personal basis. He was in the planning staff and had the Atlantic planning division of Admiral Turner's planning and Admiral Cooke's planning staff. I was on the planning staff. I was in the Pacific section and he was in the Atlantic section. So I didn't get to know him well.

He had been in the Fleet at the same time I was. He was in command of a destroyer squadron when we went down and made that dummy raid on the Marshalls right after the start of the war. Then he'd come into the COMINCH planning division.

He was a very wonderful person; I just admired him beyond all means. He was very astute, not at all loquacious. In fact, it was very difficult sometimes to get a statement of his thinking. He had the ability to express himself extremely well on paper or verbally, but he was difficult to get started. When he got started, he did extremely well.

I was delighted. We had a very wonderful time together, as far as I was concerned. I think he did a wonderful job for the Navy. He ended up as Commander Naval Forces, Europe;

a four star job, which he held for about four years.

He went into education after he retired from the Navy, as a four star admiral. He was President of the University of Long Island when he was in a plane accident and he and his wife were killed.

We went over to North Africa in February 1943. Our immediate task was to establish seven amphibious bases and to train Army troops amphibiously for the invasion of Sicily. The base furthest to the west was at Port Lyautey. Then we went across North Africa to Nemours and Beni-Saf. Then we went on to the east where we established bases at Oran, Arzeu, Mostaganem and Cherchel. The last base to the east was at Tenes.

Q: Was Bone also one of them?

Dyer: Bone was a British base.

I'll get a map and point them all out to you--Cherchel was a very small town with a very small harbor.

Q: Your main base was Arzeu?

Dyer: Arzeu, that was the headquarters. The Mostaganem to the eastward, then Tenes, Beni-Saf to the westward, then Nemours, and Port Lyautey. Then later on Bizerte and Tunis, when we captured that area, and Cherchel.

We set up these bases. The first LCILs that the United States Navy had ever had came across the Atlantic in a flotilla, 21 of them, under the command of Captain Lorenzo Sabin. He became a Vice Admiral; a thoroughly capable naval officer. The LCILs arrived in Arzew in time to participate in the Invasion of Sicily. We had a lot of LCTs and LSTs in LANCRAB-NAW, Admiral Conolly's command.

Just outside of Mostaganem was the Army amphibious base. At the time when we went into North Africa, (40 miles east of Oran), the Army had amphibious brigades. There was a great conflict of interest between the Army and the Navy over the amphibious task assignments and training procedures. A great deal of dispute had been going on during the first year of the war over who would do just what in amphibious warfare.

The Army made a proposal which was that the Army would handle all the amphibious warfare in the Atlantic-Mediterranean area, and the Navy would handle all the amphibious warfare in the Pacific area. That proposal had many things to recommend it. The primary factor in it's favor was that the Navy, being under very tight reign personnel-wise and having a tremendous need to have personnel to man anti-submarine craft, was not well positioned to provide adequate personnel to cover necessary recruit training allocations which could then be given proper technical amphibious training and then fed into amphibious type ships. Amphibious type ships (transports) are very expensive in personnel, due to the large number of small boats, and their individual boat handling davits.

Admiral King was reluctant for the Navy to take responsibility for what he would admit perfectly frankly was a seagoing capability which the Navy ought to have. We just didn't have the trained personnel to take responsibility for all Amphibious operations in both oceans. The Army wanted to take a share of the responsibility. So Admiral Kings thinking was, why not let the Army take it, and let the Army suffer all the penalities therefrom.

There were those at the lower echelon who battled this premise very strongly. Amphibious ships and craft and boats were a seagoing way of waging war, and therefore, amphibious warfare should belong to the Navy, period. That was my philosophy.

When we arrived in North Africa, in early 1943, it was still General O'Daniel of the Army who was head of the Army's amphibious contingent at Mostaganem and his command with which we did a tremendous amount of Joint training.

Along about April, maybe later, out came an order signed by Admiral King and signed by General McNarmey for the Army in which the Navy was to take over all the amphibious craft and all amphibious training. With the result that General O'Daniel, before we did the Invasion of Sicily, started the turnover of amphibious craft to the Navy in that area.

We had a rather amusing thing happen in connection with General O'Daniel. I was on a routine base inspection. The Admiral used to send me about once a month or every six weeks, to take a look at all these bases just to see how they were coming along. I'd gone over to Mostaganem. As I arrived, the Commanding Officer was extremely nervous. I hadn't been there more than about three minutes when he said, "Captain, I've got something I've got to tell you. Somebody has stolen General O'Daniel's sedan. There's a certain amount of evidence that points to the fact that it was the Navy that stole the sedan. I have conducted an inspection of this base and I can assure you that it's not in this base. Without going into all the details, the Army thinks very much that the Navy has stolen this sedan."

I said, "I'm here to conduct an inspection of the base, not to look for a stolen sedan. But, I'm glad you told me, and I'll take a look around." We had taken over a number of warehouses from the French for this amphibious base. We had also erected a number of quonset huts for a number of various purposes. The quonset huts were fairly easy to inspect; you couldn't hide a sedan in them very easily.

We went into one of these warehouses and opened the doors. There was some gear along the sides of the warehouse. I looked toward the far end and it just looked to me as if there might be something down there. I don't know what propelled me, but I walked down towards the far end. I kept walking and as I got closer I realized that a big piece of canvas had been dropped at the far end. It had been painted to look like the end of the building. When we looked behind the canvas, there was the sedan. It had already been painted grey from Army olive drab.

Of course, I had to go up and see General O'Daniel and he was just fighting mad. We had to scrape the darn thing down, and I'm sure the Amphibious Base, Mostaganem never painted it as well as it was painted before.

Q: Who was using it?

Dyer: It had been stolen by a junior grade doctor and a pharmacists mate. We shipped them back to the States.

Our officers and men who came over here to build these amphibious bases; my heart went out to them. The Bureau of Naval Personnel had ordered a lot of naval reservists who, by and large, had had pre-World War II training in the Naval Reserve. The Commanding Officers in their mid-thirties, some I guess as old as 40, who held the rank of senior Lieutenant.

They knew something about the Navy. They were put on supply ships and transports and sent over to North Africa and told they were to have base duty. There were various trained groups within the small task unit that was assigned to each one of these seven bases. When they arrived in Africa they didn't know where in North Africa they were going to go; they only had the code name of their base. They didn't have the decipherment of the code name. With the result that the Tenes people didn't know they were going to Tenes; those going to Beni-Saf didn't know they were going to Beni-Saf. They didn't know anything, except they were going to a place somewhere, where they were to establish an amphibious base. They didn't have any large amount of base gear with them. They didn't even have enough cooking equipment so they could take care of their people and feed their people with their own equipment.

These task units were moving into French-Algerian towns where we had sequestered property along the beach areas. They were under orders to establish amphibious bases. I think if ever American ingenuity, basic human resourses and initiative were called upon, they were called upon from these small groups. These amphibious base unit groups ran anywhere from 40 to 140 people depending on the size of the harbor where the base was to be established. They were called upon to work day and night and to get along with the citizens whose facilities they were using. They did a tremendous job.

Right after the base units arrived, and before they were ever ready to carry out an amphibious training program, the amphibious craft started to arrive and were allocated to the bases, depending on the size of the harbors. We were pressing very hard, because the Invasion of Sicily was mid July, and the days were going by very rapidly. The base units didn't arrive until late April or early May. They had to establish the bases, carry out the training, get ready for an invasion. They did just a tremendous job. They worked with very little, and they did very well.

We established the bases. About every three weeks, I'd drive my own jeep to all the bases and provide encouragement and ideas and such help as the Headquarters Base could provide. With nobody else, off I'd go. I'd charge down and they wouldn't know I was coming. I'd drive in and say, "Here I am, I want to take a look around."

As we drew closer to the deadline for the invasion of Sicily, of course the Army completed the defeat of the Germans in North Africa, and we moved into Bizerte and into Tunis establishing bases there. We moved our headquarters from Arzew to Bizerte. When we moved, we moved just the operational part of the staff. The mere physical problem of moving our equipment and all of our gear by jeep dictated that decision as well as the problem of space allocation to Admiral Conolly in the Bizerte base areas.

Q: Were the French facilities at Bizerte of any use to you?

Dyer: Yes, we took over a share of the French facilities. They were extremely useful. Of course, the Bay of Bizerte was very large and very helpful. The Germans had blocked the entrance to Bizerte by blowing up ships and craft. It was a major diving operation before we could open the channel up and get ships into use that Bay. The Germans did a tremendous job of closing off the Bay of Bizerte, which is a large body of water about fifty square miles.

After we got into the Bay of Bizerte and were getting ready for the invasion of Sicily, the Germans came over regularly every other night--not every night--and bombed us. Of course, the amphibious craft were extremely exposed. Right across the Bay of Bizerte from where our Headquarters were, there were oil docks. We had not been up in Bizerte too long before the Germans got some hits on the oil docks and set some of the oil tanks aflame.

One particular night when the flames were very bad, Admiral Conolly sent me, (I was a graduate of the firefighting school and was supposed to know everything about firefighting) over to fight this fire with the firefighting crew from the Flag ship, the converted seaplane tender BISCAYNE. We had one firefighting ship in Admiral Conolly's command to which we added the BISCAYNES fire fighters and proceeded over to the fuel oil dock and put out this very tremendous oil fire. I'd never seen anything like it in my life, and never had anything to do with so intense a fire real close before. Anyhow, we put the darn thing out. From then on, whenever they had a fire, the Admiral would send me to fight the fire.

Q: That was one of your other talents.

Dyer: One of my problems.

Eventually we got ready for the Invasion of Sicily and off we went.

Q: Would you tell me first just a little bit about the work of the salvage people?

Dyer: The first amphibiously oriented problem that arose when you landed on a foreign shore concerned salvage, despite that your efforts had been to learn all you could about the beach gradients in the underwater area and the obstructions off the landing beaches. It never quite worked out a hundred percent..

The degree of skill of the coxswains of the landing craft always varies widely and some of them are not particularly skillful. You ended up with broached landing craft. In other words, they are supposed to land at an angle of 90 degrees from the beach, and they are supposed to get rid of their cargo or their men or whatever it may be, and then back off the beach and go back to their ships and get another load.

It is very difficult in any kind of weather at all to hold small landing craft perpendicular to the beach. In the first place it is difficult to make a landing on a directly perpendicular course to the beach. Then it is difficult to hold the craft perpendicular to the beach as the waves strike the stern. You're held forward by the fact that you're aground. In any kind of swell, and in case of delays, it is difficult to unload without getting broached.

If you broach, in others words you get sideways to the beach, then the salvage craft are the ones who try to pull you off. By and large the salvage craft have no major difficulty with getting off small landing craft, by that I mean LCVPs or LCMs, unless they are very badly damaged when they're beaching or broaching. But once you move up into the LCT or the LCIL or the LST class of craft and get them broached, many times your salvage craft just does not have enough horsepower to pull the craft back into the deeper water.

The first salvage craft that had been made available at the beaches at the time of the initial assault landing was at Sicily. The Navy did not have them at the initial landing in North Africa. The need was so great there that it was determined that thereafter there would always be salvage craft participating in the landing operation.

We started out by having just one salvage craft to each task unit landing area. In other words, for Sicily we had three landing areas and we had three salvage craft. From Sicily, we learned we had to have more than one craft for each beach.

So eventually they set up each amphibious task force so it would have normally six craft. Three for each task unit and three more to supplement that would go from beach area to beach area. In other words, you'd have one salvage craft regularly assigned to each landing beach that would work there all the time. Then you'd have sort of a support force to move about to the beach area where the greatest problems were, or where the heaviest ships were or wherever it was you had craft to salvage.

That was the first of any real use of salvage craft.

Q: Also in clearing a harbor like Bizerte that the Germans had done a job on.

Dyer: That was more difficult, and was not salvage in the sense of amphibious beach salvage. That was a real ship or channel clearance salvage job in the larger sense of the word salvage. It called for a great deal of diving.

What they did at Bizerte was along the following lines. They thought initially in clearing the Bizerte Channel to Lake Bizerte that they would be able to restore buoyancy to the ships which were sunk and blocking the channel entrance and thus remove the ships. They eventually decided that the only thing that they could do was to blow the ships and craft apart and just reduce them to nothingness. It was a gradually flattening out process. This is how they did it.

They started with divers right down at the bottom craft, and placed detonating charges and flattened out the bottom craft. Then they flattened out the next one up and so on until they got to top craft. Eventually they got 30 feet draft ships going into Lake Bizerte.

But they did not make the ship or craft which were blocking the channel seaworthy, and thus get them out of the harbor. I don't know what they did eventually. They may have eventually just hauled away the mess. While I was there, all they did was flatten them out.

The Bizerte type Channel salvage operation was not what I was talking about previously. I was talking about salvage of amphibious craft stranded on a landing beach.

There are two or three stories about the invasion of Sicily which I might relate. In the first place we had extremely bad weather. When we moved over towards Sicily the weather deteriorated instead of improving and the seas got rougher. We had great difficulty in maintaining our speed of advance. The small amphibious craft just simply could not stand steaming full speed into that kind of sea. So that we were more than a little bit late getting into position, but we did make the landing.

As you perhaps know, we captured the Italian General in his bed. I don't remember his name anymore.

The landing was made on a night when the moon was supposed to set at roughly 1:30. The landing was supposed to take place roughly at 2:30.

This General, when he was interrogated after being captured as a prisoner, said he went out and looked at the sea roughter than all harry. He looked at the very bright moon and he said, "The yankees wouldn't be such damn fools as to make a landing tonight." And he went back and went to bed.

Q: But he expected the landing?

Dyer: He'd been alerted to the fact that the amphibious craft had sailed from Bizerte. That had been detected by the reconnaissance planes and been reported to him--that we had cleared out of the harbor. We had hundreds of craft there and nearly all of them had gone. The General took a look-see and he made his decision. The amphibious did land, and they did capture him.

One other story to tell--General Patton was the Seventh Army Commander in Sicily. General Truscott commanded the Third Division.

After our Navy and the British Navy had established the Army on the Sicilian shore, not only our Licata (Joss) landing but the other two landings (Dime and Cent) had all established their troops on shore, by then Admiral Hewitt designated Admiral Conolly, who was the junior amphibious commander, to stay and support the Army. We had to support the Army, not only logistically, but we had to support it with gun fire support.

They turned over some cruisers--the PHILADELPHIA and the BROOKLYN--and a number of destroyers and other craft to provide gunfire support.

Twice a day, I would go ashore and go to Seventh Army headquarters as it moved along the beach. They moved westward first, and then northward, and then eastward. I arranged for the fire support for the next twelve hours. In other words I'd go ashore in the late afternoon, arrange the fire support from 8 PM at night until 8 AM the following morning. Then I would go ashore early in the morning, and arrange the fire support from 8 AM in the morning until 8 PM at night.

Q: Against what opposition were you?

Dyer: The answer to that was there was a small amount of Italian defense installations. But primarily their defense was mobile. They had tanks and they had artillery and so forth. These would be located by our reconnaissance aircraft. The Army always wanted to have their advance prepared before they moved into an area. We would prepare that advance.

I had been doing that for three or four days when General Patton said, "Why don't you get your boss and come ashore and have dinner with me tonight?" I said, "I'm sure he'd be very happy to. Where will you be?" He said, "I don't know where I'll be. His headquarters was moving to keep reasonably close to the battle front all the time. But he said, "I'll have a jeep with driver on Red One (or whatever beach it was). You come ashore and the jeep will take you to where I am."

So we came ashore, from the BISCAYNE, got into the jeep, and off we went. We went along to the westward, a modest distance and came into a small Sicilian town. The jeep pulled up to a middle sized Italian house. We went up to the door, rang the bell and the Aide-de-Camp met us. He said, "The General's upstairs taking a bath, will you please go in the parlor and wait for him?" So we went into the parlor and sat down.

There was a pile of magazines in a magazine rack.

So I picked out one. It was ITALIA, which is like our LIFE magazine, except I hope it's better. It's on the same general pictorial order. I opened this ITALIA and there was a large center spread picture and I was one of the dozen or so naval officers.

The picture was of the relief of command ceremony on the USS Pennsylvania on 1 February 1940, when Admiral H. E. Kimmel relieved Admiral J. O. Richardson as Commander in Chief of the Pacific Fleet. I was on Richardson's staff.

This house that General Patton was in was one that the Army had sequestered on a temporary basis. It had a reasonable amount of facilities. We had a very pleasant dinner, and then the jeep drove Admiral Conolly and me back to our beach where we went back on board the BISCAYNE, the flagship.

General Patton, at that time, wore two wrist watches and carried two pearl handled guns. I thought he was just wonderful because he had an excellent knowledge of everything relating to use of our amphibious resources to facilitate the battle for Sicily that was then taking place. He had no trouble at all making up his mind.

At that stage of the war, General Patton was one of the few Army officers who really understood naval gunfire-- it's capabilities as well as it's limitations. The gunfire support that he proposed that we provide, we generally could do. In other words, he didn't propose impossibilities.

On the other hand, he called upon our gunfire support,

or our amphibious capabilities many times when the other Army commanders wouldn't have been willing to use us because they wouldn't have had the confidence in naval gunfire being able to do these things. He made quite an impression on me, at that stage of the war.

Q: He was a rather arbitrary person, wasn't he?

Dyer: I certainly believe he could have been quite arbitrary. But he was never arbitrary, as far as I was concerned.

The few times when my judgment indicated we should be providing gunfire or amphibious support and weren't called upon, he would say, "That's just fine, if you can do that, you do it."

On the other hand, there were times when I said, "I don't think that we can do that in the way that you would like to have it done." He'd say, "If you can't do it, all right."

He was wonderful, as far as my particular function at that time, which was to arrange the gunfire and amphibious (LCT, LCIL, LST) support. We did what he wanted us to do, I'd say 95 percent of what he originally asked for. Then we added enough of what he hadn't asked for, so that it made a little bit more than 100 percent.

Q: How did his troops seem to react to him?

Dyer: They were very fond of him. He had many of the same

approaches to his troops as Admiral Bill Halsey had to sailor men. As Admiral Nimitz said to me: "Admiral Halsey is a sailor's Admiral." General Patton was a soldier's General in my opinion.

Vice Admiral George C. Dyer, USN, Ret.   by John T. Mason, Jr.
Annapolis, Maryland   April 15, 1970

Mr. Mason: Admiral, I think you have a preface to your story of the invasion of Sicily, and you want to make that at this point.

Admiral Dyer: I thought it would be sort of desirable to give a little of the background of the HUSKY operation.

At the Casablanca conference in mid-January, 1943, HUSKY, which was the invasion of Sicily, was given a green light. It was a direct result of this decision that Captain Richard F. Conolly became a Flag officer, and I received the opportunity to become his Chief of Staff. We were both in the plans division of COMINCH headquarters.

At that time the planners in the Army high command in Washington were still yearning for a cross channel operation, and not too much interested in an operation in the Mediterranean. On the other hand, planners in the Navy high command were yearning for more operations in the South Pacific and not too much interested in operations in the Mediterranean. So actually the HUSKY operation was sort of a step child, insofar as the real desires of the military planning staffs in the headquarters in Washington.

Q: Was it primarily Churchill who was interested in the Mediterranean?

Dyer: Very much so. He was primarily interested. There were a number of political considerations that dictated our going along, in other words, supporting Mediterranean operations.

The Navy had had a terrible time finishing up Guadalcanal. And the Japs didn't start to leave Guadalcanal Island until January-February 1943, about the time that the Casablanca conference was finishing up. The Japs finally (7-8 February 1943) high-tailed it out of Guadalcanal, and the Navy began to think that they could spare some resources for further operations in the Mediterranean.

When Admiral Conolly and I arrived over in North Africa, which was in early March of 1943, the HUSKY operation was scheduled to begin on the 25th of July 1943. Actually it occurred some two weeks earlier than that. The various commands were under tremendous pressure from Washington all during this period, between February and July, to anticipate initially the July 25th landing date and later the July 10th landing date which was set on April 13, 1943.

Q: And the reason for stepping it up was what?

Dyer: The reason for stepping it up was to make possible an earlier invasion of Italy, because there were many military officers then who believed that Italy would collapse under the weight of an invasion. Actually, that's just what it did.

Everybody agreed that an invasion of Italy couldn't

be done until after we had seized the airfields of Sicily to use to provide air cover and some measure of close air support for the amphibious landing. The sooner we could take Sicily the earlier we could get into Italy and presumably bring about the collapse of the Italian government.

One story I'd like to tell--When we flew into Port Lyautey in February 1943, it was as usual "raining in North Africa." We arrived in a seaplane, landed in the water of course (the Wadi Sebon). The Navy picked us up by boat, transferred us to a jeep and took us out to the land plane field. When Admiral Conolly and I and a couple of the other members of the staff went over towards the plane that was going to fly us to Oran, a young Second Lieutenant Army Air Force aviator was standing there beside the plane. He was one of the youngest looking aviators that I had ever seen. When Admiral Conolly stepped forward and the pilot was introduced to him, Admiral Conolly looked at him and said, "Have you got your father with you?"

Q: A rather devastating remark.

Dyer: A devastating remark, but it certainly was well justified.

One other thing I'd like to say. During the early period after we arrived over in North Africa, the relations between the Vichy French and the Free French had not all been smoothed out. They were continually having small clashes between, what perhaps could be called, extremists of both sides. Additionally the Vichy French were not happy with the Americans. You never knew when you'd go through one of these small Algerian towns in a jeep, as I did literally hundreds of times, whether one of the extremists was going to take a pot shot at you. They did this from time to time. The Vichy French still objected to the Americans being in North Africa.

I was reminded of this roughly two weeks ago. My good wife and I flew out to Louisville, in connection with the Military Order of the World Wars. The chap who met us took us to his new home. His new home, which was a lovely thing, was called "Constantine." This was based on the city of Constantine in eastern Algeria, where he had been stationed during the period following the North African invasion. This home had a lot of resemblance, particularly in the outside architecture to numerous country homes in the Constantine area. Here it was nearly 30 years since he had been in Constantine, and it still had a real effect on what this volunteer soldier was thinking about in Louisville, Kentucky.

Q: General de Gaulle had come to North Africa, had he not?

Dyer: Yes. I'll tell you my one story about General de Gaulle right now. This is not at all sequential, because this happened sometime after we got into North Africa.

When we arrived over there and started putting together these amphibious bases, we were extremely short of transportation, in other words, jeeps and trucks. While we had promises of a great many coming from the United States, at hand we had very, very few. There was a tremendous need for both jeeps and trucks. Roughly 2 to 2½ months after we'd arrived over there, the shortage was terribly binding. All we had was word that some of the shipments had actually been made but the ships were not due for 3 or 4 weeks.

As we flew into Algiers to a conference which Admiral Conolly was to have with Admiral Hewitt, there were great big fields of parked jeeps and parked trucks. So I said to Admiral Conolly as a matter of conversation, "Gee, wouldn't it be wonderful if we could get some of those?" He said, "Go get them."

When we arrived and talked with some of the people on Admiral Hewitt's staff, I asked to whom did these trucks and jeeps belong and so forth, I found out that they belonged to the Free French, and that the Free French units to which they were later to be assigned, the divisions, were just forming up. In other words, the Free French were getting their people together. One thing that the French had to do, due to the fact that every Frenchman didn't drive an automobile, was have drivers' schools, in order to teach the people to drive and operate these trucks and jeeps.

I said, "We've got invoices indicating that some of our trucks and some of our jeeps have actually been loaded on board ships scheduled for North Africa. When the convoys are formed up it will be three weeks or a month and we will have some trucks and jeeps of our own. But these trucks and jeeps sitting out in these fields would be tremendously useful if we could get them tomorrow morning. Then we could pay the Free French back when ours arrive." That seemed to me like a logical thing to do. There were literally thousands, and our needs were in the hundreds. What we wanted was just a very small piece of the pie.

I processed the matter up through Rear Admiral Spencer Lewis who was Admiral Hewitt's Chief of Staff. Admiral Lewis said, "Fine, they're French and we'll have to go to the Free French. I will talk with General de Gaulle's Chief of Staff and see what we can do." And so he did.

He told me, "General de Gaulle requires that no piece of equipment of that kind get away from the possession of the Free French without his personal permission. I set up an appointment for you at 1:15 this afternoon to go over there and talk with the Free French staff and possibly with General de Gaulle.

So I went over. I had written out what I was to say and I had an interpreter from Admiral Hewitt's staff who translated it into French. I would sound off in English and say what I wanted to say (about one paragraph long) and then the Lieutenant Commander, who was the interpreter, sounded off in French. We processed this up through the Chief of Staff and then into General de Gaulle's office.

We came in and General de Gaulle was at his desk. The aide came in and announced who we were. He never looked up, never paid any attention to us. We stood there, and we stood there, and we stood there. Finally, the aide shuffled around two or three times trying to make a little noise so that the great man would again look up. Eventually this happened.

He said, "What is it?" So I sounded off in English and then the interpreter sounded off in French. When our words had been spoken, he said, "No." He looked down at his desk and that was all. We shuffled out. He never deigned to say why, or why it wasn't, a good proposition.

Q: Or even admit that you were a human being.

Dyer: That was my one interview with General de Gaulle during World War II.

Q: How did that leave you?

Dyer: Every time I flew over these jeeps and trucks afterwards, I used to have some uncomplimentary remarks to make.

Q: So you never did latch on to the materiel?

Dyer: No.

Another thing that I should say is that the amphibious ships and Navy craft that were under Admiral Conolly's command were assigned to work with and transport to Sicily the Third Infantry Division, Major General Lucien K. Truscott.

When we arrived over in Africa, there was no finished plan for the invasion of Sicily. There were two schools of thought.

One school of thought was that we should seize ports where we could discharge the logistic support directly into the ports. In the western part of the northern coast of Sicily is the wonderful port of Palermo and in the middle on the east coast of Sicily are Augusta, Syracuse and Catania. The British were slated to do their landings south of Augusta and Syracuse around Pachino Peninsula at the southeastern corner of Sicily. The British right flank was 30-40 miles south of Catania. There was much pressure, particularly I think from the naval part of the high echelon planning staffs over there (British-American) for the United States troops to land in Palermo. The initial plan was so drawn up. That was shortly after we arrived over there.

Q: Was the intention to have just enclaves, just ports, and not go into the interior?

Dyer: Oh no. The idea was to take the ports and then for the Armies to move towards each other and squeeze out the Germans in between. Also the British planned to sweep up the east coast to Messina so the Army could move over into Italy rather easily.

This was batted around. At the Amphibious planning level (the echelon above Admiral Conolly) they developed plans of their own, and so forth. About late April or early May, the landing in the interval had been advanced to the 10th of July, at some planning echelon, it was decided that all the United States troops were going to be landed on the southeast coast of Sicily. This meant that our Navy would have to support the Army over the beaches, a much more difficult amphibious chore, supporting it from alongside a dock.

The Third Division was given the Western area of the operations, so far as the United States Army forces were concerned. It's much easier to provide support from LCT and LST type landing craft over the beaches, than it is to provide support from cargo ships. The big United States ship force (transports and cargo ships) under Admiral J. L. Hall and Admiral A. G. Kirk, were scheduled to land their troops at Gela and Scoglitti. These were not ports but open beach areas with a wharf extending several hundred feet out to sea, but a little less attractive than the minuscule artificial port of Licata, which was our port. Licata, as a landing port, was just nothing at all. It was a small fishing village with one dock for coastal craft but without real dockside (shoreside) facilities. We were able to put an LST alongside the dock, but not a Liberty ship.

We worked closely with General Truscott, Commanding General of the Third Division. He was, I thought, a very wonderful leader and it really was a pleasure to work with him and with his staff.

We were sort of sorry to see the Palermo port go into

the ash can.

I've got one other story that I want to tell and that is--During this pre-invasion period, Lord Louis Mountbatten came down to our Headquarters from London. At that time, he was the senior British naval officer in their amphibious warfare operational section of the Admiralty. In the British Navy, amphibious warfare was called "Combined Operations" and Vice Admiral Lord Louis Mountbatten was Chief of Combined Operations. We had just finished developing our first plan for landing in Licata.

I had written the plan, based on my complete lack of practical knowledge of amphibious operations. I had never participated in an amphibious assault neither had any other member of our Landing Craft and Bases staff, and neither had Admiral Conolly. So we really started from scratch.

Admiral Mountbatten asked for a copy of this draft order. It was a first draft and I certainly was not too proud of it. Of course, if he wanted a copy, he got a copy.

Maybe three weeks later, when we had developed a smoother draft and one that I thought really would work, we got a dispatch asking for a copy of our plan from Admiral Sir Gerald Dickens. He was Charles Dickens' son, a retired four star Admiral in the British Navy, who had come back on active duty during World War II as a two star Admiral. He was the British naval commander at Bizerte and Tunis. We sent on to him a copy of the new plan.

About the time that we booked the Salerno invasion, and started to plan for it, Admiral Dickens, whom I saw practically daily, told me that he had a letter from Lord Louis Mountbatten. One, Lord Louis Mountbatten had turned our Licata plan over to their amphibious school with a note saying it was a model amphibious landing operation plan. And two, which perhaps was more important to me, that Lord Louis Mountbatten had recommended me for a British award. And I did get the award. The citation does say that it was a perfect example of a good assault landing plan.

Q: Admiral, the British experience had been largely in terms of commando raids, rather than an extensive full scale operation.

Dyer: That's right.

In the period before the invasion of Sicily, the German-Italian airplanes based on both Italian and Sicilian airfields used to fly over Bizerte, where we had moved from Arzeu as it got closer to the time of the actual invasion. They used to come over quite regularly, every other night. The number of planes that came over was quite considerable. I'd say the raids ran anywhere from maybe a dozen to occasionally 35 or 40 planes. They bombed by radar; they were all night raids. Some of the raids were quite accurate, and some of them were far less than accurate.

We developed, during that period, bomb shelters. They were the first bomb shelters that I had ever seen. At Arzeu we had no bomb shelters; we lived in what was a country house which was the Headquarters. But we built bomb shelters in Bizerte.

Q: Admiral, speaking about those German air bases, was not that little island of Pantellaria one of the very nuisances?

Dyer: That was captured during the period prior to the invasion back on 11 June 1943.

Q: But that was so available prior to 11 June?

Dyer: Yes. It was taken and used to provide close air support for the British landings.

In regard to your questions, and applying specifically to the landings at Licata, how helpful was our air support and how extensive was it?

You should realize that the Army Air Force was so independent of the Army and so little interested in the combat activities of the Army and the Navy, in this amphibious operation, that the orders from on high provided that requests for air support after D-Day had to be submitted 12 hours in advance to a committee located back in North Africa, where presumably they would be given consideration.

It was an impossible arrangement. And in my opinion, an indication of the arrogance of the United States Army Air Force commander in that theater of the war, Lieutenant General Carl Spaatz, U.S. Army Air Force. I believe that the actual commander of the air support command was a British officer, Air Vice Marshall, Sir Arthur Coningham, RAF. Under him was a United States XII Air Support Command who must have conceived his mission to be to avoid at all costs providing any support. Although the air support command had over 400 planes, the air support it gave was worse than pitiful. No change of moment was made as a result of this very poor showing for the Salerno operation in September.

In answer to your question--Was the enemy air force active in the area? My answer is tempered by what I personally saw happen afterwards in the Pacific, and comparing the Italian German effort with some of the real heavy action of the Japanese, for instance in the Okinawa area. So my first answer to that question is, that the enemy air action didn't compare at all.

In order to correlate my own opinion with the facts as recorded at the time, I went back to the log of the BROOKLYN. I noticed that on the first day of the invasion (this is coming out of the ship's log) during the whole day starting at 0003 when enemy aircraft were overhead of the BROOKLYN and continuing until 1822 that evening, when bombs dropped on the starboard quarter. There were roughly a half dozen air attacks in the BROOKLYN area.

Moving on to the next day, which was Sunday the 11th of July, again starting at 0226 in the morning and ending at 2247, when the log recorded planes over head, "open fire." There were about ten attacks in the BROOKLYN area.

Which indicates a reasonable amount of air activity. Of all the air attacks on those two days, however, there was only one Stuka attack. The Stuka attacks bore some resemblance to the kamikaze, not the finalist part of it, because the Stuka was always anxious to get out of there. The kamikaze was anxious to stay there. It made a lot of difference.

Nevertheless I think my second judgment, in regard to it, is that there was a fair amount of enemy air activity. I do specifically remember that they did bomb and sink an LST, and they did bomb and sink a cargo ship, during the period of the invasion insofar as what I personally saw. Undoubtedly there were other things in areas beyond my horizon.

We learned, after Italy surrendered, that a fair share of the German-Italian heavy planes based on Sicilian airfields were moved back to Italian airfields some weeks before the invasion. There were about a dozen real airfields and seaplane bases on Sicily. In addition, there was a number of small, what we would call, emergency fields. In other words, they were just cleared areas that had been smoothed out a bit. Planes could land there, but there were no airfield facilities.

Q: Were they moved back because of the vulnerability on Sicily?

Dyer: That's right.

During the period prior to the invasion, the North

African air force devoted tremendous attention to the Sicilian fields. They bombed them regularly and quite effectively.

The destruction of German and Italian planes undoubtedly was what caused the enemy to withdraw everything, except the fighters and the reconnaissance planes, to their main Italian air bases.

Q: Did Admiral Hewitt make any kind of protestation because of difficulties in enlisting Army Air Force support?

Dyer: I think he fought, bled, and died about it, but without any success whatsoever. The Army Air Force was arrogant.

They had an agreement or an arrangement with General Marshall Chief of Staff of the Army that they were to be, in effect, independent of the Army and they were to operate that way. This was a new found independence. The primary object was to maintain that independence. To fight the war, I always thought, was secondary and even tertiary. It just didn't make any sense at all.

Q: This policy then had the imprimatur of General Arnold?

Dyer: Oh, yes indeed, in fact, all the way up the line.

They had to maintain the fluidity, that was the word that they used all the time, the fluidity of the Air Force. They couldn't give any definite commitments of close air support, because they had to maintain fluidity.

Q: Actually the other side of the coin was a lack of

flexibility on their part, wasn't it?

Dyer: That's right.

In answer to your question. Where was the enemy air force based? The answer is that initially there were a goodly number based on Sicily on it's east coast. Then the bomber force retreated to the Italian mainland, and only the fighter and observation planes stayed in Sicily.

Adequate air cover for our cruisers and destroyers providing gunfire support along the north coast of Sicily, did not exist. Even when the ships did, by prior arrangements have Army Air Force planes in the vicinity, the ships had positive orders not to communicate directly with the planes. You could only communicate with the planes by going back to their base, which would pass the word to the planes. The planes had written orders, I was told. They couldn't communicate with our ships. The Army Air Force were so afraid that somebody on the spot would give an order and the pilot, seeing the need for carrying out the order, would do it. They wouldn't permit it. The Army Air Force just did not want to fight the war. They wanted to control their own aircraft to the exclusion of any sensible arrangement for coordination of fighting effort. It was just terrible.

In answer to your question - Why were no carriers or battleships used for the assault? The easy answer is that the British did provide battleships and carriers in the covering force, Force "H", which protected the invasion force on it's run from North Africa to the invasion beaches.

There were not in the British Mediterranean Fleet enough ships to provide both direct air support of the assault and proper air search and air attack from a covering force. Very logically I think, the decision was made that it was far more important to provide the safe arrival of the invasion force at Sicily and its freedom from major attack there than it was to provide direct air support of the assault.

We had support destroyers, and we had support light cruisers. One combatant ship that we had operational control over in our force was Dutch which fired 5.9 or 4.1 inch shells and would fire about 5 or 6 shells and then cease fire and signal, "I now have 166 shells left."

Q: A gunboat is something like a monitor then.

Dyer: I am not sure of the exact type of ship the Dutch ship was. There was no new supply of ammunition available in the U. S. Navy for this. We didn't make that type of a shell. The British didn't make that type of a shell. What they had was only what they'd started out with when they escaped either at the time of Dunkerque or from the Dutch East Indies. So they were very careful of the number of shells they had, and they would report them. They had hardly opened fire before they were reporting how many shells there were left, and asking permission to cease fire.

The other answer about close air support for the

Sicilian Invasion, and the easy answer, is that the United States Navy had no battleships or carriers in the Mediterranean. With Admiral King's general disinterest in the Mediterranean and the many calls of the Pacific area, and even the Atlantic area (there were Germany heavy ships still around), he wasn't about to put any carriers in the Mediterranean. The Japanese had more carriers in the Pacific Ocean than we had, even after Midway.

Q: Indeed both the U. S. Navy and the Royal Navy were stretched so thin.

Dyer: That's right, they were stretched extremely thin. I never questioned Admiral King's decision. It seemed to me, while we never had all the strength we would like, we always had enough. It was the difference between feeling that you had a comfortable over supply, which you should always have in war, we never had a comfortable supply, but we did have enough.

Q: That only came with the last stages of the Pacific war.

Dyer: That's right.

Another thing is, at that stage of the war, in the Mediterranean the Army had no great faith in naval gunfire. They didn't want any gunfire before the Sicilian landing. They were not pressing the Navy. The Navy was offering something, and they were refusing it. So you couldn't build a case for more heavy ships, when by and large, you had a product that the Army didn't want.

General Patton was the one exception in the Seventh Army that I know of, who had any faith at all in naval gunfire. He acquired a very large percentage of his faith right there in Sicily because he had some barbed criticisms to make of the naval gunfire on the northwest African coast at the initial landings. I wasn't there and I don't have any opinion in regard to their validity. In any case, in Sicily he was very good on naval gunfire.

Q: His conversion to the effectiveness of naval gunfire then carried over to the Normandy landing.

Dyer: That's right.

The Army strongly and successfully argued against a pre-landing gun bombardment of enemy held beach areas in Sicily. The Army Air Force strongly and successfully argued against being assigned the task of neutralizing the beach defenses, because they could not give of their time and energy to such mundane tasks. The Army Air Force was off in the wild blue yonder gaining control of the air, that's no fooling.

Q: What possible objection did they have to the Navy softening up the beach heads?

Dyer: The answer to that was--The Sicilian landing, insofar as the actual beaches chosen, was supposed to be a surprise landing. I don't think any senior officer thought that it would be a surprise. They hoped by not actually bombarding beaches that there would be some doubt. As a matter of fact, there was.

The Herman Goering division, which was supposed to be a crack German division, initially was up in the Palermo area, where it had been placed quite wisely because Palermo was certainly a port worth having.

In the period just prior to the invasion, I don't know just when this occurred, 5 or 10 days, they split the Herman Goering division and moved part of it eastward. It was actually down maybe at Gela or Scoglitti.

That is indicative of what the Army was trying to accomplish. They were trying to land where the enemy wasn't fully expecting them. I think to some extent that was accomplished--The Rangers that we landed at Licata captured the Italian General in his bed. At 10 o'clock the previous night, he had taken a look at the sea, rougher than all harry and the very bright moonlight. He had said, "The Americans won't be such damn fools as to land tonight," and gone back to bed. He had said this a dozen times. This wasn't something he was ashamed of, this was something he was proud of. Actually they caught him in his bed. So they were surprised.

Certainly strategically they weren't surprised. Tactically they were surprised just exactly where the landings might occur and just exactly when they might occur.

We made a big effort to get them to think we were going

to land in Sardinia. We went through all kinds of folderol to try to create that impression, including tremendous bombing of Sardinian airfields. As you know, they put a dead body out of a submarine off the Spanish coast with a message implanted on the dead body.

Q: So that the German intelligence would get it.

Dyer: And they did get it. And all that sort of thing to try to create the impression that we were going to land in Sardinia. As a matter of fact, Admiral Conolly's staff was required to make preliminary plans for landing on Sardinia. So there was a call for the necessary charts and making models of landing beaches in Sardinia.

Q: And maybe leaking some of this?

Dyer: I didn't ever hear of any leaking of it, but it could very well have been as far as I know. There was all kinds of this 'fooling the enemy' stuff going around. How really effective it was I certainly don't know.

In any case, we did not do any prior beach bombardment.

Your next question is--What role did the British play? In my opinion there's only one answer, a darn important one. They provided the Deputy Commander in Chief who was General Sir Harold Alexander, the senior Army Commander who was General Montgomery, the senior Air Force Commander who was Air Marshall Sir Arthur Tedder, and the senior Naval Commander who was Admiral Sir Andrew Cunningham. They had everything, except the top man who was General Eisenhower.

I can say quite frankly that many times I felt that the United States naval opinion was not getting through this very heavy British layer up to General Eisenhower. Whether it was or wasn't, I have no way of knowing. As a low level staff officer on the fifth level down, I used to say that whether it was true or not.

Q: Your contact, and that of your boss, must have been extensive with Sir Andrew though?

Dyer: The answer was that Admiral Conolly had quite a good deal of contact with Sir Andrew. I had quite a good deal of contact with the British Naval staff.

As a matter of fact, I learned to drink tea at that time. I didn't drink coffee before 1943 and never have since. The British no matter what was happening, at the Combined planning effort, the world could be falling apart, but when it was tea time they'd just get up and walk out of the plans room and go have tea.

The British would talk about things that didn't have too much relation to the war or anything else of great moment. That just wasn't the American naval way to do things. We used to fight the war every living moment.

Q: We do insist on our coffee breaks, nowadays.

Dyer: At that time maybe they did, but I never drank coffee. The tea breaks I always went to, and I did drink tea.

General Eisenhower was the Supreme Commander, but his influence at my level of the naval operations was not very apparent. Sir Andrew Cunningham was the Senior Naval Commander and Vice Admiral Hewitt commanded the Western Naval Task Force while Vice Admiral Ramsey of the Royal Navy, who later became head of the Admiralty, commanded the Eastern Naval Task force.

As you probably have been told before, at the invasion of Sicily more divisions were landed abreast than at any other amphibious landing in World War II. That includes Normandy and any place else that you want to think of.

The front was a hundred miles long, which is just mind joggling. There were seven infantry divisions plus parts of a couple of airborne divisions in the initial assault. All together, 13 divisions and a brigade landed on the 100 miles front.

If anything indicates that the British played the major role, the fact that the British logistic support was to be provided through ports and the American logistic support was to be provided over open beaches indicates who was in the driver's seat. The British assault landings took four divisions and a brigade. The American assault landing was three divisions, of which Admiral Conolly landed the Third Division on the left flank of the Sicilian assault landing.

To wind up the answer, I should point out that the British objectives were the essential ones in the conquest of Sicily. Their objectives were Augusta which is a big city, Catania which is a big city and Messina. Those were their three objectives.

Q: Admiral, your comment on it being the most extensive beach head of any amphibious operation, one can hardly conceive of another situation where it would have been possible to have had such a broad beach head.

Dyer: That's very true without going around a few promontories. In Normandy, of course, it could have been done.

Q: But there the opposition was so much more concentrated.

Dyer: The opposition at Normandy, and I was not at Normandy, was quite a different cup of tea because the depth of the German defense against a landing anywhere.

Sicily was not defended in depth. The decision of the German-Italian command was to have defense at the beaches and then to have a mobile force, which was to be moved to the particular beaches that were being assaulted with the thought that they would throw back the landing forces at the most difficult time that the landing force had. And that is when they are half aboard ship and the other half either enroute to the beaches or on the beach.

On the other hand, the Normandy defense was a defense in depth with proper defense every few miles, so to speak. There was quite a different proposition. I'm sure that the right plan was picked out for the Sicilian assault.

I didn't have anything to do with it, except to constantly change our plans to coincide with our naval superiors' decisions. Just like cracking the whip on the ice. Admiral Conolly's command was at the end of the whip-fine layers down.

Q: The Normandy situation was a desperate kind of almost last stand by the Germans, wasn't it? On the part of the enemy?

Dyer: It was something they had been jumping up and down worrying about ever since December the 7th, 1941.

I really do not know too much about your next question. Why were we so slow in closing the Straits of Messina?

Closing Messina was a British task. They didn't close it until General Patton had marched up to Palermo, which was roughly 100 miles northwest of where he initially landed in Gela and then along the north coast of Sicily another 100 miles. General Patton was about to take the Germans and the Italians in the flank, when the main German-Italian force which was resisting the British advance along the eastern Sicilian coast, decided that the jig was up and they retreated and crossed the Straits of Messina.

One thing that I would like to mention is a purely naval judgment. It always seemed to me that the British Navy, whose responsibility was for the Straits of Messina sector, did not do a good job preventing the use of the water the enemy had to use in moving the retreating German-

Italian troops from Sicily into the toe of Italy. There was a splendid opportunity. There was no question about the general period when the retreat over the Straits of Messina was going to happen. Once the decision to abandon Sicily was taken, the evacuation was just happening as fast as it could be done, and yet the British Navy did not break it up.

Q: Exodus certainly could have been anticipated.

Dyer: Yes.

Q: This again, I suppose, was part because they didn't have the ships.

Dyer: I do not know the answer in any detail whatsoever. But I've always thought that there was a marvelous opportunity to have accomplished what was accomplished down in North Africa, when we captured 300,000 prisoners. It would have made a tremendous effect on the war if we had captured everybody, all the Germans and Italians that were in Sicily.

Q: It would have made Naples that much easier.

Dyer: Yes, but we didn't do it.

About two weeks after the initial invasion, I don't remember the exact date, Admiral Conolly who had been responsible for the gunfire support and amphibious support of General Patton's Army was relieved by Admiral Lyal A.

Davidson. The reason assigned in the dispatch was that Admiral Conolly had a task force to command in the next amphibious landing operation, and Admiral Davidson did not. And that planning for the operation must be started.

So we went back in the Biscayne to Bizerte and threw the staff into high gear for the invasion of Salerno, which was two months later. We invaded Italy on the 17th of September.

I later saw and talked with some of the officers who were on Admiral Davidson's staff. Admiral Davidson did not say this to me at all but some of the officers on his staff said that when they were providing this gunfire support along the northern coast of Sicily and providing some of our LSTs and LCTs to transport troops to get behind the Germans and the Italians who were retreating along that north coast, that a number of times they proposed, based on the seagoing aspects, in other words having the proper beaches to put troops ashore, to make longer leap frog movements than General Patton was willing to undertake.

These officers thought that the German-Italian retreat would have gone a lot faster, if we had made longer leap frogs behind the enemy. And got behind them a greater distance. In other words, we just denied them four or five miles by landing four or five miles behind their line. While if we had gone 15 or 20, that would have been a much more worthwhile operation. There were a number of factors in this, and I'm only pointing out the naval factor.

The Germans and Italians did retreat and did get back on the mainland.

Q: Admiral, I would guess that it was a proper and wise utilization of talent and experience that you were withdrawn to Bizerte for planning the Salerno operation. You'd had experience then.

Dyer: We really did, and we had our first assault landing. We got into the second one with a lot of zest.

Q: Wouldn't you make that a part of the estimate for that reason?

Dyer: Oh, yes.

In answer to your question--Did we use our forces in Sicily with imagination? I can say that in the days before the final assault plan for Sicily was agreed upon and promulgated, I thought that the enemy troops could be defeated earlier by landing the troops from the Western Task Force at Palermo and driving eastward. Since Palermo was a first class port, the logistic support operations would have been much easier. In other words the actual time consumed, the hours that it takes to get a load of equipment, guns, ammunition ashore, when you can put a ship alongside a dock and use cranes, either cranes that you carry yourself and put on the dock or cranes that are already on the dock, is just infinitesimal compared with the time it takes to put the same amount of logistic support directly from a cargo ship or from an LCT or an LST. I was always a Palermo advocate.

Another thing that I thought was if you landed your main troop force at Palermo and drove eastward and the British landed at Catania, that you would at all times have the Germans and Italians looking over their shoulders to see who the other fellow was coming up on their rear. It seemed to me that they would have been a lot less secure with a force approaching them from two different directions. Of course, that's what eventually broke their back and why they went back to Italy. Under the initial flow, we would have had a lot more prisoners of war.

It took some days, it took two weeks or more before we got up into Palermo. We gave them plenty of notice, with the result that they destroyed the port. We had to rehabilitate the port and that took time.

Q: Indeed it did, that was a mess.

Dyer: While if we had moved into Palermo initially, we would have salvaged some of the things that they wouldn't have been able to destroy during the period of the initial attack. That's the one more thing that I would question.

The final decision, in fact the major decision always must be an Army decision. The Army makes the decision where they wanted to land all the way along. Where they finally wished to land was a practicality for the Navy and so we did it.

I'm just giving a Navy kibitz on what was really an

Army problem. For that reason, I don't particularly value it, I just say it was my opinion. I never felt I was really qualified to express an Army opinion, although I did so at the time in our own staff.

Now in regard to the question as to the extent of the mining operations. There was a mine protected Tunsian war channel along the Tunsian north coast that we used all the time. We swept it daily. I'm sure there was no great secret about it, because it was marked. I'm sure that the German submarines probably used it themselves, glad that we had a nice place that they didn't have to worry about our mines, to go back and forth.

Q: You say German submarines. Were the Italian submarines active, too?

Dyer: Yes, there were both German and Italian submarines. In the period prior to the invasion, we sank seven or eight of them that were being used agressively against our forces.

They had some successes as well. I know they sank two LSTs, both loaded, and we lost the loads. That always causes a few problems because you find out that what's in that load is extremely important for some part of the landing. I'm sure there were other loses, although I don't remember them. I just remember things that were directly related to our particular problem. The submarines were quite active, and of course we were active against them.

We had about 275 ships and craft in our JOSS Task

Force which was the name of Admiral Conolly's Task Force. The great majority were landing craft and landing ships. In other words they were LCTs, LCILs, and LSTs. Then we had some destroyers. There were a couple of cruisers, the BIRMINGHAM and the BROOKLYN, and this Dutch ship, I mentioned previously.

The LCTs had never been to sea and outside of the sight of land before, because they were brought over piggy back from the United States on the LSTs and launched over there in Northwest Africa. These LCTs had an Officer in Charge, they didn't have a Commanding Officer. The Officer in Charge was an Ensign recently commissioned in the Naval Reserve. He had about a dozen sailormen is his crew and just the barest of navigational facilities. And by and large there Ensigns did a wonderful job. I tip my cap to them.

The LCILs had two officers in them and the LSTs had seven officers in them. The LST officer numbers were increased before the war was over, but at that time they had seven. The officers that commanded the LSTs were by and large naval reserve officers of some considerable standing in the Naval Reserve. In other words, they had been commissioned before World War II had come along they were excellent people and did a marvelous job. But their help was about 0.0, because the officers that were serving underneath them were people who had been brought into the Naval Reserve since World War II had started. While they had had a variety of schooling, they had a very small amount of practical sea going experience.

I was amazed at what they accomplished. But the LSTs generally did have one officer on board who was a very reliable citizen and very capable and generally mature, about in his mid-thirties. He had been in the Naval Reserve for some time and knew his way around and could do things.

Here we had these 275 ships in the roadstead at Bizerta. To the eastward was the Tunisian War channel which had been swept of mines but with mined areas on either side of it. We had the need of a minimum length of time from when we shoved off from the Bizerte roadstead until when we arrived at Licata, so we had a need to push our formation through this mine guarded channel as rapidly as possible. Which meant that we had to have as broad a formation front as possible because if you had too long a column the JOSS Force would take too long to get through and turn north towards Sicily.

No matter how excellent our navigation might be on the Flagship in the center of the formation, nevertheless the landing craft in the JOSS Force did not have radar. The BISCAYNE was the only ship of our immediate formation that had radar on board. So we really had a worry problem.

We considered a number of formations. We eventually ended up with one that I think had seven columns of ships. Putting the columns a reasonable distance apart, in trying to get them all through the channel at the exact time, we worried about the ones on the flanks.

Q: Indeed yes. That was quite an armada.

Dyer: That was our first worry about mines. And those were our own mines, you understand.

The channel had been swept the day before we went through it. In fact, it was swept every day. So that we knew reasonably well that it didn't have any German mines in it.

Q: What about mine laying by aircraft?

Dyer: The Germans had some mine laying by air. I do not remember at the time that that was a worry factor.

Going back to mines, and trying to put down things that I could remember about mines during the Sicilian invasion, I came up with three things.

Rear Admiral Jimmy Hall was commander of the Ninth Amphibious Force. He was Rear Admiral Conolly's immediate senior, and he was Vice Admiral Hewitt's immediate junior. In other words, we were at the bottom of the ladder, the rungs of which Rear Admiral Conolly, then Rear Admiral Hall, then Vice Admiral Hewitt, and then Admiral Cunningham of the Royal Navy. Those were the four echelons of the United States naval command in the Mediterranean for amphibious operations insofar as the amphibious units based and training in the Mediterranean were concerned.

I was told by Admiral Hall that the mine sweepers at the head of his DIME force, which was the name of his task force which was headed for Gela, were so darn slow in the [strong, windy high-seas] mistral that he went on ahead of them in order to land General Patton on time. Actually General Patton said he did land him on time. I guess the facts of the matter are, he didn't. Steaming ahead of the mines sweepers really could have meant disaster, but the Italians very thoughtfully just didn't happen to mine the waters off of Gela, so he got in all right.

The second thing that I remember about mines in the invasion of Sicily is that Admiral Hewitt's plan called for laying an extensive mine field to the seaward of the big transports and cargo ships to protect them against enemy submarines. They laid 2300 mines in this mine field on the south coast of Sicily. This was after the invasion, to protect the ships that were unloading.

The thing that I remember most about his mine field-- It was laid by a classmate of mine whose name was Commander George F. (Egg) Mentz.-- is that about four days after the initial invasion the BROOKLYN, which was a light cruiser that gave her name to the BROOKLYN class, with Captain Tony Ziroli (He lives in Italy now,) got into our own mine field.

The ship was close enough to a mine to set it off. Then they thought they'd back out. So they started backing out and off goes another mine. They they thought they'd better lie to.

Q: And be rescued.

Dyer: They signaled for help. We sent some of our mine

sweepers in to sweep up our own mines, so we could get the BROOKLYN out.

Q: Did she get out without damage?

Dyer: With just minor damage. I read the BROOKLYN's ship's log the other day. The reason I read the ship's log is that the fact that the BROOKLYN got into our own mine field is not mentioned in Morrisons book on Sicily-Salerno-Anzio. It isn't mentioned in any book that I have read.

I thought, I wasn't in the BROOKLYN so maybe all this is a figment of my memory or imagination. So I asked the gal up at the historical section to get me the BROOKLYN's ship's log. I read the log of the initial day of the invasion. I read the next day and the next day. Pretty soon I found recorded in the ship's log that the BROOKLYN was just steaming along and all of a sudden, there was a tremendous explosion aft. The ship stopped and examined itself for damage. The First Lieutenant went over the side in a diving suit looking for damage. Following his examination a shipfitter went over. Then the BROOKLYN started to back out and another mine went off, and so they they decided to lie to and request help. It's all there in the log.

Q: What type of mines were these?

Dyer: These were our great big antenna mines. When the BROOKLYN started to back out, she put into her log that there was an antenna mine on a certain bearing and an antenna mine on another bearing. She was going right in between, but whether there was one that they didn't sight or not, another one went off. It shook up number two and number three turrets considerably. So then they worried about their magazines being blown up, and they decided to lie to.

The third thing I remember about mines was that we didn't have too many destroyers there at Sicily but two of them got into an Italian mine field. We had located several mine fields one of which was to the westward of Licata. It was at a place called Porto Empedocle. The Italians had some of their torpedo boats in this small port and when the word came about the invasion, they took to sea.

We had destroyers on the westward flank of the JOSS force. Two of the destroyers were the SWANSON and the ROWE. When they picked up these torpedo boats on their radars, they dashed off towards the torpedo boats, which was the right thing to do. But one of them, I do not remember which one it was, (Rowe) suddenly remembered that there was a mine field in that area. So she made a very sharp turn to avoid it and ran into the other destroyers (SWANSON). So we lost two of our very few destroyers, since they had to be returned to North Africa. That was really a blow.

Q: What repair facilities did we have at North Africa?

Dyer: At these amphibious bases, every one of them had the objective to develop repair facilities for landing craft.

At Oran, at Mers el Kebir, there was a French naval base. While it had been bombed and it had been shelled, by the time we invaded Sicily, they had brought in some new machines and equipment. It was in pretty good shape and was a reasonably capable repair base.

At Bizerte where in pre World War II days, the French had had a repair base, the base had been occupied by the Germans for some time in 1942. When the Germans abandoned it they demolished quite a good bit of the repair facilities. Nevertheless we had worked to restore the facilities and every day it was better than the day before. We had a reasonable amount of repair facilities there by July 1943.

So there were places for a reasonable repair job, all along the North African coast. We had nine amphibious bases eventually, extending from Nemours over near Morocco to Bizerte and Tunis on the east.

Then, of course, the British had bases at Bone and Philippville in Northeast Algeria.

One question that you did not ask about, was about the ill-fated paratroop jumps just inland of Gela. Some time during the ten days prior to our sailing from Bizerte on 8 July, an officer from Air Force command came down to brief our Headquarters about the first 82nd Airborne Division jump which was scheduled to take place early on 10 July, 1943.

In regard to the second jump, which was on the night of 11-12 July, the JOSS forces didn't get any advance word that there was to be any second jump until just before the airborne division got into our area. We just didn't get the word.

The smaller ships had 1.1 guns, which shot up quite a ways into the heavens. We had had a big German air raid a few minutes before the Army Air Force planes came over from 2150 to 2300. When this second landing group of paratroopers came over, we really gave them a warm reception.

It was terrible, when you learned afterwards that it had been our own people. Not only did they get shot down by the JOSS forces, but they were shot down from the Army anti-aircraft batteries located in the beach areas. Nobody got the word in our area. It was the height of military uncooperativeness, I would say.

The people at the high command all knew about this second flight, but they didn't realize the long hours required to get the word to our 275 ships and craft scattered all along that coastal area. To get the word to everyone of those ships, you've got to allow time. By time, I mean you ought to allow 12 hours advance notice. That kind of notice just didn't exist.

From the BISCAYNE, we saw an aircraft coming down, and by the time it got down to the water we recognized it as one of our own aircraft. We sent out a whale boat and rescued the people that were still alive in the plane and glider and brought them back on board the BISCAYNE.

Sufficient to say that the C-47s carrying this fine

group of paratroopers flew over the JOSS assault force in darkness, and shortly after a couple of enemy single plane attacks had made the anti-aircraft battery gunnerys a little trigger happy. I don't know what the actual loses were in aircraft and paratroopers from the three or four airborne operations. I think they carried out four, although I was really only conscious of three that passed over the JOSS area. I have heard it said that 20% of the planes were shot down.

The failure of the senior Army Air Force officers to properly coordinate their efforts with the Army and Navy commands, and to get the word out in detail well ahead of time, was, I think, indicative of military immaturity in a very large way. It was stupid.

Q: Did this have any repercussions in terms of morale?

Dyer: I don't know about the Army Air Force morale. But I think that the paratroopers morale justifiably could have been very low.

Q: They began to think it was a fruitless enterprise.

Dyer: Of course, in the first air operations, the people that were landed were scattered over many many miles. The talk, at the time, was that the first landing was pretty ineffective and that's why they undertook the second one. The second one got shot up and it was ineffective.

When the operation was all over and the Army people

wrote their reports, they tended to gloss over the things that had happened in connection with the paratroop attacks. They thought of all the good things that the paratroopers had done. They were, by and large, a wonderful group of young Americans. Within the capabilities of what one man could do landing in one field by himself with a gun, they did a tremendous job. I think they deserve, on that basis, great credit for what they as individuals did.

What they did as an operational unit, the command, I think is somewhat less praiseworthy. I think, again, it was caused not through any failure on the part of the paratroopers, but was a failure on the part of the air people who were supposed to take them over there a and drop them. They just didn't realize that there was somebody else in the war, and they had to take care of that aspect of it as well.

I was told that the planes in the first paratroop drop were supposed to come up over Malta, in order to get a bearing to head for Sicily. It was sort of a half way point to get a check on their navigation. Some missed Malta, so they didn't get that check. So the navigation was not all that one might have hoped for. When you're going to make a drop, you've got to know just exactly where you are. It's a pin point operation. It was a long air flight, and it just didn't work out.

I think it was probably the one thing about the Sicilian operation which the American command as a whole didn't do well.

One thing that I know happened well after the initial landing is that the enemy gave a lot of attention to bombing Palermo after we got in there. There would have been that problem had we moved in there earlier because it was a definite objective and comparatively easy to locate. Coming from Italy, the enemy aircraft would fly along the north coast of Sicily to get to Palermo. It took some real pastings.

Q: Would you say, sir, that the bombings which took place at that point at Palermo were more effective perhaps because the enemy had just left that port, just evacuated it, and they knew where all the salient points were?

Dyer: That's right, yes. I'm sure that was part of the picture.

Q: That's a very vivid picture of the HUSKY operation and also a very valuable one.

Dyer: I'll add just one more story and that is about what we called 'seascouts.' In the period prior to the invasion, we knew very little about the Sicilian beaches. We had to know something about gradients and something about the depth of water that we would try to get our larger landing craft into and what the beach exits were.

So we had a group of very wonderful young officers who went over to Sicily. We took them over in PT boats, until they got a reasonable distance from the beach and then put them into canoes. Then they made their approach to the beach and they landed. They walked around the beaches, trying to find beach exits.

The story that I want to tell relates to the fact that in the period just before the invasion, Admiral Conolly's command lost through their being captured and being killed, four very fine young men--sea scouts.

On the day of the invasion the skipper of an LST came on board the Flag ship, the BISCAYNE, and said, "I've got a problem on board. I've got a young officer, an Ensign, who has been crying ever since about an hour before ZERO hour. (Which was the time we launched the invasion.) I've had the doctor talk with him, I've talked with him and everybody's talked with him. We can't get him to stop crying. What'll I do?"

I said, "Put him in a boat and send him over here. We've got a bigger crying room in the BISCAYNE that you have, I'm sure."

This young fellow came over. By that time his face was all worked up from his upset state and tears were running down his cheeks. I talked with him without accomplishing a single thing.

So I went to the Admiral and said, "I recommend that we put this young officer on the first one of the big transports that are going back to the States. And that we put him on there with a letter saying, that he had been tried and been found wanting, and we recommend that he be discharged from the Naval Reserve as being unfit for naval duty."

So I drafted such a letter and the Admiral signed it. We put him on board one of the transports and home he went. As far as I know, the objective of the letter was carried out.

That night the Admiral and I were standing up on the bridge and he said, "You know the terrible thing about this is they're gone, (I do not recall the names of the four wonderful young people that we lost,) and this absolutely worthless individual we have sent back to the United States. He'll go back and probably propagate four or five others of his kind. I don't know that we arrived at the right decision." I didn't know either, and I don't know now.

Q: That's typical of war though, the flower of the youth of the nation are lost.

Dyer: That really upset me though.

Vice Admiral George C. Dyer, USN, Ret.

Annapolis, Maryland   by John T. Mason, Jr.

Subject: Biography (Salerno landing)   May 12, 1970

Mr. Mason: You were speaking of the landing on the Italian mainland, sir.

Admiral Dyer: And more specifically at Salerno. Before discussing that in any detail, I think a little background information might fit in well.

The port of Salerno is about 30 air miles south of Naples. A good many Americans take the Amalfi Drive down from Naples becuase it's one of the tourist attractions in that part of Italy. At the southern end of the drive you overlook the Bay of Salerno and the small town of Salerno.

At the time of World War II, and more specifically the summer of 1943, just inboard from the Bay of Salerno about three miles was a very important Italian airfield. It was named Montecorvino. It was, of course, the center of our air bombing effort in the period before the invasion.

Q: The softening up process.

Dyer: As far as the Salerno operation is concerned, it certainly was not a planner's dream. It really was a planner's nightmare. At least, it was at my level. My level was a very low level.

Q: Are you going to explain that statement? Why was it a nightmare to you?

Dyer: I'll tell you. First I'd like to indicate what level I was doing the planning at.

In the Mediterranean, the senior naval officer under General Eisenhower was Admiral Sir Andrew Cunningham of the British Navy. The senior United States naval officer was Vice Admiral Hewitt. Underneath him, the commander of all the amphibious forces in Northwest Africa was Rear Admiral James L. Hall. At the bottom level was Rear Admiral R. L. Conolly, who had the job of Commander Landing Craft and Bases Northwest Africa. I was his Chief of Staff. So I was at the third and bottom level of the United States naval command, and I was at the fourth level of all naval commands in the amphibious area in the Mediterranean. Counting General Eisenhower at the top, I was at the fifth level. You don't always see as clearly at the fifth level of planning as you do at the top level.

It was a very difficult planning operation for two reasons. One was that there was a great difference of opinion in regard to where the landing should be carried out. Second, there was a great difference of opinion as to just how it should be carried out. I should really throw in a third, and that is we had less than four weeks to plan the Salerno operation, from the date we left Sicily and returned to Bizerte, and the date the landing craft had to sail for Salerno from Bizerte.

I don't remember the exact date, as to when we got the final go ahead to do the landing at Salerno rather than at Gaeta or Naples, it was either mid-August or a little bit later.

Q: Was this entirely dependent upon the Sicilian campaign?

Dyer: It depended a great deal on the Sicilian campaign since General Alexander, who was the senior Army commander under General Eisenhower, was strongly opposed to the landing occurring before he had cleaned up Sicily. And also, at the same time, there were some high level negotiations going on in regard to the surrender of Italy. There was a question of coordination of the surrender with the assault landing, so that the landing would be able to take the maximum advantage of the surrender.

There was a considerable difference of opinion between our negotiators and the Italian negotiators. I learned all this second and third and fourth hand later. And there was a great unwillingness on the part of our negotiators to accept the fact that the Italians were negotiating in good faith. We just couldn't believe it, on the working level, with the result that progress towards the Italian Surrender was up and down. The hopes and fears certainly rode a sine curve.

To get back to my part of it--During the period before the final determination was made to go into Salerno,

Dyer 9 - 328

there was considerable discussion of alternatives. My boss, Admiral Conolly, was very strong on going into Gaeta. Gaeta is further up the Italian coast, 30 miles north of Naples.

One thing that I think influenced him greatly in his effort to get us to land at Gaeta was that the Bay there wasn't mined, while the Bay of Salerno was mined. That meant that for Salerno we had to sweep in ahead of the amphibious craft, the LSTs and the LCTs, the LCTs in order to get them safely on to the beach. And it meant that the landing operation would consume a great deal more time, and give the enemy extra hours to react to our assault.

The other thing that I think influenced him considerably was that we had had such inadequate air support from the Army Air Force at Sicily. The cry to land at Salerno was based on the fact that the Air Force could provide a certain modest amount of air support at Salerno.

Rear Admiral Conolly's position was that the Army Air Force had supplied so little air support at Sicily that it really didn't make any difference whether we had it or we didn't have it. And therefore, let us go into Gaeta which had advantages from the point of view of being able to get to Naples more quickly, the land between Gaeta and Naples being much more favorable for the Army to advance over.

Q: What were the deterrents to that particular landing?

Dyer: The deterrents were that the Army Air Force said

flatly that they could not provide any air support, because it was roughly 50 miles, air miles further north. They claimed that they could only spend 20 minutes over Salerno, that was the maximum they could spend over Salerno with their planes flying out of Sicily. And if they went the extra 50 miles, they wouldn't be able to provide any air support.

The determination against Gaeta was an Army determination. In any amphibious operation, the Navy is required to land the Army where the Army wants to be landed, if it is possible from the naval point of view.

Q: You said a little before that the beaches at Gaeta were not mined. This would indicate that the Italians didn't think it was a feasible place to land either.

Dyer: I don't say that the beaches weren't mined, because I don't remember. I'm saying that Gaeta Bay wasn't mined, while the Bay of Salerno was mined.

Another factor was that the landing was to be made in two major sub-divisions. The American troops were to be landed in the southern half, and the British troops were to be landed in the northern half. The landing craft from Admiral Conolly's command were landing British troops, and specifically the British 46th division.

Our United States Army commanders insisted that there would be no preliminary gunfire bombardment.

I think a factor of some weight in deciding for the

landing at Salerno was that the Army felt that the gunfire support after the landing in the Salerno area would be more effective than at Gaeta because of the contour of the land where all the ground defenses had to be gathered into the level beach area. The reason being that all the Salerno-Agropole area is sort of like the inside of a cup on its side. About three miles from the beach to the east are the first row of hills backed up by 2000 foot mountains. The white sand beaches provided this very lovely landing area. Any ground defenses had to be right within that area.

The physical geography around Gaeta was in no way the same. Gaeta was much more broken up in the background with improved possibilities for defense.

The British Army commanders were much less stubborn about preliminary gunfire bombardment, but General Eisenhower had an order that said you couldn't shoot until shot at.

There was British destroyer gunfire support up in our area which was designated "Uncle", as soon as the German guns opened up on us.

Q: Admiral Hewitt is said to have not gone along with the Army point of view about the prior bombardment of the coast defenses.

Dyer: You want to remember that in the British Army and the British Navy, their experience at Gallipoli had made a profound impression on them. You could find hardly any Britisher who would argue that it was possible to make a successful assault landing against alerted and prepared beach defenses. When any discussion was made in regard to landing at all, the British would immediately go back to Gallipoli and quote you letter and verse in regard to their experience there. They had had a very sad experience.

On the other hand, in our Navy and in the Marine Corps, there was increased confidence in being able to land against strong defense because of what we felt that we had mastered and the British had not, and that was the art of adequate gunfire and air support.

As you know, in August 1942 we made our initial amphibious assault landing at Tulagi in the Solomons against a prepared Japanese defensive position. While we suffered a reasonable number of casualities, we did take the place after considerable initial delay and calls for gunfire support.

At the time we were planning the Salerno landing in August and September 1943, our South Pacific Amphibious Force had just completed the landings in New Georgia. This commenced the 30th of June. In these landings we were making an attack on what was a strongly defended Japanese position at Munda. In fact, it took us six weeks to take it. We had the idea that we could take it. We accepted that we could take a strongly defended beach position.

The next place that we went into was the Gilberts, where we had Tarawa.

Q: That was a pretty tough nut.

Dyer: That, of course, was one of the toughest of them all. But there was an accepted belief in the naval part of the Amphibious team that we could take a strongly fortified position.

On the other hand the British, both Army and Navy opposed it. I believe that the British Army was stronger in its opposition than the British Navy. They both had a belief that taking a strongly defended and alerted place just couldn't be taken by an amphibious assault.

This really moves into your next question, which is "How important was naval gunfire support? The Royal Navy apparently supplied most of the naval vessels and supported the operation. How effective were they?"

It was difficult for me to judge since we had only a very few United States naval ships in the northern sector of the operation providing gunfire support. We had U. S. gunfire support ships in the immediate area where I was, in the early days of the invasion. The gunfire support was supplied by the British Navy, other than what we supplied from the BISCAYNE. She had one five-inch gun.

The only impression that I came away with was that the British use of gunfire support was much less generous than the United States Navy. In other words, we just poured it on until our observers ashore said, "Cease fire," or "Lift fire," or whatever. We just kept it going. While the

British naval system was to fire a limited number of salvos and then to quit, and that was it. They had provided their support.

Q: What was the reasoning back of that?

Dyer: The reasoning was that they had far less adequate suppliers of ammunition in England than we had in the United States.

Q: And far less wherewithal, too.

Dyer: Yes, that's what I mean. In other words, they were fighting on rations and they had to be careful. We just poured it on.

That is another thing that should be mentioned in regard to gunfire support. When we went into Sicily, General Patton was the top Army commander from the operational point of view and General Bradley was the Corps Commander underneath him. We sold both of them, Patton more than Bradley, the usefulness and capabilities of gunfire support. They were just amazed, and they were most pleased.

But when we went into Salerno, these two Army generals were not in the picture. We had a new Army General in top command, Lieutenant General Mark Clark and under him Major General Dawley commanding the VI Corps and General Middleton, commanding the 45th Division. Here was almost a complete new team, who didn't want any part of preliminary gunfire bombardment prior to the landings.

Q: They had to be educated all over again.

Dyer: They had to be educated starting completely fresh.

There's one thing that I want to put in that should have been put in before. This is about not going into Gaeta.

The British Army were the ones who made the final decision as far as we were concerned, and as far as my staff level was concerned. They didn't want to go into Gaeta, they wanted to land at Salerno. They said that the defenses at Gaeta were too strong.

As it turned out, with the Italians surrendering nine hours before we landed, the defenses at Gaeta wouldn't have been a fact or because the defenses at Gaeta weren't manned by Germans, they were manned by Italians, while the defenses at Salerno were manned by Germans. The defense problem wouldn't have arisen at Gaeta.

And I'm sure that our movement into Naples from the landing on the beaches, if we had landed at Gaeta would have been far more expeditious than it was when we landed at Salerno and had to work north through the hills and small mountains intermingled. Anyhow we made the amphibious assault landing at Salerno.

There's the background.

We started planning for the landing at Salerno on the 9th of August about three weeks before we had to sail from Bizerte. Of course, we were about a three day sail with our LCTs and LSTs up to Salerno.

Salerno had three hazards. First, the bay was mined. Second, the air cover promised was slight. And third, there was to be no preliminary gun bombardment in the southern half of the landing area.

The British accepted, and they were willing that there be a limited amount of preliminary gun bombardment in the northern half of the area. That was where we were doing the landing, where Admiral Conolly was landing the British troops.

Q: So this whole element of surprise was negated by this fact, wasn't it?

Dyer: There couldn't be any surprise, that was our point of view, that there couldn't be any surprise. Because in the first place, the German-Italian planes flew air reconnaissance over the whole northern African coast. Here we were at Bizerte with 300 amphibious craft, plus a few other ships. It was quite obvious that the major sailing of the smaller craft was going to take place from there. All they had to do was to scout us when we left.

I think Admiral Hewitt is the one who said that all the enemy had to do was to take a pair of dividers and swing them from North Africa and from Sicily, and figure where the limits of the air cover would be. Since the problem of our getting air cover was being discussed in the press at that time, they'd realize that we'd have to land at Salerno if we were going to land anywhere in Central Italy.

The Italian planes tracked us all the way up to Salerno. They made air attacks on us all the way up. There was no element of surprise in regard to our assault landing in any way, shape, form, or description. There was no element of strategic surprise, and there was no element of tactical surprise.

The decision was made at a level above that of my boss, CORLANDCRABNAW. We didn't have anything to do with it except to accept it. Actually we had only destroyers in our area to provide the gunfire support in the first twenty four hours of the Candrig.

Later after the first few days we had three cruisers in Bay of Salerno, the PHILADELPHIA, the SAVANNAH, and I believe the BOISE.

Q: They had initially been involved in the Bari takeover, hadn't they?

Dyer: The BOISE, I think, was the one that went in to Taranto. The other two were with the Southern Attack Force. Admiral Hewitt was with the Southern Attack Force. Admiral Hall was the amphibious commander immediately under Admiral Hewitt. He landed General Mark Clark, and we landed British Lieutenant General McCreery.

One little thing I'd like to remark about that. The initial British corps commander was nammed Horrochs. At

Bizerte, the Germans or Italians or whoever were there had built shelters.

Every time one of these air raids came over, all the officers would go out and stand in the vicinity of the shelters and watch the raid and the bombs falling. It was probably one of the most asinine things I ever did.

This British Leiutenant General was standing in the group that I was standing in, watching the air raid. Suddenly, he was machinegunned. A bullet came down and hit in his shoulder at an angle and went right through his chest area at an angle, and out the other side. Everybody thought he was going to die right away, but he didn't. I don't know whether it was months or years before he died, but he lived long enough to be shipped back to England.

Then they ordered in this new British Lieutenant General McCreery. The thing that I remember best about him was that as soon as he arrived and was given the plan, he had a conference of all the senior officers of his corps. Admiral Conolly and I were invited to this conference. This was about four or five days before we were going to sail. He got up on his feet with one of these little short whips that the British officers carry and whipped his legs. He said, "I have read the plan. I don't like it, but we are going to do it. It's too damn late of change it." And it was.

As far as I was concerned, I was very much relieved because if he'd wanted to change the troop landing plan, we'd have had to change all the amphibious craft and landing craft schedules.

On Admiral Conolly's staff, his Plans Officer was the son of Admiral William H. Standley former Chief of Naval Operations, Commander W. H. Standley, Jr. The Operations Officer was Commander Charles A. Buchanan out of the class of 1926. He became a Rear Admiral in time and served with distinction.

Standley was a very excellent planning officer. We would normally plan from early morning up until about midnight or one o'clock each night. Then Charlie Buchanan and I would go to bed. We'd get up at six o'clock in the morning and go to work again.

Standley would stay up and imbibe. When he got up in the morning, he was always the worse for wear. He had an excellent mind, he was a good planner, but he had a basic defect. It didn't pay him any dividends. Charlie, who I think was a class junior to Bill Standley, was closer to him than I was. He tried to get him not to do this.

Q: It was his relief from the tension, I suppose.

Dyer: Yes, that's right.

In answer to your question, "How important was naval gunfire support?", it is my humble opinion that first class naval gunfire support is an essential for any amphibious assault.

I was not in a position to judge how effective the

Royal Navy was in supplying this support, because I only observed a few British destroyers providing it during the early days of the Salerno landings. They were, what I would call, parsimonious in their use of ammunition.

As you perhaps know, the Sele River was the dividing line or the boundary line between the British landing and the U. S. landing. This had both it's advantages and disadvantages.

The disadvantages of it were made clear when one day the German tanks used it to come down to the beach area to run over the Allied beach landing areas. The German tanks did this in the immediate area where our Naval Beach Groups located. After their attack was over, Admiral Conolly told me to go ashore and reestablish the beach control organization because the beach was in pandemonium. We had provided some slit trenches. Some of our people got into them, but quite a few of them didn't. The tanks had just raised cain with everyone that wasn't in a slit trench.

I'll never forget the Sele River.

Perhaps I should give a general answer. In my opinion, the landing was made with only partial gunfire support. I don't know of any of the later difficulties that were directly related to that partial gunfire support. Since by and large, on the southern half of the landing the American troops advanced fairly rapidly until they had really conquered the whole plain level back to the hills. So that I can't point out that later difficulties were directly related to the lack of gunfire support. On the northern half of the landing, the British made very slow progress right from the very start.

We landed some Rangers north of the British divisions. They had a fairly easy time in the early part of the assault landing.

Q: Did the British actually meet with strong opposition immediately?

Dyer: Almost immediately. They suffered quite a few casualities. Another thing was that a lot of their people surrendered. They found themselves in positions that were deemed untenable and surrendered. I think one day nearly 500 people surrendered. So everything was not the way it should have been.

Question three is, "Apparently the Army did not want an advanced bombardment of the beach area because they wanted to preserve the element of surprise. Would I comment on that?" I have already done so.

"Apparently Admiral Hewitt was not in agreement with this point of view." I can say that I'm sure of that. He was a very sound naval officer. In fact, he was a highly intelligent and well trained professional--a brilliant leader.

Your next question is, "What role did shore-based aviation play in the landing? What role did sea-based aviation play in the landing?"

The Army had been subjected to severe criticism after the Sicily assault landing because of the terrible performance that the Army Air Corps had put on during that affair.

Q: You said that this was in the press before.

Dyer: The answer to that is it was in the press. It appeared in several of these so-called 'think' articles that come out of briefings or background briefings of the various Headquarters. As I remember the criticism appeared in one of Hanson Baldwin's articles in the NEW YORK TIMES. These articles indicated, in a soft way, that there had been certain deficiencies or inadequacies in the Army Air Corps support of the Sicily assault landing in the views of the other Services. Of course, the Army Air Corps did not agree with these comments. At least, not then.

One thing that I know that General Eisenhowers Headquarters did is that they appointed some kind of a new air commander for the Salerno landings. His name was House. I don't know what ever happened to him, because I never heard of him again.

In an effort to meet this criticism, the Army did appoint this General. He was given a modest amount of authority.

They also changed the air support system considerably from that effective at Sicily, in that the British Coastal Command was given the chore of providing the air cover for the Fleet. In other words, the U. S. Army Air Corps was relieved of that responsibility and it was turned over to the British Air Force. It was turned over to the people who had been in the Fleet airarm, but who were not part of the British Air Force.

During the assault landing at Salerno, there were planes from British carriers supporting the landing. The British had two big carriers and some small carriers present in the area. They provided some of the air cover and they also provided some of the air support.

Again, I do not remember too well the details of this. It seemed to me that by and large that the German-Italian air force operated pretty much at will in the Salerno Bay Area. In the craft scattered along the Bay of Salerno we were subjected to a tremendous number of air raids.

I saw a story in the Army history the other day which said that the Army said that the enemy air raids averaged 50 a day.

We lost some ships and amphibious craft, and merchant ships and we had others damaged.

The Germans had a new air controlled flying bomb. They would fly this flying bomb over, and a German plane would fly above it. Then the control plane would match images on a radar. When radar image of a ship was in a certain position in connection with this bomb, then the bomb would tip up vertically and down it would come at tremendous speed. There wasn't anything you could do about it, except watch it come down, because you couldn't shoot it down with your anti-aircraft guns. This was beyond the fire control capabilities. You didn't have any data in your fire control computer which would handle such a situation, where you had such a complete change of course and change of speed. You continued to shoot at it with the man-controlled guns. In other words, if you had a 50 caliber gun you could still shoot at it, but that was ineffective.

Q: At what height would they operate these?

Dyer: They came in at about 8 to 10 thousand feet, then the bomb turned to the vertical and came down at a tremendous speed.

We lost a number of merchant ships that were carrying supplies.

Q: Then it was a very hazardous undertaking to have the large British carriers operating in those limited waters, wasn't it?

Dyer: Yes. When I was exec in the INDIANAPOLIS, which was in 1940-'41, the British battleship, WARSPITE, having been damaged by an Italian torpedo attack in Alexandria, Egypt, was routed through the Pacific Ocean by the British around to the Puget Sound Navy Yard for repairs. She came through Pearl Harbor and I went aboard her and acquired an interest in her. She was in the Mediterranean again when I was there in '43, and during the Salerno operation she took aboard in her stern sheets one of these radar controlled bombs. I remember her name distinctly. I don't remember the names of any of the others hit by radar controlled bombs, except the SAVANNAH. Which, of course, also had a radar controlled bomb that came down and went right down through the top of the turret and exploded the magazine. Very fortunately, it didn't blow up the ship.

Q: Am I right in recalling that the ILLUSTRIOUS was there?

Dyer: She was there, yes.

Q: And damaged too, wasn't she?

Dyer: That's right.

Admiral Hewitt, in his report on the Salerno operation said, "Enemy's regular and persistent bombing and strafing attacks effectively interrupted unloading activities." I think that probably summarizes the situation fairly well. The going was pretty tough.

One thing that has disturbed me in the period subsequent to the war, is that I read a book by General Mark Clark, in regard to the Salerno landings. In this book, he denies that he ever seriously contemplated evacuating the beaches at Salerno. My memory is quite different.

Along about D plus six or seven, Admiral Conolly called me into his office and said that the Chief of Staff of one of the Army's divisions and a lesser staff officer from General Mark Clark's Headquarters had come aboard. They had said that they desired that the Navy plan immediately for an evacuation of the troops.

Q: From the beachheads?

Dyer: From the beachheads, and that is almost impossible. Because when you land you run an LST or an LCT up on a beach at a good speed. It's fully loaded, you have a lot of momentum which carries it where you want it to go. Then you unload the craft. And then you back off with a very lightly loaded craft. That's one thing.

But when you are up on the beach in an LCT or an LST in an unloaded craft or ship and then you re-embark troops and their equipment, you put a tremendous number of additional tons in the LCTs and the LSTs. These craft have a very small engine backing power with which to get off the beach, and they just can't do it. An engine always has twice the power to go ahead than it does to back. So that evacuation from a beachhead means that you can take aboard only about half of the load that you actually put on the beach from the same landing ship or craft and still back off.

So since we have just finished a landing, two re-enforced divisions down there in the southern part of the beachhead and General Clark wanted to take them back on board ship and craft, we had an impossible situation insofar as the Navy was concerned. Because as soon as the amphibious craft were unloaded, we had started them back to Bizerte to pick up additional stores to bring back for the troops use. This had been going on for about five days. A good many of these LSTs fully loaded were back up to Salerno 60 to 72 hours from the initial landing. We didn't have a lot of empty ships sitting around in the Bay of Salerno just waiting to do something, like an evacuation.

Providing the logistic support of an Army corps is a big proposition. When you are going to suddenly say, "I've got to evacuate," you just don't have empty landing ships and craft. You should have twice as many landing ships and craft in order to evacuate the corps as you did to land them, because you have to evacuate them with crafts only half full in order to get them off the beaches.

With such information as we had and such landing ships and craft that were available, Standley, Charlie Buchanan, and I worked all night on developing the naval aspects of this Op plan for evacuation. We gave it the code name of 'Brass Hat'. That name I never will forget, because I hated and still dislike the term, 'Brass Hat'.

Admiral Conolly, as soon as he was advised of General Clarks desires, sent a dispatch to Admiral Hewitt advising him of the Generals' desire. Admiral Hewitt got in a British destroyer, I think it was the HILLARY, and came dashing back up from Algiers and brought along with him General Alexander and a number of other officers of his staff and the Army Staff. They got back up there some 24 hours after this thing had been decided by General Clark and we had been told of it.

Q: You were at Algiers then?

Dyer: No, I was off the beachhead in the Bay of Salerno. Admiral Hewitt was at Algiers, I was off the Salerno beach.

When Admiral Hewitt left the Bay of Salerno for Algiers, he designated Admiral Conolly to continue to provide the logistic support and the gunfire support, and such air support as there was available, which was about .0, .0, .0.

Rear Admiral Conolly was the boss man locally, the senior United States Naval officer in the area and that's why General Clark sent his representative to him. Rear Admiral Conolly was the Senior Officer Present off the beaches. The others had all gone back to North Africa, where they had their own things to do. It was highly desirable also to get these ships out of the area and away from the German bombing attacks.

Particularly after the SAVANNAH was hit, Admiral Hewitt was anxious to get the ANCON out of the area, because she was the only command ship in the Mediterranean. So it was quite natural for him to want to preserve her for later operations.

This conference on Operation Brass Hat is what I want to tell you about. It was held in the BISCAYNE. At Arzeu before the Sicilian operation we had built on the topside of the BISCAYNE, making her quite top heavy, this so-called War Room. Into it on this day were crowded General Clark's staff, the Corps Commanders Staff, the two Divisions Commander of his two divisions and representatives of General McCreery and of his two divisions. General Alexander brought with him some of his staff and Admiral Hewitt brought with him some of his staff. They were crowded in this very limited War Room.

The first thing on the program was to have the representatives of General Clark present the situation as they saw it ashore. Then Admiral Conolly's representatives, of which I was one, presented the situation as we saw it from the seagoing point of view.

This I will never forget: General Alexander, who is not a large man, he is like myself, a small man, had not said a word all during these presentations. When the presentations were finished he got up and he walked to the front, which was about three paces because they were all crowded in this small war room and he turned around. He took this little whip, he cracked his leg with it, and he said, "There will be no evacuation. Now we'll proceed from there."

He sold himself to me right there. He made the decision, and now General Clark writes a book and says--a lot of things that I believe do not coincide with the facts of the matter.

Q: In retrospect, how could General Clark forget this fact?

Dyer: The answer is I'm sure he doesn't. I don't see how he possibly could.

The result of the conference was that everybody made more effort. A lot more air support was brought in. General Eisenhower evidently applied the whip up there in Algiers. Things they said they couldn't do before, they did do, in air support.

Q: In other words, it was a crisis.

Dyer: That's right.

They loaded craft in Algiers with new troops and they

loaded them in Sicily. They brought them up in everything that would float and run. They got them there and landed these additional troops. The people that were there held on and the tide of battle turned.

There was a German panzer division with a very competent General, whose name I don't remember. He really gave our boys the devil. He almost won. He announced that he was going to win. He had our troops on the run, he said. He was looking at the back of General Clark's mind, I think.

Wiser councils prevailed.

The next question is, "Just a short time before the landing began, General Eisenhower announced on the radio that the Italians were out of the war. Did this have any psychological repercussions on the troops?"

I would say that it had tremendous psychological repercussions on the troops. They could hardly go ashore determined to do or die, when the enemy had just turned in his suit. The fact that the Germans hadn't turned in their suits was not readily apparent to the GI until somebody shot at him. So I think the GIs did a wonderful job of picking themselves up from a period where they were just walking ashore and raising the flag to where they had to fight for everything they got.

Q: Would you say that this incident that you just related in respect to General Mark Clark, that this was a part of the psychological reaction?

Dyer: I think probably some lack of drive to get just every

inch that they could get in the first six hours, twelve hours, eighteen hours ashore wasn't there because some of the people just weren't convinced. Every trooper, as he was landed, had to wait until he got shot at before he was convinced that he was back in the war. Therefore, there must have been considerably less drive.

Q: When your own segment of the front where the British were landing, you said before that there were as many as 500 surrendering in one day, was this related in any sense to the psychological reaction?

Dyer: It could have been.

The reaction of the Italians to their country's surrender was just instantaneous.

One other thing which sticks in my craw is that the night when we anchored the BISCAYNE in Salerno Bay, my Admiral said the BISCAYNE must be the closest ship to the beach. And he was right.

We dropped our anchor about three thirty in the morning. As soon as "first light" broke, out came a small boat from the beach, with four or five Italian officers in fresh uniforms. Up they came and onboard.

Q: Flying a white flag?

Dyer: The small boat was flying a white flag.

Up they came. They had one officer who spoke quite good English. I met them. My heart just went out to them.

I couldn't do anything except treat them with the greatest courtesy, because they were in a terrible position. There were professional soldiers as well as naval officers amongst them.

The first thing that I told them was that I wanted the information on the mines that were in the area. A naval officer amongst them produced the chart, he had it right up underneath his trousers. He pulled it out, and there was the chart with all the mines. I was very grateful.

We had already had an LST run into a mine. The Commanding Officer of the LST did a wonderful job after he had hit the mine. He plowed ahead full speed until he hit the beach, and tried to get rid of his cargo before his ship was totally submerged. While he hit the beach well out, we were able to save quite a bit of his cargo.

The Italians produced this map. If we'd just had a zerox system, it would have been just wonderful. But we didn't have any zerox in those days.

I turned it over to the staff Chief Quartermaster and told him to make a couple of copies of it right away quick and to get one to Admiral Hewitt, who at that time was in the Bay of Salerno.

Commander Buchanan analyzed the Italian map and we put out a signal to all ships present showing where the lines of mines were.

Although we had swept through them and buoyed the channels where we had swept, it was favorable information to know where the mines were that hadn't been swept.

One of the Italian Army officers who came aboard had a list of where all the guns in the hills were. They brought forward a lot of useful information.

I sent them down to the wardroom and gave them coffee and tried to make them feel a little bit comfortable.

Q: They were in jeopardy personally with the Germans.

Dyer: Yes.

The next question is, "Was the Italian population helpful to the American forces?" I really don't know the answer to that. I didn't have any contact.

About three days after the initial landing, I went ashore into Amalfi harbor because we were looking for places where we could land craft without having to beach them. You can unload some types of craft much faster alongside a dock, than you can on a beach. The British had announced that they had captured Amalfi harbor, so I went ashore and toured the docks and harbor area. The Germans had blown up the docks to some extent, but our Army engineers immediately went to work to restore them. As a matter of fact, we made quite a good deal of use of this small Amalfi harbor.

That was the only time that I came close to any of the Italian population. I rode through a part of Amalfi. I also got out and walked around. During that time, I guess I saw maybe 25 Italians.

I had no way of actually getting a personal reaction. They were all smart enough to wave and look at me, but I had no conversation. I couldn't speak Italian, and they couldn't speak English. So all we could do was just look happy at each other.

Q: May I interject another question, which has to do with General Eisenhower's announcement on the radio of the Italian surrender. Obviously he understood the implications of a public announcement of that sort at this moment as the landings were about to take place. What was the overriding necessity then for doing it at that moment?

Dyer: You mean making the landing at that time?

Q: No, the announcement.

Dyer: I thought that the announcement was made because the Germans had become very suspicious of the Italians and were taking over the commands at various places. As you know, the German bombers came out and sank the ROMA, one of the great bit Italian battleships, with a tremendous loss of life. The Germans bombed some of the other Italian ships. The Italian Fleet had no air cover and the Germans showed considerable willingness to get down low and to bomb.

I think that the timing was probably based on General Eisenhower's knowledge of the necessity of doing something right soon. I'm no witness on that.

Q: You strongly suspect that the fate of the Italian Fleet was one of the factors?

Dyer: The Allies and the Italians wanted to save the Fleet. And they did save eighty percent of it.

The next question is, "What was the extent of mining operations in the area? Was it a real detriment to our efforts?"

The answer is that it meant that we had to arrive off of Salerno considerably earlier than if there had not been mines there. And therefore, that the Italians, by air reconnaissance, were able to determine where the exact landing was going to be sooner than if there had been no mine sweeping effort.

I think you could say it was a real obstacle to a quick landing. Had we been able to arrive at the Bay of Salerno at two-thirty or three o'clock in the morning for a three-thirty landing, in other words, shoved the landing craft off from the landing ships at three-thirty, that would have been one thing. But we arrived up there along about nine or nine-thirty in the evening. You just can't hide 300 ships.

The Germans made a number of attacks on the Fleet, dropping flares on us while we were lying there waiting for the mine sweeping to be completed.

Q: When you were planning this operation, obviously our intelligence had informed you that there was considerable mining there in Salerno. When you received these Italians who surrendered and received the mining charts, how closely did they correspond to the kind of intelligence that you had worked with?

Dyer: I wish I could answer that question with accuracy, but I can't.

When we started in and the mine sweepers started to pick up mines, we established certain lines on the charts that seemed to be indicated by the mines that were being swept. So that we had, I would say, ten or twenty percent of the mine information when the Italians handed us the charts.

What we had was not intelligence information, it was operational intelligence information. In other words, we had deduced it from actual mines. The information that we had prior to the landings was not specific, it was an educated guess.

Q: I see. That's an answer to the question.

When a port is mined like that there are safe channels, are there not?

Dyer: Yes.

Q: But when a landing is expected, is there also then random mining?

Dyer: Yes. They just close the channels.

The next question is, "Why were no American carriers or battleships involved in the operation?"

The answer to that is that we had no carriers available in September of 1943 which were not very much involved in Pacific operations. The U. S. Navy and Admiral King had opted for the Pacific and everything that our Navy did in the Mediterranean was done reluctantly, in my very humble opinion.

While we had old battleships in the Atlantic, they were escorting our troops convoys and protecting them from German raiders. While our Atlantic battleships had all done some gunfire support work, they were not peeled off from their escort chores and sent into the Mediterranean. They were kept to their convoy protection duties.

We just didn't have any battleships or carriers there. The British had carriers. The British Fleet was there. A chap who later became the Commander in Chief of the Mediterranean while I was over in the Mediterranean in 1947 and 1948, Sir Algernon "Fauntleroy" Willis was there. He had command of Force "H", including the battleships and carriers at that time. Sir Philip Vian, a British Rear Admiral, had command of the carriers.

I'll tell you a story about Admiral Willis that has nothing whatsoever to do with Salerno.

When I went over to the Mediterranean in 1947, I went in to Gibraltar. I had command of a division of cruisers and a squadron of destroyers, a little task group. I sent out an information signal to the ships in my command before I went into Gibraltar saying, "The Flag Officer commanding Gibraltar is Rear Admiral Archer. The Flag Officer commanding the Mediterranean fleet is Admiral Sir Algernon Fauntleroy Willis. I say it again, Sir Algernon Fauntleroy Willis." Actually his middle name was not "Fauntleroy" but "Usborne".

We got into port late, five o'clock in the afternoon. I sent a signal over to Admiral Willis asking when it would be convenient for me to call upon him. And he replied, the next morning at ten o'clock.

So the next morning I went alongside his flag ship in my barge and bounced up the gangway. When I walked through the line of side boys, Admiral Willis was there. He said, "My name is Admiral Sir Algernon Fauntleroy Willis. I say again, Algernon Fauntleroy Willis."

He told me that one of the members of his staff had been ashore with somebody from the American flotilla and they told him the signal I sent. We became fast friends. He was a most understanding and competent naval officer, with a keen sense of humor.

I thought the Salerno assault landing was an extremely good operation, insofar as the Navy was concerned because the operation had been put together in a very minimum of planning time. We were able to supply the logistic support that kept the Army happy with very limited seagoing resources since the support had all to be done with small ships and craft - not the initial support, but the follow-up support -- and merchant ships. It had to be done at a considerable distance from our nearest home bases, which were Bizerte and Algiers. It was a logistic success of a very considerable extent.

I again learned that our cruisers and destroyers which supported the Southern Attack Force landings did a tremendous job under very difficult circumstances. The Army was quite happy about that.

Q: That causes me to ask a question. Why was it, since it seemed to be such a closely allied operation in Sicily, that the Army changed Generals, and Patton and Bradley were no longer involved in this particular landing?

Dyer: The only reason that I can tell you is that they had said, at the highest level, that the Salerno landing would take place as soon as the Sicily operation was completed. Certainly if Generals Patton and Bradley were to be on top of the operations in Sicily, they could not be on top of planning the landing operation at Salerno. In other words, you can only do one thing extremely well at one time.

Q: Would the same rule of thumb apply to the naval high command?

Dyer: The answer to that was, I think, to a lesser extent inasmuch as our Naval operations was of shorter duration. In other words, the Navy had a tremendous peak to reach, but the Army had a long continued operation to plan for. This was the march on Naples and the conquest of Italy. They had a much more extensive operation than we had. Our operations reached a tremendous peak load, but the peak held for a comparatively short time.

Q: The operation came to a precipitous close for you personally. Will you tell me about that sir?

Dyer: To give you a little background on that: On the

BISCAYNE, on the Flag Bridge there was on either side and directly opposite the chart room doors, two 50 caliber machine guns, one on each side. Manning one of these was a great big brawny machinist mate.

When we were in Bizerte, and the Germans used to send over their Stukas to make their air attacks, we used to lay a tremendous amount of smoke in a smoke screen.

When we had an air attack and we had laid heavy smoke, you couldn't see anything. I was on one side of the bridge and I heard the Stukas coming in on the other side, in a dive. You can place where they are by their noise. I was going from my side of the bridge, the port side, moving to the starboard side where the Stukas were. In the narrow passageway connecting the two wings of the bridge, I met this great big gunner who should have been at his gun.

Q: Was he moving in fright?

Dyer: He was moving in fright, yes. When those Stukas come in, they can frighten you.

Whenever afterwards we used to have an air attack, I used to station myself right behind him and coach him because he was not a good gunner. He was a machinist mate. He was up there because the ship didn't have the ratings which an ordinary ship that was going to fight anti-aircraft battles had.

Q: And yet it was a command ship.

Dyer: In a very limited way, it was a command ship.

Admiral Conolly was on watch twelve hours a day, from seven in the morning until seven at night. I took the twelve hours at night, from seven at night until seven in the morning.

That day I had gotten up and shaved and showered and eaten a meal. Then I immediately went up to topside to read the dispatches, because that was the thing I wanted to do. What had happened while I was asleep?

I went up and into the chart house and was reading the dispatches, when the general alarm sounded.

On the far side of the low hills which surrounded the Salerno plain, there were a number of enemy air bases which our planes had bombed and rebombed. But the Germans were still operating planes out of them. The German planes would fly very close to the ground until they'd get to these hills, and then they'd come up and over the hills and bomb and strafe the ships. Our ships had roughly a minute or a minute and a half to actually start shooting at them, before the planes had attacked the ships.

The general alarm went off and I rushed out to get behind the gunner. I was just going through the door of the chart house to get to my station behind the gunner, when zowie, I got hit in the left leg. I said, "I'm hit."

They laid me down on the deck, then got a hospital corpsman and took me back aft because some other people had been hit. The doctor came along with this great big needle. I said, "Don't you put that into me. I want to know what's happening." The next thing that they did was to put me on Admiral Hewitt's Flag Ship to be taken care of.

Q: How badly were you damaged?

Dyer: I spent four months and thirteen days in the hospital. My leg bone was somewhat shattered.

The ANCON decided they couldn't handle me so they put me onboard the ST. ANDREW, which was a British hospital ship.

I shall tell one story about the Saint Andrew, and then I'll quit for this day.

The night before I was put onboard this hospital ship, perhaps the second night before, the Germans had come and bombed the hospital ships. The British had two hospital ships which were merchant marine manned. The Germans had bombed one of these two hospital ships, all outlined in lights with a big red cross on the top. It was no mistake.

It started to get dark and one of the nurses on the ship came in and said, "The master (he was Scotch) will not turn out the lights."

In this previous bombing on this other ship, they had dropped the bomb and it had gone right down into the doctors' quarters. It had killed 11 or 12 doctors.

Q: They could bomb a ship like that with ease, because it wasn't defended.

Dyer: So she came in and she was quite hysterical.

When I came aboard, they told me that I was the senior

patient onboard. Two or three people had come in and told me that I was the senior patient onboard.

I said, "As the senior patient onboard, will you ask the Master of the ship to please come down to see me?"

So he came down. I said, "You are playing war according to the rules. The Germans play without any rules. You have seen what happened to the other ship. (It was the ST. ALBANS). You should turn out your lights."

He would show me that he had an order that he wasn't to turn out his lights. I said, "I've been in the Navy about 25 years, and I believe in obeying orders also. But there are times, if you're really bright, that you don't obey orders literally. You carry out their intent. The intent is to save you from being attacked in error. The Germans have showed that they are not attacking in error. They are attacking you intentionally. They'll be back here."

They had made a raid two or three hours before. About every two or three hours, we got an air raid.

I said, "They go back and load up their bombs, and this time you're lights will be on. They will pick you out and you'll get bombed. I've been wounded, but I have no desire to die. I just think that you ought to go up and turn out those lights."

No, he couldn't do that. When he disappeared, I told the nurse, who came back in, the sad news. I said, "How's to get me the senior doctor onboard?" He had already been in to see me once, but he came back.

I told him what I'd done. I said, "What I ask you to do is to go up and argue with this master. And ask him to come down again. Tell him that you and I will talk to him." So he did.

The Master came down again. But he was a Scotchman, and he was very determined. I kept looking at my watch, figuring what time the German planes would come back because you could do that. They were very regular.

I just said, "What will it merit you if you die defending what in effect is a foolish order at this moment, not a foolish order in general, but a foolish order at this minute. Because the other fellow isn't playing according to the rules. If the enemy is playing according to the rules, you obey your order. If the enemy isn't playing according to the rules, you use your common sense. I suggest that you get underway at your best speed. Keep your lights on until you're clear of the task group that's scattered around. Then turn out your lights."

The next thing I heard, the ship was underway. Still the lights were not out, I could see the glow on the water. But after we got out there, he turned out his lights.

Q: And you weren't bombed.

Dyer: We weren't bombed.

Q: How long did you remain on board the hospital ship?

Dyer: They took me to Bizerte. They put me in an Army field

hospital. There, they set my leg for the first time.

Q: You must have been in great pain then in the interim.

Dyer: They gave me shots. I had a numb feeling, sort of a dull pain, like when they numb your jawbone and pull your tooth. But I was not in any great pain.

I was there, and one day in walks Admiral Conolly. He said, "I'm flying back to the States either late this afternoon or tomorrow." I said, "How about taking me with you?" I was in the Army field hospital in Bizerte and I certainly didn't want to stay there.

He said, "Fine. I'll send a dispatch to Admiral Hewitt and ask authority." So he did. In no time at all, in plain language dispatch, he got an answer.

They loaded me on the plane and flew me back to New York. The story should end there, because by the time I got to New York I had orders to report to the Naval Hospital, Brooklyn.

Commander Fritz Gleim, who was coming back with Admiral Conolly, together with Bill Davidson, the Flag Lieutenant, carried me. I was in a stretcher, and they carried me into the waiting room at the airport. I wanted to hold a telephone conversation with my classmate, Johnny Roper, who was the Captain detail officer in the Bureau of Naval Personnel. He later was Vice Admiral Roper, Chief of Bureau of Naval Personnel.

They had great difficulty. Finally found a couple of chairs that they could move and set my stretcher down so that I could use the telephone. I could listen and holler back up. And I talked with Johnny Roper.

I said, "I don't want to go to Brooklyn. I want to go to Washington and report to the Naval Hospital at Washington."

He said, "Now you go to Brooklyn, and we'll get out orders for you in a couple of days to send you down to Washington." I said, "I don't know of any reason why I can't proceed in advance of orders, and I'll get down there. Then you can confirm it." He said, "I'll do that."

I flew with Admiral Conolly down to Washington. I had told Johnny Roper, "Please have an ambulance meet the Admiral's plane." And he did. I got in the ambulance and went out to Bethesda.

Every two or three days I'd call him and say, "How about those orders? The doctor keeps asking me for a set of orders, and I haven't got any orders. I've got to have a set of orders."

The doctor would come in and say, "We've got you here and we haven't even got a piece of paper on you."

Q: Completely illegal.

Dyer: I didn't ever have a set of orders until they detached me from the Naval Hospital, Bethesda in order to be the prospective Commanding Officer of the light cruiser ASTORIA, the Mighty Ninety, CL90.

Q: Why did they fail to issue orders for the hospital?

Dyer: I can't give you the answer to that. All I know is that I never had them. And I stayed in the hospital until the middle of February, 1944.

One other thing that I would like to say is that when I was in the hospital, Johnny Roper kept calling me and telling me about all the fine shore jobs he had lined up for me. I kept telling him, "not I, I'm going back to sea."

He said, "Oh, you've been to sea. You've got evidence that you've been to sea. We've got a lot of people that haven't been to sea yet." I said, "Now listen, Johnny. I'm going to go to sea. You don't want me to have to go down and see Ernie King and tell him that you won't send me to sea, because Ernie will send me to sea."

Then he started offering me jobs at sea. He finally called me one day and said, "I can give you the AUGUSTA, if you can get out of the hospital in two weeks."

I knew the AUGUSTA was going to be Admiral Kirk's Flag ship at the Normandy landing. She was a heavy cruiser. I thought that was a good job.

I came out of the phone booth and the doctor's office was right at the end of the hallway. He was in the office and I hotfooted it down there. I went through the door and he said, "The answer is "no." If you think I'm going to let you leave this hospital and go onboard ship, when you're still limping and have them all call you "Gimpy" Dyer, you've got another thought coming."

I think I was really very fortunate in that I missed that job. When the war was about over, I was selected to Flag rank in June of 1945. There were no Captains selected from the

Atlantic by this particular Selection Board in its initial effort. All were selected from the Pacific, where I went. And from where I was selected.

So I showed basic bad judgment in saying I'd take the job, but I was very lucky in that I got to go to the Pacific.

Q: The Atlantic didn't fare very well, did it?

Dyer: It didn't fare well at all and I regret it, because they missed some very good people.

Actually they ordered Edward H. Jones, 1917, to command the AUGUSTA. He didn't get selected, although he was promoted on retirement to rear admiral.

Vice Admiral George C. Dyer, USN
Annapolis, Maryland

by John T. Mason, Jr.
October 15, 1970

Mr. Mason: It's good to be back Admiral and have this opportunity of resuming your most interesting story. In chapter 10 you're turning your attention to the Pacific War. You had returned to Washington, and to the hospital.

Admiral Dyer: The hospital was very wonderful to me. They brought down a bone specialist from Philadelphia and he worked on my leg. In due time I was getting around much better than I had ever thought that I would be. After I had been there a month or six weeks, I started to be sure that I was going to get back to active duty because I had not been at all sure when I came into the hospital.

Q: Nor had the doctor been sure.

Dyer: That's right.

I started to worry about where I was going to go. I kept getting these pieces of paper from various people that picked me out as their relief, because throughout the COMINCH organization you had to have a relief who could be made available in order to get yourself to sea.

Q: You were the author of that original memo?

Dyer: That's right.

I'd get these little chits. So and so would say, "How about relieving me?" But I had made up my mind, the Lord willing, that I was going to get to sea and a Command in the Pacific.

The first thing that happened was that Admiral Moon, who was ordered to Command an Amphibious Group in the Mediterranean, came down to the hospital to see me and asked me to be his Chief of Staff. I had just come from a Chief of Staff to Rear Admiral Conolly in an Amphibious Group, and also in the Mediterranean. So I was sure that was one thing I was not going to do over again. Although it was very interesting and stimulating and kept you close to the war, that was one thing I knew I wasn't going to do again. More particularly, and I say this very softly, I was sure that Admiral Moon would be his own Chief of Staff and that I really wouldn't have a job. He was completely different from Admiral Conolly.

Admiral Conolly made, with no problem at all, all the big decisions. He didn't pay any attention to the details. The Chief of Staff handled all the details. Just to illustrate, in all the time that I was with him, he only signed two letters. I signed every other letter than went out of that office, and literally thousands of them went out. He never signed the letters.

Q: He was one of those fortunate men who could delegate authority.

Dyer: That's right, and be happy with it.

Admiral Moon I had known as a Midshipman. He was my three striper. He was a first classman, and a three striper in my company. He was the most meticulous individual, very bright, star man at the Academy. But he was a "do it yourself man." He did everything himself. And he had continued to do everything himself all during his career.

Q: That ultimately was his downfall, wasn't it?

Dyer: That's right. He got to worrying about the details and shot himself. Anyhow I told him, "No can do."

Johnny Roper, at that time Captain Roper, who was later Chief of the Bureau of Naval Personnel, was the Captain Detail Officer. Johnny was a classmate and an old friend. I thought very highly of him and I thought he thought very highly of me. He eventually became convinced that I was going to go to sea. Because every time he would call up and offer me a shore detail, I would say, "Johnny, I'm going to go to sea again. I'm going to go to sea in Command of something. If you don't do it on your own, I'll go down to COMINCH and get somebody there that can tell you to do it, to so detail me." He finally accepted that. He quit trying to get me to accept a shore detail.

One day he called me up and he said, "If you can get out of the hospital in two weeks, I can give you Command of Admiral Kirk's flag ship, the AUGUSTA, which was for the Normandy invasion." Of course, that was a good detail.

I came out of the little phone booth where he had called me and at the end of the hall was the doctor's office. My doctor was in there and he was looking right down the hall. He had the whole ward up there. When I walked through the

the door he said, "The answer is 'no.' I know by the look on your face that you've just been offered a good sea detail and that you want me to let you go to sea. I'm not going to let you go to sea and hear you called 'Gimpy Dyer." You're going to have to stay here at least another month until I can work that limp out of you." And he did.

So that is how I didn't go to the AUGUSTA. But as a matter of fact, it worked out extremely well.

Johnny called me one day and said, "We're putting a new cruiser division into commission, Cruiser Division 17. J. Cary Jones is the Division Commander. You can either have the flag ship or the ASTORIA." I said, "I will take the ASTORIA."

I knew J. Cary Jones reasonably well. I knew him not only professionally, but he was a great stamp collector and I was a stamp collector. I used to see him and talk with him.

The PASADENA was the flag ship, and my classmate Dick Tuggle had command of it. Felix Johnson, who lives down south here about thirty or forty miles, was the skipper of the SPRINGFIELD. A chap in the class of '17, Robert Lee Porter, was the skipper of the WILKES-BARRE, which was the other ship of the Division.

Q: This was a brand new type of cruiser?

Dyer: No, basically they were an improved CLEVELAND type, the CLSS type. The ASTORIA went into commission on the 17th of May 1944.

I want to add something to this right now. As of today,

26 years later, the SPRINGFIELD is the flagship of our Sixth Fleet. In other words, the biggest and best that we have is the flagship of our most important Fleet, the Sixth Fleet, 26 years old. Out in the Pacific, the WILKES-BARRE, also a ship of the same Division, in commission 26 years, is the flagship of the Seventh Fleet. That is indicative of how old our fighting Navy, so-called, really is.

Q: Yes. There was much publicity on that just recently.

Dyer: It's just terrible to think that we're forced ot use ships that are that old as the flagships of our two most important Fleets.

Q: Admiral what are the distinguishing characteristics of this class of cruisers? How did they differ from previous ones?

Dyer: They didn't differ greatly. They were of the CL-55 CLEVELAND class of cruisers. Those now still in commission have all been fitted with some rocket launchers. But when they first went into commission, they had just their six-inch guns, (6"/47) of which they had twelve. They had also a very good five-inch anti-aircraft battery, twelve 5"/38. They were roughly 30½ knot ships, although designed for 33 knots. They had a fine engineering plant. (General Electric geared turbine, 100,000 horse power).

Q: What displacement?

Dyer: Their so called "standard displacement", "treaty ton basis" was 10,000 tons. They were theoretically about 13,750 tons at full load. Actually they operated at about 15,000 tons. In other words, they were overloaded from the day they were designed. Because they kept developing new things during the war and if you heard of a new thing, you'd try to get it on your ship. So that they were very much overloaded, but extremely good shooting ships.

They had wonderful engineering plants, once they had ironed out the initial bearing problem which arose from inadequate white lead in their bearings, when they first went into commission.

The ASTORIA, CL90 has been decommissioned, she's still around, but she's not in full commission, and probably never will be. She is currently designated a "Fire support ship."

Q: Just a digression, sir, I know it's a complex reason, but primarily why has our Navy been permitted to go on this way using the old and outmoded ships?

Dyer: They haven't been able to get the money to buy new ones. In the first place you want to realize that the Navy came out of World War II very much sold on the value of aircraft carriers. For a large part in the intervening years, the top man in the Navy has been a naval aviator or someone who owes his advancement due to the fact of his acceptance of the naval aviation point of view.

When the chips are down and the decision is, "Do you

want a carrier which costs a billion dollars, or do you want four cruisers which will cost together a billion dollars?" The answer from the top man in the Navy has been, "We'll take the carrier." Because the Navy hasn't been able to get both, as a matter of financial politics and budgets getting through the Congress, against a growing peace movement in the United States.

Q: So primarily it has been an emphasis on the carrier, to the detriment of the line ship.

Dyer: That's right.

The fact is that the Congress turned down the latest carrier, after they had gotten it through the House, but it had not gotten through the Senate. In the Conference Committee, the House gave way and the carrier was lost.

Q: Is this the Eisenhower?

Dyer: No, this was the one after that.

So actually the Navy got nothing out of the big effort. They did have the money in for this carrier as it passed the House, but no authorization or money from the Senate for it. Eventually the authorization was dropped.

I don't know what the ultimate answer is. I do know that you can't run ships for ever and have them first class. Ships age.

Q: Maybe the fact that it's quite apparent now that we're up against a first class Navy, we'll do something about it.

Dyer: Of course, they did get this year (1970) extra money through the efforts of Senator Stennis and Congressman Rivers. They did produce some extra money for the Navy this year. They had first started out to get a billion dollars, and they ended up by being very happy to get roughly a third of that for building program.

To go back to the story - The ASTORIA went into commission on May 17, 1944. Admiral Milo F. Draemal was the Commandant of the Fourth Naval District.

She started out very happily with roughly 1300 people in the crew and about 80 officers. I had about five regulars out of that 80, and had about 50 pre-World War II sailor men in the crew. There were, of course, quite a number (150 maybe) of the '40 and '41 period, because the Navy had expanded quite rapidly. Those people had come in in '40 and '41 and gotten quite rapid promotion with the enlisted rank.

Q: I see why you underscore the pre-World War II personnel.

Dyer: They were the people who served in the Navy during the time of it's depression and they were old time sailor men. In any case they were a very willing outfit of both officers and men.

I had a number of amusing things during the period when I was just commissioned. One thing, I got a letter from the Chief of the Bureau of Engineering, who was Vice Admiral E. W. Mills.

He had a friend who later became (1946) Secretary of the

Interior, Julius A. Krug. Krug was a young fellow who was a fresh caught Lieutenant Commander in the naval reserve. He wanted to go to sea in naval ship. He wanted to fight the war. He would resign his present job with the War Production Board and go to sea in the Navy.

Mills wrote me a letter and I wrote back and said I wasn't interested. The man had never been on board ship before in his life. He wanted to come aboard ship as Lieutenant Commander. Mills insisted he could be the First Lieutenant.

I had been a Damage Control Officer as a first Lieutenant and I knew the real background of nitty gritty knowledge you had to have to be a useful Damage Control Officer. So I said, "No."

Then this chap walked into my cabin one day in Philadelphia and gave me a real sales pitch. He was a salesman, if I ever knew one. But I just dug in and said, "No." I told him, "In this ship we have one Captain and one Commander, the Executive Officer. We have six Lieutenant Commanders, Heads of Departments. I feel that all the young reserve officers should be able to look at every Lieutenant Commander on this ship and say, "There is an officer who knows something about the Navy and to whom I can look to get some good sound naval advice." If you put on a uniform of a Lieutenant Commander, you don't become a Lieutneant Commander that quick, you're merely disguising a civilian as a Lieutenant Commander. I'm not going to breach that wall."

Q: Why had he concentrated on you?

Dyer: Mills, who was the Chief of the Bureau of Engineering, I had served with on various occasions. He evidently had picked me out as somebody he thought would handle this chap, and it would be a place where he would be properly handled. I think I would have, if they had insisted. If they had insisted on doing it, I would have had to take him and handle him. I was very fortunate that they didn't insist on it. That was just one of the things that happened.

Another thing which Mills asked, which I was extremely happy to cooperate with. He wrote a letter to a number of Commanding Officers, one of whom was the Commanding Officer of the ASTORIA. He said that the Bureau had developed some protective suits which were supposed to be shrapnel proof suits, due to the fact that the Bureau of Medicine and Surgery had reported wounded by flying shrapnel. He would like to have these protective suits put on and tested. They would have to be really tested to tell whether they were worthwhile.

I was a chap who had been wounded, I knew you could get wounded. Most people think the other guy gets wounded, but I never get wounded. I knew you could be. So I wrote a letter back and said I'd be delighted to test them.

We went on our shakedown cruise with the Training Command. The place where you carried out your shakedown training was in Trinidad, where it was hotter than all Harry.

Q: This was within the big harbor there?

Dyer: There and outside. You trained both in the Bay and

outside the Bay, depending on training you were carrying out.

The suits covered you from head to foot, particularly protected in the breast and back, with heavy head protection and so forth. They were hotter than all Harry to wear.

Of course, the men perspired and the suits became smelly. They were really something. Gradually you could observe, in looking down at your gun crews, on the five-inch guns they were not being worn. They were to be worn, presumably, by all people on topside who would be exposed to shrapnel. Of course, I wore mine and the bridge crew wore theirs. I could understand the sailor man's reluctance to wear the suits.

One thing that I insisted on, and that was that every officer wear his. I didn't let a single officer get away with not wearing his. If I spotted an officer topside during general quarters without it, he immediately got a message from me. With the result that rather than have that, they all wore them during general quarters.

We got out to the Pacific. One of the first times that we were in action, the Gunnery Officer got a great big piece of shrapnel right over his heart. His name was Lieutenant Commander Kenneth E. Meneke. This raised black and blue spots and so forth, but didn't kill him, and didn't break his flesh.

Q: Dramatic illustration, wasn't it?

Dyer: So I took this suit and had it stuffed and put it right at the head of the chow line. There it stood day after day after day, for an illustration of there was a man whose life had been saved by this suit. The day after the suit appeared, a lot more people wore their suits topside, and eventually everybody wore them. We got into a position where we just told people to do it, and they did it because they knew there was a good reason behind it. In other words, they'd become convinced.

Q: Would they put them on at the beginning of an engagement, or what?

Dyer: When the general alarm went off, you never knew whether it was for real or for phony, they put on their suits. They wore it to their general quarters station, and they wore it until they secured from general quarters.

To tell the story to the full end--The great problem that existed in our anti-aircraft battles with the Jap air attacks was that the ships were constantly maneuvering. The Jap planes would dive down and the guns would follow them down. If the Fire Control Officers were not sufficiently adept to cut off the fire in time to stop the guns before they fired into other ships, the result was that a very large number of people in our Navy were wounded by our own fire.

We were in one of these go rounds out there, after we had been out in the Pacific a number of months, when the Jap planes after making their attack came down and flew right between the lines of the light cruisers that were protecting the carriers. Some ships didn't cut off, and they put a five inch shell right into the ASTORIA's bridge just eleven feet from where I was standing. It filled the bridge full of shrapnel, of course. The shell exploded when it hit the light armour that we had and was scattered all over. I had thirteen pieces of shrapnel in my suit.

One of the requirements to get a Purple Heart was that you had to draw blood. I looked very carefully because I had a Purple Heart, and I would have been very proud to get a second one. But I couldn't find any, I had some black and blue spots, but I didn't get another Purple Heart.

We took pictures of the hole that had been made in the ASTORIA's bridge. I stood at the apex of a triangle of enlisted men at the forward end of the bridge, and right before the radarscope and the voice radios. Some of the people who were in the rear end of this echelon got Purple Hearts. I've got a picture of the ceremony, where I handed out the Purple Hearts. I always said, "I was running the fastest, and they were the ones that got caught."

They were very valuable suits. I wrote this very glowing letter and sent the pictures and all that sort of thing. But I was the only ship that made a favorable report.

Q: They were used in other ships?

Dyer: Oh yes, they were used on half a dozen ships.

Q: What was their future? Were they widespread after that, or what?

Dyer: To the best of my knowledge, they never became used widely. They were very irksome to wear.

To go back, on the way to Trinidad, this was a chain of events that I did not know until some years later. The need for the invasion of the southern France called for an extra cruiser. Admiral C. M. Cooke told me this story. They had the dispatch all written out telling me to break off my shakedown cruise and head for the Mediterranean. I had two destroyers with me. And to join the cruisers supporting the invasion of southern France.

They had already written the dispatch, it had been initialed for release. Admiral C. M. Cooke was holding the dispatch, when they handed him another one from me which had just come in saying that I had wiped my main bearings and stripped the turbine on the port side. Of course, that was a major casualty.

The first dispatch they wrote after that told me to return to the Navy Yard, Philadelphia to have the repairs completed. But I originated a dispatch and said that I would like to continue the shakedown on one engine. Permission was granted to do that and I went on down and continued my shake down. Then went back to Philadelphia. As I pointed out in my dispatch - It would take some time to get the new bearings and new turbines and so forth, and I could be conducting the shakedown, and they could be assembling the material. When I got back to the Yard, they could do what had to be done. And that was the decision.

When we got back to the Philadelphia Yard, it was a major operation to install new turbine blades and to install new main bearings.

At this time there was a real question in my mind as to whether the loss of oil pressure had been handled properly in the engine room, and had resulted in the handling of the turbines so that they were slowed down immediately and brought to a stop. So even if they lost oil in the lubricating system of the bearings, it wouldn't result in stripping the turbine. So we worked on drilling for that.

We got the new turbine blades in, and went down through the Canal and up the west coast. We were coming into San Diego Harbor when we had exactly the same casualty, except that we did not strip the turbine. In other words, the bearing wiped, due actually to a defect in the bearing, but there was no major damage and we went on to San Francisco.

Q: Had this been a replacement in Philadelphia?

Dyer: Yes.

After I reported a second bearing casualty, we were sent up to the Mare Island Yard. I found out that two other cruisers in the Division had had the same bearing problem. The Bureau found that out. I didn't know that, but they ordered Captain Joseph S. Evans, who was a very wonderful Engineer, as the Senior Member of a special Board of Inspection and Survey to come out and take a look at this thing.

They found out that the Bureau, due to a shortage of the right kind of material to put in the bearings, had authorized a reduction in certain aspects of the bearing material. This was 25 years ago or more, and I cannot tell you just exactly what it was. The word "antimony" is the one that sticks in my mind, which was the thing they were short of.

They gave us brand new bearings. We stayed in Mare Island roughly three weeks, while they manufactured new bearings and shipped them by Navy Air out to Mare Island and installed them. In addition they gave us a spare pair of bearings of the new ones. In other words, we not only got in the new bearings, but we had new spares. We operated all the rest of the time in the Pacific, and never had a bearing problem.

Q: If you had, and had a spare on board, could this have been taken care of at sea?

Dyer: Yes. We rolled them in and out in drill.

Q: It doesn't pay, as usual, to get a substitute.

Dyer: They had determined the right material and then they had thought they could do this and that, but it cost them many thousands of dollars. A new bearing in a cruiser is expensive, but stripping a turbine when the bearing drops down and the turbine blades impinge on the turbine frame, that's tremendously expensive. That's hundred of thousands of dollars rather than thousands of dollars. We only stripped the turbine blades once.

Captain Evans really saved my life because when this happened the second time in the ASTORIA, of course, it came to Admiral King's attention. He told Admiral Edwards at that time, and Admiral Edwards told me this story: He said, "Maybe we ought to relieve Dyer." There was a question, "Was the crew handling the casualty promptly enough?"

We did handle it the second time and no problem resulted, except, of course, we lost the bearing when it melted due to the improper constituency that was in it. That, of course, clogged the circulation of oil and you had to shut down the shaft and stop the turbine before the bearing dropped enough to strip the turbine.

He wrote up a report which, as far as I was concerned, said, "No fault is to be found in the ship's handling of this casualty." Those were saving words, as far as I was concerned.

The Navy was having a tremendous "absent without leave" problem, due to a reluctance of the American citizens to actively participate in the war. You talk about their not wanting to fight in Viet Nam, there were just literally thousands that didn't want to fight in World War II, and don't let anyone tell you otherwise.

Q: What was the motivation for this?

Dyer: Let me tell you this story - When I put the ASTORIA in commission, I had a bright idea. At least, I thought it was a bright idea. It turned out to be "stinko profundo."

I thought it would be a wonderful thing to get some of the sailor men out of the heavy cruiser ASTORIA, survivors at the Battle of Savo Island, for whom the cruiser I commanded was named for, and get them into the crew of the new ASTORIA. Imbued as I was with a desire to pay back these Japanese so and sos for what they'd done to me, I thought that the ordinary sailor man would have the same idea.

Q: And it was a direct continuity.

Dyer: So the Bureau very kindly ordered six, the senior one of which was a Boatswain's mate, a line Petty Officer Second Class whose name was Lemon.

Before we sailed for our first Shakedown Cruise down to Trinidad, I got all the crew together and told them we were due to sail. I told them I wanted every one of them on board ship and I knew there was an absent without leave problem, but they would really show that they were a panty-waist, if they were not aboard the USS ASTORIA when she sailed for shake down. I said, "You're not even sailing for a war zone. You're sailing in the safe Atlantic."

So actually we only had four sailor men who were absent without leave when we went down. As a matter of fact, a couple of them were what I call "legitimate missing the ship." They were drunk and not physically able to make it. Police had picked them up on the street and they were actually in the jail at Philadelphia. So I only had two that consciously missed the ship.

Q: Incidentally, what was the punishment that was meted out to an A.W.O.L.?

Dyer: It depended a great deal on the Commanding Officer. I treated them severely. That's the answer to that.

Then the next big sailing was when we sailed from Hampton Road for the West Coast. Again I gave them a big how do you do. I got them all together, told them what hour we were sailing, gave them plenty of notice, and told them I wanted them all on board. We sailed for the west coast with only four missing. Which again, was a comparatively small number.

When we got to San Diego and sailed from San Diego to San Francisco, we had six missing and one of them was my man Lemon. So I sat down and wrote a letter to the Chief of the Bureau of Personnel.

I had had the Executive Officer and the Division Officers investigate. They gave me statements from a number of other sailor men about how Lemon had been saying for some weeks that he was not going to sail back out into the actual fighting area. I said that all the resources of the Bureau should be put to work to locate Lemon and to restore him to the USS ASTORIA wherever she might be. I had been told, in fact, some of these sailor men said, that Lemon said he was going to report in at New Orleans.

The Commandant at New Orleans name had been Frank T. Leighton. He was the same Leighton whom I had relieved when he was on Admiral King's staff when I was a Commander. Admiral Russell Willson had called me in and said, "Admiral King has directed that you go down and relieve Admiral Leighton." I relieved him as a Commander. The Chief of Staff in New Orleans was an old submariner that I had known for many years, whose name was Johnny Longstaff, out of the class of '20. The Commandant of the 8th Naval District in late 1944 was Rear Admiral A. C. Bennett. He and his Discipline Officer were just letting these sailormen miss ship on the West Coast, and when they reported in at New Orleans, just slapping them on the wrist and not giving them any real punishment.

So I pointed out to the Bureau that New Orleans was a haven for the deserters from the war area, and something should be done about that.

I got a letter from the Discipline Officer of the Bureau of Naval Personnel, who was Captain Armand J. Robertson. He sent me a copy of a wonderful letter that he had sent to every Commandant in the United States with this indictment of the Eighth Naval District which I, a Captain, had penned. His letter was extremely well written.

He told me that if Lemon showed up anywhere in Naval jurisdiction that the Bureau would produce him and they'd produce the other five people if they ever showed up in the Naval jurisdiction and get them back on board the ASTORIA.

In Robertson's letter, he had developed the facts upon which I had only asserted that this was what sailormen said. He had a lot of specifics.

Lemon did show up in New Orleans, before this was all in the mill, and he was assigned very moderate punishment. The Bureau started him back towards the ASTORIA.

To finish the Lemon story - We were fueling the ship when the tanker came alongside and said they had transferees for us. (This was at sea somewhere out in the Philippine area or the Sea of Japan. I don't remember the exact location we were. We went to sea for long periods of time. I was at sea 68 days once and 61 days another time. Months sort of float into each other.) The Bureau routed him out, Lemon, and they routed out all the other five, and they all came back.

This list came over and Lemon's name was on it. When he came aboard, I got on the loudspeaker and I said that, "Boatswain's mate Second Class Lemon was back aboard." He hadn't been disrated, which was the first thing they should have done. He was a Second Class Line Petty Officer deserting in time of war, and he hadn't been punished for the offense he had committed. He was legally beyond any punishment that I might be able to assign him. I turned him over to the crew. I told the crew, "I have assigned him where none of you will be under his command, because I think he's unfitted for command." I made him Captain of the boatswain's gear storage space, called the "Forward Hold."

The crew put him in coventry, wouldn't talk to him. About a month after he came aboard, he asked for a Captain's mast which any sailor man could do in those days. The Exec brought him up to the Captain's mast. He said, "Captain, I've been punished enough. By this time I'm very, very sorry for what I did," and so forth and so on. He had a good song and dance. I said, "As far as I'm concerned, I'm not going to do a blooming thing about it. When the crew relents on you, they'll relent on you. When they figure that you've had enough punishment, they'll let up on you. Not I, because I don't think you've had enough punishment." I detailed my extremely low opinion on what sailor men with his time in the Navy, and he had eight or nine years in the Navy, what I thought of him.

Maybe another month, again he came to Captain's mast and

he asked for a transfer. I said, "You can put in a written request for transfer. I will disapprove it, because I think you're getting your just reward. I'm just as fond of this crew as I can be for what they're doing to you."

About a month later the Exec told me that they were now talking to him. He was still in the ship when I left.

Q: How did they handle the other five?

Dyer: The other five were all people who had been drafted or had enlisted for the war. They were all Seamen Second Class. I don't think anything ever happened to them. If it did, it wasn't of any great significance.

You were constantly getting orders from the Department to transfer to the United States certain numbers of people to outfit new ships. About every ten days you'd get one of these dispatches. You'd have to take your trained people and sometimes the untrained ones, because there was a certain number of seamen and firemen they sent back, and send them back. The only thing I did was I said, "Don't ever permit their names to be on these lists. They may be perfectly worthless, and they are probably so because of what they did, but they've got to stay in this ship as long as I'm in this ship."

They stayed as far as I know. I never actually made any effort to follow this. I presume that the Exec carried out my orders. I never heard anything about it.

On board ship out there in the Far Pacific when you go up on the bridge when you leave port, and when you stay there for 60 days or more, you're an operational man. You have to assume that everything below is going to happen the way it ought to happen. So that you don't follow the details like you do in peacetime, where you have to nurture every man individually. I didn't do that at all.

To go back to sailing from San Francisco - When we sailed from San Francisco, I sailed in company with two heavy cruisers, I was a light cruiser, and there a Division of destroyers for Honolulu. I was the junior skipper. My radio call was "Low Life." Captain Harry D. Hoffman, (Class of 1918) who was the Officer of Tactical Command, would come on the voice radio and say, "Low Life." He really talked to me like I was "Low Life."

When we sailed from San Francisco, we sailed with eight absentees. When we got close to Hawaii, all the cruisers and destroyers were gathered under the Command of CruDesPac. That was Rear Admiral W. H. P. Blandy. He sent a dispatch for Commanding Officers to report to him upon arrival at Pearl Harbor.

The sailing with eight absentees worried me all the way to Honolulu, and I really mean it. I had concocted half a dozen speeches that I was going to make on why we had eight absentees because I had really worked on the crew by making talks to them to keep the number of absentees very low.

We walked into Blandy's Headquarters, three skippers to pay their respects and to be told what we were going to do and we weren't going to do. The three skippers were Carl Fink, in my class, Hasty Hoffman, out of 1918, and myself.

Admiral Blandy just gave the first two of them the very

devil. One of them had sailed with 68 absentees, and other one 57 (as I remember the numbers). So he gave me a letter of commendation for sailing with only eight, after I had really just worried about it all the way over to Hawaii, because in my opinion we should have sailed with none.

Q: Had the High Command in Washington taken any cognizance of this problem?

Dyer: If they had, it wasn't within my knowledge, except what later came out of Robertsons' letter.

After we got into Pearl Harbor, one thing that you had to do was to go through the Kahoolawe Firing Range down at the Island of Kahoolawe where you were really given training, although you had received a tremendous amount of instruction in this from the Training Command, on conducting close fire support. It was an excellent course, just a wonderful course they had worked out.

During the course of the ASTORIA's going through this Firing Range thing, they put you through it and marked you on everything you did. If you didn't pass, then you had to go through a second time. During the firing, we developed a turret casualty.

They had to send back to the Naval Gun Factory in Washington to get the particular new pieces that they had to put in the turret, with the result that I did not sail with the other two cruisers to the Far Pacific. As a result, I missed the battle of the Philippine Sea, to my great regret.

Dyer 10 - 392

When I was due to sail, I got my sailing orders, I was directed to sail independently without destroyer escort from Pearl to Ulithi. So I went over and talked to the Assistant Operations Officer, who was Howie Collins much later, Rear Admiral H. W. Collins. (He is now the Secretary of the Retired Officers Association.)

I said, "Howie, I want an escort." Commander Collins said, "I can't give you an escort." I said, "I want an escort." The same reply came back, "I can't give you an escort. Sorry, you'll just have to sail without one."

So I went back and wrote a dispatch to the Commander in Chief, Pacific and said, "Having been ordered to sail without escort from Pearl to Ulithi, I request escorts," and I got them.

The INDIANAPOLIS, when she was ordered to make the same thing, except she was ordered to sail to Guam, if she had requested escort, in my opinion she would have had escorts instead of being sunk by a Japanese submarine when she didn't have any escort.

You put the man on the spot. Otherwise the burden is on you, the Commanding Officer, you've accepted the order. I said, "Having been ordered to sail without escorts, I request escorts," and I got them.

Escorts being two destroyers. They're hard to come by and sure there was a scarcity of them. But I thought I should have them, and I got them.

I went on out. When you arrived in Ulithi, in those days, anyhow, they actually truck in the instructions that governs what you're going to do from then on. They give you a pile of instructions.

We were operating in two Fleets, the Third Fleet and the Fifth Fleet: The Third Fleet commanded by Admiral Halsey, and the Fifth Fleet commanded by Admiral Spruance. They rotated and their Staffs rotated.

When I left Ulithi, I went out with the ALABAMA, a big battleship, Commanded by Captain Vince Murphy, with escorts and so forth. We fell in with the Task Group at night. If you can imagine, if you had never operated with a Task Group, it's large, as these Task Groups and Task Forces were.

In the first place the Task Forces were made up of two or three, normally three, Task Groups, some times even four Task Groups. You had 300 ships gathered in a very small area and they're going at high speed, when you come in to join them it's really something. And if you join them at night, it's really double something.

I had had the great advantage of having gone to the Radar School. That was one thing - When I was ordered to Command the ASTORIA--Before I went over to North Africa I had asked to be ordered to the Fire Fighting School, and I asked to go to it again because I had fought a number of fires over in the Mediterranean.

I went to the Fire Fighting School, and I also went to the Radar School and I learned to read radar. Really to be able to look at it and know what it means, when you have all kinds of ships on it, you really have to have a marked skill if you're going to do that well.

We joined up with the Task Group, that was one of the hairiest times I ever had because I was assigned a position in the middle of these fast moving ships. To move your ship safely, safe to them and safe to yourself, requires a high degree of skill. I was so grateful for that Radar School that night, I just thanked them and the good Lord a half a dozen times, because it would have been almost impossible if I hadn't had that training. It was very wonderful training.

I moved into the Task Group. I was in both the Fifth Fleet and the Third Fleet. We did the Iwo Jima operation and we did the Okinawa operation. We did bombardments of various islands. We did a lot of chores.

One of the things that I remember best was the day that the FRANKLIN was badly damaged. The BIRMINGHAM, as you remember, went alongside of her and fought the fire and got badly damaged herself. Tommy Inglis was the skipper.

The Task Force Commander, who was Rear Admiral Frederick Sherman, moved one light cruiser from one Task Group to another Task Group because the BIRMINGHAM and another ship had fallen out to fight the fire in the FRANKLIN. I was the one who was directed to go from my Task Group to the other one.

We normally cruised at 25 knots. My actual speed was about $30\frac{1}{2}$. I cranked up full speed and off I went. Normally there's twenty-thirty miles between Task Groups. Some Jap plane evidently sighted me out there all be myself, without any destroyer escort or anything else. He sent word back and, in due time, the Bogies were reported. The cover that was over the Task Groups was vectored out and took on these Jap planes. As always, or nearly always, some of them got through.

One of the closest calls I had was these two planes that got very close to the ship, headed right for us very obviously kamikaze bent. We destroyed one of them, when it was about 1,000 yards from the ship where it exploded and disappeared. The other one came boring in, burning all over, but still coming on. It got in about 300 yards from the ship. It got inside the range where your five-inch shell explodes. Everything in the ship, of course, was shooting at it, including the 50 caliber guns, 30 caliber guns, and the five-inch, and everything else. It was deflected and came down 30 or 40 feet on the side.

It splattered the ship with all kinds of machine gun bullets until the very last minute. They were shooting at us, they had good aim, they couldn't have much else. That was really the closest the ASTORIA ever had to a real kamikaze attack.

Q: You say they, was there more than one Japanese?

Dyer: There were two planes that started initially.

Q: In each plane was there more than one Japanese?

Dyer: Just one. We recovered the pilot, the dead body. I circled around lowered a boat, and got the Japanese pilot out. He was dead.

Evidence, you had to produce evidence that you'd sunk

these things or they wouldn't give you credit. There were too many times, of course, when we didn't have the evidence.

Q: My point was, there was only one pilot in a Japanese kamikaze plane?

Dyer: That's right. We only recovered one.

One thing I'd like to mention in the same incident: The Chaplain was a great camera bug. His battle station was down at the dressing room, where he says good-bye to the boys that are about to die. He was a great camera bug, and in the middle of this action he was on top taking pictures. The pictures were wonderful, but he picked up some shrapnel in his spine.

My first thought was to transfer him to the Hospital Ship by destroyer. The senior doctor's name was White.

Dr. White came to me and said, "The Chaplain is just pleading to stay with the ship. He doesn't want to go to a Hospital Ship and then be transferred home. He wants to stay with the ship. As far as the operation is concerned, I assure you I am perfectly competent to do this operation just as well as it can be done anywhere. I recommend the patient stay with the ship." I said, "Sure, I'd be glad to keep him. You do the operation and we'll keep him." So he did the operation and about six weeks later the Chaplain was up and around and well enough to hold services.

During the period that he was not on board, the Exec held most of the services. One of these periods we were at Ulithi at anchor and I held the services.

When the Chaplain got well enough to hold services, I went to the services. The subject of his sermon was, "The Lord plays no favorites." Don't you think that was wonderful?

I want to tell you something about the ASTORIA. When the ship was going into commission I said, "The ASTORIA has got to have a name," a nickname. So in the ship's paper we announced a contest for a name for the ASTORIA. Her number was CL-90.

We put a box out on deck. I appointed one Chief Petty Officer, one Petty Officer First Class, and one Petty Officer Second Class--fortunately not Lemon--as members of the board to pick the name since it ought to be a sailor man's name. We put the box up and said when we would open it, and then this group of three would decide.

I went by the box one night and dropped in a typed name, "The Mighty Ninety." There were all kinds of other names. The committee picked "The Mighty Ninety" as their name. I never told anybody that I was the originator of it, I was afraid to. So she was named "The Mighty Ninety," and that's what she was called.

Q: I hope you will tell me about some of your recollections of the Iwo Jima operation itself.

Dyer: I was there when the Marines put the flag up on Mount Suribachi.

The first thing that happened at Iwo Jima--They had this fire support schedule all worked out.

Q: You were under Admiral Blandy at that point?

Dyer: The answer to that is "no".

The Gunfire and Covering Force was under Rear Admiral Bert Rodgers. Blandy was on the echelon above Rodgers in command of the Amphibious Support Force.

Blandy again had the Amphibious Support Group at Okinawa and Rear Admiral Mort Deyo had the Gunfire and Covering Force. By and large the people who were at Iwo Jima did not make Okinawa, because the Iwo Jima operation did not cease until the 21st of March and Okinawa commenced on the 1st of April, 1945.

I was ordered up to relieve a battleship. As I moved into the berth sea area, which she had been occupying, the first thing that happened to me was that some Japanese guns on the beach opened up on me. The first shot just cleared my fo'castle and landed in the water on the far side.

I had not sent my dispatch to the Commanding Officer of the ship that I was relieving, because you were to send it when you were all ready to open fire. He could cease fire and you open fire. I know that I sent the dispatch, "I hereby relieve you of this hot spot."

Of course, we were assigned targets by the Shore Fire Control Officers. All we did was to try to fulfill their needs. They would spot for us and do everything else.

Q: And the Japanese batteries were very hard to locate, weren't they?

Dyer: Impossible to locate because all you ever saw was the

flash. You wouldn't see the flash half of the time. The guns were in caves. The flash was killed by the side of the caves. You just didn't see their guns.

There are two things that I remember about Iwo Jima. We were providing support at night. You had a quota of shells that you could fire during any hourly period. Then you had a certain emergency quota. Based on your judgment, and on information that you got from the shore, you could throw in this emergency quota or not. But there was only one emergency quota for your period of firing.

Q: This was all predicated on logistics?

Dyer: Yes, the available ammunition.

And you had a quota of star shells. The star shells, again, you had an emergency quota that you could throw in. We shot all night. From dark 'til dawn, we were providing the gunfire support for the Marines. Their cries were for these star shells, keeping things illuminated, because the Japs were really giving them fits.

The real test of your judgment was in knowing that the call at four o'clock in the morning might be more urgent than the call you had yielded to at ten o'clock the previous night. You had to judge when and how to allocate those small rations of emergency shells that you had.

It was a real toughie, and could be made by nobody else except the Commanding Officer. You had to use every bit of your judgment and knowledge to do it.

Q: That's where a computer might have been handy.

Dyer: I don't know about that. A computer is no good, except for what you can put into it. It can't produce more than you put into it. If you don't put good knowledge into it, you don't get good answers out of it.

Q: And, of course, no experience to go on in a situation like this.

Dyer: It made a very real impression on me. You stayed up all night, because you got constant calls. You never could respond to all the calls that you got. You would hear the Marines on the lower echelon pleading with their Gunfire Control Officer by voice radio for this and that. You tempered your judgment in regard to what you should or shouldn't do.

We re-ammunitioned each day we were there, in other words, they knew how many shells there were in the bucket. When you went off the line, the bucket was empty. You had to go over to the Ammunition Ship for re-ammunition and then go back.

We had had a small number up to that time at Iwo Jima of night kamikaze attacks, but the threat persisted. In the early days of Iwo Jima, they had damaged the SARATOGA. They had sunk one of the LSTs and they had really gotten around. So that you were concerned about planes.

Q: And also weren't you concerned about the kaiten, the little Japanese submarines?

Dyer: Not at Iwo Jima, no. At Okinawa, the answer is "yes."

I don't know that at that time (Iwo Jima) I had ever even heard of them. It was only when we came into the Okinawa area, that we got into them. Suicide boats, they were called.

The other thing was that the Marines had great difficulty getting up Suribachi. The Gunfire Support people had great difficulty doing anything. They were just shooting into the side of a mountain with no great success. While the Gunfire Support at Suribachi undoubtedly made it dangerous for Japs to do anything except sit in holes and shoot at people they could see, by and large it was done by the courage of the individual Marine who went up and lobbed a grenade into a hole. Then a couple of minutes later, somebody lobbed two or three in. Eventually somebody had enough courage to go in and see whether anybody was still alive. It was pretty grim, the chance of Gunfire Support putting a shell into the very small holes that they had.

In the Korean War, the North Koreans weren't nearly as smart. Their gun apertures were a great deal larger. In Wonsan Harbor, it was a lot easier to put a shell into one of those gun apertures than it was at Mount Suribachi.

We shot an awful lot of ammunition at Iwo Jima. I don't know that we accomplished too much in the day time, but we did accomplish, I think, a very real chore at night.

I never will forget the cries, I'm talking about real cries, that came out from some of these Marine Units when the Japs were making night rushes at them, how they wanted illumination and gunfire support.

Q: The ASTORIA was there for the entire operation?

Dyer: On no. We were there, I think, only four days.

We did not participate in the initial two or three days of the landing operation. I can't give you the exact date, I can look it up in the log. It was all run on a schedule. We knew ten days or two weeks ahead that D plus such and such a day, we would come on the line. They rotated the ships up on the line or back with the fast Carrier Task Forces. We were in the fast Carrier Task Force at this time.

Q: In order to complement and supplement your previous remarks on morale and so forth, how did the crew of the ASTORIA stand up?

Dyer: They just loved it. They grumbled, of course, but just as proud as peacocks. They knew they were doing something. They knew they were accomplishing what the ship was built for, and it made them very proud. And I think darn happy. Like every Captain, I was proud of my crew. When I left the ship this is what they gave me.

Q: This is quite a tribute, and I'm going to read it!
June 9, 1945

"Let it be known to all men that George Carroll Dyer, a Captain of the United States Navy, while serving as Commanding Officer of his valiant and fighting ship, the USS ASTORIA, has by his courage and untiring efforts inspired and led this ship and crew through strenuous days of training and into battle against the enemy. These efforts have greatly aided the establishment of the fine reputation this ship now holds in the Fleet. The "Mighty Ninety" has successfully met and stopped all enemy resistance on every front she has yet fought.

Know you all that as Captain George Carroll Dyer leaves this ship on this 9th day of June, in the year of our Lord 1945, his merits of leadership, determination, and courage shall live on in those of us who remain behind. It is with regret that we see him depart. God speed and good luck in his new assignment. May we be fortunate enough to serve with him again."

The officers and men of the USS ASTORIA.

I hope that the signature of Lemon was attached. Was it?

Dyer: It had no signatures. This was secured by them from San Francisco, after I had left the ship and sent to me in Washington.

Q: Admiral, perhaps at this point would be a good place to comment on this second point: Discuss your estimate of the value of the ASTORIA as a screening ship and for shore bombardment, as compared with an eight-inch cruiser.

Dyer: For shore bombardment actually no comparison whatsoever, because the eight-inch shell does have a little oomph behind it and can really do a great deal more damage ashore than the six-inch. As a screening ship and protective ship, the ASTORIA and her class I would say were close to equal to the eight-inch cruisers.

But you couldn't trade me a six-inch cruiser for an eight-inch, if I had the eight-inch. Eight-inch is far more valuable, and by and large a better ship all around. Although in the protective screening duties the six-inch was reasonably equal to it.

Q: Now when we're talking about screening, how did the destroyer stack up in this picture?

Dyer: The destroyer stacks up, in my opinion, as being better than either the six-inch or the eight-inch cruiser. The only real minus of the destroyers point of view is that if you have an enemy surface fleet to deal with you don't have the proper vehicle to deal with the enemy heavy ships. You've got to have a heavier ship for actual screening purposes, because the destroyers is an anti-submarine ship as well as an anti-aircraft ship. She has a dual purpose and does both of them extremely well. Despite the fact that they are darn expensive, they are essential if you're ever going to move logistic support forces, or combatant ships across the oceans. You must have them.

Q: Discuss the question of gunnery and the rate of fire. Would it be preferable to shoot more slowly and carefully? Is that a pertinent question?

Dyer: I think it's probably a pertinent question, but I would say that the answer would depend entirely on what you were shooting at. The great difficulty is that it's awfully hard to get a major caliber gun hitting a target. And if you're shooting at a fast moving target, the thought is if you can just get a hit before you get off of the hitting, you get in two or three hits with a fast shoot. On the other hand, if you pause and shoot slowly then you're bound to be off. In other words, fractions of seconds moves your target out of range.

Q: So the question of accuracy doesn't really enter into it there, it's speed.

Dyer: They're both extremely accurate. And I'm sure in order to do good gunfire support work you've got to be close, and you've got to fire quite slowly, deliberately. Because you are semi-stationary and the target you're shooting at is stationary. On the other hand, you never can tell when you may have to use that shooting against a fast moving ship, and therefore, you have to have a gun with both capabilities. If you built a gun to shoot very fast, you know that it can shoot slowly.

It's a very real problem, but you can't have a ship for every case or a gun for every case. You've got to have a wide range of capabilities, both in the ship and in the gun.

Vice Admiral George C. Dyer, USN, Ret.   by John T. Mason, Jr.
Annapolis, Maryland   November 5, 1970

Mr. Mason: Good to see you again this morning Admiral for Chapter eleven. Perhaps you're willing to comment on one of those questions.

Admiral Dyer: The campaign for Iwo Jima was a costly operation. Was it useful in the scheme of things and worth the cost?

My answer to that is very definitely, "Yes."

I think you have to take a broad look at the picture out there and realize that if we were going to make an invasion of Japan, it probably had to be made up through the Ryukus, i.e.: Okinawa. And you should visualize the Island of Okinawa as being a center for Japanese air attacks considering those from Kyushu which was to the north, and those from Iwo Jima which was to the east, and those from China which was to the west. And realizing the problem of taking Okinawa with only sea based air against overpowering Japanese land based air which could be used for close air support. You would see the advantages if you could knock out one of those Japanese air bases (Iwo Jima). You would have accomplished a one-third reduction of the ways in which you could be attacked by air when assaulting Okinawa.

I've always thought, and I don't have any knowledge of this whatsoever, that the code name for the Iwo Jima operation which was DETACHMENT must have been framed by some planner who thought we'll just detach from Japan one of the main base areas which they had and which they could use to defend Okinawa.

That's one reason why I think it was essential to do Iwo Jima. The planning for Iwo Jima was done at the same time that the planning for Okinawa was done. It would have been impossible to have done the Iwo Jima operation and then, as had happened before in our Pacific campaign, go back to Guam or Pearl Harbor or, where we might want to go, and plan the next operation. They were being planned simultaneously.

Of course, that is one of the wonderful things about the Iwo Jima operation - the job that Admiral Richmond Kelly Turner did at that time, because he was the Amphibious Commander of both operations. Also the same thing could be said of Admiral Spruance, he was the sea borne Commander for both operations. They had to ride two different horses at the same time. They were riding General Buckner, who was the Army Commander for Okinawa, and they were riding Howling Mad Smith, who was the overall Landing Force Commander for Iwo Jima.

It showed, in my opinion, the great skill that our planners had acquired by that stage of the war, where they could well plan two different, difficult operations at the same time.

Q: It also shows the vast increase in production of material.

Dyer: Yes, and the personnel. The people who had planning skills.

Another thing was, of course, at that time of the war the

B-29s were just beginning to come into their own. We were using the Mariannas to attack the mainland of Japan with B-29s. A good many of the B-29s were getting either minor damage or severe damage, during the time they were over the Japanese Empire. A good many of those planes that made it up to Japan, dropped their bombs and started home, never made home. Because the damage took charge on the long flight home, and they crashed and went down in the sea, and we lost a great many people.

Actually we opened the air bases there at Iwo Jima before we had officially captured Iwo Jima (16 March 1945). And a good number of B-29s, thirty six, were saved by landing on Iwo Jima by that 16 March date. So that over a long period of time, Iwo Jima served as a tremendous rescue station of our B-29 effort against Japan.

Q: That's a very interesting point.

Dyer: Iwo Jima was a terrible operation, in that so many people lost their lives (6800). But once you decide that a specific operation is necessary to advance your strategic plan, the cost is really something we have to accept when you do that. The estimate of people who were to be lost at Iwo Jima (2500) actually was about half of what it turned out to be. In other words over twice as many Marines and Navy lost their lives as it was estimated would lose their lives in the operation. It was far more costly.

Q: Was this in part because we didn't anticipate the kind

of defense . . .

Dyer: We didn't anticipate the ferocity of the Japanese defense. They defended every foot of ground, just tremendous courage and skill with great resourcefulness.

Q: The very ferocity of their defense -- did this indicate their appreciation of our overall strategy?

Dyer: I think it does. And I think at the higher level of Japanese command they appreciated that when we took the Mariannas, the war was lost. At the so-called working level - the Lieutenant Colonel down to second Lieutenant level, and also a great many of the Japanese enlisted men - I think realized that when we took Iwo Jima the die had already been cast. In other words, that we had closed in and that nothing except defeat was going to happen as far as Japan was concerned. So it had a tremendous psychological value through the officer strata of both Army, Navy, and Air Force of Japan.

Q: The ferocity of their defense in this Island, was it greater than what they had demonstrated previously?

Dyer: In my opinion, the Japanese always die hard. In other words, compared with Americans, an American will surrender (I hate to say this) ten times as easily as a Japanese.

But I think their high command had so embued the officer structure at Iwo Jima that they died harder there than anywhere else and more skillfully. Because the initial doctrine of the Japanese marines was to resist at the beaches. Of course, it was proved at Tarawa that that was a phony doctrine and one that was quite unsuccessful.

So they then adopted a different doctrine - For instance when we landed in the Mariannas, there was no great fight at the beaches. The fight was back of the beaches in prepared positions, where they had something to prepare. They had hills and rocks and ravines and valleys and everything else. And they did a tremendous job in regard to fields of fire and all that sort of thing.

Of course, at Iwo Jima, actually our people landed from east to west. But when we turned north, that was quite a different thing. Or when we turned south to Surabachi, quite a different proposition.

The ferocity of their defense defies imagination, how hard they died. Each person practically had to be torn to pieces individually.

Q: They died to the last man.

Dyer: That's right. It just was tremendous.

But despite the fact that many very wonderful Americans lost their lives, it had a great effect in shortening the war. It made Okinawa a lot more possible than it would have been, had the Japanese still held Iwo Jima.

And it made the Air Force assault on Japan a lot better, because the air men's morale was raised, in that they had for some time submarines scattered along that route from the mainland of Japan back to the Mariannas. And they could land be picked up, and many of them were. The submarines did a wonderful job, but a submarine has a limited speed and the plane has to ditch and people get lost in ditching and all that sort of thing.

The good old land base that Iwo Jima provided was most valuable. In my opinion it was very much worthwhile. And it was extremely well done by the Marines and by the Navy, although there was bitter discussion later.

As you know, old Howling Mad Smith claimed that the Navy didn't give them enough prior gun bombardment.

But as a matter of fact, the actual answer to the question - The Marines did land without too much opposition. We did put the Marines where they could do their job, and therefore, the amount of prior gun bombardment was adequate.

If they had been repulsed, then it certainly would have been inadequate, but they weren't repulsed. I think that's the answer.

I don't know whether you ever knew General Weller, Marine. He was a Colonel at the time, maybe a Lieutenant Colonel I don't know. He was the man on the Marine Staff there working with the naval gunfire people. Some years after the war was over, and after Howling Mad Smith had published his criticism of the prior gun bombardment, General Weller wrote a very fine article for the Naval Institute, in which he claimed that the gun bombardment was adequate.

Number 9 - In the campaign for Okinawa, something of the same question - What was the purpose of going there? Was it a suitable base for future operations against China, the Japanese mainland, and Taiwan?

I wouldn't think it would be a good base for operations against Taiwan, because Taiwan is just too far away. But it was a good base for operations against China or against the Japanese mainland.

Kyushu to Okinawa was about 175 miles.

Q: It's almost just another Island in the Japanese chain, isn't it?

Dyer: That's right.

You want to remember that our close air support planes and our fighting planes of that era, that was just about it. For working purposes, you used 200 miles.

The Japanese didn't put their airfields right on the end of Kyushu, so you had to go in a little ways to get at a Japanese airfield.

On the other hand, going down to Taiwan was twice that distance, and a little bit more. You couldn't do it. It was not a suitable base for operations against Taiwan.

Q: In retrospect, when engaging in retrospect, it's much too easy to forget the fact that they were short legged planes in those days.

Dyer: Yes.

It was the nearest large Island base to Japan that we could plan on taking before we moved into Kyushu. It was big enough, the Japanese had five airfields on it when we arrived and we put a lot more after we got there.

We started to land the 1st of April, Easter Sunday, 1945. Of all days to pick out to make a landing. It hurt me landing on the first of April.

Okinawa had enough defensive air that we had to really make an all out effort to control the Japanese air prior to landing. We not only controlled it, by and large, we extinguished it on Okinawa.

And we did a great deal to the Japanese air bases in Kyushu. But you want to remember that as soon as a Kyushu landing strip was put out of commission, all that it meant was that the Japanese gathered a few more men, women, and children and had them rebuild it. Within 24 hours the bloomin' airstrip was usable again. Something that we would probably say was impossible, but they actually did it.

Of course, you destroyed maybe the planes that were on that field, although they had revetments by that time and the amount of damage you got was limited. But they could fly in from way up in northern Hondo down into the main Island of Japan and then down into Kyushu.

So that what you had to get from Okinawa was a place where you could supply close air support and a tremendous overfly of bombing planes and everything else for a landing on Kyushu. It was ideally located, give or miss 25 or 50 miles, for that purpose.

Q: When you talk about the Japanese civilians being employed in reconstructing the airfields and so forth, you're saying in effect that they showed the same kind of spirit that the soldiers showed in their ferocious appearance.

Dyer: Tremendous spirit, and they were all available. They didn't have to sit around and argue with a union which would tell them that the bell had rung and it was the end of an eight hour day. They all turned to with tremendous spirit, and did the job that had to be done, and they did it under dangerous circumstances.

I have the greatest admiration for the courage of the Japanese people. You may not like them, but if you're at all honest, you'll admire their courage.

Q: What about the role of your own warship, the ASTORIA?

Dyer: At Okinawa we provided gunfire support.

Q: This was a softening up process?

Dyer: No, after the landing.

In the period before the landing, we bombarded some of the Chichi Jima, north of Iwo Jima in the Bonins.

Q: What value did it have, as a defensive position?

Dyer: The Japanese had a seaplane base and they had a partially built air base there. They also had coast defense guns and that sort of thing.

We had photographs of these gunning places, coast defense guns and so forth, and the shore facilities. They had been hammered by aircraft any number of times, B-29s and B-26s.

The B-26s participated in the pre-Iwo Jima landing. They could just about make it with the loads of bombs that they carried. Of course, Chichi Jima was only about 40 miles north of Iwo Jima.

We went in on one of these bombardment things. This is a fact - the ASTORIA was a wonderful shooting ship. There were many wonderful shooting ships. We had the ability to open fire quickly, shoot rapidly, and to hit. Those are the necessities.

The thing I remember most about bombarding Chichi Jima - Every Division of cruisers has a lame duck, and we had a lame duck. We had an allowance of ammunition to shoot for this thing. The old ASTORIA opened fire, zoom. We expended all the ammunition and we hit, before one of the ships was able to open fire. The Division Commander was J. Cary Jones. (He's still alive and around). He was really a bit upset.

: What comprises a lame duck cruiser? What makes if worthy of that appellation?

yer: One thing J. Cary Jones did - You fueled every three or four days. At a certain moment he would say, "Rampage," which as my radio voice call, "Go fuel."

He would take the time from when he issued that word until you got alongside, got your fuel lines out to the tanker, the time you took to oil, and the time it took you to get away, and whether you parted any lines or so forth. He kept an SOB book with that information in it.

He told me by signal and he also put it on my fitness report, that I was the fastest fueling ship. And this ship was always the last.

He would ask me, "Why is so and so's ship . . .?" He was actually interested in finding out. I said, "Admiral, if you'd like me to, I'll put some of my people on board, under your orders, and they can come back and tell you why." And so he did just that. He was interested in reducing the length of time.

The same thing happened in gunnery. He said, "Why in the world can't the so and so open fire?" I'd say, "Here's the system that I use."

I stood right up on the bridge, and I listened at the same time to three bridge radios. I listened to three different circuits, each loud speaker controlled a circuit. So that when anything happened on any of those three circuits I heard it.

You've got to learn to train yourself when two people are talking to hear both of them and understand what they say. Because one man is talking on one circuit, which is a different case he has than the other. You've got to train yourself. I couldn't do it today, but I could do it at that time. I was alert to what things were happening.

Another thing, for instance, you'd suddenly get an order from the Task Force Commander to launch a search plane. I kept my senior aviator sitting, one aviator in the plane, with the engine all ready to go, even when we were on stand-by notice. The other aviator was up with me in the bridge area. As soon as something came over the three voice radio circuits that looked as though somebody was going to have to send a search plane, I was alerted. I alerted my aviator, he started to listen in on the stuff, and when the thing worked down the Division Commander would very quickly say, "How soon can you launch?" You had a safety precaution, you couldn't launch within five minutes. I would always say, "I can launch in five minutes. The other people were reporting, "Ten, twelve, or twenty minutes," before they could launch. This guy was always at the end of the line, he never got himself organized.

Q: His reflex action was slow.

Dyer: Slow, yes.

Of course, it takes a bit of doing to get your people to feel that they have got an integral part in winning this war and they've got to give their best efforts at every moment. They've got to be keen to do the thing, not to fight away from doing something.

Because there are poeple that go through the whole war trying to keep away from where the action is. And there are other people who try to keep where the action is.

Q: How did you achieve the placing of men on board his ship without telling him?

Dyer: We just went alongside. The Division Commander sent a signal for "Rampage" to place observers on board.

Q: So that he knew?

Dyer: He knew all about it. It wasn't anything that was done under the blanket, it was done right out in the open. I'm sure the Commander Officer knew why he was being observed because I'm sure in private conferences with his Division Commander he was told this.

J. Cary Jones was not one to hide your defects. He trotted them right out where everybody could look at them.

Q: How long an operation was Chichi Jima?

Dyer: It was an operation which, as far as the ASTORIA, consisted of run into there, the bombardment, and coming back. In other words it took two hours and a half to run in, maybe seven to ten minutes to do the bombardment, and good-bye.

Q: Was the intelligence or the charts furnished you accurate enough?

Dyer: Their photographs were excellent, and we had been provided with them. They did a good job. The preparation done at the Division Commander's level was excellent. He was on his feet.

Q: And then you went immediately to offer support on Okinawa?

Dyer: The answer to that is that I cannot tell you the exact sequence. I do not believe I went immediately. I think I went back and joined the Fast Carrier Task Force.

We were around Okinawa for a long time. I was there in

the Fast Carrier Task Force for all of April, all of May, and early June, the first few days of June, before we went back to Ulithi. I think I was at sea that time about 71 or 72 days.

Q: You really deserved a rest at Ulithi, didn't you, after that, being on the alert all the time?

Dyer: I got relieved of Command on June 11, 1945.

Along about the first of June orders came in for me to be relieved and go back to Admiral King's Headquarters.

Q: Was there anything in connection with the gun support on Okinawa that is worthy of mentioning now?

Dyer: Actually it was all pretty routine, particularly for ships that had done that before. And we had done it before.

Let me say that the gunfire support on Okinawa was nowhere near as urgent as that at Iwo Jima. At Iwo Jima the Marines cried for every shell. They just kept pressing and pressing and pressing the ships to shoot more, more, more. Of course, the problem on Iwo Jima was more difficult perhaps that the problem at Okinawa.

Q: It was even desperate, wasn't it?

Dyer: Yes.

At Okinawa it was something that you felt you were expert on, and went ahead and did it in, I think, a very professional manner. But you didn't have the tremendous cries. You could hear people just crying over that voice radio for gunfire or star shells. You didn't have that at Okinawa.

You had certain chores that you wanted to do, and you went in and did the chores. The fire control people of the beach did their jobs. It all went off sort of routine like.

Q: I suppose the size of the Island itself had some bearing on this situation, didn't it? There was more manoeuverability for the Marines.

Dyer: That's right.

We expended our ammunition, and routinely got some more over at Kerama Retto, which was where the base was. Admiral Jerry Wright's Task Group had established a base. (I think it was Admiral Kiland. Admiral Jerry Wright was there, but Admiral Kiland was the boss man). They had ammunition ships, and you went over there and picked up your ammunition to take back.

Q: Was the ASTORIA subject to any Japanese attack?

Dyer: The answer is we were not. We had the one kamikaze attack, I think I told you about that. That happened when I was in the Fast Carrier Task Force. It was not at Okinawa.

By and large the Japanese attacks were broken up by our destroyers and destroyer escorts and small craft, about 50 miles away.

Q: Those were the picket ships?

Dyer: Oh, yes. Those were the boys that really took up the

Japanese attack. Not that some Japanese planes didn't get through. We spend an awful lot of time at general quarters, due to the fact that the attacks were only a minute or a minute and a half away.

Q: Whose brilliant idea was it, the use of the so-called picket ships?

Dyer: I do not know who's the father of the idea, or whether anyone is the father of the idea. It was used by Admiral Turner. They kept pushing the pickets further and further out.

Admiral Frederick Sherman, of the Fast Carrier Task Forces, and Admiral McCain, and before him Admiral Mitscher had all used pickets.

The picket idea started out with one destroyer. Then with one on each bow, two destroyers. Then as we got more destroyers, we got more destroyers in the Task Force and the Task Groups, we started getting as many as three pickets. So actually it was an adaptation of what was done in the Fast Carrier Task Forces to a land situation.

Q: Had it been employed at all in the South Pacific?

Dyer: It was employed prior to the Battle of Savo Island. There were two destroyers designated pickets, the only two destroyers with radar. They were designated the picket destroyers. Had their been more radar equipped destroyers and had the Commanding Officers been more forewarned or alert let us say, they might have served a real purpose. As it is, neither one of them served a useful purpose, but they were there.

Q: They really came into their own at this time.

Dyer: Pickets came into their own during the Central Pacific campaigns.

Q: The next question - 10 - The Navy suffered at Okinawa in some measure because they had to stay on the scene. After putting the troops on the Island, the naval ships had to protect the supply lines and were subjected consequently to kamikazi attacks. Was it worth it? Could it have been done better?

Dyer: Some people think anything could have been done better. But considering the state of the art and the number of ships we had available and the land forces that we had available - The problem at Okinawa was that the landing took place on the first of April 1945. Do you recall what day the Germans surrendered in Europe?

The European War was still going on, and therefore, the people who were controlling the distribution of forces in the United States were mainly European oriented. The Navy, sort of alone, with modest help from the Army and the Air Force, was fighting this terrible Pacific war.

The people in Washington were saying, "You just wait until we finish this European one, and we'll give you all the troops you want."

But the Navy wanted to move along while the Japanese were really reeling under a series of very heavy blows. We had the momentum and we didn't want to lose it.

And so, therefore, you had to divide up the pie and the amount that was left for the Pacific was always the smaller piece, and sometimes very much smaller.

When you had used a great deal of your amphibious troops in Iwo Jima, there just weren't too many amphibious troops left. And that is what Okinawa got.

So the timing is all a question of whether you say, "Yes, the momentum had to be kept on," or "Momentum was desirable, but it could have been postponed until more people were available." The more that you can overwhelm an enemy, generally the less your loses will be.

I happen to belong to the school of thought that thinks we did well to keep our momentum rolling.

Q: And your opinion should have greater credence than that of others, because you were involved in both theaters.

Dyer: That's right.

It was done practically simultaneously with the last effort against Germany.

I think that it was done quite well. I think it was very much worthwhile, because it certainly brought to the individual citizens of Japan the fact that the ring was closing in tighter and made them much more willing to accept the Emperor's decision to surrender. When you consider the

Japanese people and consider what they really had to take in order to surrender and to consider the very wonderful attitude under which they surrendered, here they were people who had fought to the last man and all of a sudden the Emperor says, "Surrender," and they surrendered. And they cooperated. They don't surrender and back fight, as might well have happened. They surrendered and cooperated.

Q: And even smiled about it.

Dyer: That's right. And were orientally pleasant, let us say.

Q: An incredible kind of discipline, wasn't it?

Dyer: Yes. And I think a great deal of the background of that attitude arose from knowledge which the propaganda programs couldn't hide. The fact that we had landed in Okinawa and that we had captured it, so soon after having landed in Iwo Jima and captured it, and the inevitable next step which was Kyushu and then Hondo, was just bound to have it's influence. And I think prepared the Japanese people for surrender like nothing else could have done. When you're far away, maybe it will happen, but when the people are getting close to you and these things happen in comparatively rapid sequence, it starts to bore into even the thickest that something has gone wrong and that you'd better be prepared for something else.

So I think it was very much worthwhile. I think that the timing was excellent. I think that the Navy did it's job at Okinawa, and proved that it was a Navy. The Navy lost more people at Okinawa than either the Marines or the Army. We lost, of course, a tremendous number of ships, but we proved that we were a fighting Service. And that, whatever the enemy had, we could take and give back a bit better. And that's the primary test of a fighting organization.

Q: So the experience of the ASTORIA at Okinawa was somewhat unique, in that you were not attacked by the enemy as others were and suffered. What was the attack aircraft, mainly kamikazi?

Dyer: Yes. They came down from Kyushu. Some of them came down from the mainland, just touched down at Kyushu and got a load of gas and came on down. They also had the "Baka-bomb" there.

We had a Baka-bomb shot at us, which was one of these very high speed vertical bombs.

Q: Was this a new weapon?

Dyer: Yes, new to the Japanese. They had gotten it from the Germans. The Germans had quite an effect with the Baka-bomb at Salerno. But the Japanese didn't use them until we got to Okinawa.

Q: Does this indicate the fact that there was a free interchange of ordnance information?

Dyer: I think there was much interchange information.

The last question is - You once said as recorded by Ned

Potter, when an officer operated under Admiral Spruance he always knew what to expect but that was not the same case under Admiral Halsey. Do you want to discuss this further?

I think probably the answer to that is, having gotten a barrage of criticism on my prior remark I could answer, "No."

But I actually think the answer to that is, "Yes." And if you will notice that there were a few people who stepped forward in the Naval Institute and said that what I had said was correct.

When you have not operated in a Fast Carrier Task Force and you move into the Fast Carrier Task Force, they had a multitude of instructions to cover a multitude of situations.

In Admiral Spruance's Command, you learned the lessons were poured into the instructions and came out for the newer people. The people that were there already knew that, but the newer people didn't know it. They hadn't had the experience. And therefore, the instructions had to be just constantly modified, and they had to be constantly brought up to date. In other words, you had to take one piece of paper out, and put another piece of paper in.

It required excellent staff work and it required an awareness of that general principle that you had a lot of new people and you had a lot of old people. You had a lot of new ones constantly coming in and they had to be properly indoctrinated in the first twenty minutes.

In other words, here was a great big pile of instructions, a thing this high. You were given the instructions when you ot to Pearl, and you had three to five days before you joined the Fast Carrier Task Force afterwards. And you had that period to indoctrinate yourself and your people who were standing bridge watch and gun watch and everything else.

There were a lot of things that required split second decisions. You didn't have time to run and see what the instructions were, you had to know what the instructions were, and you had to do what the instructions said. Because by and large, the other ships around you were going to do just that, and you had to be in step to support your Task Group and your Task Force Commander.

So it was my impression, having served both with Admiral Spruance and Admiral Halsey, because the top men changed from time to time, that in Admiral Spruance's Command, in which Captain Charles J. Moore was the Chief of Staff initially and then he was relieved by some air man, the system was established that worked very well. The instructions were up to date, they were definite, and they were clear. And you knew if you studied the instructions, which most naval officers will do, Ninety percent of them will study instructions, some will get more out of them than others, that's just the run of the mine thing. But ninety percent of them will study them and study them hard.

When you moved into Admiral Halsey's command, you got a considerable bigger bunch of instructions. The top page one said, "Modify paragraph three C of page four D of instruction number 912 of 344," and perhaps gave exactly the same information, but it took forever to find out what the right answer was.

You had to go through three or four changes of mind that this was the thing that was supposed to be done.

Q: So therefore, under the duress of battle you didn't do it.

Dyer: The answer was it just didn't get done. You just were not always aware of what was coming, what he wanted you to do, even though you were trying as hard as you could to do what he wanted. Admiral Halsey was a wonderful leader who everybody admired. You wanted to do just what he wanted you to, but it was difficult, even when you made a heck of an effort. And I made a heck of an effort. As a matter of fact, my relations with him were just wonderful.

One thing I remember - We were down in the China Sea and it was rougher than all harry, and we were supposed to have a fueling operation. A number of the ships had tried to fuel and had parted their oil lines, and had sprayed oil all over everything. Finally Admiral Halsey came up on the voice radio, it was his voice, he said, "Rampage you make a try at it. If you can't do it, nobody can do it." So I went up and I didn't make it. I hooked up, but the sea was just too rough, and I rolled apart my oil lines.

In other words, he knew who I was and I knew who he was, and our relations were good. I'm not saying this in any criticism of him, because I thought he was a wonderful leader. I think he turned the tide in the South Pacific and probably was the only one of two or three naval officers in the whole Navy that could have turned the tide in the South Pacific.

But I'm just saying, and I still stick to it, it was

a lot easier for a new officer to move into Admiral Spruance's Task Forces than it was to move into Admiral Halsey's Task Forces.

Q: Admiral Spruance had the more understanding point of view?

Dyer: I don't say that, I say that he had very definite instructions. He knew what he wanted you to do, he had it all down in print insofar as it could be covered in print, and he expected you to follow and he didn't kibitz what you were doing. He was silent. He was not a kibitzer.

I'm sure if somebody did something wrong he said, "What do the instructions say?" If the instructions said it was all right what he did, he kept quiet. He changed the instructions if he wanted something done. It was a lot easier.

Everything is a strain. People don't realize the strain you operate on, on a 24 hours' basis.

When we got underway from Ulithi, I got up on the bridge and I never left the bridge until we went back to Ulithi again, whether it was 40 days or 60 days. You're on a bridge on a 24 hours' basis. You're on your feet much of that time, you're under strain.

Q: You, I would judge, were rather unique. Were the other captains that conscientious that they were up on the bridge all that time?

Dyer: I don't want to make any comment, because I wasn't on their bridges. I know where I was.

I had one time, and this is where my naval career pretty

near ended - They used to take the heavy ships out of the Task Force formation and exercise the heavy ships in what could be called a simulated battle of the Philippine Sea or something like that. Then you would move back towards your Task Force and at a certain moment they would tell all ships to take positions. Generally you were six to ten miles away from your position, when you got that order.

We'd finished our manoeuvres and were turned around headed back. I had to have my 'mornings-morning', and that's something. You've got to keep your system working. So I left the bridge and got the Exec up there, and turned the thing over to him, and went into have my 'mornings-morning.' I had been sitting there for a few minutes, I finished up, and then I decided I was going to shave. So I started to shave.

My Signal Officer, a senior Lieutenant who had been a Chief Signalman who's still alive, came up to my cabin and said, "Captain (right off of the bridge, I was only about ten or twelve feet from the operating part of the bridge) you'd better get out on the bridge."

So I got out there. And my Lord, the Exec had gotten the ship -- Admiral Spruance's flag ship, the INDIANAPOLIS, was on my right coming down to swing into it's position, which it would become the guide of the formation. On my left was Swede Monson, with his battle cruiser, the MONTANA. This hole was getting smaller and smaller. It was quite obvious that I wasn't going to get through. There wasn't anything I could do.

So I came up on the voice radio and I called Swede Monson

and I said, "Swede, back down with everything you've got. I am coming through." Ten seconds later the old MONTANA was jumping up and down backing down, and I slithered over on to her side. Because the INDIANAPOLIS was the Fleet Flag with four great big stars up there. Swede kept backing that ship down and I swept by within about 20 feet of his bow, and he was still going ahead. Then when the INDIANAPOLIS swung back up, I swung back up and got into position.

I owe my professional life to Swede Monson, who's now dead. If he hadn't been on the bridge and done what I asked him to do the moment I asked him to do it, it would have been good-bye for me. I sat down that day and wrote a letter to the Bureau of Naval Personnel to detach my Exec, and they did.

Q: He was helpless in the situation.

Dyer: He was doing it right five minutes before.

Admiral Spruance never said a word to me. He could have come up and just blasted me. He never said a word to me. That's pretty wonderful.

Q: Was that in contrast with Admiral Halsey?

Dyer: Oh, yes.

Q: Halsey would have reacted differently?

Dyer: And loudly. And he would have had perfect justification.

It was the fact that Admiral Spruance didn't react, that's the thing. Because the normal reaction would have been to really blast me, because I had disrupted the whole formation.

The destroyers saw the MONTANA backing, they backed, and let the little old ASTORIA go through. The only thing I could do was to go through. I rang an emergency, "Full speed ahead."

But that's the difference, and you never forget a thing like that.

Dyer 12 - 433

Vice Admiral George C. Dyer, USN, Ret.   by John T. Mason, Jr.
Annapolis, Maryland   November 24, 1970

Mr. Mason: Good to see you this morning again, Admiral.

Last time I think you concluded you remarks about your period in the Pacific at Okinawa and other places. Now I think you want to resume your story, coming back to Washington.

Admiral Dyer: I got my orders back to Admiral King's Headquarters. I got back to Washington and reported into Admiral Edwards, who was the Deputy CinC. He said the Flag Selection Board was sitting and depending on what the Selection Board did would determine what my job would be.

He said, "Meanwhile, I've got a whole desk full of dead cats here, and you can go to work on these dead cats." I said, "What do you really want me to do? Do you want me to try to solve the problem or do you really want me to give it the final waste paper basket endorsement treatment?"

He said, "If you think the problem can be solved, I want you to try to solve it. If you think it should be dropped in the waste paper basket, you draft a final action by Cominch and either I'll sign it or Admiral King will sign it and we'll end it up. There're all problems with lots of angles. Don't think that any of them have got simple solutions. If they had simple solutions, they wouldn't be in this drawer."

: Sounds like a very profitable project to put you on.

Dyer: Then he reached out down to his bottom drawer and pulled out two or three pieces of paper all heavy with lots of endorsements, and staff recommendations. These particular ones were all in regard to recommendations for awards for foreign officers. He said, "We have had no policy in regard to awards for foreign officers, except if it is the question of heroism we have gone ahead and made the award, irrespective of the nationality. We have made no awards for very excellent performance of duty. So you start on that basis."

He shuffled among some of these papers and pulled out one of them and said, "Here's a real dead cat." It was a recommendation for an award for the Dutch Admiral Helfrich, who had been down in the ABC territory in the early days of the war.

Q: Admiral Helfrich.

Dyer: He said, "Before anything is done on that, you should talk with Admiral Hart, who is now Senator Hart."

There was a big pile of reommendations regarding any and all things. I spent the rest of the day rifling through these things and looking at them and trying to form some first judgment in regard to any of them. Eventually I picked on the awards thing and though, "My Lord, the war's coming to and end and we've got to have some kind of a policy here. We've got to do something." So I started with the awards and worked on that for literally weeks.

I'll merely illustrate the complications. I got in touch by telephone up in Connecticut with Senator Hart, whom I had known as a young officer. He was just violent on this

Dutch Admiral. He said, "If the Navy Department has any idea of giving him an award, you let me know and I'll come down and talk to anybody, including President Truman, Secretary Forrestal and so forth and so on." He was strongly against any award to Admiral Helfrich.

Then the question of the Russians. What awards for the Russians? Knowing many of the things that they had done, which had been almost impossibly antagonistic to both the short term and long term interests of the United States, I believed that were largely done as a matter of their general policy, rather than any private decision of individual officers. That was another field most difficult to arrive at a reasonable and justifiable position.

That was one of the first things that I did.

Q: Roughly how many foreign officers were involved in this?

Dyer: About 300. There were large groups of them.

For instance, there was a great desire to give awards to people who had been recommended by our combat officers, not due to their personal combat heroism but due ot a very fine performance of duty. For instance, the British carrier group people that worked over in the Pacific.

Q: Admiral Frazer.

Dyer: But once you started something like that, how do you separate the Free French from the Vichy French? Some of the Vichy French had been very cooperative, and had been very helpful. Other ones had been real stinkos. So it was a real can of worms.

Eventually after many weeks, I drafted a staff paper. Actually the award was the only thing I worked on (or largely the only thing) because it became extremely involved. I had to decide on a policy for people that we felt were really our Allies as well as people that were legally our Allies, but that I felt hadn't really given us wholehearted support. Then we had the so-called fringe benefit military people in South America.

To illustrate, there were Australians who had been most helpful in the South Pacific campaign. For instance, the Coast Watcher people up in the Solomons. There was no real question in regard to of the desirability of giving them an award, but one had to establish levels of awards and decide what people could be given under certain circumstances and grind it out.

I turned to on that. And very shortly thereafter, I heard that I had been selected. Actually Admiral Edwards never told me that my name was on the list. One morning he just said, "You can stop worrying now." Because it's perfectly natural that everybody worries.

Then, of course, the whole selection list got tied up over selections of reserve officers and Mr. Forrestal's previous aides not having been selected. It got to be a very messy thing, and I did not get confirmed by the Senate, and I didn't put my stripes on until the 5th of November, 1945.

I had been told that when I was promoted I was going to

be Chief of Logistic Plans. Then I went down to that office and that is the lead into your question, which says . . .

Q: May I ask one question first before that? Were there any other dead cats that you were able to handle in that interim period?

Dyer: I drafted a number of staff papers including one on the organization of the postwar Navy and one on the rank of Commodore in the post war Navy. These were hot subjects which Admiral Edwards pressed me to work on. The only one of the "dead cats" that I ever really felt that I had arrived at a sound conclusion, drew up a piece of paper which was approved and signed by Admiral King and stood up for some months, was for guidance in regard to medals for foreign officers. That was it during that four month period. I should add that there were a number of other letters which I picked out which the end of the war had made no longer a matter of bitter dispute or strong argument. Therefore, I could prepare a closing endorsement which Admiral Edwards could sign without any policy diction. He said, "That's it," and signed it and sent everybody a copy.

There were a minor number of questions that related to post war plans for various things, whether we would or wouldn't plan for this in the post war era. And what we should try to do to make the Army and the Air Force feel happy when it was all over and stop digging at our heels, just kiss and quit talking about it. Those sort of things I drafted, I guess there were eight or ten.

Two things were decided on at that time, and both of them relate to your questions. In closing down the war, undoubtedly there were a number of decisions made for the post war period. What about plans for demobolization. One thing of great concern was what the organization of the Fleet would be in the post war period.

As soon as I was made a Flag officer, I was made head of two boards. One was a board which was to designate the rank of the Commanders and the organization of the post war Fleet. In this something interesting happened. I was one who believed very strongly in the rank of Commodore.

As you perhaps know, the current (1970) proposed personnel legislation will create that rank in the peace time Navy. It almost got into the peace time Navy in 1946, and I'm going to tell that story.

I drafted what the organization would be - the Atlantic and the Pacific. We set up a South Pacific Force. And we set up the main Atlantic Fleet and Pacific Fleet, with appropriate sub-divisions.

It had been my experience that the British handled a lot of minor difficult chores having officers whom they wanted to test out for Flag careers by making them Commodores. They were Flag officers, just like the Army Brigadiers. They could be given a job in a minor capacity, and then observed as to how they moved. Because there is a tremendous difference between being a Captain and being a Flag officer. The buck stops on your desk and you're the man who must make a real decision. I thought that the British system was excellent.

For many of these minor forces that we had, I provided a Commodore as the Commander.

We have always had a matter of, let us say, a running feud between the Commander of a Naval District and the Commander of a large Navy Yard or Ship Yard in that District. So I provided a Rear Admiral for the Naval District and a Commodore for Command of the Navy Yard, Shipyard, or Naval Base.

Q: And this ends the dispute.

Dyer: That would have solved the problem.

The one thing that Admiral King kept saying whenever I talked with him, which wasn't too frequently, was that "I want to keep the number of Flag officers down." That was in accordance with his long established policy.

So I drafted this organization thing and it was circulated in the Department first, and received the support of the Bureaus. The idea was to get their comments and those from the Deputy CNOs, revise it and then send it out to the Fleet.

It had been circulated in the Department and we had gotten quite a few of their comments, and there were nit-picks here and there, yes. Which would certainly be anticipated and expected and were asked for.

But all of a sudden we get a dispatch from Admiral Towers, who at that time was CinC Pacific. He said that he has heard that there was an orgniazational chart floating around in the Navy Department which calls for the creation of the rank of

Commodore in the post war Navy, and that he and Admiral Halsey have talked this thing over and they both are very strongly opposed to it. And he would like to have the opportunity of coming to Washington and talking about it.

A dispatch went back saying that as soon as the departmental comments are in and adjustments have been made, it is the plan of Cominch to circulate this to all the Fleet Commands. And it would be done so, roughly in another couple of weeks. And this was done.

It hadn't anymore than gotten to Pearl Harbor, when a request came in that Admiral Towers would like to come to Washington and discuss it with Admiral King.

As I remember Admiral King was to go out about the 5th of January of '46, and Admiral Nimitz was to take over. Admiral King was a non-personnel man, and Admiral Nimitz was a personnel man.

There also was a bill already introduced in Congress which carried out Admiral Kings decision to create the permanent rank of Commodore. Because after I had sold it to Admiral King, he told me to talk with the Assistant Chief of Naval Personnel, who was Jimmy Holloway, and with Vice Admiral Randall Jacobs, Chief of Naval Personnel, to get this incorporated in the Personnel bill. So it was done.

So these things were all coming to a head. And in comes Admiral Towers.

I participated in one conference, at which there were maybe twenty-five officers present, during which this matter was discussed. Amongst them were a lot of people like myself, who had just been promoted to Rear Admiral who were Rear Admirals of the lower half, and who, under the provisions of the bill in Congress, would have reverted to Commodore.

I thought, as far as I was concerned that was quite all right. I was perfectly willing to do it. But there were many people in that group who were quite unwilling to revert back to Commodore. Because we had a lot of Commodores. We had over a hundred Commodores on active duty during the war. These Rear Admirals of the lower half had no desire of any kind to revert to Commodore and have to take their chances on again becoming a Rear Admiral. In other words, go through a selection process in order to become a Rear Admiral.

Q: It also meant a pay cut, did it not?

Dyer: The answer to that - it would have meant no pay cut under the pay legislation that existed. But it would have put you through the selection sieve again.

The sentiment of this group was perhaps about fifty-fifty. But the ones who thought they were going to have their throats cut talked the loudest and the strongest.

This conference had taken place before Admiral Towers arrived and was the schedule which Admiral King and Admiral Edwards had set up in order that they might, I think, sound the thing out. They had broadened the first conference enough so they brought in a lot of Rear Admirals of the lower half.

Q: What sort of returns did you get from the Departments?

Dyer: The Departments, by and large, supported the idea, with minor nit-picks. And BuPers supported the idea, Admiral Jacobs and so forth.

Admiral Jacobs was Chief of Bureau, and Jimmy was his Deputy.

When Admiral Towers came, he just raised cain with it. All I got in on really, as I say, was the end result - which was to throw the thing out.

So that was one board I headed.

Q: What was the gist of Admiral Towers' opposition and Admiral Halsey's?

Dyer: In the first place, the rank of Commodore had sort of acquired a bad name. This perhaps needs a little background.

About eighty percent of the Commodores in our Navy at that time were officers who had failed of regular selection to rear admiral, maybe two or three or four times. And then each had been spot promoted by fiat to Commodore, and largely assigned to shore jobs. Although some of them were at sea, as Chiefs of Staff to Vice Admirals, and others as Commodores of Amphibious Ship Squadrons.

You take th list as of the 1st of July, 1945 of Commodores, (107), and see how few of those people went on to Rear Admiral. (18). Marked exceptions I recall are Arleigh Burke and Ruthven Libby. Actually if the rank of Commodore was going to be used as a sieve through which you were going to pass people, to rear admiral, you would certainly expect to have sixty or seventy percent selection pass through the sieve.

Q: A different philosophy was applied.

Dyer: That's right.

A lot of people who certainly were excellent naval officers, but lacked that little extra spark that separated them from the ones who were selected to rear admiral, just gave the rank a bad name.

I can name half a dozen people who went though Commodore during World War II and ended up three-stars or higher, such as Arliegh Burke. On the other hand, eighty percent of them never got promoted to Rear Admiral except upon retirement.

So Admiral Tower's objection was that we were putting a hazard on a lot of people who had been tried in war and done well, in other words they were Rear Admirals who had been selected to Rear Admirals, and forcing them to go back to the rank of Commodore and that was just unfair.

Anyhow it carried the day, whatever it was. I did not participate in the final moments of the decision making. They knew what my position was. I had said it and written it and everything else. I think it was some of the senior people in the Navy who were at that time fifteen years older than I was, I was forty-seven and they were sixty. They made what they thought was the right decision.

Q: Do you happen to recall what the position of Admiral Nimitz was, or did he take a position?

Dyer: Admiral Nimitz had said that the rank of Commodore was quite acceptable to him. But he was not the same type of a fighter that Admiral King's people were. King's people were all advocates, and they'd fight down to the last breath. But Admiral Nimitz was a pacifier.

I had the greatest admiration for him. And I think he was just the right man at the right place, and he did a wonderful job. But he did it with a different personality. Even people that he had to do something unpleasant to, he did in a pleasant way.

I think his story to me about Admiral Ghormley - he was a chap whom he had looked up to his whole life, and he had to relieve him. He relieved him and I'm sure they remained fast friends until the day both of them died.

I interviewed Admiral Ghormley three times up in the Bethesda Navy Hospital. He had nothing except praise for Admiral Nimitz.

When you can do that, you've got something. And Admiral Nimitz had it.

That was one of the boards. The next board, which was called the Dyer Board, and which you still see references to in papers on personnel, made the determinations on specilization in the Navy Post World War II. Which is another one of your questions.

In the pre-World War II Navy, we had a much sharper line between the specilists and the non-specialists. There was a greater degree of risk for promotion to be a Line officers than it was to be a specialist.

Nearly every specialist became a Captain, and a large percentage of them became Flag officers. They started out with comparatively few out of each Naval Academy class, maybe three or four or five. Probably forty percent of them would become Flag officers.

It was quite irksome to the General Line officer to see a chap who opted for an easy going engineering life promoted to Flag rank.

I have a classmate that's a retired Flag officer right now, that's still alive. I heard him say several times, "I'm going to shift to EDO (Engineering Duty only) and become a Flag officer." That's just exactly what he did.

They had a small group. They had adequate vacancies to handle them, and they promoted them. They actually had a system of elimination. They eliminated the people who deteriorated physically, mentally, or morally. All those that did a good job moved right up along.

So there was considerable feeling on that forever. On the other hand, there was a feeling throughout the whole Navy that we did not have enough specialists.

For instance, in the pre World War II Navy, intelligence work was a dead end if ever there was a dead end. Actually I know only three people of my general era that went into intelligence (more than one cruise) who became Flag officers. I should mention that Admiral Spruance had a cruise in the Office of Naval Intelligence. Admiral Kinkaid had several cruises, one as Naval Attache and one in Intelligence. And John Cassidy, in my class, who I think relieved Admiral Kinkaid in Rome.

But the number of people were distressingly few.

I think, for instance, McCollum is a perfect example. If he had had a little bit more general line duty, he might have got selected.

I know two people, one of whom is still alive, who were on the Selection Board that considered McCollum. This one chap has told me this story about half a dozen times about how hard he worked to try to get McCollum selected, because of the very wonderful job in intelligence that McCollum did. But McCollum was just hampered by too much shore duty, and not being present when the blood and gore was passed around. So he didn't get selected. He was promoted after retirement.

There was a strong feeling that we had to have intelligence specialists and we did not have them. And the Dyer Board did that.

Q: Sam Frankel is an example of that.

Dyer: The other thing was language. Sam Frankel is a language man, rather than an intelligence man. He's a combination of both, because he's been so employed. But primarily, he was a language man.

There was a feeling that we didn't do enough to encourage people with special talents in language and protect them as they moved along. Because if they had a special talent in language, they were apt to repeat in a duty station. Repeating in a duty station is just terrible. Do the same thing, go away and do something else for three or four years, and then come back and do it again - you haven't grown very much or enlarged your point of view or anything else, or enlarged your experience. So that's deadening. So the idea was to bring in a small percentage of the language people into a specilized area of promotion.

The next thing was hydrographics. During the war we developed some hydrographic ships. And we borrowed them from the Coast and Geodetic Survey and so forth. And we borrowed officers. And we did a tremendous amount of surveying.

It was a talent which the old Navy had had, the Navy before I was active in it as a young officer. But ten years before I'd been in, the period 1900 to 1914, very frequently our ships were sent into a harbor which we didn't have good charts for. And the officers and personnel on board chartered the harbor, and we produced a chart.

For instance, we produced our first chart of the Admiralty Islands off of the old cruiser WEST VIRGINIA. Young Kelly Turner was one of those who was down doing it, working in the hot sun, and so forth. He wrote a letter to his mother, and I have the letter.

We did have that talent, but we lost it. Because we had other things we thought were more important.

During World War II, we had to borrow people in order to provide us with this necessary talent. So the thought was to have a very small percentage of hydrographic specialists. And that was authorized in the congressional bill, as was the division of the engineers into basic engineers and aeronautical engineers, which are two quite different groups with quite different talents.

different talents.

This Dyer Board proposed six divisions of Naval talent.

Q: The naval constructors were taken care of prior to this?

Dyer: They had been taken care of prior to the Dyer Board; that was water over the dam. We didn't do anything about that.

We also provided percentages so that the specilists would not have to undergo as much selection as the Line, but they would have to undergo a reasonable amount of selection.

The individual staff Corps, in the pre-World War II Navy, largely determined what their rates of selection were. The Supply Corps always maintained a very severe selection, and maintained it's officers in position in step with the Line.

You take, for instance, the engineers. They were selected two, three, and four years behind their Line contempories. but they had a much higher degree of selection. They slowed up the pace.

The thought was to keep everybody in step, but to permit the Staff Corps to have lesser steps down in the percentage of officers in each grade. In other words, if the line officer has forty percent senior Lieutenants and six percent Captains, that was a reduction of seven to one. The Dyer Board recommendation was to provide the engineer with maybe seven to two and a half.

That was the skinny behind the thing. I can't remember the details now, it was nearly thirty years ago. Nevertheless the Dyer Boards recommendations were largely approved and effectuated, the recommendations were incorporated in the Personnel Bill and largely stand today. It was the post-war effort to provide in the Line of the Navy the necessary talents, for actually producing a first class Navy.

I had all kinds of problems as Chief of Logistic Plans, primarily in regard to trying to get the Navy back into size and trying to get it on a reasonable financial basis.

Q: What guide lines were provided, if any, in terms of political considerations, monetary ones, budgetary ones?

Dyer: The guide lines were quite straight in that the Bureau of the Budget in effect said, "The Navy Department next year can have thirteen billion dollars, and you divvy it up. But you can't have any more."

You could make out the finest justification for fourteen and a half billion, it didn't make any difference. You were going to get thirteen billion, and that was what it was going to have to be.

It allowed a reasonable amount of freedom, except that it led to a very great pressure between the individual agencies of the Navy Department as to who would get the money and just how it would be allocated.

Q: Was this planning for peace time predicated on a peaceful world? Or was there any anticipation . . .

Dyer: The answer to that is that the Department was very strongly divided in that. I wouldn't want to apportion the percentage of strength. The formation of the United Nations had a very real effect on the people in the Naval Services.

For instance, when I came back from Command of the ASTORIA, I landed in San Francisco. I went up to the St. Francis Hotel and I went in and asked for a room. The clerk said, "No rooms."

Charlie Lockwood had said, "If you ever want a room at the St. Francis, you go see the manager and tell him you're a friend of Charlie Lockwood's. And I'll gaurantee you'll get a room."

So I went up on the mezzanine deck and went to see this chap. I said, "I'm a friend of Charlie Lockwood's. I served with him twice, and he said if I'd come to you I'd get a room." He said, "How long are you going to be here?" I said, "I've heard that the United Nations conference is meeting here. I'd like to attend a couple of those sessions, at least a couple of nights." He said, "Okay," and he wrote on a piece of paper and signed it, and I took it down and got a room.

As I was riding down in the elevator from the mezzanine deck to the ground deck in the St. Francis, I was, of course, the last person to get in the elevator on the mezzanine deck, I heard somebody say, "Captain Dyer." I turned around and there was John Spencer.

John Spencer was the legal advisor to Haile Selassie. John asked what I was doing in San Francisco. I said, "Well, I've just arrived. Right now I'm trying to get into the United Nations conference, after I get settled in my room." I still had my bag in my hand. He said, "I'll get you in there, no problem."

So I sat with the Ethopian delegation.

I heard one thing which I will never forget. And that is Senator Conolly arguing as to why the veto should be in the charter of the United Nations. Because basically I was opposed to the veto. I listened to Senator Conolly argue why we should have the veto. He was much wiser than I was, I can tell you that.

The feeling which the creation of the United Nations - spread throughout the Naval Service might be summarized: Here were people that had fought a hard war, their stomachs were full of it. They came back and their hopes were high for peace. There was a very real sentiment for - "Let us anticipate that the post-war world will be peaceful."

The Soviets, of course, soon disillusioned everybody by rigging elections in the Balkans and overthrowing the governments there, and so forth.

But initially anyhow, in the period right at the end of the World War II, there was a very strong feeling that we should plan for and support with all our might and main getting the Navy down to size. Nobody wanted to abolish it, I don't mean to say that. But they all thought of the Navy of 1941 as being a pretty good Navy, and let's get down to something about that size.

The reduction was not fought down to the last tooth nail, it couldn't be. Plans, I think, were formulated with some altruism in them, yes.

In regard to personnel, everybody realized what had

happened after World War I, when we had disarmed so rapidly. The post World War II plans had three different stages during which the Navy personnel was to be cut down.

And the plans envisaged adequate time for the ships to be put out of commission in proper shape, so they would be usable again.

Mr. Forrestal, in my very humble opinion, did not support the Service adequately in insisting that a good job be done in putting the ships out of commission. All he was interested in, was getting the people out of the Services.

Q: But the Services had anticipated this emotional approach, and they wanted to slow it down.

Dyer: That's right, worked hard to slow it down.

This plan had been drafted probably early in '45, long before May of '45. As you know, the War Plans provided that we should try to so wage the Japanese War that it would be brought to completion one year after the peace in Europe. We'd have peace in Asia then.

Actually the end of the Japanese War came much more rapidly. The Japanese surrender depended on a number of factors, I think. I don't think the atom bomb was the one or the only one which decisioned the Japanese to sue for peace. I think it certainly was a good laxative to them. They were in a very weakened condition, and somebody gave then a laxative, which was the atom bomb. And it gave them a ready excuse to hang a surrender on. They hung it.

I think by the time Okinawa was over, there certainly were no Japanese military people of any stature who were willing to say that Japan had a chance of ever winning the war or bringing it to a stalemate. They knew they were going to lose, and the question was how would they lose the most gracefully.

Q: What about the service fleet? Do you want to talk about that?

Dyer: I do not believe, and I'm a logistician and have worked in logistics all my life, that you will ever be able to provide a military organization in which the logistician will occupy a place on equal status with the combat soldier or sailor. It just isn't possible for people who are five miles, or fifteen hundred miles, or five thousand miles away from the fighting to get the same credit as the man who does the fighting.

The man who does the fighting in a spectacular way, like the air man, or in the future whatever the missiles may be, is going to be the man who is going to get the top assignment.

Also you want to realize that in the military service, not everyone is fitted to be a combat personnel man. There are people who can fight extremely well for short periods of time. There are other people who can fight for short periods of time, but who can't live with the fight. Their body mix is such that they wear themselves out. They cannot live by taking short snatches of sleep, and irregular meals, and so forth. Their system just won't adjust to it. Their body deteriorates, their mind deteriorates. And they become less effective, and they have to be taken out.

I'd say if you had a hundred flag officers in the Navy today and war started tomorrow morning, that there would not be one in ten of your top people who would turn out to be the ones who can carry a combat fight for any long length of time. By a long time, I mean longer than nine months or a year.

The Bureau of Naval Personnel, during World War II, set up a very excellent policy. And that was that after a year or thirteen months in a combat zone, you were taken out. As you know, that's been applied to Korea and being applied to Vietnam.

On the other hand, you also read, if you read close enough, that there are a reasonable number of people in Vietnam who are staying on or requesting a second cruise and so forth.

Harry Hill, right here in town, is a perfect illustration of a man who came into combat in '42 and stayed in it until the end of the war. In other words, he did three years.

Frederick Sherman, who also came into the war in '42, I can't tell you the exact month, stayed until the end of the war. He did better, and better, and better.

There are people like Commodore Henry Flannagan, who was an ex-sailor man, and an ex-Chief Yeoman, who became just a wonderful fighting man.

Commodore Herbie Knowles is another one, another of these cantankerous individuals. Herbie and I were shipmates in submarines. Herbie was one of the most cantankerous of the cantankers. Yet he adjusted to the war. He's one of the few people that, as far as I know, was there when the first bullets were fired.

and he was still out in the combat zone when the war was all over. His system could adjust to it.

So that you can't have everybody in the combat area. You've got to have people who can do the logistics job, and that's a tremendously different job than the combat job.

At the last football game, a chap came into the stands and sat down. I said, "Hello Admiral," to him. He looked at me and said, "Hello." After about five minutes he turned around to me and said, "You're Admiral Dyer, aren't you?" I said, "yes, sir. And you're Admiral Carter, aren't you?" He said, "Yes."

He was out of the class of 1908. He said he was 87. He was a logistician and a wonderful one. He had the logistics down in the South Pacific, and then moved to the Central Pacific. Wherever you looked, Admiral Carter was around to help you out. He just had the particular make-up to do a fine job. He was the co-author of BEANS AND BULLETS.

You can't just have one talent. Logistics covers entirely a broad guage. In Carter's book he says that Kelly was the best logistician he ever knew, and I think he was. Turner had a tremendously comprehensive mind. He saw the trees, and he always saw the forest. He never was lost either way. And he was a wonderful logistician and that was a major factor in his success.

You know General Hogaboom, USMC. General Hogaboom said that Kelly could tell you the cubic feet of every piece of Marine equipment that moved overseas. He said that he had tested him, he'd studied up the things. He'd go over and test him and Kelly would tell him how many cubic feet that would take to go into his ship. That's a knack, that's a knowledge.

It's something that Admiral Halsey could have spent the rest of his life, and still wouldn't have known half of them. Some people have that talent and others don't.

I think what you want in wartime is someone, for instance, of Admiral Nimitz's great qualifications who could judge people and put them where they could do the best job. And then keep them there.

During World War II when the Bureau firmly announced their policy of rotating people ship to shore and when the orders came out, Admiral Turner sometimes refused to pass along the orders to people to let them carry them out - people that were doing the job, who were able to handle the war. So he got into furious difficulties with the Bureau.

The problem is if you get a team together and get some people at the top who have some knowledge, and so forth and so on, it's desirable to keep them together.

So I don't think there'd ever be a Navy where Service Force people would be the same people that are combat people. In other words, they'll be the people who can be good Service Force people. And there will always be enough of them get promoted to encourage the others. They will never get the same percentage of promotion thatthe combat officer gets, because they won't do the same things that attract the same attention.

Q: A point well taken.

Admiral in the planning for post-war and the kind of Fleets necessary and so forth, did you take into consideration, did you have any knowledge of the fact that the Royal Navy was going to be so depleted in areas like the Indian Ocean and other places, and these vacuums that we have had to fill in?

Dyer: The answer is certainly that I didn't have any such knowledge. After I left Logistics Plans, I became Chief of General Plans. While as Chief of Logistics Plans I might very well have had that knowledge, as Chief of General Plans I should have had it, if it was available in the Navy Department. And I can say very distinctly that I have no remembrance of any such thing.

We did exchange information with the British. In other words, we had a post-war plan and they had a post-war plan. And we exchanged such information through the Combined Staff, which was there in Washington. We very frankly said what we planned on doing, and I hope they very frankly said what they planned on doing. But certainly they didn't visualize any such reduction in the British Navy. And of course, we didn't visualize any such tremendous increase that we have had in the United States Navy.

Q: I suppose part of the answer is that the rapid disintegration of the British Empire hadn't begun at that time.

Dyer: That's right. And after all, Mr. Churchill had said he had not become the King's First Minister in order to preside over the disintegration of the British Empire.

I didn't have any such ideas. I have always been very fond of the British.

While I was Exec of the INDIANAPOLIS in Pearl Harbor in pre-World War II days, the WARSPITE came in. She had been attacked in the harbor of Alexandria by underwater . . .

Q: Those Italian one-man torpedo.

Dyer: That's right. And they brought her in - she'd come around Singapore and then over to Hawaii. She was going to Bremerton Navy Yard.

I had an opportunity to go onboard her and talk about damage control and other things. I just admired their spirit.

I had actually first run into the British Navy when I was in submarines, out on the China Station. The British L-boats were stationed on the China coast.

Once a year they came down to Manila and tied up alongside the BEAVER, or the RAINBOW, or the AJAX, whichever our tender was. We would go up to Hongkong and tie up alongside their tender and spend four or five days or a week or as long as we could. We got to know some of their people quite well.

They were quite a different Navy than we were, but they had their points.

Of course, when I was on Admiral Richardson's Staff, Lord Louis Mountbatten came out to the Fleet and stayed with the Staff awhile. He ate with us and talked with us. He had another Commander or Captain with him, I don't remember who it was, and we talked with him.

I had a very high opinion of the British Navy, and nothing that happened in the war changed that opinion. They have their own idosyncracies. Two things happened during the war that illustrate some of their idiosyncracies.

When I was flying over to North Africa, we flew through Bermuda. Admiral Jules James was down at Bermuda. There was a defense arrangement that provided for a Combined Command at Bermuda. The British had a Vice Admiral down there. Jules James was a Rear Admiral. The Vice Admiral had a Commodore Chief of Staff.

The Vice Admiral took sick, so they decided they'd have to move him to a hospital back in London. (I'm not sure that London was his destination, but anyhow they moved him out of the Island, out of his command.) So James made all preparations to take over, because the basic agreement provided that the Senior officer of the two countries would have command. But when he showed up at the Command Center to take over the Commodore said, "Well, sir, they just made me a Vice Admiral." And they had. They moved him up to Vice Admiral, so he continued in command.

I'll tell you another story - just before we were to go in to Salerno. They had a British Commodore, who later became a four-star Admiral in the British Navy, Commodore G. N. Oliver Royal Navy, in command of the amphibious ships and craft that were to land the British 46th Division (Northern Attack Force).

About four days or a week before we were to sail, I said to Commodore Oliver, "I think, in view of the fact that we have

Dutch officers and American officers and British officers, we should have a succession to command. So that if anything should happen to you, it would be known as to who was to take command."

So he said, "Excellent idea, excellent idea. We will find out, and we will issue a list." A couple of days later the list came out.

Much to my surprise, because I was a junior naval Captain, after all I had just been made a year before I went over there, I was the next in command. So I became a bit more interested in what was happening, in case . . .

About twelve hours before we sailed, along came another piece of mail, a revised list of seniority. There was a British officer who was second in seniority and he had just arrived from the Admiralty. The British flew him in, just in case.

Q: They were very flexible.

Dyer: They're wonderful.

Now you asked - what about the vast amounts of material in the Pacific and elsewhere? Was there any decision to leave much of it there, and if so, why?

There was a decision made to leave much of it there. Part of that decision, I'm sure, although it was made at several levels above where I was operating, was due to commercial pressure. Because shipping many of these things, which were needed for base installations had a commercial use. In other words, they could be put in a factory, in a town, in a shop - machine tools, plumbing, sewerage facilities, all that sort of thing had a regular commercial application.

Q: Widgeons are widgeons, aren't they?

Dyer: And so the pressure was not to bring all that stuff back in order that it would not be thrown on the market at cut-rate prices and undermine the established standards of wages and prices. Because everybody thought when the war was over, there'd be a tremendous increase of unemployed. And I think there was.

There would be, of course, some pressure to stop the very strong inflationary effect which was in existance at the end of World War II, as much as there is at the present stage of the Vietnam War.

Q: I suppose it was looked upon as stock-piling, whether it was on Guam or where it was.

Dyer: The quantities were just tremendous, you couldn't imagine how great they were. And so the decision was to leave a great deal of it where it was, disintegrate it or give it to the Indians, and bring back a few things that had only a naval application.

Q: There was a factor, if there were vast amounts of things abroad and they were given away, this did something to the foreign market for that particular thing, didn't it?

Dyer: It actually worked as a two-edged sword in that area, since many of these islanders had not been too long accustomed to these things. Here were things, if the islanders had used them once they'd want to use them again. It created a long range market.

The next question is - were there plans in the making for the Mediterranean? The answer is - yes, with the Atlantic and Pacific fleets. I've covered that in some detail.

Q: The plans for the Mediterranean were something of an innovation for peace time, weren't they?

Dyer: That's right.

Admiral Jules James, I think, was the first Commander, Naval Forces Mediterranean. Admiral Bernard H. Bieri was the second one.

The Command in the Mediterranean was considerably smaller than it is now, but it did consist at that time of one carrier and a division of cruisers and a squadron of destroyers and some train. It did not have any amphibious ships, they were added later. Of course, it didn't have multiplicity of carriers, or supporting ships.

Q: Now this was considered a supplement to the Royal Navy in the Mediterranean.

Dyer: That's right.

Q: Were there talks with the Royal Navy on this?

Dyer: Oh, yes.

While I was in the Mediterranean, which was in 1947 and '48, we had Combined planning sessions and all that sort of thing at Malta.

Admiral Sir Algernon Usborne Willis was the Commander-in-Chief of the British Fleet. He was a very fine gentleman with a very excellent sense of humor, and a very keen individual, as far as I was concerned.

Q: What was the thinking involved there? The Royal Navy had done an adequate job in the Mediterranean prior to World War II. Why was it thought necessary to have U. S. units there after World War II?

Dyer: The formulation of the North Atlantic Treaty Organization - the United States Navy after World War II was over, just couldn't bring itself to believe that there was any other Navy that was quite equal to it. We particularly couldn't believe that there was any air arm of the Royal Navy that could be even close to the air arm of our Navy.

So while the British had the British fleet in the Mediterranean with the headquarters in Malta, certainly with the correlation if you're going to have a NATO organization to fight on the beach, you also were going to have to have a NATO organization afloat to fight at sea, our Navy had to be in it in the Mediterranean. In the period when I was over there, the French were part of the NATO organization and participated in the major NATO exercises.

I certainly didn't do any great amount of thinking about why the United States Navy was in the Mediterranean. What I thought was - we certainly been in the Mediterranean during World War II and we ended up with forces in the Mediterranean

My thought was that if we were going to maintain a strong defense line against the movement of the Soviets getting further to the westward, that part of that defense line had to be seaborne.

That was why so much effort was devoted by bringing the Turks and the Greeks into NATO. As you remember originally, NATO was formed without them. They came in subsequent to the initial formation. And a great deal of effort went into getting them to do just what they did.

Q: Yes, it was stretching the concept, wasn't it? They were hardly Western Europe, North Atlantic.

Dyer: That's right.

The next question is about the Fleet Service Force. You say - do you think we have learned any lesson as the result of our experience in the Pacific?

I think the Navy has learned many lessons in regard to logistics, in both World War II, the Korean War, and the Vietnam War, although I am no authority on the latter. The new Director of Naval History, Vice Admiral Ed. Hooper, is an ex-Op-4 in the Department, and an ex-Commander Service Force, Pacific Fleet. In other words, he held the big logistics job in the Department and the big logistics job at sea. He's both a logistician and a combat officer. So that shows progress in the logistical detail area.

Your next question, I've already answered it, which is in regard to specialization.

The only one that I really haven't answered is - number one, which is "a larger and more graphic picture of Admiral King, keeping in mind my desire to gather as much as I can about him for some future biographer."

I merely tell you one aspect of the future biographers' part of that. I talked with Mr. Hoyt last week. Hoyt is the chap who's just done Nimitz admirals. He says that on Admiral Hill's recommendation, he got in touch with one of the King daughters. She told him that the family did have quite a few family letters, but if they were made available that each of the daughters that had these letters would want to be able to pass on (i.e. censor) the text of the biography. That ended his efforts right there, and it would have ended mine.

All of Admiral King's personal papers which he retained and did not turn over to the Director of Naval History when he died have now reached the Naval History Division through Mrs. King. Mrs. King's dead, and Joe the son passed them on. I would think the King letters to the daughters would have to wait another generation maybe before they become available.

I think also that trying to do anything about Admiral King, the family aspect of Admiral King, is going to be most difficult.

When he was Cominch, he used to go home once a month. I really don't have anything factually to add in regard to those visits. There used to be a bit of joking at the lower staff level about it, but I don't have any facts. But I think the fact that the man only went home once a month when his wife was living in the same town is indicative of the difficulty of the relationships.

Q: His stated reason was that he could concentrate better on the yacht.

Dyer: Yes, that's right. And he did, he was a tremendous worker.

Another thing is that he did a lot of thinking about things. He would have three or four things on a memo, and he would sit and wrestle with them. It's surprising what he was able to develop out of his thinking about a problem.

Q: Did he, in your estimation, have a superior intellect? Was this his basic equipment?

Dyer: I think his basic equipment was his superior intellect. He was a very savvy boy at the Naval Academy. And in some ways he was a great student, in that he was a great acquirer of facts. He was much more interested in facts than he was in opinions.

Although he looked for opinions from people and he was open to opinions. but he was open particularly to opinions which were well based, factually based. I mean you're merely saying that I like this, didn't have any influence at all. If you liked it because, and then could name three or four solid things, you made some progress with him.

I told him once, "Every great man is entitled to have one blind spot, and your blind spot's personnel.

Q: And how did he take that?

Dyer: He looked at me and said, "Who's saying what?"

Q: Implying you were equally as tough.

Dyer: The fact that he would let you say things like that to him and not cut your throat, I think is indicative of the fact that he was a much broader man than a lot of newspaper people seem to intimate.

Q: But it was only a very selective few who could say a thing like that to him. Was that not so?

Dyer: I think so, yes.

Q: Why this tough stance of his?

Dyer: I think that he had a great problem, and some people discipline themselves by doing difficult things.

I point it out in a very minor way, the fact that I have never smoked and I have never drunk coffee. Now that's not easy to do in the Navy. You've got to discipline yourself and you've got to do it kindly without being obstreperous about it - but it takes real self discipline.

He had a drink problem, as you perhaps know. I think that he had a disciplining problem, and he had learned to control it within the limits that he had set for himself. And I think that he was constantly disciplining himself.

I'm not one of those who thinks that every problem can be solved with sweetness and light and a little extra money. I think there are some things that are not solved that way.

And I think that he operated somewhat on the same basis - that this was the right decision, and there was no sense in having a long-winded discussion in regard to it, and it was a difficult decision to make and he was going to make it, and he made it and that was the end of it. Why wrestle with it for fifteen minutes to arrive at a conclusion which was correct or an action which he had decided had to be done.

No one ever knows what goes through another man's mind, but that was what I thought many of the times - that he cut things short because he hated to have it have it dragged out and wrestled with, when he knew what was going to have to be done.

Q: Does this imply that he was an impatient man?

Dyer: I think he was a very impatient man. No one ever gets me to say he wasn't impatient. He wanted it done yesterday. He wanted memorandums prepared which would take two hours, to do well, he wanted it prepared in five minutes.

Again I think basically, he decided that the only way that we would win that war was to press. Not to take things as they came, to do a good job sure. But he figured if we could save a little here and save a little there, it would all add up to getting the job done. And it was basically shown that his pressing to get the Japanese off balance, and once having gotten them off balance, pressing to keep them off balance. It wasn't easy. Here he had Admiral Nimitz recommending delaying this and delaying that. He was constantly saying, "No more delays, that's the day." It wasn't easy, but it accomplished the objective. It was the same way with Admiral Turner.

Q: This was his concept, this was his commission. Was it a commission derived from F.D.R. or was it a commission of his own design?

Dyer: I think it was derived of his own design. I think F.D.R., if anything, tended to ameliorate anything from the plan.

Q: What was their relationship?

Dyer: I think their relationship was one of mutual respect. He realized the broadness and the difficulty of the President's position.

I think he, in the later days of the war, realized the fraility of the man who was dealing with him because several times the word was added, "If he lives." I think he had diagnosed, as you do when you look at someone and feel that he's about to pass on, not necessarily tomorrow or three weeks from tomorrow, but there are signs that he's over the top and down the hill.

I think he was a very keen individual, Admiral King. As I said, I thought his blind spot was personnel, in that he had several friends that he stuck with through thick and thin who were just not worth sticking with.

I'll illustrate that by telling one more story. When I was relieved as Executive Officer of the INDIANAPOLIS, I was relieved by a Commander out of the class of 1916 who had been the Executive Officer of the OKLAHOMA at Pearl Harbor (Commander J. L. Kenworthy). He arrived on board about 0800 and I was due to be relieved that day prior noon. He was there when the ship came alongside the dock. I was to fly out that afternoon at 1300 on the Pan-American plane.

My orders had come in when I was at sea, and I had thought that Admiral Nimitz would cancel them, but he didn't. He tried to, but they were uncancelled by the Department.

There was great urgency for me to turn over to this officer as rapidly as possible what he should have if he was going to be the Executive Officer. I made a very real effort to do this.

When I got ready to be relieved I went into my Commanding Officer, who was E. W. Hanson, class of 1911, and I said, "Captain I have never said this before, and I hope I never say it again, but I do not believe that the officer who is designated to relieve me is capable of relieving me. Because I do not believe that he has recovered sufficiently from the sinking of the OKLAHOMA, so that his mind can be put on the job. I hope I am proved wrong, but I should in honesty tell you what my impression is."

About two weeks after I had gotten back into Washington, I got a long winded Western Union telegram from this Commander. It said, "I have been returned to Mare Island under guard by these crazy people (and so forth). They think I'm a nut, and I'm ordered to St. Elizabeth's in Washington. I'm an old friend of Admiral King's and I wish that you would see Admiral King and get me ordered as the Commanding Officer of the Naval Ammunition Depot, Fort Mifflin, just outside of Philadelphia.)"

I took the dispatch in and Admiral King read it. I told him about my relief and what I had told Captain Hanson. I said, "I'm ashamed to tell you this, but this is the truth, just what I told Captain Hanson. I think that the sinking of the OKLAHOMA has unbalanced his mind."

All Admiral King said to me was, "Call the Bureau and have Kenworth, ordered as Commanding Officer of that Ammunition Depot." So I called the Bureau and he was ordered up there.

He wasn't there more than a month, when he was down in St. Elizabeth's. He used to call me on the phone. Here I was sitting in a mass of papers, and trying to do a thousand things, and here would come this long-winded. . . I would finally say, "I cannot talk to you another instant. I'm going to hang up. Good-bye."

He'd write me long-winded resigtered letters from St. Elizabeth's. He always had something that he wanted Admiral King to do or not to do.

Even after that chap was in St. Elizabeth's, Admiral King kept trying to get him out of St. Elizabeth's. It was just terrible, in my opinion.

That's one of the reasons why I told him his blind spot was personnel. I didn't tell him at that time, I told him much later.

Q: So it wouldn't be related to that incident.

Dyer: But he did have very distinct blind spots, he had great loyalty to sometimes quite unworthy people, in my very humble opinion.

Dyer #13 - 473

Interview #13

Vice Admiral George C. Dyer, USN
Annapolis, Maryland

by John T. Mason, Jr.

December 10, 1970

Mr. Mason: Good to see you again this morning, Admiral.

Last time you gave me an account of your duties with CNO and had completed that chapter with a vivid picture of Admiral King. You want to go on with your sea duty which followed?

Admiral Dyer: In the first place I should mention how I happened to go to sea.

When Admiral Nimitz came into the Navy Department as CNO, one of the early things that he wanted to do was to get the Departments down to size. More accurately, I should say to get the various Bureaus down to size and to get OPNAV down to size. His approach was that he couldn't really talk tough to the Bureaus until OPNAV had set the example. So he set me up as senior member of a board to work on actual allowances in the OPNAV divisions, sections and sub-sections.

I had some very capable officers working with me, and also some capable civilian employees who were in the personnel business. We visited each sub-section and examined the workloads. We worked for several months and came up with the recommendation.

Admiral DeWitt C. Ramsey, the Vice Chief of Naval Operations, was my immediate superior as Chief of General Plans. On the organizational diagram, he was the immediate senior of the Chief of the General Plans Section, and the next person up on the ladder was, of course, the CNO.

So, I talked with Admiral Ramsey and told him that when I got this personnel reduction worked up I'd show it to him, and then I would send it to all the many sectional and divisional heads and let them make a reclaimer. Then after they had made their reclaimer and that had been considered and I had drafted the final report, then I would present it to Admiral Ramsey and then to the CNO. And this was done.

Everything went along I thought quite well, with the exception of Vice Admiral Radford, who was at that time DCNO Air. (Op-05) When I went through the DCNO Air Division, it was apparent that they were well overstaffed and I made a lot of recommendations in regard to them just the same as I did for all the others - Op-01, Op-02, Op-03 and Op-04.

When the reclaimer went out all the other people made some claims and some of the claims were allowed.

Admiral Radford sent for me and said, "I'm going to pay absolutely no attention to this thing. It's of no value whatsoever. I need every person I've got. I'm not going to give up a single person." I thought that was a harassing attitude, so I put in my recommendations as arrived at, and signed the report of the Board.

The report went to Admiral Ramsey and Admiral Ramsey approved it. He had all the DCNO's in and got their recommendations before doing this. Then we had a big meeting with Admiral Nimitz.

Admiral Forrest Sherman was Op-03 at that time. Denfeld was Op-01. Farber was Op-04. Of course, Radford was Op-05.

So Admiral Nimitz gave them all the opportunity to say their piece. By and large, I'd say 80 to 90 percent of the recommendations, even after the reclaimer, they accepted. There were one or two people in each of the offices that they just insisted that they couldn't get along without. Some times Admiral Nimitz said, "Okay," and some times he said, "No, it would stand the way it was recommended."

He started right with Op-01 and worked through to Op-05. Admiral Radford in effect said, "I'm not going to pay any attention to this." Admiral Nimitz adjourned the conference on that basis.

Q: He didn't lock horns with him.

Dyer: He didn't lock horns with him at all. He never stood up to him for a minute. He never said, "Everybody else is taking a cut, and there's no reason why Op-05 can't." He just didn't.

It completely disillusioned me. I just was upset. So several days after it was over, I went in to see Admiral Ramsey and he was very much upset.

I said, "Well, I fired my shot, and it hasn't got anywhere. I'm going to go to sea." He said, "I'm not going to let you go to sea, unless I can get somebody in here who I'll be happy with. But I can understand how you feel that you position is untenable because in effect Radford's gotten away with murder."

So I went over to the Bureau of Naval Personnel, and said, "If I go to sea, what can you give me?" They said, "Every flag officer at sea wants to come ashore. So we're delighted to have someone who wants to go to sea." So they gave me three names as my relief; and three jobs I might go to.

I went back to Admiral Ramsey with the three names and said, "The one that I recommend that you get to come in and relieve me is "Germany" Curts. He had command of Cruiser Division Ten. It wasn't the best job of the three people's names they gave me, whom I would relieve when I went to sea, but he was the best one in my opinion of the three to be the General Plans Officer.

That's how I happened to go to Cruiser Division Ten. I went down to Norfolk in December of 1946, the last of December, and relieved him. The Division was under orders to go to the Mediterranean and it sailed almost immediately for the Mediterranean.

Vice Admiral B. H. Bieri at that time was Commander Naval Forces, Mediterranean. Then he was relieved by Forrest Sherman, who came over there as Commander Sixth Fleet. When Admiral Bieri left, they changed the title of Naval Forces Mediterranean to the Sixth Fleet. And Forrest Sherman came in to command.

The Sixth Fleet was considerably more active than Admiral Bieri had been with the Naval Forces, Mediterranean. One thing that Sherman did, which I was delighted to participate in, was that he had a monthly tactical problem.

He and his flag ship and the carriers - he divided the forces up various ways. We had little tactical problems with what was a much smaller Sixth Fleet than it currently now is.

Q: Where did you operate for these problems, in western or eastern Med?

Dyer: We operated primarily in the area around Malta, out of Sicily, out of Naples, but occasionally went over to Crete, and operated out of Crete, south of Greece. At that time the Greek civil war was going on.

When I went over to the Mediterranean the first time, it was December '46 when I left Norfolk. One of the first things that happened after arrival in the Mediterranean was that I was sent by Admiral Bieri over to Greece and told to work with General Van Fleet in connection with the use of the Greek Navy in the civil war.

I did not know General Van Fleet, had never seen him. And, of course, he had not fought in the Pacific War at all. He was completely a European War soldier. He had had practically no relations with the Navy. I found his knowledge of what had happened in World War II, insofar as the Pacific War was concerned, was at a very low ebb. So after my first talk with him, I decided I've really got a problem here.

The second time that I went up to see him and talked about what the Greek Navy could do, I hit upon this very simple formula. I said, "Now Greece is a peninsula. And any time that the Army is fighting ashore and your side has control of the sea, you can land behind the enemy's lines no matter where those lines are and turn his flank. The problem here, as I see it, is that all we have to do is get the Greek Navy to get into some very simple amphibious operations, because mostly they won't have to land over defended beaches. They'll have to land in undefended small ports or harbors. Put the troops ashore and keep turning the enemy's flanks, landing behind them. Cut their logistics support lines by cutting the rail lines (which in every peninsula always run down the coasts). Here we must cut cown the logistic support which is coming down through Yugoslavia and Albania and Bulgaria. This war is really ideally situated for use of the Navy. And if you can get the Greek Navy to do this, there's no reason why in three months or six months we can't have these buggers on the run." He bought the concept.

Actually just giving the Greek navy something to do - they were so happy to be useful in the struggle that there was really no problem. Of course, they didn't have the right kinds of ships.

Q: They had some submarines.

Dyer: Yes, but that wasn't what we needed. We needed amphibious craft, we had to get some small amphibious craft. We had to use everything the Greek Navy already had.

We continued to turn the communist flanks and continued to push the communists back, and, of course, eventually got them well back to the borders. General Van Fleet, of course, was delighted.

When I landed out in Japan, at the time of the Korean War, General MacArthur and Turner Joy told me to go over and report to the Army Commander in Korea. And it was General Van Fleet.

So I landed in Seoul, and they had a Jeep and an aide there to meet me. He took me up to the Commander-in-Chief's Headquarters.

I had made arrangements by dispatch to go down to 10th Corps Headquarters that night to discuss gunfire support, because Task Force 95 which I had Command of out in Korean provided gunfire and close air support for the 10th Corps.

So I was very anxious to pay my courtesy call to General Van Fleet and get down to the 10th Corps Commander to talk business.

I rode into the Army Headquarters area and walked into General Van Fleet's outer office. There was his aide-de-camp there. I told him who I was and that I was just paying a courtesy call on the way down to the 10th Corps Commander.

He said, "General Van Fleet has the Chief of Staff of the Australian Army in there. Just leave your card. I'm sure that he will take the gesture without any further action by you and you can just go right on down to 10th Corps Headquarters." I said, "Well, I would like to say "Hello" to General Van Fleet before I go down." The aide-de-camp was very hesitant.

I said, "You just take my card in and if he doesn't want to see me, I'll be out of this office in five seconds and head for the 10th Corps."

At that time, helicopters could not fly at night, you had to helicopter in the daytime. I was going by helicopter down to the 10th Corps Headquarters.

The aide-de-camp took my card in and came out and said, much to his disliking, "The General will see you." So I walked in.

The Chief of Staff of the Australian army was sitting over here on the left, and General Van Fleet was sitting behind his desk. I walked into the office and General Van Fleet stood on his feet and held up both his arms and said in a loud voice, "Korea is a peninsula." He had learned his lesson.

To go back to Cruiser Division Ten, the Greek war went very well and the Sixth Fleet tactical exercises went very well.

The system that Naval Operations had set up then was that ships ordinarily were in the Mediterranean for four or five months, and then came back to the United States. You might have an upkeep and overhaul period in a Navy Yard, or you might have certain Naval Reserve cruises, or something to keep you busy anyhow over here. Thus, there was a chance for the people to get ashore and to see their families. Then you went back over. Ordinarily most of the people who made those cruises only made two of them, then they were relieved and went on their merry way.

So each time I came back I got a dispatch from the Department to come down and report in, and I did. Bill Fechteler by that time was the Chief of Naval Personnel, so I went in to see him. When I came back the second time he said, "Well what do you want to do now?"

What I said, perhaps was a mistake. At least I gave him an honest opinion. I said, "I've gotten to know a great many of the shore side personalities in Greece, in Italy, in Tunis, and in Tangiers. Insofar as I understand my mission, I did much better the second time I was in the Mediterranean than I did the first time. And I believe that I would do it even better if I went over there for a third time."

He said, "This is practically unheard of, somebody who wants to stay at sea and not come ashore. But I'd be delighted to have you. What you say is probably correct, and as far as I'm concerned you can go back over."

So I went back over and I actually completed two years in command of Cruiser Division Ten. I was relieved by Mary Miles (1922) in Trieste in late December of 1948. I flew back and arrived in Washington Christmas Eve, 1948.

Q: Tell me sir, why was this reversal in feeling? Men didn't want to stay at sea now, they wanted to be on shore.

Dyer: Fifty years ago a great proportion of the Navy was at sea. When I'm talking about the Navy, I'm talking about the line officers of the Navy.

In 1915, 75 percent of the line officers of the Navy were at sea. You couldn't make a reputation ashore (you could lose it), you made your reputation at sea.

Ashore was a place that you went to be educated, which many thought less than desirable, because there never was the strong urge for education in the Navy that there was in the Army. But people who believed in being educated wanted to go ashore to be educated and go to Postgraduate School, Naval War College, Army War College and that sort of place.

Most people viewed shore duty as a place that you came and had an awfully good time, then swept all but the memories under the rug and went back to sea. And that at sea was where you really did your work and where you made your reputation.

When the Navy turned more complex, when the ships turned to more complexity, fire control became more complex, communications became more complex, engineering became more complex. The Navy had to have a great many more enlisted men who went to technical schools, and they had to have a great many more officers who required technical training ashore.

So that there was a need for a change in this mix of 75 percent at sea and 25 percent ashore. Gradually more and more people were required ashore and then more and more people had a less yen to go to sea.

And I'll say this, that, I notice it in my daughters, the wives of naval officers have a great more influence today about what their husbands do than they had in my day where the wives accepted the fact that their husbands went to sea and viewed any shore duty as really manna from heaven. But now when you go to sea, that's great privation, that's the last thing you really want.

And today a good many of the people, and I say this with great humility, who make a reputation, make their reputation ashore and not at sea.

Q: And this was becoming quite apparent after World War II?

Dyer: Very apparent.

Another thing, for instance when I was Chief of Logistic Plans - I cannot recall the exact figures. But when World War II started in Europe, I think there were less than 300 officers in the Navy who were in govenment quarters ashore. By the time the war was over, the numbers was up in the thousands. It's gotten worse.

For instance, we had dinner here a few months ago with the skipper of the PUGET SOUND. This skipper of a single ship had government quarters in his home port. Now if that isn't the complete reversal of the Navy as I knew it, I'll eat my hat.

I never had a set of quarters until I'd been commissioned 31 years (1949). I was a Flag officer, and had been a Flag officer for four years before I had a set of quarters.

Q: Yes, I've heard that repeated over and over again by senior officers.

Dyer: I've said it over and over again. It's so much different what people do now. People decide on the jobs they want by the set of quarters they're going to get.

There's been a great change in the Navy in the fifty years that I've been associated with it, insofar as the attitude toward the Service. By that I do not mean in any way that there were never people who upon reaching adulthood did not find themselves in a position where they didn't want to continue their service in the Navy.

I don't think it's possible to take 200 or 500 or 1,000 young people who think they want to be in the Navy, and then actually subject them to conditions that exist even not in the Navy, and find all 1,000 of them want to be in the Navy.

Another thing is that you see a great many comparatively young officers who are retiring. I've known a number right here at the Naval Academy. A couple of these I thought were outstanding officers and had a reasonable chance to become Flag officers. Yet the family influence and the influence of a pay scale which I thought was very generous, they retire from the Navy and take a civilian job, because they thought they could get more money some place else and their wives pressure them and make them unhappy with the Navy.

We've had at least three instances here of officers who I thought in each case were well on the road to becoming Flag officers, and each one retired with 22, 23, or 25 years service and took a job. They wouldn't wait.

It's just a change of attitude toward devotion to a Service and willingness to sacrifice for that Service. Sacrifice is not a generous commodity at any time in any age, but it's getting rarer and rarer in my opinion.

Q: Before you leave the Cruiser Division Ten in the Mediterranean, would you say something about relationships with the Royal Navy and so forth there?

Dyer: I had very wonderful relations with the Royal Navy. I've got a couple of stories that I'll have to tell.

The first time that I went into Gibraltar, which was early in '47, I had Command of a Cruiser Division with four cruisers in it. (They only now have three). And I had a squadron of destroyers, which at that time was nine destroyers - eight destroyers plus the squadron leader.

When I got reasonably close to Gibraltar, I came up on the radio and sent a dispatch to the FOIC (Flag Officer in Charge) of Gibraltar and told him I was coming and when I would arrive and so forth, and requested anchorage assignments for my ships, mail, etc.

I got a dispatch back giving the usual information. And it also had a paragraph saying that the Commander-in-Chief of the British Mediterranean Fleet, Admiral Sir Algernon Usborne Willis, was present in the harbor, in whatever his flagship was.

I sent the information out to all the ships telling them the various anchorage that had been assigned and that sort of information. And I put a paragraph on telling all of the Commanding Officers of the ships in my company that the Commander-in-Chief of the British Mediterranean Fleet was present in the harbor and his name was Admiral Sir Algernon Usborne Willis.

We arrived late in the afternoon. By that, I mean it was half past four. I immediately sent a dispatch to Admiral Willis and said I'd be pleased to call at whatever time would be convenient to him. He set up the time as nine-thirty the next morning, which was quite logical.

I went ashore right away and paid my call on Admiral Archer, who was the British Flag Officer in command there.

The next morning with my barge all shining like a rose, I dashed over to the battleship flagship of the British Mediterranean Fleet, went alongside promptly at 0930, bounced up the gangway, through the line of side boys, and there was Admiral Willis at the far end. As I approached him, he held out his hand and said, "I am Admiral Sir Algernon Usborne Willis. I say again Algernon Usborne Willis."

Q: Incredible name.

Dyer: I found out that some of my people had been ashore in a bar with some of his staff people. And they told them about this dispatch which I'd sent. In which I gave his name, and then I said, "I say again," and I repeated his name. They'd come back and told him.

That started a wonderful friendship. Every time we got anywhere close together, he always had some kind of shindig or party for us. I went on picnics with him and all that sort of thing.

Q: When you got to that stage, what did you call him?

Dyer: I never called him anything except Admiral Willis.

One day, we came into Malta, which was his regular headquarters, and where he had a tremendous Admiralty house. He said, "We're going to have a picnic tomorrow, and would like to have you come. After the picnic, we're going to go to the horse races." They had races once a week, at least they had them on Sunday, in Malta.

We went on this hiking picnic. They carried the lunches and all the necessary libations. Following lunch, we walked down the hill to the race track.

The race track in Malta is an unusual race track in that part of it is cut through a hill. As you know, Malta is very hilly. Horses disappear at about the half mile mark, (a half mile after they've left the start), and then show up about a quarter of a mile from the finish. In other words, there's about a quarter of a mile hidden in between. Of course, they have judges stationed there to observe the horses and jockeys.

We arrived at the race track. And I found out that one of the races was the Admiral Sir Willis race, the big race of the day. The track officials met us and we all went down and walked through the paddock and looked at the horses.

So when we finished, Admiral Willis asked me, "Which one are you going to bet on?" I said, "I'm going to bet on number six." He said, "Oh six, that's next to the longest shot in the race." I said, "I don't care. I'm going to bet on number six." He said, "How much are you going to bet?" Their system of betting is not the same as we have.

I said, "I'm going to bet five pounds. I'm going to make one bet this afternoon, I'll bet five pounds." At that time the pound was four dollars so the bet was to be twenty dollars. I went up and bought a win ticket and the horse was about fifteen to one. Number six was a roan, I guess that's what they call a horse with red hair. When the race started, Number six was last when he went by the finish line the first time. He was a long legged horse, with tremendous hips. But as the horses moved toward the half mile mark, he passed a couple of horses. When they disappeared into the hill he was running about fourth in the race, and I thought doing quite well.

When the horses appeared again, and you could see them well, (we had brought our binoculars), my gosh number six was challenging for the lead. But he wasn't immediately going past the lead horse. They were head and head, head and head, head and head, down to about fifty yards from the finish.

You know, the British jockeys ride in a saddle position which might be called standing up, as far as our jockeys are concerned. This jockey was standing up and he hit this horse with his whip hard enough to knock him down, but the horse gave a couple of tremendous jumps and won by a head.

Of course, the crowd around Admiral Willis immediately wanted me to pick out the winner of the next race when we all went down to the winners circle together. I said, "I can't pick out any. I only bet that one race."

So every time I'd come in on a weekend in Malta, I'd get a signal from Admiral Willis. He'd say, "Come on over for Sunday dinner, and then we'll go to the races." I always said, "No more races for me, I've shot my wad."

It was a very wonderful cruise. I got to know quite a few of the Italian officers, who really were pretty much in the dumps at that time in 1947 and '48. Their Navy was being split up amongst the powers as a result of the peace treaty. The Russians were fighting about getting more and more of their ships. The British and the Americans, due to the fact that the Italians had come over to their side in the latter part of the war, were trying to protect them a bit. The Italian Officers were really down, insofar as the size of their Navy was concerned. They didn't have any money. Their officers were pitifully paid. In any case, I got to know quite a number of them well.

As a matter of fact, within the last week I just sent Christmas cards to four Italian officers. It's been 22 years since I was over there. There were some very wonderful people amongst them.

The same thing, I think, was true of the Greek Navy. The Greek Navy, of course, has been through many spasms, I would call them. Because primarily the King of Greece was very close to the Greek navy, therefore, the Greek Navy tended to be very oriented toward the King. This period when the King had been ousted and fleeing to Italy and all that is quite bad for the senior officers of the Greek navy. Some of whom were purged or forcibly retired. It had been a difficult period for them.

One of the things that I should say, Lord Louis Mountbatten was a cruiser Division Commander at the same time I was in the Mediterranean. I had known Lord Louis when I was on the Commander-in-Chief's Staff out in the Pacific. He had come out, I cannot remember whether he was a Commander or a Captain, but I believe he was a Captain at that time, to exchange information and to watch some of the maneuvers that we had and so forth. And I had known him at that time, never well at all. I was just one of a number of Staff officers when he reported to the Commander-in-Chief and was in the flagship, but at least I knew him.

So when I got into Malta the first time, he was in there as a Division Commander. We exchanged calls and he invited me over for lunch.

I said to him, "One of the problems that I'm running into is the question of my total inadequacy in languages. I never had any skill at the Naval Academy or any time since in languages."

He said, "Well, I will give you a suggestion. When I was the Viceroy of India, I had to do a great deal of inspecting of Indian infantry units. Every one of them had a different dialect. I couldn't begin to cope with that."

"But each morning when I was going to inspect a unit, written on a little card right in front of my breakfast plate were three phrases, which were written in English but which were phonetically understandable insofar as the dialogue of the people that I was going to inspect."

"One phonetic phrase would say, how long have you been in the Army? The next phrase would say, do they feed you well? Are you married?"

"The soldiers would be just amazed to have me say these things. They'd reply. Of course, I wouldn't know what the reply meant, but that didn't make any difference."

"No conversation. I'd just ask one question to one man, and he would reply. And then maybe I would move onto the next man with the next question. And then ask the third question and again move on. By the time I'd gotten out of his hearing, I'd ask the first question again."

"It worked out wonderfully well."

About that time I was going over to Greece. The Greek Navy detailed a Lieutenant Commander to be my aide. So I was all fired up with this idea of Admiral Mountbatten's. The Greek Navy aide had a number of invitations for me to speak to various Greek groups.

So for each occasion I wrote out roughly two short paragraphs, each one with about three sentences. I said, "I want these translated into phonetic Greek. Then I'll memorize them. Then I'll rehearse them before you. Then I want you to bring in some other Greek officer, and I want to rehearse them to him. First, I want to speak them to him. And then have him tell me what I said."

Q: That's a brave undertaking.

Dyer: But a very profitable one. The Greeks would clap and yell and shout, when I'd finished my talk. It was really amazing.

I did the same thing when I went down in Tunis. Then I went back to Italy, and again did the same thing. As I became practiced in the art, I expanded it. I had a good memory, and I could make a five minute speech, all in the language of the country I was visiting. I'm sure it was far from being perfect, but the fact that I made the effort, that was the thing that they appreciated. Here was someone who was willing to make an effort to speak in their language.

I just thought that was a wonderful system, and have told many people about it since. Hopefully, that was one of the gadgets whereby I tried to make myself liked or appreciated by the people of the country where ships of the United States Navy were visiting.

Q: You became a person to them.

Dyer: That's right. It worked out extremely well.

The last time that I came through Gilbraltar on the way home from my third cruise, the Flag Officer in Charge of Gibraltar said, "I heard you're going to be the Director of Naval Intelligence when you get back to Washington."

I said, "That would be a very fine detail and I'd be happy to have it, but nobody's told me anything about it." He said, "Oh, I heard this from two different people coming through here - that you're the next Director of Naval Intelligence."

Tommy Inglis, at that time, was the Director of Naval Intelligence, but he had been in the job long enough to be expected to be relieved.

When I got back to Washington, I report into Rip Struble, Op-03, who was the immediate senior at that time to the

Director of Naval Intelligence. That's whom my orders told me to report to, the Deputy Chief of Naval Operations for Operations, Op-03.

Rip said, "Before you move into your next job, (without mentioning what my next job was going to be), I've got a temporary chore for you to do which will probably take you about two months.

"The Joint Chiefs of Staff are trying to formulate a document to supercede the present existing publication, JOINT ACTION ARMY-NAVY. The Army and the Air Force have each appointed working representatives, and you will be the Navy's working representative."

"We want you to cover amphibious warfare, air support, and so forth and so on."

So I said, "Okay." This was in 1949, seven days a week. I worked with these people, and we worked seven days a week.

Q: What made it so pressing? What was the deadline?

Dyer: The Joint Chiefs had set up a dealine. As usual, it was somewhat unrealistic. We had several officers named to be our assistants.

But the great problem was there were fundamental differences between the Navy system, for instance, of close air support and the Air Force's.

There were fundamental differences in the Army in regard to amphibious troops. Of course, I'd had a lot of amphibious experiences during the war, and I had firm opinions how best to do these things. The Air Force and Army representatives were similarly fortified. Although the Army representative by and large didn't, due principally to the fact - it was General Bull, that he had not participated in amphibious operations except in the landing in Normandy.

Anyhow, we battled through, and it took three months to do it. We got this document all done, and the working representatives all agreed.

I was a working representative, I was not the boss man in any way. Rip Struble still wasn't the boss man, he was a DCNO. The Chief of Naval Operations, of course, was Louis Denfeld at that time.

We drafted our document. The Army and the Navy signed it at Rip Struble's level. The Air Force completely threw out what their working representative had agreed to and went right back to the initial Air Force position. The Air Force refused to sign.

So then it went up to the Joint Chiefs themselves. They held it for about a month, and then they threw it out.

Q: Threw the whole thing out?

Dyer: Threw the whole thing out. It was five years or longer before they had a finished document mutually agreed upon, about "Joint Actions".

Q: Yet it was a rush job.

Dyer: That's right.

During this period the next thing I knew was that Admiral Fechteler, who was Chief of Bureau of Naval Personnel, called me in one day and said, "When you finish this work on this "Joint Action" Committee, we're going to send you down to be the Navy Deputy at the National War College."

I said, "That's fine with me." He said, "You go down and see Admiral Hill. We want to get you down there about a month before Admiral Hill leaves."

General Bull was coming in as the President of the National War College to relieve Admiral Hill. I had worked extremely well with General Bull on the Joint Action Committee. We had had some differences of opinion, sure, but we had at all times been congenial about them. So I was delighted at that prospect.

So I went down and saw Admiral Hill. I'm sure that Admiral Hill was surprised when I walked into his office and said, "Admiral Fechteler has said that I'm going to be the Navy Deputy." I think that he'd picked out somebody else. I don't know that for a fact, but I certainly got that feeling from the first interview I had with him. He didn't really say, "Aye, yes, or no."

The next day I got a telephone call from Rip Struble. Rip said, "What in the world are you doing down at the National War College? You're going to be the Director of Naval Intelligence."

I said, "The Chief of the Bureau of Naval Personnel told me to go down. I haven't got any orders. He told me to go down and tell Admiral Hill that I was coming down there."

Rip said, "You're going to be the Director of Naval

Intelligence." I said, "It's immaterial to me. I'd be delighted to do either job." And I would have.

Both activities were in fields that I liked, education and intelligence. I felt that I had some background, some knowledge, and that I was reasonably well qualified to do either. So I was happy as a lark.

The next thing I knew, Bill Fechteler came in and said, "Rip Struble's been here just raising cain with me for telling you that you're going to go down to the National War College. I wouldn't have any strong feelings one way or the other about your being Director of Naval Intelligence, but I just think you're outstandingly well qualified for the National War College. You've always had a yen on education and that's why I thought you should go down to the National War College."

Rip sweated and fumed. Finally they called me in along with Rip. Bill Fechteler said, "Rip's agreed that you can make the decision as to which place you're going to go to. As far as I'm concerned, it's either one. If you want to be Director of Naval Intelligence, you'll be so named."

I said, "I really would like to go down to the National War College and stick my head in a little more education before my brains stop working." So that's where I went.

I had two wonderful years down there. As a matter of fact, I got a piece of paper from the Joint Chiefs saying I could stay three years. Of course, I didn't know the Korean War was going to come on.

The Korean War came on, I started to get hot feet and

wanted to get out and get in it. General Bull kept saying, "I've got a piece of paper," and he'd haul it out and show it to me. He'd say, "You're going to stay three years."

So finally I went up and saw Admiral Forrest Sherman, Chief of Naval Operations by that time. I said, "I want to get in this Korean War. I don't know how long it's going to last, but I'd like to get detached and be sent out there."

He said, "I'm in favor of your getting into the war. I think you can contribute something to it. You always did extremely well over there in the Mediterranean with those tactical exercises. I think it's a good idea. I'll talk to the other members of the Joint Chiefs."

Roughly a couple of weeks later and after I had nudged his aide a couple of times saying, "What's happening?", the word came back that I was to go out and take command of the United Nations Blockade and Escort Force out in Korea.

Q: Let's turn back and tell me about the National War College.

Dyer: As you know, Admiral Hill did a tremendous job. He was the first President of the National War College. I just think he was an ideal choice, because he was a person who was able to get people of strongly divergent points of view to talk to each other in a sensible logical way.

In the period right after the war, in the period particularly when the Air Force was being formed up, the Air Force was just a little empire by itself.

Really they were just exactly like the youngsters are

today. They won't listen to you, they won't even let you tell what the story is on your side. The Air Force was just exactly the same in that period.

Some of the naval aviators were exactly the same way. They didn't want to talk with the rest of the Navy. In fact, when I had been the Logistic Plans and then the General Plans Officer, I was shown and had the opportunity of reading various statements by Flag officers in the Navy calling for a separate Naval Air Corps with separate promotion lists, separate this, separate that, from the rest of the Navy.

Fortunately, they never got any, what I would really call, of the top flight naval aviators to join that group. But they had people, and people that were willing to sign their names to pieces of paper.

Q: I suppose the incident you sighted in connection with Admiral Radford is an illustration of this - his independence.

Dyer: That's right.

Admiral Hill had just smoothed out so many of those things. I don't mean to say that he yielded to the Air Force point of view, because he didn't. But he argued against it with great knowledge, and I think with very excellent results.

There were in the first class, particularly, some Air Force officers who Admiral Hill told me might just as well have been in Siberia while they were taking that course, because they paid practically no attention to what was being taught. But they were in the minority.

The majority of the Air Force officers were realizing that they were part of a team, and they would get the farthest if they played as part of that team.

Q: As a foot note - how do you analyze this cocky attitude on the part of the aviators?

Dyer: This cocky attitude is true of some of the people in naval aviation. Fortunately, only a small proportion. When you get up and fly around in the wild blue yonder, it's awful hard to know what's really happening on the ground. When I hear a naval aviator talking, I don't know how much combat flying he's done, or how much participating in dive bombing attacks he did. The Navy's great ability in this dive bombing paid such tremendous dividends. In dive bombing, you're dealing in split, split seconds. What you see and what effect it has on you may be quite different than the same thing if you viewed it much more slowly and under much less stress.

The cocky ones talk big about what they did, it's very hard to get them down to the facts of really what had happened. They had impressions of what they would like to have happened, but they didn't always know what had happened.

Q: I suppose you could label them in quotes, "the now boys."

Dyer: They were. They had sold themselves to the American public in a tremendous way. Particularly, the Air Force had had a wonderful public relations team.

For instance, I don't know if you've ever given any

thought to the early bombing attacks of the Air Force at the Battle of Midway. I was in COMINCH at the time, I was Admiral King's Intelligence Officer.

Before the Navy had in any way gotten any publicity whatsoever, the Air Force had publicity on the streets of how their bombers had gone out and bombed and sunk all the Japanese ships and all that sort of thing. They'd never hit a single ship. Not only had they not sunk them, but they hadn't even hit them. And yet here was this publicity about their sinking these ships and there wasn't much left for the Navy to do and all that sort of stuff, which they always worked in with the proper language. They just had a tremendous image. That particularly bombing attack at Midway really did nothing but alert the enemy to the fact that we knew the Japs were coming. The Air Force had a big opportunity to do damage. It didn't.

For instance, I participated in a briefing, in which they brought back a Lieutenant Colonel and a Major from that bomb flight. Those poor guys were trying to tell the truth, and the people that were debriefing them wouldn't listen to them. They kept supplying answers which these people wouldn't stand on their feet and deny. They would just hedge on it. Then the publicity would be, "Yes, sure, they hit them." It was just terrible.

Q: I know that various members of Admiral Nimitz's Staff remonstrated with him about the secrecy of that operation - that he should speak out and refute the Air Force story, but he didn't do it.

Dyer: Oh no.

The great majority of the people who came down to the National War College were at that period of time were really first rate.

Q: And it was a very exalted concept, the establishment of this College.

Dyer: That's right.

It was during my two years there, in fact, I wrote an article for the Naval Institute showing how the Naval War College - of which I was a graduate - was getting practically no Flag Officers out of it's graduate students. And what was the sense of having a Naval War College, if you didn't send some of your best people to it.

So that the last year I was at the National War College, the Naval Deputy was always a member of the selection committee. We were told that we had to leave some of the cream to go up to the Naval War College. So the Naval War College could get back some of it's reputation. The National War College had been running nearly five years by that time (1951).

Q: What was the quota per class at National War College?

Dyer: At that time (1949) we had twenty from each service, plus I believe, fifteen from the State Department, a man from the Budget Bureau, a man from the Agriculture Department, a man from the Treasury, and a man from the Department of Commerce. We had three Canadians and three British officers there, a very fine group.

But the class that followed the last year that I was there, in which I participated as a member of the Naval selection group, had some very fine Naval people in it, some that went on to high rank. But it didn't have nearly everyone that was available at the top, which was what the earlier classes had had.

Q: What about the caliber of the instruction in those years? I've had Admiral Hill's story about how he went out and selected them from all over the country, the cream of the faculty. Was that continued?

Dyer: It sure was. I made trips to the University of Minnesota, to Chicago, to Harvard enlisting these people.

At that time we could only pay them what the maximum Civil Service pay was, and it was about $14,000 or $15,000. The best of their people at these schools were already getting more money than that. So we got people that were willing to give up their sabatical year to come down and spend roughly eight months at the National War College.

Q: Did you run into any anti-militaristic attitudes on the part of the faculty?

Dyer: The answer to that is; basically, "no."

But occasionally as you shopped around and talked to various people, you came away with the impression of somebody who didn't want to get his furs ruffled by the military or didn't want to move into an area where he felt that he was under any compulsion to do anything at any time except for his own inner desire to teach might qualify him to do. Sure, there were some people like that. There've been some people like that since the year one.

Q: I imagine today it would be more difficult to recruit.

Dyer: Far more difficult, yes.

Dyer #14 - 504

Vice Admiral George C. Dyer, USN, Ret.   by John T. Mason, Jr.
Annapolis, Maryland   March 4, 1971

Mr. Mason: Good to see you again this morning, Admiral. Today I think you're going to talk about the Korean campaign, and your participation in it.

Admiral Dyer: You have given me a number of questions. The first thing that I want to say - your first question relates to blockades. The force which I commanded was known as the United Nations Blockade and Escort Force, but actually that just names two of the tasks that the command was assigned.

Mason: Let me ask first - was this an assignment that you were pleased with? Did you seek it?

Dyer: I was just delighted. To tell you a story on that - I was at the National War College as the Navy Deputy. The President of the National War College was Lieutenant General H. R. Bull, a wonderful Army officer out of the class of 1913 who had been Operations Officer, G-3, for General Eisenhower over in Europe.

The Korean War started in July of 1950, after I had been there only one year. I was scared to death that the war would get over before I could get out in it.

So not too long after the war started, I started to talk to General Bull about getting relieved. Because when I came down there the practice at that time was that the Joint Chiefs asked the Departments to detail the officer for a period of three years. It had certain advantages to go down there for three years.

I was sure that by that time the Korean War would be over and I'd never get in it. So I asked him about letting me go at the end of two years. Finally, I'm sure, to get rid of me, he said if I could arrange it he would let me go.

Q: You mean you had to arrange for your relief?

Dyer: No, I didn't have to arrange for my relief.

I went over to the Bureau of Naval Personnel to see the Chief of Bureau of Naval Personnel, Vice Admiral Laurance T. DuBose. He said, "You're down there under a JCS piece of paper, and I can't do anything about it. I'd be quite willing, as far as I'm concerned. Why don't you go over and see Lynde McCormick, who is the Vice Chief of Naval Operations, and see if you can't either get him to do something on his level or get him to let you get into see the Chief of Naval Operations and see if you can't get Forrest Sherman to do something."

So I went over and saw Lynde McCormick. He said the same thing that the Chief had said. He said, "However, you can go in and see Forrest Sherman."

I went in and saw Admiral Sherman. He said, "There are only about half a dozen naval officer's jobs out there where the officer is actually participating in the war. No sense of getting you relieved, until I can work something out. However, I'm delighted that you want to get out there, and I will do what I can to work something out, but it will take time. You're just going to have to go back and relax. When I work something out, I'll give you a call."

I went back, just fussed and fumed, and just waited. At least a couple of months later one day his aide, who I believe was Neil Dietrich at the time, called me and said, "The Admiral wants you to come up and see him."

I went up and Admiral Sherman said, "I think I can give you Command of the United Nations Blockade and Escort Force, Task Force 95. If that's agreeable to you, I'll work with the Joint Chiefs. I don't think there'll be any problem. We'll get you another piece of paper, and you can go." I said, "That delights me." So my orders were issued.

Admiral Sherman told me at this time, and he told me also when he came out to Korea, which was about ten days before he died, he said, "When the Seventh Fleet opens up, which is going to happen pretty soon, I'm going to order you to command the Seventh Fleet."

Of course, I was just walking on air when he said that. Then he went off to Italy and died, and that was the end of that.

The tasks which the Commander Task Force 95 and the Commander United Nations Blockade and Escort Force had, I wrote down ten of them the other night and I'm sure there were more - blockade, number one; escort, number two; number three was gunfire support.

The Force was made of 100 to 130 ships varying from time to time, from day to day. The largest ships that I had regularly were a division of British cruisers, CAs. My flag was normally a heavy cruiser, but I shifted flags in the year or a little bit more that I was out there about twenty times. Some times I had a CL. But the British always had a division of heavy cruisers there.

Q: You flag ship sometimes was a British ship, was it?

Dyer: I flew my flag only temporarily on a British ship.

Then the fourth job was air support. I had the jeep carriers. I didn't have the big carriers at all, I only had jeep carriers. I had an Australian jeep carrier, a U. S. jeep carrier, and a British jeep carrier. In other words, I had a division and depending on circumstances I had either one or two jeep carriers on the line.

Then in the fifth job, I had Command of all the islands north of the old boundary between North and South Korea. There were a number of very important islands on the east coast, which were between the south Korea border line and the Soviet border line, which we occupied. We used them for two purposes - one was to send in guerrilla warfare people, and the other was to send in intelligence people to get intelligence reports.

The sixth job I had was that I had charge of the guerilla warfare on the east half of North Korea. I made any number of helicopter flights into talk with guerilla war leaders, and to try to get them to do something - that was the main effort. There was plenty of "want-she" but very little doing.

Q: How were they trained, who trained them?

Dyer: As far as I knew, they had no basic or specialized training. They were just people who were agin the government, all Koreans. They were all North Koreans presumably, although we did have a few South Koreans in the units, but they were mostly born in North Korea.

There were a lot of people that were anti-communist. They hadn't gotten over the change from non-communist leadership to communist leadership, so they took up arms.

One of the biggest jobs I had was the mine sweeping. All the mine sweepers, of which we had about forty, Korean and U. S. and some British were doing the mine sweeping.

Of course, one of the strong features of Russian warfare has always been mine warfare. They'd been feeding the mines down the rivers and creeks which feed into the Sea of Japan just continually.

When I arrived out there, the basic policy was that you never went where there was a mine field. My good luck was to get Admiral Turner Joy to approve a new policy, which was to sweep the mines out where we went or wanted to go. And that involved a tremendous chore, of course. However, he approved it and stuck by it. We did a tremendous amount of mine sweeping and cleared up an awful lot of that area.

Q: What type of mines were used mainly by the Russians?

Dyer: Their normal was an anchored mine, and their second was an influence or a pressure mine. What they always started out with was to mix them. So that if you swept into a mine field working against one type, you most always found the others.

Q: Did you have casualties on this job?

Dyer: The Koreans lost a number of mine sweepers. We didn't lose any. If you want to read about it, it's in THE SEA WAR IN KOREA, by Cagle. In fact, a great deal of what I did is told in this SEA WAR IN KOREA.

The next is the intelligence activities. Of course, we did an awful lot of that. I never had very much faith in our Korean intelligence sources.

I had a missionary's son on my staff who was very helpful. There were two boys, one was in the Army and one was in the Navy. They, of course, spoke Korean extremely well.

And I had this Lieutenant in the naval reserve on board my flag ship. He interrogated the refugees and the few intelligence people that we got ashore and got back, because a good many of them we never got back. We sent them, but they never came back. I don't know to this day whether they were captured and killed, or whether they were deserters or double agents or what they were.

We got an awful lot of fastastic tales out of these refugees. They were quite obviously trying to pull somebody's leg, as far as I could figure out.

Another thing that we did - I had Command of the River Patrol on the west coast, in which we daily swept up the Han River. We had a lot of trouble with that from swift current, shifting channels, and enemy fire. The Han River Patrol was maintained largely by the British ships that were under my command.

Q: The mines were laid in the river -

Dyer: Not too many, because the river was very swift. That was the main problem. You got shot at an awful lot, because they would come over land with a gun and put it in the bushes and when you got close, they'd let you have it.

The tenth job that I had a great deal to do with was the interdiction job. The main logistic support line from the Russians on the east coast came down through Wonsan and turned west at Wonsan, where there was a junction, and went over to Pyongyang, the capital of North Korea. They ran trains all the time.

Theoretically you ought to be able to stop it, and we put in plenty of effort trying to stop it.

The thing that's best illustrated at Wonsan - the ability of the communists to provide logistic support - it just defies belief, but this is what happened. Right after dark the communists would take the rails out of where they had been hidden in caves and so forth, and lay the tracks. Along about eleven thirty you could hear the trains start to move. They ran the trains from then until about four o'clock in the morning, when they would stop the trains, pick up the tracks, and put them away. These were large narrow gauge trains.

We spent tons of thousands of tons of ammunition trying to hit trains in Wonsan. Every once in a while, every 13th or 15th or 17th night, by george, we'd hit a train. We'd hit some ammunition and it would blow up. And we'd have a tremendous victory success. Then the next night, they'd run the trains.

Q: Were the tracks laid on ordinary rails?

Dyer: The tracks were rails, they had ties, and so forth. It was just unbelievable.

The eastern coast of North Korea is full of mountains and gulleys and bridges. We knocked out dozens and dozens of bridges. They just rebuilt them and ran the bloomin' train over them three or more nights later. It was almost impossible to believe, but the communists did a fine job of providing logistic support.

The aviators would bomb them all day and bring you back photos showing there wasn't any bridge there. The second night they'd run the train over the gulley.

There were a number of places where there was fairly wide rivers, so called, or creeks where they couldn't do something like that, they'd portage everything across. They had thousands of people, just thousands.

They hid the railroad cars engines and tracks, in tunnels in the daytime, and at night they put the pieces all together and ran the trains. These were steam engines.

The Air Force ran this anti-logistic operation called STRANGE. Our Air power and gunfire knocked out all kinds of bridges, rails and roads. But the North Koreans still provided logistic support.

I sympathize with our fly fly boys in Laos trying to knock out communist logistic support, because it's the same sort of thing.

Anyhow, the job as CTF95 was a very wide ranging job, with a tremendous number of things happening all the time. I worked at it extremely hard.

My problem in Wonsan - Wonsan is a very large harbor and it has large cliffs at both north and south of the inner harbor, with the largest cliffs on the northern side was to keep the harbor swept so our craft could shell from close inshore, and to keep our wonderful crews in the destroyers and minesweepers working hard at an endless task. The communists used to drill through the face of the cliff and stick a gun out of a very small aperture and then shoot at us. Of course, our objective was to try to put a bullet in that hole. That's a pretty difficult trick, hitting a twelve inch hole - three to five hundred feet up from the water's edge.

Q: What size gun did they use?

Dyer: The largest that they ever had in that particular place was a little larger than a six inch. It's a millimeter gun of about a 6.7 or something like that. It could do some damage.

Q: Were these limestone cliffs, or what?

Dyer: They were hard stone.

We spent an awful lot of time and effort shooting at them.

They'd float down mines every night or every other night, and we'd have to sweep in order to go close in shore. It was a very complicated, interesting, and reasonably dangerous operation.

I thoroughly enjoyed being at Wonsan, although I didn't spend too many long periods as I had over 1200 miles of coast to be familiar with in there. I forget how many days each month your ship had to get shot at, in order for the enlisted men to get extra pay. The extra pay was on that basis, if you were under fire ten days or nine days or some such number of times a month. The one sure way to qualify was to spend a detail at Wonsan. I qualified nearly every month that I was in Korea, but of course, officers received no extra pay.

Q: How closely did you work with General MacArthur?

Dyer: Actually General MacArthur got fired just at the time I got out there. I worked with his relief.

Most of the work was done with Admiral Joy and Admiral Martin. Admiral "Beauty" Martin had Command of the Seventh Fleet, and Turner Joy was Commander Naval Forces Far East.

I made up my mind that we needed to have more air power at Wonsan so that we could get at these cliff guns and so forth. The big carriers were involved in this work way up north on the bridges and electrical power and dams and so forth. So we conducted a two day strike against Wonsan with only the Jeep carriers.

I didn't know this at the time - after we conducted the

strike and made the reports and so forth, Admiral Radford, Commander-in-Chief of the Pacific Fleet, sent a dispatch to Admiral Martin, Commander of the Seventh Fleet, saying he considered it very inappropriate that a non-aviator was conducting strikes. He didn't say anything further, and Admiral Martin never said anything to me about it.

So the so-called intelligence we got indicated the strike had been very successful. We worked on some of the caves where they stowed the rails and ties and so forth, where a lot of the people gathered, and where they had machine shops and everything else in Wonsan.

Roughly about five weeks later, when I could get my jeep carriers together again, I conducted a second jeep strike on Wonsan. I not only had the problem of having one U. S., one British, and one Australian jeep carrier, but I had their overhaul and upkeep schedules and all that sort of thing to coordinate.

When this one had been reported to CinC Pacific, Admiral Radford sent a dispatch to Admiral Martin saying that this was a direct order - I was to conduct no more such operations, that they were to be conducted only by naval aviators.

I had been in any number of strikes during World War II through my service in the Fast Carrier Task Forces, as Commanding Officer of a light cruiser. After the first strike, Beauty Martin had said, "I didn't see anything that was done wrong. As a matter of fact when I told him I was going to conduct a second one, he sent over a naval aviator to be on board during the strike. I thought he was just coming down to see the show. He wrote back to me and said everything went just fine, no complaints.

Then Admiral Radford sent back to the Department to get somebody else out to relieve me. Actually his Chief of Staff came out to relieve me.

Q: He's somewhat biased, isn't he, in terms of aviators?

Dyer: He was somewhat biased against George Dyer, because I had had that problem in the Department in regard to the reduction of personnel in the Op-05 Division of Naval Operations.

Anyhow, that was how my cruise ended. When I went back through Pearl Harbor, I arranged my schedule so as to have two days in Pearl Harbor, I talked with Admiral Radford. He never said a word to me about the air strikes which I had conducted. I never heard of his feeling about non-aviators conducting strikes until after Beauty Martin (who was at San Diego as Commander Air Forces, Pacific), when I took over the Training Command said, "Raddy has never forgiven me about letting you make that second strike. He just raised cain with me about it."

I came back from Korea in early June 1952 and was given the Training Command of the Pacific Fleet.

Q: Before you say anything about that, would you look at these questions?

Dyer: The first one question was - why was the blockade deemed necessary and was it effective?

In the Vietnam War, the Russians and the Chinese are keeping the North Vietnamese going with the large scale logistic support move in large merchant ships into Haiphong.

The purpose of the blockade of North Korea was to prevent the Russians and Chineses from accomplishing this logistic support of the North Koreans in an easy effort.

The blockade make them do it the hard way and less effectively.

Between our air searcher, and our surface patrol, there was no big ship running of the blockade. There was some movement of supplies and small numbers of North Korean troops from up in North Korea down to the battle line. Also there was some end running of intelligence agents and guerilla forces well down into South Korea.

The blockade on an over basis, I would say, reasonably effective. But it was closer to being a seventy to eighty percent job, than being a hundred percent job. Because unless you had a lot more forces than we had, it was quite obvious that it would be perfectly possible for them to run four or five hundred sampans during the night whatever distance they could gain either with motor power or with sail and move things down the coast, and we couldn't stop them. When we learned that there were small "sampan forces" doing just this, I had to come up with some idea as to how to stop this movement.

The first idea that I had was that it the North Koreans didn't have any sampans, they couldn't do the moving. So the thing to do was to destroy the sampans.

We started working on the literally dozens of fishing villages along the east coast of Korea, and landing a small party of sailor men. Maybe there were half a dozen sampans there. You can't blow up a sampan with a hand grenade, it's just too tough. You can blow it up with maybe five or six, but the sampans are a very tough thing to completely destroy. The wood burns very slowly.

Q: What are they made of - teak?

Dyer: Teak is not native to Korea. So probably not. They are made of very tough wood, some native wood, that has many of the properties of teak. You can hit a sampan with a five inch shell, as we frequently did, without destroying it. Damaging it, yes, but not destroying it.

We spent a tremendous amount of effort trying to destroy sampans, and we did destroy many of them. In my opinion, it was a twenty to thirty percent operation. We made it more difficult for the North Koreans to operate the sampans, since they could only move at night.

We destroyed a few sampans each day, and the next day they had a few less than they had the day before, because we were able to largely stop any building of new ones. They generally built them right down on the beaches, and you could put a bomb underneath of them and blow it up. If they were in the building stage, you'd wreck them.

Q: And they were hauling these supplies that came by these trains over land?

Dyer: That's right. Very frequently, of course, they'd gather a bunch of sampans to move across a creek, a small river, to get the stuff moved.

The blockade was deemed necessary to prevent logistic support moving into the battle area. I think it was a perfectly sound reason on which the blockade was established, and we made quite an effort to make it effective.

Daily we ran ships, destroyers, frigates, and PT Boats on patrol. That was another thing. And one of the peculiarities is that we had nine nations in the United Nations Blockade and Escort Force - Australia, New Zealand, Canada, Holland, Columbia in South America, Thailand, Great Britain, South Korea, (the French for a awhile, then they backed out just like they backed out of the naval part of NATO), the United States was number nine.

Q: That with the U. S. would be nine. How did Columbia happen to get in there?

Dyer: I don't know. They had a frigate and they had a wonderful set of officers.

One thing that I'll never forget - that we were out there during the period of the annual Navy Relief Drive, and the Columbia frigate contributed a hundred dollars to the United States Navy Relief. They were a very fine group.

The Canadians threw all kinds of curved balls into the TF95 proceedings there. Their frigates, destroyers, could only do certain things. The Commanding Officers had to go up and see the Ambassador in Tokyo at regular intervals and get political instructions. We'd send them a signal and tell them to do something, and they'd reply saying it violated their political instructions and they regretted they'd be unable to comply.

Q: Why that attitude on the part of the Canadians? One doesn't usually associate them with that.

Dyer: No, but it was true.

The second question - Were there any valuable lessons to be learned from the experiences, lessons that might have proved useful for the Cuban missile blockade or for Vietnam?

I think there were lots of lessons for Vietnam, and I think that by and large, the Navy paid some attention to them.

What was the composition of your Force? There was generally a Division of heavy cruisers (British), a squadron of destroyers (British) and some British minesweepers and river patrol craft. The United States Navy provided a cruiser flagship, two to four squadrons of destroyers, destroyer tender, a jeep aircraft carrier, and about 24 minesweepers, including a division of DMS. In addition, a few amphibious types such as an LST were attached from time to time. I've named some of the units. Plus the Korean navy, which consisted of roughly about fifty small to very small ships. Their largest ship was a frigate. All of the Task Force 95 was essentially the smaller ships - destroyers, frigates, mine sweepers, even PT boats, and all that sort of thing. They worked extremely well together.

One thing that I learned was when you were talking with a Korean and you tell him what an operation is going to be, and how you would like him to carry it out, and he says, "Yes," it doesn't mean he's saying, "Aye, aye." He merely says, "I have understood you." Whether he does it or not is quite a different thing.

I had operational control of the Korean navy, and I had wonderful relations with the Korean navy. I learned my lessons, maybe slowly, but I learned them well. They don't operate exactly the same as we do in their mental process. I don't mean to say that there's any deficiency on their part, they just work different.

It took more effort to get something done by the Thailanders than it did in any of the other navies, except for the Canadians with their political instructions. If a Canadian ship was permitted to do something, he did it extremely well.

I have one long-winded story, which I'm not going to tell because my voice is giving out, in which we had one of our islands on the east coast attacked by the communists. The island forces called for help and my nearest big ship was Canadian. I sent him a dispatch to go to their rescue. He came back with a dispatch saying that he would proceed to the area, but in accordance with his political instructions he would take no offensive action because it was too close to the Soviet border.

Q: Were Canadians participating almost against their will in this joint effort of the United Nations?

Dyer: I think they were doing a lot of window dressing on both sides of the picture. In other words, they were afraid not to participate because it was a United Nations effort and they were afraid to participate for fear they might antagonize the Soviets or the Chinese.

Q: And lose their wheat customers.

Dyer: What was the composition of your Force? The largest regular one was this division of British cruisers. I had a British flag officer serving underneath me, a very fine one.

Then I had normally three or four squadrons of U. S. destroyers. And I always had two squadrons of British destroyers.

Then I had frigates, which is the next largest group. The Koreans had maybe ten frigates, I can't tell you exactly how many. We had about ten more frigates out there. The British had some frigates. The New Zealanders had frigates. The Australians had a frigate, they also had a jeep carrier. The Thailanders had a gunboat and a tender.

When the war was over, the Thailanders sent back one of their Princes and he gave me the highest award of the Thailand country, the same award that they gave General Westmoreland, the Royal Order of the White Elephant. My wife had to sign a piece of paper saying when I die, she'd send it back. They only have 150, and they keep the 150 in circulation.

Q: What was the origin of the frigates in the Korean navy?

Were they Japanese?

Dyer: They were all ours.

Q: Where had their officers been trained?

Dyer: A lot of them had been trained in the Japanese navy in World War II. As a matter of fact one of the Korean rear admirals, Kim Sam Song had been a Lieutenant in the Japanese naval reserve. Initially, he had been a merchant marine sailor. After World War II was well started, the Japanese did the same as we did, put most of their merchant marine officers into the naval reserve.

Kim Sam Song was sunk twice by us, once when he was a merchant skipper and he survived that. And then he became a Lieutenant in the Japanese naval reserve and was serving in another merchant ship, and again, one of our submarines sunk his ship. That time he swam eleven or twelve miles to shore. Kim Sam Song was his name. He's dead now.

In 1951, he was the operations officer of their whole navy. I worked with him very closely. And I've got several mementos from him which I will show you.

Dyer #15 - 523

Vice Admiral George C. Dyer, USN
Annapolis, Maryland

by John T. Mason, Jr.
May 11, 1971

Mr. Mason: Admiral, last time you told me about your participation in the Korean War, and brought that story to a conclusion with the change of command. Now you return to the United States, and will you resume your story at that point?

Admiral Dyer: I would be less than frank if I did not say that I was deeply disappointed when I was ordered to the Training Command of the Pacific Fleet. I had a long letter from the Chief of Bureau, who was Vice Admiral Laurence T. Du Bose, saying he was disappointed also since he had planned on ordering me to command Cruisers Destroyers, Pacific Fleet, but that he had been unable to secure my detail to that job. My classmate, Johnny Roper, had been ordered to the job from Chief of Bureau of Naval Personnel in mid April '51 and relinquished it in June 1952 to Rear Admiral Curts.

After I'd been in Training Command for a short time, Johnny Roper went as Commandant of the 11th Naval District. When he became sort of sub-par physically, he was retired and I relieved him as the Commandant of the 11th Naval District.

I was in the Training Command roughly a year. I had just reported to the Command when I got a telephone call from Cincinnati. It was my mother and father's family doctor, Dr. Brown, and he opened the conversation by saying that he had bad news for me.

I presumed, of course, that it was my mother because my

mother had been doctoring heavily for ten years, and my father went to the doctor a couple times a year and that was it. I said, "Mother?" And he said, "No, your father." I had always been very close to my father and just thought the world of him, so it was a very deep shock for me.

I called Admiral Radford, who was Commander-in-Chief Pacific, and told him what had happened and asked for emergency leave. I went back to Cincinnati and picked up father's body and took it to Arlington, and then came back to Cincinnati and stopped very briefly, and then came back to the Training Command headquarters, which was down in San Diego.

The best thing that I know about the Training Command, as far as my year in it was concerned, was that it did have subordinate Training Groups all over the West Coast of the United States and at Pearl Harbor, Guam, and Japan and Korea. Therefore, I was able, at regular intervals, to make several swings around the circuit to get out and visit and inspect these Training Groups.

The other good thing about it was, entirely without my having any part to play in it, that I was notified that a division of Peruvian frigates would come up and have a month in the Training Command. I had no knowledge of the Peruvian Navy, except that we had for a long time had a Mission down there and that it had been quite successful in it's work.

This division arrived, the Commander was Captain Llosa. We had laid out a strenuous program for them and we carried it out. This was a purely training program.

When they arrived, they needed quite a number of minor repairs. At that time at the Destroyer Base in San Diego there was a large training activity down there, and we had a lot of good relations with the repair activity at the training base. So I was able to get a considerable amount of cumshaw work on the Peruvian ships, which the Commanding Officer of the repair base, aided and abetted by his immediate senior, who was Commandant of the 11th Naval District, undertook for the Peruvians, and they were very grateful.

Q: Had we furnished them with the frigates in the first place?

Dyer: They initially were our frigates.

We had a number of social entertainments for the officers. We had all kinds of activities for the crews, smokers, sight seeing trips, dances, etc. It was a very happy occasion for All Hands.

Q: What sort of training did they seek?

Dyer: They wanted detailed technical training in such features as anti-submarine and anti-aircraft. In other words, we had submarines from the local contingent of submarines in Submarines Pacific that provided targets for them to make training approaches on.

We had technical personnel who not only helped them with their equipment - how to use their equipment, how to get the most out of their equipment - but also to teach them skills in anti-submarine work.

We held gun practices and proved them with both air and surface targets. We had mooring practices in handling their anchors. We had radio drills and signal drills. We had technical instruction in keeping their manufacture of water in their auxiliary plants. We had various types of training activities to improve their skills in everything that needed to be done in a frigate.

Q: How adept were they at maintaining their ships?

Dyer: I think that basically they were pretty good, but just like in our Navy there's always something new in how to maintain a piece of equipment and how to get the most out of it, that can be learned from someone that is really skillful.

The Training Command personnel are specially selected Petty Officers and Chief Petty Officers and some Warrant Officers. They add a great deal in our Navy, and they were able to add even more to the Peruvians.

I was surprised at some of their skills, and a bit disappointed in some of them, but they took full advantage of the month. They worked hard and came along extremely well. We gave them planned test at the end of the period, and I was quite well satisified with it. My subordinates were extremely well satisfied with the test. The Peruvians were just enthusiastic about it.

As a result of that the Peruvians asked to come up for two months the following year. The plan was worked through the Department and the Department finally approved it, because it got enthusiastic endorsements from myself and from Admiral Roper.

Then during the next year I moved over to be the Commandant of the District. Working through Rear Admiral Earl Stone who relieved me as Commander of the Training Command, we did even better. We did a lot more repair work because I was the immediate senior over the Destroyer Base skipper and was able to pressure him to do more than perhaps he would liked to have done.

The Peruvians came the second year with a new turnover of officers. They had their best officers in those ships. Many years later the Peruvian Navy invited Mrs. Dyer and myself to come down there. Captain Llosa, whom we had known again in Washington because he came up as the Naval Attache, and the second Squadron Commander, (Tirado) had both became Rear Admirals in the Peruvian navy. Later one of them, Llosa, had become the Secretary of the Navy and the other one, Tirado, had become the Chief of Naval Operations of the Peruvian navy.

They invited Mrs. Dyer and myself down to Peru and we went. They met us on the dock, and we were down there at Lima for sixteen days. The amazing thing was the very large number of officers who had come up on those two cruises who had become Flag Officers in the Peruvian navy.

Q: It was kind of a postgraduate course for them, wasn't it?

Dyer: During the time we were down there, in one function or another, they all entertained us. I think there must have been at least nine or ten of the officers who were Flag Officers.

Q: In very short order you had been exposed to units of two Latin American nations, Columbia and Peru. Did any others wish to participate in this Training Program on the Pacific Coast?

Dyer: Yes. They had a lot of requests after the Peruvians had gone back, but the difficulty was who was to pay for it. That was the bind.

The one thing about the Peruvians which was a bit different than some of the others was that the Peruvian navy seemed to be able to get more funds than other navies did. The other navies were anxious to do this, but they wanted Uncle Sam to bear all the expense. The Peruvians at least made a gesture, and a worthwhile one, in bearing part of the expense.

Q: Perhaps they had a little more money to go with anyway.

Dyer: It may very well have been. I do not know that, but I do know that the Argentine navy made an effort to do this. Of course, we had a much larger mission down in Brazil than we had anywhere else in South America. I don't know what we have as of today. The Argentines have worked closely with our Navy for many years.

When I was in the Submarine School at New London in 1918, there were three Argentine officers in that submarine school. I corresponded with one of them for thirty years. He finally got involved in one of these political maneuvers, which have occured quite frequently down there. Of course, in my letters I always told him for years that the military ought to stay out of politics. I worked on this, I never wrote a letter without stressing that. I still think it's important. He finally got completely on the other side of the thing. He didn't answer my letter. I sent him a Christmas card and he didn't send a card back. I've still got his letters because they always had nice stamps on them, so I saved them.

Q: How many ships did you have in the Training Command at one time, how many ships involved in training? How big an operation was it?

Dyer: Training Command as a command does not have ships in it, except as they are ordered by the Type Commanders to report temporarily to the Training Command. You not only don't have anything regularly with you, it changes every morning.

Normally, it changes every Friday when the ships come out having finished their tests, depending on how long they've been with you.

Type Commanders may find there's some deficiency in some aspect of a ship that they have in their command. They'll order that ship to the Training Command for a week, just a single ship to work on that particular thing.

On the other hand they have a regular period when they sort of re-train, and that is a much longer period. Normally it's three weeks, they come in and spend three weeks with you.

Q: So you have to have a fairly large staff which covers all aspects of Navy work.

Dyer: I had a large staff, I would guess about thirty officers. You have a very high number of enlisted men, many of them Chief Petty Officers and Petty Officers First Class.

We had training centers at Long Beach and at San Francisco and at Puget Sound. Then we had a training group in Pearl Harbor. We had a training group in Guam. We had a training group in Olongapo. We had a training group in Yokosuka, one in Sasebo, and one in Pusan.

So that the big commanders, such as Commander of the Seventh Fleet, could order his ships to whatever Training activity was most convenient - to Pusan or Sasebo or Olongapo or whatever it might be.

I flew out to Olongapo and inspected the activities there. The Pacific Fleet Training Command handled everything except the aviation training activities. We had nothing to do with aviation training, that was entirely under the Commander Air Pac. We trained carriers in the other aspects of carrier activity.

Q: You had to keep abreast of all the new ordnance coming out from Washington.

Dyer: We had to keep abreast actually of all the new of everything. The Training Command had many interesting aspects to it, but my objection was that I knew that it's history had been that it had been a dead end job. I thought I knew also that Admiral Radford had been responsible for my being pushed into it because of the conflict that had arisen during the Korean War.

Dyer #15 - 531

Q: I suppose it was always put in charge of a senior officer.

Dyer: Yes. I was relieved by Rear Admiral Earl Stone. It's one of the Type Commands of the Pacific Fleet.

Q: I can see where it wouldn't be entirely satisfactory to you because you were too much of an activist.

Dyer: That's right. And also you're working to get results for somebody else's immediate benefit. It isn't anything that you can say, "I took the ship from the bottom and raised it up to the top," because you didn't have that sort of a job. Other people sent you all of their problems and you tried to correct them for them.

I worked very hard at it and as far as I know did it quite satisfactorily, but it just wasn't the kind of a job that would give you the opportunity to see the results because you turned the people over to other commands and they were the ones who actually found out how well you'd done your job. You never had the opportunity to get a second look, unless the ship came back possibly a year later. I wasn't there that long to do that.

From there I went to Commandant of the 11th Naval District. When I arrived I relieved Admiral Roper who physically retired. He had been temporarily relieved by a naval aviator, Rear Admiral George Henderson who was Commander Naval Bases 11th Naval District. He had been there for three months before I showed up.

When I did show up the officer who was in charge of the Naval Reserve activity in the 11th Naval District came to me and said, "The Naval Reserve activies in this District suffer from a lack of command attention. We have three hundred and some odd reserve activities in this large District. There're countless ones of them that have never seen the Commandant of the 11th Naval District."

I had had, as I said before, two years out in Michigan as the Inspector-Instructor of the Naval Reserve, and I had formed close friendships with a number of outstanding Naval Reserve officers and thought they had a real place in our Navy. I thought that if there was anything that I could do to help the Reserves that I wanted to do it.

With the result that I told the head of the Naval Reserve section on the staff for him to lay out a schedule for me whereby about three times a week I would fly out to Yuma, Arizona, or wherever it was, and that I would fly out right after working hours and get there and have dinner with the officers of the Reserve activity. Then I would inspect the activity. Then I would get the officers together and deliver a talk to them, sort of a pep talk, and then lay myself open to questions and stay there as long as they wanted me to.

Q: That was a great boon to the Reservists.

Dyer: That was quite a program, and I worked on it for over a year, fifteen months to be exact. It was a very strenuous schedule, because I got home late. Most of the time I flew home that night, got home late. Actually it was a killing schedule.

Q: Did your wife not try to restrain you?

Dyer: I presume so. It drove my blood pressure way up.

I was deeply interested in the Reserves. I realized that many of their gripes and stories of neglect were very true. I was deeply grateful to them because during World War II and during the Korean War I had commanded ships or divisions or task forces with a very high percentage of Reserves, who largely were turning in outstanding jobs. They were interrupting their lives of civilian enterprise for the second time in the Korean War.

I thought we owed a great deal to them. So I tried, by paying attention to them and participating in their activities and respecting them and giving them, I hope, some new enthusiasm for sticking with what was a difficult job in many cases, to spur them on and keep them tied to the Navy. I sure worked at it and I think I was quite successful at it.

I had a number of things that were quite interesting. One of the things that I required was that these officers wear uniforms when they came to drill. At that time it was within the discretion of the Commandant to require them. I found that many of these officers had never worn uniforms for that purpose. The uniforms were pretty terrible, and I made some pretty salty remarks about it when I inspected them and I gave them deadlines to meet.

Q: Did you have repeat appearances at these various places?

Dyer: Yes, some of them I had repeat appearances.

The head of the Navy League was a young fellow who came from Los Angeles. He got the gripes from many of the reserve officers who were required to get themselves new pieces of uniforms, as well as to improve their uniforms. He went back and made a plea to the Secretary of the Navy.

The first thing that I knew was that I got a letter from the Secretary of the Navy which said that this was causing discontent among the Reserves and that I should cease and desist. That was quite upsetting.

About two days later I got a letter from this chap and he said, "I presume that you have been disturbed by the letter which you have received from the Secretary of the Navy which I was largely the instigator of. I had told him what a terrible person you were, and so forth."

"On the plane coming back to the West Coast I was sitting next to a chap in civilian clothes, but I found out that he was an ex-sailorman in the Navy. I asked him the question - if you had to name the most wonderful naval officer that you have ever served with, whom would you name? Needless to say, I was greatly amazed when he said - Admiral George C. Dyer."

"I talked with him all the way across and I came out of this conversation with a quite different opinion of you than I had before I came into it. I am sending you a copy of the letter that I have written to the Secretary of the Navy in regard to this."

He had written such a letter and he sent me a copy of it. The letter just told what had happened and that he had some second thoughts about what he had done, and he was a bit regretful that it had happened, and he hoped that the Secretary in due time would withdraw the prohibition against my requiring people to be in uniform.

The ex-enlisted man was Lieutenant Commander Francis V. O'Leary. He died within the last year, in fact, he died in February or March of this year, 1971.

Actually the Secretary of the Navy never recinded the order, so I couldn't insist any longer, I merely could encourage them. But that didn't keep me from traveling around.

The great problem at that time in the Naval Reserves was the Bureau of Naval Personnel had what in effect was an Officer-Instructor-Inspector at each of the larger Naval Reserve activities, and some had staffs as well. The people that had been ordered to these jobs were far from being the best in the Navy, and one wouldn't expect they would be the best because it was bound to be apparent that it was a dead end job. Also the Bureau had quite a number of Naval Reserve officers on active duty in the Fleets and Shore Establishment where operating standards had to be net.

My point of view of the detail matter is that we should, in about ninety percent of the cases have Naval Reserve officers on active duty at these Naval Reserve activities because those seeking active duty generally were the eager beavers of the Naval Reserve outfit. They also were in much better positions to tell another Naval Reserve officer that this was the standard and that this standard was what he had to meet than to hear this from some third or fourth rate regular officer, who frequently was a violator of the standards himself.

Q: It was a 'go and do thou likewise' sort of thing.

Dyer: Yes.

We had a number of such extremely excellent people in the naval reserve organization, and I sought to very markedly enlarge that number and was reasonably successful. Although by and large the Bureau wouldn't move anybody out of a billet until he was either due to be finally retired or could be eased out of the job without too many teardrops being cast about.

In any case if you didn't do anything else, it would have been really a full time job. They had a very excellent Captain in the Commandant's organization, who had been working hard at the job and continued to work hard. With a very large number of units you have great difficulty giving individual attention which you need to give.

The Commandant has a lot of other chores to do. The chore that finally did me in, at least I'm convinced it did me in, was that I had a legal officer in the days when the line officer had something to do with the legal standards of the Navy. He no longer has very much to do with it. We had a continuing general court martial with officers on it, senior officers who sat down at the destroyer base, and day after day after day they tried people. The Legal Officer of the District is the immediate superior in command, and therefore, he reviews the actions of the court and recommends to the Commandant the final action, that is, final up to the Secretary of the Navy for review by the Judge Advocate General's office.

This Legal Officer of mine was always finding some technicality - he wanted the case thrown out, or the case approved and the sentence thrown out.

My primary thought in the matter always was - I want justice done. If a man's guilty of an offense, he should be punished. If he isn't guilty of an offense, he ought not to be punished. The primary thing to be decided here was - was he guilty of the offense, and if he was guilty of the offense it was up to the Navy to do something about it.

I was in a constant series of arguments with my Legal Officer. He would send up prepared endorsements for me which I wouldn't sign. I read all these cases, and it takes time. The cases come in that are very thick. You've got to read all the testimony. You've got to form a judgment, and that takes time.

I would call him in and have long winded discussions with him. It got to the stage where after I'd been there fifteen months or more I told him, "Now I've talked to you about this, I don't want any more prepared endorsements to come up for me to sign in which there's some technical thing that you think should cause me to throw the case out. I want to find out what the facts of the case are, I want to know what the testimony is, I want to know has the court martial arrived at a judgment which is within reason, and if the judgment isn't within reason based on the testimony given and they've given punishment my action should be tempered with mercy, but it should not free the one who has been guilty of doing something against the Articles for the Government of the Navy."

On the morning when I had my first stroke, he had come up with another case. I had called him in and we had had a ten minute go 'round, during which I had expressed my opinion of him and his lawyer judgments.

When he walked out of the office I realized something was happening to me. I became faint, and I had enough sense to buzz my buzzer for my Chief of Staff just as I was passing out and went down on the deck. He came in and, of course, got the ambulance from the hospital. By the time the ambulance had gotten there, I was revived. They took my blood pressure and it was way up, and so forth. It had been high for ten years, my blood pressure.

When I came back from the war and reported to Admiral King's headquarters, they had a doctor there and he examined you once a month. He examined all new officers as they reported, and the first time he examined me he said, "I don't know whether you know it or not, but you've got high blood pressure." I said, "I don't know any reason why I shouldn't have high blood pressure." And I didn't.

I never left the bridge when we went to sea until we came back to port and in the far Pacific we were at sea never less than sixty days and as high as eighty-one days, under constant tension. I didn't see any reason why I shouldn't have high blood pressure.

At that time the lower of the blood pressure readings, which is supposed to be around eighty, was up around one hundred and five or six. The top was around one hundred seventy or one hundred eighty. It didn't come down much during the monthly examinations I had, although he gave me various things to do, and I tried to do them.

I was worried when I was examined physically for promotion to flag rank that I wouldn't pass my physical examination, but I told the doctors my sad story and they passed me.

I was ordered into the naval hospital on two occasions when I took my annual physicals, because of high blood pressure. They would give me a routine to follow, which consisted of spending a lot of time in bed and so forth and so on.

Q: That only added to the tension I'm sure with you.

Dyer: Each time the blood pressure came down a bit, and they were heartened and I was heartened.

It just went over the boiling mark at this particular time, and I had a stroke. So I found myself at the naval hospital, San Diego.

I was very anxious to get back on active duty, of course, quite logical as far as I was concerned. I didn't want to retire. I was 57.

The Commanding Officer of the Naval Hospital, San Diego had drawn up a document recommending me back to active duty. He had written a letter to the Chief of Bureau of Naval Personnel telling him that I was coming back to active duty and there was no need to order a relief and so forth.

I was sitting in my chair reading a perfectly harmless mystery story when I had another stroke, six weeks after the first one. I was just about to go back to active duty. The corpsmen hoisted me up onto the bed.

Dr. James, Rear Admiral Walter F. James (Mc) was the Commanding Officer of the naval hospital in San Diego. He came in and shook his finger in front of my nose and said, "Now George, no doctor in the United States Navy would certify you for active duty. The only thing you've got to do is to learn to live. Lie back and relax."

Dr. Davis, who is now Chief of the Bureau of Medicine and Surgery, Vice Admiral George M. Davis (mc) was my doctor. He's a very excellent doctor, as you might guess. He gave me all kinds of rules. I made up my mind as far as I could, I would live with those rules, and for about the first four years I observed them no matter what.

Q: You applied just as much diligence to that as you did to your career beforehand.

Dyer: Yes, the object was to live. While I undertook certain jobs and did certain things - I wrote a biography of Admiral Richardson.

The first thing I should say is that I wouldn't be alive today, if it wasn't for that wonderful wife of mine, who fell in to this very difficult routine and supported me in it. If she hadn't taken a real interest in it, and really worked at it - it takes real work from a woman's point of view, I wouldn't be here today. Many things that she liked to do, I didn't do.

I pay tribute to her.

I was retired the first of February '55. I didn't feel well for the first four months after I retired, I felt badly most of the time. Then I began to feel more human.

Along about September of that year (1955) I got a letter from Rear Admiral John B. Heffernan who was the Director of Naval History in Naval Operations, Navy Department. He said, "We're trying to get some biographies written. Would you be willing to undertake writing a biography of Admiral James O. Richardson?"

I had the greatest respect and admiration for Admiral Richardson, and I owed him a great deal, because he had been a tremendous help to me in becoming a better naval officer. Because of the high standard he set, he appealed to my ideals. He also gave me many, many helpful hints. He just was wonderful. So I felt that I owed him that job.

Since I had done a lot of minor writing on active duty, it was because of that, that John Heffernan suggested that I might be willing to undertake it.

I said that I thought I would be ready to start about the first of the following January, and if that was agreeable to him I would undertake it. He wrote back and said that would be fine.

So the first of January '56, I started to write Admiral Richardson's biography. I was then living at 4 Chase Road, Annapolis, Maryland, and have continued to live there.

I, of course, had to go into Washington regularly. I

had to go into the Naval History Division, which at that time was in the old Navy Department down on Constitution Avenue, and get source material and so forth. Admiral Richardson cooperated a hundred percent.

In about two years I did it, turned it in, it was accepted, and I was paid.

Before I finished Admiral Richardson's biography, I got a call from the Editor of the Naval Institute, who lives right here in town, out of the class of 1914, Roy Horn. Roy Horn said, "How about coming over here to talk to me? I'd like to use some of your talents." I didn't know what it was, but I went over.

He said, "We have a call from the Bureau of Naval Personnel for a book on Naval Logistics which can be given to a reserve officer to prepare him for their examinations." At that time all naval reserve officers, as well as all line officers, had to take a written examination for promotion. He said, "There's only one problem - the Bureau says that the book has to be completed by the 31st of December 1959. The subject is Naval Logistics (which I had had a great deal of experience and training in)."

I said, "That's not too far away due to the fact that I'm not quite finished with what I'm doing now. But anyway, I'll give it a try." I signed a contract on the first of June 1958 to complete the book by the 31st of December 1959, just eighteen months.

I wrote NAVAL LOGISTICS and I turned it in on the 30th

of December 1959. I had told them all during the latter part of this writing chore that I had promised my wife that I would take her on a trip around the world, and that we had made our reservations to sail on the 1st of April, 1960 and that they had to get the thing into galley proof so that I could proofread it before I left. The Editor of the Naval Institute, who by this time was Rear Admiral Horace H. Jalbert, of the class of 1914 said, "No problem."

I turned it in, by that time Roy Horn had ceased to be Editor. H. H. Jalbert had become the Editor of the Institute. He had gone to the naval hospital and was in the hospital then.

Early in February, 1960, after they had had the manuscript about five or six weeks, I called and said, "I haven't gotten any galley proof here and time's approaching for me to sail on this trip. How about it?"

They said, "Jalbert took the manuscript with him when he went over to the hospital and nobody has done anything on it. He has read far enough into it to tell somebody on the staff that it's darn good, but that's the only thing we know about it. We'll go over and retrieve it right now, and have somebody finish reading it, and see if we've got any changes to suggest. We'll get it up to the printers to get galley proofs right quick."

They never said a word to me about any changes, nor did they make any in the text, not a single one.

Along about two weeks before I was to sail, I got a fairly good bunch of proofs, and Adaline and I read them and marked them up. Then we got a second group, and then a third group.

We got right up to the sailing date and I said, "I told you about this a long time ago, and we're going to sail," and sail we did. The Naval Institute said they would get a professional reader, and they did hire a Navy wife to finish the job.

When we got to Singapore, we received the finished book. So of course, like every author, I sat down to read it. In the first 181 pages that we had proofread, we had one proof error. In the rest of it there were countless. In the first print, there must have been at least twenty-five errors in this part and in several cases, sentences had been changed. They turned it over to a woman here in town. She proofread it. She didn't know anything about logistics. If it didn't sound right to her, she re-wrote it. It's got several of the most terrible things in it.

Of course, that upset me beyond measure. Here I was out in the Pacific - all I could do was to write the Naval Institute a snazzy letter.

Fortunately, the first issue of 6,000 copies sold out in about a year. The Naval Institute thought it was going to continue to sell well so they had me do a revision, so I could correct the errors.

By that time Mr. McNamara had come into town. He was going around to all the logistic agencies and mixing things up. I had a section of the book devoted to logistics in the Department of Defense including diagrams, graphs, and that sort of thing. They all had to be changed and so forth and so on.

The general principles, the NATO logistics, the SEATO logistics and that sort of thing - they all stayed. Mr. McNamara's logistics - they were all changing every Monday morning.

I did the revision of it, but by that time I had started on Kelly Turner. I did the revision while I should have been doing Kelly Turner.

Q: What started you on Kelly Turner?

Dyer: It's all told in the introduction to the Kelly Turner book.

Judge Eller (Rear Admiral E. M. Eller, U. S. Navy Retired) had come in as Director of Naval History in Naval Operations by that time and was doing his very wonderful job as a historian for Naval History. He was trying to get autobiographies or biographies of all the principle naval personalities of World War II. Kelly Turner or anyone who was in top command in the Pacific was certainly one of the principle naval personalities.

Kelly Turner had written to him and I quote the letter that he wrote in which he said that - all one had to do was to read some of the autobiographies to know what poor literature and poor history they were. He said, - as for having a ghost writer he wouldn't have any part of it. He was just going to let it rest at that.

Judge Eller kept after him and finally sent him a copy

of the biography which I had done on Admiral Richardson, which of course, hadn't been published. Admiral Richardson's requirement was that it not be published until he died. He is now past 93.

Q: And incidentally the title of the Richardson book is what?

Dyer: ON THE TREADMILL TO PEARL HARBOR, the biography of Admiral James O. Richardson.

Anyhow, he suggested my name at Turner, as one who might do his biography. So Admiral Turner told me that when he got that letter from Admiral Eller he said to himself, "Dyer is just enough of a son of a bitch to do a good job." So I told Judge Eller, "All right."

That story I've got in the introduction to the Kelly Turner book.

I had served with him twice and he knew me reasonably well. He cooperated until the time of his death. He was a very wonderful person. I'm delighted that I've done this.

It's taken me ten years to do it, but I think I've done a good job in that I have gone around and talked to literally hundreds of people. I have all points of view in the book, and I publish them as they said them. In other words I don't try to make a great man, he becomes a great man in my opinion.

He had his defects, and he was getting along in years. He had been the type of a man who could work literally twenty hours a day. I'm not talking about theoretical twenty hours, I'm talking about literal twenty hours. He got up at four o'clock in the morning and he worked until midnight. He turned out a supurb performance.

As he got along in years, and as the war bore down on him, he turned to the bottle. And he nursed it. He first started with just the cocktail. He was largely a non-drinker. He just wasn't interested, it interfered with what he wanted to do, so he wasn't interested. You can't find anyone that ever saw the man take more than one drink until the middle stages of the war, and by the end of the war he was nursing the bottle. He needed a stimulant to permit him to do what he knew he wanted to do.

He was devoted to his Navy, his country, and to the people that met his standards. He was very hard, he was impossible with third and fourth rate officers. He was difficult with second rate officers. With his first rate officers he just raised cain part of the time. He just was devoted to the people that served him well.

Q: But his addiction to drink was the price he paid to keep up to par in his latter years.

Dyer: That's right.

Q: I hope you'll go on and write a biography of somebody else.

Dyer: I'm going to take a little time off when I finish in deference to my companion and wife of fifty years.

Index

Series of Interviews

with

Vice Admiral George C. Dyer

U. S. Navy (Retired)

Alden, Prof. Charles S.: 26-27

Alexander, Gen. Sir Harold: Deputy C-in-C, Med, 302-303; his decisive action taken at conference in BISCAYNE on possible evacuation of the Salerno beach-head, 347-348

Amalfi Harbor: captured by the British - allies made good use of the facilities, 352

Amphibious Warfare: discussion of Army-Navy jurisdictional problems, 265-267; difficulties faced by the small naval groups who came to North Africa to establish amphibious training bases, 269 ff.

USS ANCON: Dyer, when injured off Salerno, put on board...later transferred to the British Hospital Ship, ST. ANDREW, 361

Ansel, RADM Walter C.: 256-257

USS ARIZONA, BB: Dyer assigned to Electrical Division in 1928, 122; story of wardroom mess and Dyer's service as mess treasurer, 126-131

Army Air Force: in operation HUSKY, 293 ff; lack of communications about Airborne Division Jump back of Gela, 318-320; see also entry under Salerno campaign; Conolly urges landing at Gaeta regardless of their support, 328-329; criticism in press, elsewhere forces changes at Salerno, 341-343

Arzeu (Arzew): headquarters base in North Africa for invasion of Sicily, 264-265

USS ASTORIA: 365; new cruiser in commission on May 17, 1944 - Dyer in command, 371-373; 375 ff; repair work in the Navy Yard at Philadelphia, 381; problem with Boatswain Mate Lemon and other survivors of CA ASTORIA, 385 ff; firing range instruction in

-1-

Hawaii, 391-392; Dyer asks for escorts on cruise to Ulithi, 392; kamikaze attack on unescorted ship, 394-396; ship is given nickname - MIGHTY NINETY (CL-90), 397; Iwo Jima operation, 397-398; problem with ammo allocation, 399-400; attitude of crew towards Iwo Jima engagement, 402; citation crew gave Dyer when he left ship, 402-403; value of ASTORIA as a screening and protective ship, 403; question of gunnery, 404-405; her role in Okinawa campaign, 414 ff; technique employed for rapid launching of search plane, 416; near collision with INDIANAPOLIS and MONTANA, 430-432

USS AUGUSTA: Dyer offered command of AUGUSTA (Kirk's flagship for Normandy landings) but missed it because doctor would not release him from hospital, 366-367, 370

Austin, Joseph Eliot: trial captain for Lake TB Co. - relieved of his job as result of trials of S-15, 100-103

Aviation - role as part of a team: Dyer comments, 497-499; uses Air Force publicity over Battle of Midway as illustration of remarks, 500

B-29: use of B-29 in operations against Japanese shipping - value to them of Iwo Jima bases, 408, 411

Badger, Adm. Oscar C.: Exec on USS INDIANAPOLIS, 174; 176-177

Bagley, Capt. D. W.: Acting Commander, DD Scouting Force, 171

Baka Bomb: Japanese use for first time at Okinawa, 425

Baron, Lt. Comdr. William P.: deep sea diver operating from WIDGEON, 145-146

Barr, Comdr. Eric L. (1911): skipper of R-5

Bemis, Comdr. Harold M.: Division Commander, E-boats and N-boats out of New London (1919), 76

Bieri, VADM B. H.: Operations Officer for Adm. J. O. Richardson (1939), 183-184; in 1947 - command of U.S. Naval Forces, Mediterranean, 476-477

USS BISCAYNE: flagship of Adm. Conolly for invasion of Sicily, 278-279; 308; resucues U. S. paratrooper plane shot down at Gela, 319-320; 332; at Salerno beachhead, 350; receives delegation of Italian Naval Officers who come under white flag, 351-352; manning of machine guns near bridge in Stuka attack, 359; injury to Dyer in Stuka attack from Salerno, 360

Bizerte: becomes headquarters for invasion of Sicily, 270-271; Germans had effectually blocked harbor, 271; firefighting in harbor area, 271-272; Germans conduct nightly air raids before invasion of Sicily, 292; planning for Salerno goes forward (Aug. 1943) at headquarters with landing craft assembled, 334-335; Dyer in Army Field Hospital there, 363-364

Blandy, Adm. W. H. P.: CruDesPac, 1944, 390-391, 397-398

Bode, Capt. H. D.: Incident (1918) at SS base in New London, 41-43

BRASS HAT: Code name for proposed evacuation of Salerno beachhead, 346 ff.

Briggs, Capt. Zeno E.: 107-108

British Forces at Salerno: problem of surrendering, 340

USS BROOKLYN: gives gunfire support to troops on Sicily, 277; log of BROOKLYN covering enemy air attacks at Licata, 294-295;

damaged in U. S. Minefield off Licata, 315-316

Brown, VADM Wilson: Task Force Commander whom Adm. Pye ordered to cancel raid on Marshall Islands, 198-199; his subordinate commanders, Conolly and Frederick Sherman, urge that it not be cancelled, 199-200; favored request of Pat Wing II that reconnaissance flights be cancelled, 211

Bull, Lt. Gen. H. R.: 494; succeeds Admiral Hill as President of National War College, 495, 497, 504-505

Bureau of Navigation, Planning Staff (1939): 180-181

Burgy, Lt. W. C.: skipper of USS N-6 (1919), 51-54; receives a general court martial and public reprimand, 54

Burke, Adm. Arleigh: was a Commodore in 1945 - one of few to advance from that rank, 442

Bush-Selzer Engine: used by Lake Torpedo Boat Co., in submarines, 62-64

Carpender, VADM A. S. (Chips): Chief of Staff (1936) to Adm. Richardson, 158, 163; detail officer, BuPers (1941) - gives Dyer assignment as Exec on INDIANAPOLIS, 201

Carrier Task Groups: Adm. Richardson, 1939, as Commander, Battle Force, develops technique of task groups with carriers at center, 184-185

Chichi Jima: ASTORIA bombards prior to Okinawa landings, 414, 418

USS CHILDS: develops gunfire system, 151-152

Clark, General Mark: did not want naval bombardment prior to landings at Salerno, 333; in post war period denies he ever seriously contemplated evacuation of beaches at Salerno, 344-345; Dyer's recollections of conference on board Hewitt's command ship on subject of an evacuation, 344 ff.

COMINCH Headquarters: Dyer returns from Pacific in June, 1945, 433

COMINCH Security Officer: Adm. King alarmed at reports of pending operation against North Africa, 239-240; discovers army much less stringent in its control of information on this operation, 240; comments on Departmental Security, 241-242; policy memo on staff service in Washington, 258-259

COMINCH Staff work: 219-222, 226; relations of Intelligence and Plans to Operations, 228; 239

Commodore Rank, U.S. Navy: Dyer's efforts to establish rank of Commodore in post-war Navy, 437-441

Conolly, Adm. Richard: Squadron Commander of DDs in T.F. assigned to Marshall Islands raid - objects to cancellation, 199-200; 258; takes Dyer as his Chief of Staff for operation against Sicily, 261, 263, 271, 283 (see also entries under HUSKY); detached immediately after Sicilian invasion to prepare for Salerno, 307-308; his decision on Ensign who was sent home, 322-323; his arguments in favor of allied landing at Gaeta rather than Salerno, 328, 344, 346-347, 360; his ability to delegate authority, 369

Cooke, Adm. Charles M.: head of War Plans (1942), 262, 381

Crawford, Comdr. John G.: ordered to staff of Adm. Edwards, 217-218

CruDiv 10: Dyer relieves Adm. Curts in command of CruDiv 10 (Dec. 1946), 476 ff; Dyer asks for second year in command, 481; relations with Royal Navy in Med, 485-486; Dyer adapts Mountbatten practice of memorizing phonetic sentences for use with navy men of different nationalities whom he had to inspect, 491-492

Cunningham, Admiral Sir Andrew: Senior Naval Commander, Med, 302, 304

Curts, Admiral M. E. (Germany): Dyer relives him in Dec. 1946 in command of Cruiser Division 10 and departs for Mediterranean, 476

USS D-3: Hancock gets command of D-3 for Dyer, 70, 75; some characteristics, 75-76; recruitment tour of New England ports, 77-80; Dyer leaves D-3 after four months for Hampton Roads and a larger command, 84

Daggett, Capt. R. B.: 256

Dashiell, Capt. G. W. D.: skipper of R-1, 57

Davidson, VADM L. A.: relieves Adm. Conolly in command at Sicily, 307-308

Davis, VADM George M. (Med. C.): Chief of Bureau of Medicine and Surgery (1971), doctor to Adm. Dyer at time of his strokes, 540

Dawley, Gen. E. J.: commanded Army VI Corps at Salerno, 333

Deep Sea Diving School: Dyer selected from Naval War College for special course before taking command of WIDGEON (ex-minesweeper), a SS rescue ship, 139-140; qualifies to dive to 200 feet, 143

De Gaulle, General Charles: story of Dyer's audience with General for purpose of borrowing much needed jeeps and trucks, 286-288

DeMott, Capt. Max B.: 29-30

De Steiguer, RADM Louis R.: commandant, Portsmouth Navy Yard (1922), 105

DETACHMENT: code name for Iwo Jima operation, 406-407; see also
    entries under Iwo Jima campaign

Dickens, Adm. Sir Gerald: British Naval Commander at Bizerte and
    Tunis, 291

DIME Force: name for Task Group under Admiral Hall, 314-315

Donovan, Col. William J.: 235-237

Downes, RADM John: Division Commander, CruDiv 5, 175-176

DuBose, VADM L. T.: Chief, Bureau of Personnel, 523

Duct Keel: on S class submarines, 104-105

Dyer, VADM George C.: family data, 1-8; early education, 11; early
    business experience, 12-14; more family data, 17-18; religious
    associations, 19-20; promotion to LTJG, 92-95; selection for
    RADM (1945), 436; first stroke, 538; second stroke, 540;
    retirement (1955), 541

Dyer Board: made determinations on specialization in post war navy,
    444-449

Edwards, Adm. Richard (Dickie): Assistant Chief of Staff for Operations (1942) to Admiral King, 216; takes Comdr. John G. Crawford as his assistant, 217-218; 220, 222, 260; as Deputy CinC, assigns Dyer multitude of thorny problems upon return to Washington in June, 1945, 433-434, 436

Eisenhower, Gen. Dwight D.: Commander in Chief, Med, 303-304, 330, 348

11th Naval District: Dyer becomes Commandant, 531; Naval Reservists ask him to activate their units, 531-532; Dyer's difficulties with Legal Officer and his recommendations, 536-538; his first stroke, 538; second stroke, 540

Evacuation discussion, from Salerno: 344 ff; Dyer analysis of almost insuperable problems involved, 344-346; after General Alexander's decision a renewed effort on part of Allies turns tide, 349-350

Evans, Capt. Joseph S.: senior member of Board of Inspection and Survey who solves bearing problem on ASTORIA, 382-383

Fahr, Commodore Charles M.: 94

Fechteler, Adm. William: Chief of Naval Personnel (1947), 480-481, 495

Fletcher, Adm. Frank Jack: Assistant Chief, BuNav (1939), 182

Foreign Awards: development of Navy policy on this subject, 434-436

Frankel, RADM S.: 446

French forces - Vichy vs Free: 284-285; attitude towards Americans, 285; Free French equipment denied to U. S. Forces, 286-287

French Frigate Shoals: see entry under USS RICHMOND

Friedman, Edwin, Capt., USNR: class of 1915 - target of much hazing and discrimination, 22, 24

Gaeta: planners for Italian invasion gave some consideration to a landing there, 327-328; British army opposed to Gaeta landings, 334

Gallipoli: lingering influence on British as they plan Italian landings, 330-331

USS GAMBLE: minelayer, 149; Dyer takes command, 150-151; inventory of crew's mess, 152-154

Gela, Sicily: landing point in Sicily of Gen. George Patten, 306, 318

German Fly Bombs: used for first time at Salerno, 342-343

Ghormley, VADM Robert Lee: Nimitz comments on, 224-225

Gilmore, Capt. Morris D.: (Gracey), skipper of N-5 (1918), 46-49

Goodwin, Lt. Comdr. Harry (USNR): class of 1915, 23

Greek Navy: Gen. Van Fleet uses Navy to outflank communists along coastal planes, 477-478, 489

Haas, Comdr. Walter S. (Gobo): skipper of N-7, (1919), 49

Haiten (suicide boats): use at Okinawa, 400-401

Hall, Adm. J.L.: with amphibious landing forces, Sicily, 290; 314-315

Halsey, Flt. Admiral William: his operational instructions system compared with that of Adm. Spruance, 426-429; disapproved of plan for post war rank of Commodore in Navy, 442

Hancock, Lt. Comdr. Louis: named skipper of S-2 (1919) building at Lake Torpedo Boat Co., 62-63, 65-70

Hansen, Capt. Henry Otto: gunnery officer on USS GAMBLE, 151-152

Hanson, VADM ED. W.: skipper of INDIANAPOLIS (1941), 206; 470-471

Hart, Adm. Thomas C.: his talk with midshipmen during WW I encouraged enrollment for duty with submarines, 37

Hawaiian waters - Patrol Plane Search (1939-40): see entries under Adm. J. O. Richardson

Heffernan, RADM John B.: Director of Naval History, asks Dyer (Sept. 1955) to write a biography of Adm. J. O. Richardson, 541

Hein, Capt. H. R.: skipper of N-6 (1918), 44-45

Helfrich, Dutch Admiral: Adm. Hart's reaction to U. S. Navy award to the Dutch Admiral, 434

Hepburn, Adm. A. J.: 137-139

Herman Goering Division, a German army division on Sicily: 301

Hewitt, Adm. H. Kent: North African landings, 253-255; protests lack of Army Air Force close support in Sicily, 296; 304, 330, 333, 335, 340; his response to Gen. Clark's proposal for an evacuation of Salerno beaches, 346-347

Hill, Adm. Harry: head of National War College, 497; his ability to deal with differences within services, 498

Historical Records: government handling of, 190-192

Hoey, Capt. Granville B.: developed Hoey Navigation position plotter, 29-30

Hooper, VADM Edwin: held at one time top logistics job in Department (Op 4) and at sea as Commander, Service Force, Pac Fleet, 464

Horne, ADM F. J.: Commander, Aircraft Battle Force in 1937, 171-172

Horrocks, Lt. Gen.: in command of British Army's X Corps while still in planning stages for Salerno - wounded at Bizerte and replaced by Gen. McCreery, 336-337

House, Brig. Gen. Edward, Jr.: landed a fighter-director team on Hewitt's flagship to provide air support at Salerno, 341

HUDDLE: code name for proposed Santa Cruz operation in Solomons, 239

Hurley, Comdr. Michael: machinest on WIDGEON, 141

HUSKY: code name for invasion of Sicily, 282; background information, 282 ff; objective in speeding up invasion of Sicily and Italy, 283-284; early ideas on nature and place of landings, 289-290; crystallization of plans, 290; U. S. Army Air Force support over Licata, 293-294; enemy attacks, 294-295; independence of Army Air Force in Mediterranean, 296; close naval support for the landings, 297-298; lack of Army faith in naval gunfire for the operation, 299-300; hundred mile long front, 304; main objectives, 304-305; mining operations, 311-312; JOSS Force, 313-315; paratroop jumps, 318-320; sea scouts, 322-323

USS INDIANAPOLIS: flagship of Adm. Tarrant (1937-38) - Dyer serves as First Lieutenant and Damage Control Officer, 173 ff; Dyer assigned as Exec(1941), 201-202; participates in abortive plan for raid on Marshall Islands, 198 ff; Dyer's attitude towards a state of readiness, 205-206; skipper backs him in his plans, 206-207

Inglis, VADM Thomas B.: Director of Naval Intelligence (1948), 492-493

IS-WAS: a hand device used in firing torpedoes, 81, 83

Italian Navy: low state of affairs (1947), 488-489

Italian Surrender: 349; psychological repercussions on campaign, 349-350; reaction of Italian military, 350-351; Eisenhower's announcement on radio, 353

Iwo Jima Campaign: witness to flag raising on Mt. Suribachi, 397; evaluation of this operation, 406-411; Iwo operation planned simultaneously with one for Okinawa, 407; value of airfields on Iwo, 410-411

Jacobs, VADM Randall: approves idea of post war naval rank of Commodore, 440, 442

Jalbert RADM H. H.: Editor of Naval Institute, 543

James, RADM Walter F. (Med. C.): commanding officer, Naval Hospital, San Diego, 539-540

Japanese courage: ability of civilians to repair airstrips under most difficult circumstances, 414-415

Joint Action - Army-Navy: publication of Joint Chiefs of Staff - effort in 1949 to revise, 493-494; Dyer served as Navy representative, 493-494

Joint Intelligence Committee: Dyer served on as a Commander (1942) - army objected and Adm. King spot promotes Dyer to Captain, 230-231

Joint Security Committee of JCS: 249; Dyer's first task to ascertain number of Navy Dept. personnel who knew of North African plans, 250

Jones, VADM J. Cary: in command of CruDiv 17, 371; 415-417

JOSS Force: name of Conolly TF for Licata landing, 312-313; 317; fail to receive advance notice of 2nd paratrooper jump at Gela, 318-319

Joy, Adm. Charles Turner: 508, 513

Kenworthy, Comdr. J. L., 470

Kimmel, RADM H. E.: cancels patrol plane search in Hawaiian waters immediately after taking command from Richardson, 189; Dyer's estimate of his failure to maintain proper state of readiness in ships, 208-209; when he relieved Adm. Richardson did so only in command of Pacific Fleet, 208-209; fails to maintain air reconnaissance around islands, 209 ff; discouraged bringing of families to Hawaii, 214; Dyer's estimate of his share of responsibility for Pearl Harbor disaster, 216

Kim Sam Song, Korean Admiral: operations officer for Korean Navy, 522

King, Fl. Adm. E. J.: Dyer ordered (Jan. 10, 1942) as King's Flag Secretary, 203; relieved by Comdr. George Russell and then becomes Intelligence Officer, 216-217; King fires head of his operational intelligence office and puts Dyer there, 218-219; dismisses Adm. Frederick Sherman, 223 - later promotes him, 223; comments on King's standards for duty, 224; contrasted with Nimitz, 224-225; his alarm over word spreading in Washington about forthcoming North African invasion, 239-240; forthcoming North African invasion, 239-240; 247-249; his reaction to Dyer memo on staff service in Washington, 258-259; attitude (1942) towards Army control of amphibious operations in Mediterranean, 266; approved idea for post war rank of Commodore, 440-441; further account of King's personality, 465-472

Kinkaid, Adm. Thomas: skipper of INDIANAPOLIS (1937-38), 174; 176; demonstrates diplomatic skill in dealing with personnel, 176-177

Kirk, Adm. A. G.: with amphibious landing forces, Sicily, 290

Knowles, Commodore Herbie: 454

Korean Navy: use in Korean War with United Nations Force, 521-522

Korean War: Dyer's desire to take part, 497, 504-505; becomes Commander, U.N. Blockade and Escort Force, 506

Krug, The Hon. Julius A.: 376; his desire for an assignment on ASTORIA, 376-377

Kyushu: with taking of Okinawa Japanese mainland is in easy striking distance, 412-413; 423

USS L-10: Dyer gets command at SS base in Hampton Roads (1920), 84-85

USS L-15: Dyer sent as executive to new SS with D. R. Lee (Doc) as skipper, 88; building at Lake TB Co., 92; Asiatic Station incident (Oct. 1922) - CinC, Asiatic relieves skipper and names Lt. J.G. Dyer as his relief, 98-100; story of L-15 trials at Lake TB Co., 100-103

Lake, Simon: see entries under Lake Torpedo Boat Co.

Lake Torpedo Boat Co.: 55, 62; financial problems, 62-64; 100 ff.

Lame duck cruiser: 415

Landing craft: discussion of status at outbreak of WW II, 255-257; use in HUSKY operation, 312-313

Leighton, RADM Frank T.: summarily relieved by Adm. King of duties as operational intelligence officer, 218-220

Licata, Sicily: landing port for U. S. forces, 290; Dyer gets British commendation for assault landing plan, 291-292; comments on air support for landings, 293, 301

Literary efforts: Naval History asks Dyer to write biography of Adm. J. O. Richardson, 541-542; Naval Institute asks Dyer to do book on Naval Logistics (1958), 542-543; revision of Logistics book, 544-545; Biography of Admiral R. Kelly Turner, 546-547

Lockwood, ADM Charles: invites Dyer to come aboard new V-3 (1926) as electrical engineer, 114-115; 116; on Court of Inquiry investigating the sinking of the S-51, 118; fails in his solo test at Naval Air Station, San Diego, 121-122; teaching at Naval Academy (1934), 156

Logistic Plans: Dyer named as Chief of Logistic Plans upon selection as RADM in 1945, 449 ff; had no foreknowledge of post war period, 462-463

Lowe, Capt. F. S. (Frog): on Adm. King's staff (1942), 221-222

MacGruder, Commodore Cary W.: Executive at PG School, 1929-30, 132

MAGIC: reports not included in data for COMINCH Operational War Room - use in reports of Joint Intelligence Committee, 229

Malta: headquarters of British CinCMed, 486; Dyer attends horse races and bets one winner, 487-488

U. S. Marine Corps: Dyer applied for Marine Corps upon graduation, 35-37

Marshall Islands: original planning concept for invasion, Nimitz revision, 246

Marshall Islands Raid, proposed: part of War Plans in case of conflict, 197; week after Pearl Harbor attack Task Force gets underway to implement plan, 198; Pye's order to cancel - discussion in the fleet, 198

Martin, Adm. H.M. (Beauty): in command of 7th fleet in Korea, 513-514; Adm. Radford displeased with Martin for permitting Dyer to make air strike against Wonsan, 515

Massey, Mrs. Thalia: 147

Materials - Post War decision on disposal: 460-461

McCollum RADM A. H.: hindered in his selection to flag rank by virtue of too much shore duty, 446

McCormick, ADM Lynde D.: VCNO, 505

McCreery, Lt. Gen. Sir R. M.: British officer commanding the Xth

Corps for landing at Salerno, 336-337

Mentz, RADM George F. (Egg): navigator on USS RICHMOND, 168, 170; lays protective minefield off Sicilian Coast, 315

Middleton, Lt. Gen. T. H.: commanded Army 45th Division at Salerno, 333

Mills, VADM E. W.: 375-376; promotes use of shrapnel proof suits, 377

MINELAYING - TACTICAL INSTRUCTIONS FOR: Dyer rewrites publication while on duty in USS GAMBLE, 156

Minesweeping - Korea: 508-510

Mining and Minesweeping Operations: Sicily, 311-312; 314-315; protective minefield for big transports, 315; Italian minefield at Porto Empedocle, 317; party of Italian military and naval officers board BISCAYNE in Bay of Salerno and turn over chart of Italian mines in the area, 351; 354-355

Momsen, VADM C. B. (Swede): takes over Dyer assignment on BB WYOMING (1936) for Midshipman cruise, 159; skipper of battle cruiser MONTANA, 430-431

Montecorvino: Italian airfield near Bay of Salerno (1943): 325

Montgomery, Gen. B. L. (Monty): senior army commander in Med, 302

Moon, RADM Don P.: asks Dyer to serve as Chief of Staff for his amphibious group in the Med, 369-370

Mooring Board: definition and use on USS ARIZONA, 123-124; use in USS RICHMOND, flagship of Adm. J. O. Richardson, 166-167

Mostaganem: Army amphibious base located there, 264-265; for Sicily invasion, 266

Mounbatten, Adm. Lord Louis: British Chief of Combined Operations, 291. (1947) Cru Div. commander, Med., 489-90; his method of dealing with various dialects and languages his men spoke 490-1

Mt. Suribachi: mountain on Iwo Jima, 397, 401; difficulty it presented to the U.S. Marines, 401

Murray, ADM S.S.: together with Dyer switched to Submarines when told they could not go to Marine Corps upon graduation, 37

N boats - Submarines: Cruise on, 38-40 (1918); 44-6; incident involving the N-5 in Thames at New London, 47-9; N-boats equipped with listening tubes, 49-50. N-7 in near collision with N-6, 51-3; the "automatic" blow on the N ships, 52-3; further details on the N boats, 55; Congressional Act authorizing construction of the N boats (1914) suggested number be deployed in Gulf, 55

National War College: Dyer named Navy Deputy while Adm. Hill still President 496, 501; required to leave some promising naval officers for assignment to Naval War College, 501-2; faculty recruiting, 502-3

NATO: made it necessary for U.S. Navy to be represented in Med. in post World War II period, 463

Naval Academy: Early determination to attend the Naval Academy, 2, 7; appointment from Oregon, 8-10, 14; trip to Academy for entrance, 15-17; gouging inquiry (1915), 20-1; hazing and anti-semitism, 22-3; the elephant race, 24; hazing inquiry, 25;

early scholastic experiences, 26-29; summer cruises, 30-31. Dyer on teaching staff in Steamship Dept., 156-157

Naval Aviation: Dyer interested in Aviation in late 1920s but not qualified physically, 120-122

Naval Gunfire: importance of, 338-9; use of such support at Salerno, 339-40. value of in Pacific, 404-5

Naval Recruiting: Dyer takes the USS D-3 on tour of New England ports for recruiting purposes, 77-80; sent to Detroit as Recruiting Officer and officer-inspector of the Naval Reserve, 107-8; handling the financial accounts for the station, 112-4

Naval Reserve - 11th Naval District: Dyer as Commandant begins series of visits to various reserve units, 532; difficulties with SecNav and various reservists, 534-5

Naval Reserves: work with the Reserves in Michigan, 1924-26, 109-112

U. S. Naval War College: 134-137

U. S. Navy Plans - Post World War II: 449, 451

Needham, Capt. Ralph C.: 27-29

USS NEVADA - BB Midshipman cruise ship, 30-32, 34

Nimitz, Fl. Admiral C. W.: 178, 201. his approach to personnel problems as contrasted to Adm. King, 224-5; role of Nimitz in planning, 215-6; approved of post war rank of Commodore, 443-4; contrast with Adm. King, 468-9; as CNO wanted to reduce personnel in Navy - names Dyer head of a special board to recommend reductions in OPNAV first, 473 ff; fails to stand up to refusal of Adm. Radford to cooperate with recommendations, 475

O'Daniel, Major Gen. John W.: head of Army's Amphibious contingent at Mostaganem, 266; his sedan stolen on the base, 267-8

USS OGLALA: Flagship of minesweeping force at Pearl Harbor, 149-50

Okinawa: 411 ff. suitable base for planes attacking mainland of Japan, 412; price navy paid, 422-3; discussion of timing for the campaign, 423-4

Oliver, Adm. G. N. - Royal Navy: 459-60

ON THE TREADMILL TO PEARL HARBOR: Dyer's book dealing with Richardson, Pearl Harbor, Patrol Plane Searches, etc., 190, 204

ONI - status prior to WW II, 227-8; 231-3; pre WW II work compared with Army's G-2, 237

OPNAV - General Plans Officer: Nimitz as CNO sets Dyer up as head of Board to work on personnel reductions for OPNAV divisions, 473 ff

Oran: North African repair base for use at time of Sicilian invasion, 318

Osterhaus, RADM Hugo W.: succeeds Capt. Wortman as Commander of SS Base at Pearl Harbor, 147; the annual fleet problem, 147-9

Palermo: first planned objective for American Forces, 289; discussion of the value of an initial landing there, 309-10; subjected to severe bombing raids by the Germans when we landed forces there, 322

Pantellaria: former German air base - became base for close air support for British landings on Sicily, 293

Paratroop Jumps: 318-21

Patrol Wing II: based on Pearl Harbor (1939-40), 186, 188; 209-212

Patterson, Capt. Theo T.: 89-90. relieves Dyer of Certain aspects of COMINCH staff job, 262

Patton, General George: participated in planning for N. Africa, 248, 252, 254; Patton on beach in Sicily in command of 7th Army, 277-8; understood value of naval support gunfire, 279-81, 300. did not respond to suggestion that he make longer leap-frog movements on north coast of Sicily, 308

Pearl Harbor Disaster: Dyer, as Flag Secretary to Adm. King (Jan. 10, 1042) asked by him to make a report on the Pearl Harbor disaster, 203-4; lack of readiness on ships, 208-9; failure to continue air reconnaissance instigated by Adm. Richardson, 208 ff; Dyer's estimate of blame for the disaster, 215-6; his findings on status of intelligence in the Navy prior to WW II, 226 ff

PG School: course of study, 1929-30, 121-2; Dyer wins right to go from PG school to the Naval War College, 133

USS PHILADELPHIA: gives gunfire support to the landing in Sicily, 277

Picket Ships: 420-1

Pye, VADM Wm. S.: succeeds Adm. Snyder as Commander, Battle Force when Adm. Kimmel takes over from Adm. Richardson, 197; orders cancellation of Marshall Islands raid, 198-200

USS R-1: Dyer assigned to her, 55-7

USS R-5: Dyer serves in her for several patrols, 58-60; example of

USS R-5: Dyer serves in her for several patrols, 58-9; example of navy discipline on board the R-5, 59-60

Radar School Training: Dyer cites value of this when he joined Task Group at night in mid Pacific, 393-4

Radford, Adm. Arthur W.: DCNO Air (Op-05) - refuses to consider recommendations (1946) for reduction in personnel, 474-5; objects to Dyer using carriers for strikes against Wosan defenses, 514; after second such strike orders they be stopped - no more such strikes under command of non-aviator, 514; has Dyer relieved of his command, 515; 524

Ramsey, Adm. DeWitt C.: VCNO as C-ief of General Plans, 1946 - 474-475

Richardson, Adm. J. O.: becomes commander, Scouting Force, 161; his manner of dealing with his staff, 161-165; Dyer article on subject in PROCEEDINGS, 166; President Roosevelt sends him (1939) to sea as Commander, Battle Force, 182; Jan. 6, 1940 takes command of U. S. Fleet, 185-6; his insistence that patrol planes search Hawaiian waters daily, 186; difficulties involved in patrol, 186-7; efforts of aviators to get a cancellation, 188-9; his attempt to get more aircraft for patrol purposes, 189; verbal sketch of J. O. R., 192-3; he misjudges FDR, 194-5

USS RICHMOND: flagship of Adm. J. O. Richardson, 167; Fleet Exercise involving French Frigate Shoals, 168-171

Rodgers, Comdr. John: Commander Submarine base at New London (1918), 36

Roosevwlt, President F. D.: misread by Adm. Richardson, 194-5;

account of President's sudden change of mind and dismissal of Adm. Richardson, 195-6. Dyer's estimate of his share of blame for the Pearl Harbor Disaster, 216

Roper, VADM John: officer assignment, BuPers (1942), 259-60; 364-6. retires from 11th Naval District Command because of ill health - Dyer succeeds, 531

USS ROWE - DD: damaged in collision off Porto Empedocle, 319

Royal Navy - comments: 457-9; recollections of Joint Command arrangements, 457-60

Russell, VADM Geo. L.: relieves Dyer as Flag Secretary to Adm. Kings. 216

S-Boats: details on theri background and use of ideas from captured German U boats, 60-1; trial run of the S-2, 64-5; fire in motor room, 66-8, 70-1

USS S-4: 142; exercise in salvage operations at Pearl Harbor, 143-5

USS S-15 (Submarine): 29; her adventures in Manila Bay, 117-8

Sabin, VADM Lorenzo: 265

HSM ST. ANDREW - hospital ship: at Salerno Bay - Dyer transferred there, 361; attempt to get the ship;s master to circumvent German night bombing attack, 362-4

Salerno: landing operations - 1943, 325 ff; difficulty in planning, 325-6; complicated by negotiations for Italian surrender, 327; discussion of reasons for Salerno landings rather than Gaeta, 329-30; confidence of U. S. planners that landings could be made on fortified beaches, 331-2; naval gunfire support - British practice, 332-3; British coastal command given task of providing air coverage for the fleet at Salerno, 341; Dyer's recollections of enemy air attacks over beachhead, 341-2; Clark's proposal for evacuation of the Salerno beaches - conference on the ANCON, 344 ff; lack of availability of U.S. Capital ships, 355-56; 357; reason for the Army changing generals, 358

Salvage Problems - North African area, 272 ff; use of salvage craft with landing craft, 273-7; channel clearance of Bizerte, 275-6

USS SARATOGA: flagship of Adm. Horne, (1937), 171-2

Sardinia: allies make feint towards Sardinia in an effort to surprise enemy on Sicily, 302

Schlossbach, Comdr. Ike: on board the N-5 (1919), 56-57

Scofield, Adm. Frank H.: 194

Sea Duty: comments on changed attitudes, 481-5; availability of quarters for officers - contrasted with earlier days, 483

Sea Scouts: young officers who reconnoitered Sicilian beaches prior to allied landings, 322-323

Sele River: boundary between British and U. S. landing forces at Salerno, 339

Sellers, ADM David F.: Superintendent of the U. S. Naval Academy (1936), 159

Sherman, Adm. Forrest: relieves VADM B. H. Bieri in command of Naval Forces, Med - name changed to 6th Fleet, 476; initiates tactical problems for fleet units, 476-7; Dyer gets him as CNO to obtain his release from National War College to take command of United Nations Blockade and Escort Force in Korea, 497; also 505; tells Dyer that he intended to order him in Command of 7th Fleet when vacancy occurred, 506

Sherman, VADM Frederick: skipper of USS LEXINGTON - objects to cancellation of Marshall Islands raid, 199-200; serves briefly on Adm. King's staff, 221-2; career in the Pacific, 223. TF commander with the Pac Fleet, 394

Shrapnel Proof Suits: promoted by Chief of Bureau of Engineering, 377; use in battle on the ASTORIA, 377-80

Sicily - invasion of: 263 ff; tales of the actual invasion, 276-8; background to operation HUSKY, 282 ff; see also entries under HUSKY

Smith, General Holland (Howling Mad): Landing Force Commander at Iwo Jima, 407, 411

Smith-Hutton, Capt. Henri Harold: released as POW and assigned to COMINCH staff (1942), 261-2

Snyder, Adm. Peck: Commander Battle Force (1941) under Adm. Richardson, 196; refuses to serve under Adm. Kimmel and is relieved, 197

Spaatz, Gen. Carl: commander of the Army Air Force in Mediterranean Theatre, 293-5

Spruance, Admiral Raymond: Dyer makes point that under Spruance lessons of war were being fed into the instructions constantly for benefit of new arrivals in battle area, 426-7; made no public notice of near collision of the ASTORIA with his flagship, 431-2

Standley, Comdr. W. H. Jr.,: Plans Officer on staff of Adm. Conolly at Bizerte, 338, 346

Stark, Adm. H. R.: CNO's version of the Richardson dismissal by FDR, 195-6; writes in Dec 1940 that air reconnaissance around Pearl Harbor not necessary "at this time," 211; Dyer's estimate of his share in the blame for Pearl Harbor disaster, 216

Stein, Comdr. M. H. (Abie): 133

Straits of Messina: 306

STRANGE: name of Air Force Anti-logistic operation in Korea, 511-2

Strauss, ADM Joseph: skipper of BB NEVADA - later Cinc, Asiatic Fleet, 32

Strong, Major Gen. George V.: head of Army's G-2, 229-31

Struble, Adm. Arthur D. (Rip): Op-03 in 1947, 492-3; 496; wanted Dyer named as Director of Naval Intelligence, 496

Stuka: German Stuka attacks compared with Japanese Kamikazi, 295

Submarines: summary of U. S. Submarine Complement, Jan. 1919, 72; recruitment for service in Submarines - tour of D-3 in New England, 77-80; diving compensation, 81-2

Submarine Division 8: Dyer called from duty on USS INDIANAPOLIS to command SS Division 8 (1938) which was then de-commissioned in 6 months, 178; program engaged in by Submarines at Pearl Harbor in 1938, 179-80

USS SWANSON - DD: damaged in collision off Porto Empedocle, 319

Taffinder, VADM S. A.: Chief of Staff to Admiral J. O. Richardson (1939), 183-4; 201; indecisive about reconnaisance flights around Pearl Harbor in 1941, 211

Tarrant, Adm. Wm. T.: 172-3; 176

Taylor, Captain Conant: 57-8

Tedder, Air Marshall Sir Arthur: Senior Air force commander, Med. 302

Thomas, Raymond G. (Roaring Bull): Inspector of Machinery, Lake Torpedo Boat Co., 67-8, 70

Thurber, Capt. H. Ray: relieves Dyer of Security features of COMINCH staff job, 262

Tibbals, Clarence L. Chief Gunner's Mate: served during 1932-3 with Dyer on the WIDGEON - aware named for him offered at the Naval Academy, 141

Towers, Admiral John: objects to the post war rank of Commodore, 439-40; 442-3; kills the proposal, 443

Training Command, Pac. Fleet: Dyer given command in June, 1952, 551; disappointment over as assignment, 523; trains a division of Peruvian frigates, 524-8; other Latin American navies request same training facilities, 528; scope of training command efforts, 529-31

Truscott, Maj. Gen. Lucien K.: in command of 3rd Infantry Division for Operation HUSKY, 288-90

Turner, Adm. R. Kelly: skill in planning dual operations - Iwo and Okinawa, 407; early in career helped with charting of Admiralty Islands, 447; 455-6

U. N. Blockade and Escort Force, TF 95: Dyer takes command, 506; duties, 506 ff; details to be found in Adm. Cagle's "The Sea War in Korea," 509; discussion of reasons for the blockade and problems involved, 516-7; problem destroying North Korean sampans which were used in running blockade, 517-8; use of naval ships from other countries, 518; difficulty with Canadians, 518-20

USS V-3: Dyer in 1936 becomes Electrical Engineer, 115

Van de Carr, Capt. James C.: Division Commander of Submarines, Hampton Roads, (1920), 85

Van Fleet, General James A.: in command of Allied forces in Greece during Civil War (1947) - Dyer sent to him by Adm. Bieri and convinces him of need to use Greek Navy in outflanking the communists, 477-8; aware of similar problems when in command in Korea, 479-80

Vinson, The Hon. Carl: 181

Von Heimburg, VADM E. H. (Count): 139

War Plans - Navy: Dyer assigned there by Adm. King (1942), 218; planning for North Africa, 233-4; planning for the Solomons' operations, 234 ff; cooperation with OSS, 235-7; original Solomon's plans called for landings on Tulagi and Santa Cruz but not Guadalcanal, 238; very detailed planning involved in early operations, 243-4, 245; role of Nimitz in the Pacific campaign and in planning, 245-6; more on planning for North African invasion, 247-8, 252-3; conflicting weather forecasts, North Africa invasion, 252-3;

HMS WARSPITE - BB: 343-4

Washington, Adm. Thos.: Cinc, Asiatic (1922), 96, 99

Watts, RADM Wm. Cl.: Commander, Mine Force, Pearl Harbor, 149-50

Whitehill, Walter M: came to Washington to write history of COMINCH staff, 251-2

USS WIDGEON: operations in Hawaiian waters, 140-9

Willis, Adm. Sir Algernon V. (Fauntleroy) 356-7. Cinc British Mediterranean Fleet (1947), 485-8

Wilson, Adm. Russell: Chief of Staff to Adm. King (1942), 216, 220

USS WISCONSIN - BB: Midshipman cruise - coaling operation, 30-1

Wonsan: attempt to break up logistic support of the North Koreans, 510-511; the harbor and its defenses, 512-3

Withers, RADM Thomas, Jr.: 138

Wortman, Capt. Ward K.: Commander of SS Squadron #4 at Pearl Harbor, 146

www.ingramcontent.com/pod-product-compliance
Lightning Source LLC
Chambersburg PA
CBHW082221090526

44585CB00020BA/2127